Charles Spurgeon, 1864

the LOST SERMONS *of*
C. H. SPURGEON

the LOST SERMONS of
C. H. SPURGEON

*His Earliest Outlines and Sermons
Between 1851 and 1854*   *Vol.3*

Edited with Introduction and Notes by CHRISTIAN T. GEORGE

B&H
ACADEMIC

NASHVILLE, TENNESSEE

The Lost Sermons of C. H. Spurgeon, Volume 3
Copyright © 2018 by Christian George and Spurgeon's College
Published by B&H Academic
Nashville, Tennessee

Standard Edition ISBN: 978-1-4336-5093-2
Collector's Edition ISBN: 978-1-4336-5095-6

Dewey Decimal Classification: 252
Subject Heading: SPURGEON, CHARLES H. \ SERMONS \ CHRISTIAN LIFE–SERMONS

Special thanks to Spurgeon's College, spurgeons.ac.uk

The web addresses referenced in this book were live and correct at the time of the book's publication but may be
subject to change.

The marbled paper for the cover of the collector's edition was created by Lesley Patterson-Marx,
lesleypattersonmarx.com

Printed in China

1 2 3 4 5 6 7 8 9 10 RRD 23 22 21 20 19 18

To my all-time pastor, professor, and lifelong friend, Charles T. Carter,
pastor emeritus of Shades Mountain Baptist Church in Birmingham, Alabama,
where I was converted, baptized, licensed to preach,
married, and ordained to the gospel ministry

CONTENTS

CONTENTS

CONTENTS

FOREWORD

The Lord often works in mysterious ways. At least, He certainly has in my life, and this was exactly the case with my first real introduction to Charles Spurgeon. Of course, I lived far too late to be introduced to him face-to-face, but I did come to know him through his sermons. Here's how.

It was around fifteen years ago, at the point of my journey that had me wandering in a kind of spiritual wilderness between my early years in the Dutch Reformed tradition and my eventual home in the Reformed Baptist tradition. I had taken my first-ever position at a church in one of those brand-new digital-era roles related to the Internet and social media. My job was to learn, master, and deploy all these amazing tools we realized were perfect for reaching the unchurched masses here in the Greater Toronto area.

One day I was dispatched to an associated church to speak to their pastor, who was interested in updating their website with some new information. I learned he had decided to make some significant changes to the structure and personnel of the church. He had been doing a lot of reading that had convinced him the time was right to embrace a new kind of Christianity. He wanted something less institutional and more organic, something less structured and more egalitarian. He wanted to minimize preaching to maximize sharing. He wanted to move on from the church-growth model to fully embrace the emerging model.

He and I spoke for some time, and I jotted down all the notes I would need to adapt his site accordingly. Then, as I stood to leave, he offered me a book. It was by one of the leaders of what was then just gaining fame as the Emerging Church. This was the book that had changed his life and was now motivating the sea change to his ministry. But that was not all he offered me. He pointed to a series of ten hardcover volumes, said he wouldn't be needing them anymore, and asked if I'd like them. I took them as well. They were ten volumes of sermons by Charles Spurgeon.

I returned home to read that slim volume that advocated a whole new kind of Christianity. It repulsed me. I put it aside and [instead] started into those volumes of sermons, which I soon learned advocated a very old kind of Christianity. They electrified me. Spurgeon called me to remember and embrace the gospel of Jesus Christ. He called me to understand and enjoy sound doctrine. He called me to have every confidence in the Bible. In the end, he convinced me to search for a new church. He changed my life and did it through simply preaching the Word of God.

The sermons of Charles Spurgeon were used by the Lord to transform my life. It is for that reason I'm thrilled to see even more of them become available. May the Lord use them to change your life and mine.

TIM CHALLIES
Pastor, Grace Fellowship Church
Toronto, Ontario

EDITOR'S PREFACE

In 1859, an American minister named Rev. H. traveled to London to meet the famous pastor of the New Park Street Chapel. When Spurgeon discovered his guest was from Alabama, his "cordiality sensibly diminished." A six-month American preaching tour would expedite the construction of the Metropolitan Tabernacle, but could Southerners tolerate Spurgeon's stance against slavery? When Spurgeon asked his guest this question, the Alabamian said he "had better not undertake it."[1]

This advice might have saved Spurgeon's life. The same year, S. A. Corey, pastor of Eighteenth Street Baptist Church in New York City, invited the twenty-four-year-old to preach at the Academy of Music opera house for $10,000.[2] News of Spurgeon's visit was met with anticipation in the North and hostility in the South. According to an Alabama newspaper, Spurgeon would receive a beating "so bad as to make him ashamed."[3] On February 17, 1860,[4] citizens of Montgomery, Alabama, publicly protested the "notorious English abolitionist"[5] by gathering in the jail yard to burn his "dangerous books":[6]

---

1   "Spurgeon's Anti-Slavery Mission to America," *The Times-Picayune* (October 22, 1859).
2   See "Spurgeon and His $10,000 Offer," *The Brooklyn Daily Eagle* (February 5, 1859).
3   "They Want Spurgeon," *Daily Confederation* (October 30, 1858).
4   There is some confusion about the date of the Montgomery burning. Some British newspapers claimed it occurred on January 17 ("Mr. Spurgeon's Sermons Burned by American Slaveowners," *The Southern Reporter and Daily Commercial Courier* [April 10, 1860]). American sources reveal the more likely date of February 17 ("Book Burning," *Pomeroy Weekly Telegraph* [March 13, 1860]).
5   The full quote is, "A gentleman of this city requests us to invite, and we do hereby invite all persons in Montgomery who possess copies of the sermons of the notorious English abolitionist, Spurgeon, to send them to the jail-yard to be burned, on next Friday (this day week). A subscription is also on foot to buy of our booksellers all copies of said sermons now in their stores to be burnt on the same occasion" (*Montgomery Mail*, repr. in "Spurgeon's Sermons—a Bonfire," *Nashville Patriot* [March 15, 1860]). See also "The Barbarism of Slavery," *The Cleveland Morning Leader* (July 3, 1860), and *Randolph County Journal* (July 5, 1860). The burning of Spurgeon's sermons in Montgomery solicited caustic responses in Northern states, such as in New York's *Poughkeepsie Eagle*: "There will—unless this fanaticism is soon checked—be a general bonfire of another Book, which has something of a circulation [in the] south, and which declares it to be every man's duty to 'let the oppressed go free'" (March 8, 1860).
6   For a more comprehensive account of the burning of Spurgeon's sermons at the Montgomery, Alabama, jail yard, see "Burning Spurgeon's Sermons," *The Burlington Free Press* (March 30, 1860).

Last Saturday, we devoted to the flames a large number of copies of Spurgeon's Sermons. . . . We trust that the works of the greasy cockney vociferator may receive the same treatment throughout the South. And if the Pharisaical author should ever show himself in these parts, we trust that a stout cord may speedily find its way around his eloquent throat.[7]

On March 22, a "Vigilance Committee" in Montgomery followed suit and burned Spurgeon's sermons in the public square.[8] A week later Mr. B. B. Davis, a bookstore owner, prepared "a good fire of pine sticks" before reducing about sixty volumes of Spurgeon's sermons "to smoke and ashes."[9] British newspapers quipped that America had given Spurgeon a warm welcome, "a literally brilliant reception."[10]

Anti-Spurgeon bonfires illuminated jail yards, plantations, bookstores, and courthouses throughout the Southern states. In Virginia, Mr. Humphrey H. Kuber, a Baptist preacher and "highly respectable citizen" of Matthews County, burned seven calf-skinned volumes of Spurgeon's sermons "on the head of a flour barrel."[11] The arson was assisted by "many citizens of the highest standing."[12] In North Carolina, Spurgeon's famous sermon "Turn or Burn"[13] found a similar fate when a Mr. Punch "turned the second page and burned the whole."[14] By 1860, slave-owning pastors were "foaming with rage because they [could not] lay hands on the youthful Spurgeon."[15] His life was threatened, his books burned, his sermons

---

7   "Mr. Spurgeon's Sermons Burned by American Slaveowners." See also *The Morning Advertiser* (April 2, 1860). A similar statement is found in a letter from Virginia minister James B. Taylor: "Wonder that the earth does not open her mouth, and swallow up Spurgeon. . . . Pity that that cord from the South is not applied to his eloquent throat!" ("Review of a Letter from Rev. Jas. B. Taylor, of Richmond, Va.," *The Liberator* [July 6, 1860]).

8   "News from All Nations," *The Bradford Reporter* (March 22, 1860).

9   "Book-Burning in Montgomery, Ala.," *Randolph County Journal* (March 29, 1860). See also "Another Bonfire of Spurgeon's Sermons," *The Wilmington Daily Herald* (March 12, 1860).

10 *The Morning Advertiser* (April 2, 1860). See also "The Rev. C. H. Spurgeon in Scotland," *The Morning Advertiser* (March 11, 1861).

11 For a more accurate version of this account, see "Mr. Spurgeon's Sermons: Why They Were Burned by Virginians," *The New York Times* (July 9, 1860).

12 "Virginia News," *Alexandria Gazette and Virginia Advertiser* (June 22, 1860). See also "Burning Spurgeon," *Richmond Dispatch* (June 5, 1860), and *Brooklyn Evening Star* (June 22, 1860).

13 Spurgeon preached the sermon "Turn or Burn" (*NPSP* 2, Sermon 106) on December 7, 1856.

14 "Our Politeness Exceeds His Beauty," *North Carolina Christian Advocate* (July 10, 1857).

15 "Espionage in the South," *The Liberator* (May 4, 1860).

censured,[16] and below the Mason-Dixon Line, the media catalyzed character assassinations. In Florida, Spurgeon was a "beef-eating, puffed-up, vain, over-righteous pharisaical, English blab-mouth."[17] In Virginia, he was a "fat, overgrown boy";[18] in Louisiana, a "hell-deserving Englishman";[19] and in South Carolina, a "vulgar young man" with "(soiled) sleek hair, prominent teeth, and a self-satisfied air."[20] Georgians were encouraged to "pay no attention to him."[21] North Carolinians "would like a good opportunity at this hypocritical preacher" and resented his "fiendish sentiments, against our Constitution and citizens."[22] *The Weekly Raleigh Register* reported that anyone selling Spurgeon's sermons should be arrested and charged with "circulating incendiary publications."[23]

Southern Baptists ranked among Spurgeon's chief antagonists.[24] *The Mississippi Baptist* hoped "no Southern Baptist will now purchase any of that incendiary's books."[25] The Baptist colporteurs of Virginia were forced to return all copies of his sermons to the publisher.[26] *The Alabama Baptist* and *Mississippi Baptist* "gave the Londoner 4,000 miles of an awful raking" and "took the hide off him."[27] The *Southwestern Baptist* and

16 The following reports suggest that the censuring of Spurgeon's sermons became widely publicized in American newspapers: "Beecher has charged that the American edition of Spurgeon's sermons, does not contain his sentiments on slavery as the English edition does. A comparison of the editions has been made, and the charge has been found correct" ("Spurgeon Purged," *Ashtabula Weekly Telegraph* [November 26, 1859]). In April of the following year, the newspaper reported that "grave charges have been made of interpolations and modifications in the American edition of his sermons, to suit American squeamishness, and secure currency to his works" (April 14, 1860). See also "Ex-Spurgeon," *Ohio State Journal* (November 29, 1859).

17 "A Southern Opinion of the Rev. Mr. Spurgeon," *The New York Herald* (March 1, 1860).

18 "The Great Over-Rated," *The Daily Dispatch* (August 17, 1858).

19 "Spurgeon on Slavery," *The Bossier Banner* (February 24, 1860).

20 "Spurgeon and the Lady," *Charleston Courier* (June 15, 1858).

21 *Macon Weekly Telegraph* (February 25, 1860).

22 "Rev. Mr. Spurgeon," *The North Carolinian* (February 18, 1860).

23 "Rev. Mr. Spurgeon," *The Weekly Raleigh Register* (February 15, 1860).

24 Spurgeon was ten years old when tensions over slavery resulted in Baptists from the Southern state conventions gathering in Augusta, Georgia, to form the Southern Baptist Convention (SBC) in 1845 (see A. H. Newman, *A History of the Baptist Churches in the United States* [New York: The Christian Literature Co., 1894], 443–47). On June 20–22, 1995, the SBC adopted a resolution in Atlanta, Georgia, acknowledging that "our relationship to African-Americans has been hindered from the beginning by the role that slavery played in the formation of the Southern Baptist Convention," and "Many of our Southern Baptist forbears defended the right to own slaves, and either participated in, supported, or acquiesced in the particularly inhumane nature of American slavery." It also stated that they "unwaveringly denounce racism, in all its forms, as deplorable sin" ("Resolution on Racial Reconciliation on the 150th Anniversary of the Southern Baptist Convention," 1995; accessed May 18, 2016, www.sbc.net/resolutions/899/resolution-on-racial-reconciliation-on-the-150th-anniversary-of-the-southern-baptist-convention).

25 *The Weekly Mississippian* (March 14, 1860).

26 "Spurgeon Repudiated," *Newbern Weekly Progress* (March 20, 1860). See also "Spurgeon Rejected in Virginia," *Cincinnati Daily Press* (March 28, 1860).

27 "Prof. J. M. Pendleton of Union University, Tenn., and the Slavery Question," *The Mississippian* (April 4, 1860).

other denominational newspapers took the "spoiled child to task and administered due castigation."[28]

In the midst of this mayhem, Spurgeon attempted to publish several notebooks of sermons from his earliest ministry. His promise to his readers in 1857 would not be fulfilled, however, due to difficult life circumstances in London. How poetic, then, that 157 years after *The Nashville Patriot* slandered Spurgeon for his "meddlesome spirit,"[29] a publishing house from Nashville would complete the task he failed to accomplish. How symmetrical that Spurgeon's early sermons would be published not by Passmore & Alabaster in London but by Americans. And not only Americans, but *Southern* Americans. And not only Southern Americans, but Southern *Baptist* Americans with all the baggage of their bespeckled beginnings.

As a Southern Baptist from Alabama, allow me to confess my own bias. I have spent the majority of my vocational life studying Spurgeon. I have found in him (and share with him) a genuine commitment to making Jesus Christ known to the nations. Like him, I too am deeply invested in the church and claim the same evangelical impulses that fueled Spurgeon's ministry. I admire his stance for social justice, love for the marginalized, and commitment to biblical orthodoxy.

Spurgeon's language is not always theologically precise. At times his colorful, allegorical, and experimental rhetoric make academic treatments challenging. However, Spurgeon was not a theologian in the systematic sense and never claimed to be. He was a preacher. And as such, his ultimate concern was not crafting perfect manuscripts—though he spent a great deal of time redacting his sermons for publication. His greatest concern was, as his famous title hinted, becoming a *Soul Winner*. With pen and pulpit, Spurgeon indentured his literary and intellectual abilities to service of the church. His uncanny gift for rendering complex ideas in the working-class vernacular distinguished him from many of his contemporaries and gave him instant audiences.

Spurgeon's preaching emerged not in the ivory towers of Cambridge but in the lowly villages surrounding it. He was more concerned with feeding sheep than with feeding giraffes.[30] Spurgeon started his ministry as a country, not city, preacher. His congregants at Waterbeach Chapel were farmers and laborers. Even after moving to

---

28 "Mr. Spurgeon," *The Edgefield Advertiser* (February 22, 1860).

29 "Spurgeon's Sermons—a Bonfire," *Daily Nashville Patriot* (March 15, 1860).

30 "We must preach according to the capacity of our hearers. The Lord Jesus did not say, 'Feed my giraffes,' but 'Feed my sheep.' We must not put the fodder on a high rack by our fine language, but use great plainness of speech" (C.H. Spurgeon, *The Salt-Cellars: Being a Collection of Proverbs, Together with Homely Notes Thereon* [New York: A. C. Armstrong and Son, 1889], 56); "Some brethren put the food up so high that the poor sheep cannot possibly feed upon it. I have thought, as I have listened to our eloquent friends, that they imagined that our Lord had said, 'Feed my camelopards.' None but giraffes could reach the food when placed in so lofty a rack. Christ says, 'Feed my sheep,' place the food among them, put it close to them" (*MTP* 56: 406).

London, Spurgeon retained his early earthy idioms and used illustrations common to the Victorian experience.

His preaching flourished in cholera-ravaged Southwark near London's warehouses, distilleries, and factories. This gave Spurgeon a finger on the pulse of the population that, when combined with his own physical and mental ailments, produced a level of empathy uncommon to his contemporaries. Spurgeon "never suffered from having never suffered."[31]

At the height of my illness in 2013, Spurgeon's earliest sermons had a profound effect on me. During a series of surgeries, my eyes chanced upon a phrase in Notebook 1: "Think much on grace, Christian."[32] Over the twelve months of my recovery, these words brought such encouragement that I doubt they shall ever be forgotten.

Whenever new discoveries are made—whether lost diaries, letters, hymns, poems, or sermons—there is an opportunity to further our knowledge of a particular subject or person. In 2011, only a handful of doctoral students in the world were writing on Spurgeon. Today roughly two dozen are entering the field. Much work is yet to be done. Caverns of untapped resources await exploration. My hope is that the publication of Spurgeon's lost sermons will inspire future generations of scholars to mine the theological treasures still untapped.

I am also hopeful that this project will promote a reinvigorated sense of unity, mission, and Christian witness throughout evangelicalism. The recent surge of interest in Spurgeon could and should be leveraged for the kingdom. Spurgeon can become an agent of healing. Everyone can, and does, claim him, regardless of theological stripe, tribe, or camp. Spurgeon's appeal extends not only across denominational barriers but also into the broader evangelical tradition. With the upcoming accessibility of Spurgeon's sermons on the revamped website www.spurgeon.org, and also with the advances in scholarship at The Spurgeon Library of Midwestern Baptist Theological Seminary, younger and older generations face exciting new opportunities to stand together as witnesses to the world in celebration of what God has accomplished in history. Who knows? Perhaps it was for this reason that the sermons were lost in the nineteenth century and found in the twenty-first.

In 1860, an article entitled "Mr. Spurgeon and the American Slaveholders" offered the following words: "Southern Baptists will not, hereafter, when they visit London, desire to commune with this prodigy of the nineteenth century. We venture

---

31 Christian George, "Raising Spurgeon from the Dead," Desiring God, December 5, 2015; accessed May 18, 2016. http://www.desiringgod.com/articles/raising-spurgeon-from-the-dead.
32 See "God's Grace Given to Us" (Sermon 14).

the prophecy that his books in [the] future will not crowd the shelves of our Southern book merchants. They will not; they should not."[33] In 1889, Spurgeon uttered a prophecy of his own: "For my part, I am quite willing to be eaten of dogs for the next fifty years; but the more distant future shall vindicate me."[34]

The more distant future *did* vindicate Spurgeon. His sermons *do* crowd the shelves of Southern bookstores. As Carl F. H. Henry rightly noted, Spurgeon has become "one of evangelical Christianity's immortals."[35] Throughout Alabama, Virginia, and the United States of America, the books of "the notorious English abolitionist" still burn—casting light and life in a dark and dying world.

After the Emancipation Proclamation of 1863, Spurgeon's reputation improved among Southern Baptists. Many of their churches were named after Spurgeon's Metropolitan Tabernacle, such as Mark Dever's Capitol Hill Baptist Church in Washington, DC, which originally was called "Metropolitan Baptist Church."[36] Southern Baptists such as John A. Broadus, founder of The Southern Baptist Seminary in Louisville, Kentucky, flocked to Elephant & Castle to hear Spurgeon preach. After his 1891 visit, Broadus said, "The whole thing—house, congregation, order, worship, preaching, was as nearly up to my ideal as I ever expect to see in this life."[37] In June 1884, the faculty of that seminary penned a collective letter of commendation to Spurgeon:

> We thank God for all that he made you and has by his grace enabled you to become and achieve. We rejoice in your great and wonderful work as preacher and pastor, and through your Orphanage and your Pastor's [*sic*] College; as also your numerous writings, so sparkling with genius, so filled with the spirit of the gospel. . . . And now, honored brother, we invoke upon you the continued blessings of our covenant God. May your life and health be long spared, if it be his will; may Providence still smile on your varied work, and the Holy Spirit richly bless your spoken and written messages to mankind.[38]

---

33 *The Christian Index*, repr. in "Mr. Spurgeon and the American Slaveholders," *The South Australian Advertiser* (June 23, 1860).

34 "The Preacher's Power, and the Conditions of Obtaining It" (*ST*, August 1889), 420.

35 Carl. F. H. Henry, quoted in Lewis Drummond, *Spurgeon: Prince of Preachers* (3rd ed.; Grand Rapids, MI: Kregel, 1992), 11.

36 See Timothy George, "Puritans on the Potomac," *First Things*, May 2, 2016, https://www.firstthings.com /web-exclusives/2016/05/puritans-on-the-potomac.

37 A. T. Robertson, *Life and Letters of John Albert Broadus* (Philadelphia: American Baptist Publication Society, 1910), 243.

38 Ibid., 342.

In 1892, B. H. Carroll, founder of Southwestern Baptist Theological Seminary in Fort Worth, Texas, reflected on Spurgeon's enduring legacy: "The fire has tried his work. It abides unconsumed." He added, "When Bonaparte died, Phillips said: 'He is fallen.' When Spurgeon died, the world said: 'He is risen.'"[39] The notable theologian Augustus Hopkins Strong had such admiration for Spurgeon that, on June 17, 1887, he brought John D. Rockefeller to London to meet him. After two hours of fellowship, the two Americans concluded that "the secret of Mr. Spurgeon's success was his piety and his faith. Above all else, he seemed to be a man of prayer."[40]

In 1934, George W. Truett, pastor of First Baptist Church, Dallas, Texas, was the only speaker invited to deliver a fifty-five-minute address at the Royal Albert Hall in London for the centenary of Spurgeon's birth.[41] Truett's successor at First Baptist Dallas, W. A. Criswell, once claimed that Spurgeon was "the greatest preacher who has ever lived." He added, "When I get to Heaven, after I see the Saviour and my own dear family, I want to see Charles Haddon Spurgeon."[42] Billy Graham once applauded Spurgeon for being "a preacher who extolled Christ—everlastingly."[43]

Charles Spurgeon *has* come to America. Through the rotations of a thousand gears of grace, his early sermons have spanned a century and a sea to be read by new audiences. Like Abel, who "still speaks, even though he is dead" (Heb 11:4 NIV), Spurgeon still has something to say. "I would fling my shadow through eternal ages if I could,"[44] he once declared. And indeed, his shadow has spilled into our age. Few preachers are as frequently cited, "memed," tweeted, and quoted (or misquoted) as Spurgeon is. Future historians will be right to see the publication of his *Lost Sermons* as belonging to an extraordinary and unexpected narrative of redemption.

The publication of these sermons will reach full potential when they guide readers not just *to* Spurgeon but *through* Spurgeon to Jesus Christ. Insomuch as John the Baptist's words become our own, "[Christ] must increase, but I must decrease" (John 3:30 ESV), and insomuch as the sermons inform minds, reform hearts, and

39 These two quotations come from B. H. Carroll's 1892 address "The Death of Spurgeon" (J. B. Cranfill, comp., *Sermons and Life Sketch of B. H. Carroll* [Philadelphia: American Baptist Publication Society, 1895], 25, 44).

40 Crerar Douglas, ed., *Autobiography of Augustus Hopkins Strong* (Valley Forge, PA: Judson Press, 1981), 300. See also *ST*, July 1887: 369.

41 See Keith E. Durso, *Thy Will Be Done: A Biography of George W. Truett* (Macon, GA: Mercer University Press, 2009), 214. Truett had also delivered an address entitled "Spurgeon: Herald of the Everlasting Evangel" at the Marble Collegiate Church in New York City on May 8, 1934 (see "Centenary Program in Honor and Recognition of Charles Haddon Spurgeon" in The Spurgeon Library archives).

42 W. A. Criswell, quoted in *NPSP*, 1:book jacket.

43 Billy Graham, quoted in *NPSP*, 3:book jacket.

44 W. A. Fullerton, *C. H. Spurgeon: A Biography* (London: Williams and Norgate, 1920), 181.

transform lives, then the energy will be worth the expenditure, and future generations will glimpse not only Spurgeon's shadow but the *Son* that caused the shadow.[45]

B. H. Carroll once said, "The great crying want of this day in our churches is *fire*."[46] If we can share Carroll's desire for fire, then Helmut Thielicke's words will still ring true of Spurgeon: "This bush from old London still burns and shows no signs of being consumed."[47]

Christian T. George
Associate Professor of Historical Theology
Curator of The Spurgeon Library
Midwestern Baptist Theological Seminary
Kansas City, Missouri

---

45 I have used some of the verbiage in this paragraph and in the preceding one on numerous occasions in interviews, blogs, social media, and in my interview for Stephen McCaskell's documentary on Spurgeon, *Through the Eyes of Spurgeon*; accessed May 18, 2016, www.throughtheeyesofspurgeon.com. However, I originally wrote this material for the contextual introduction of the timeline "The Man and His Times: Charles Haddon Spurgeon" that hangs on the wall in the entrance of The Spurgeon Library at Midwestern Baptist Theological Seminary in Kansas City, Missouri.

46 Cranfill, *Sermons and Life Sketch of B. H. Carroll*, 42, emphasis added.

47 Helmut Thielicke, *Encounter with Spurgeon* (trans. John W. Doberstein; Stuttgart, Germany: Quell-Verlag, 1961), 4.

ACKNOWLEDGMENTS

O ver the past eight years, I have become indebted to numerous individuals who have lent time and talent to the formation and publication of this project: David Bebbington took an interest in this project from the beginning, and I am grateful for the encouraging way he has shepherded these sermons. Steve Holmes, my doctoral supervisor at the University of St. Andrews, has also provided timely advice and guidance over the years. Tom Wright, Ian Randall, Mark Elliot, and Ian Bradley were instrumental in sharpening my writing and honing my thoughts on Spurgeon's Christology. Timothy Larsen, Brian Stanley, Mark Hopkins, Michael Haykin, and Tom Nettles widened my understanding of nineteenth-century evangelicalism in ways that directly benefited this present volume.

J. I. Packer, Chuck Colson (1931–2012), and Mark Dever have offered broad direction to my research. I am indebted to their mentorship, support, and investment in my life. To those at St. Andrews who witnessed the embryonic stage of this research, I also remain grateful: Liam Garvie, pastor at St. Andrew's Baptist Church at the time; my doctoral colleagues at the Roundel; the students I tutored at St. Mary's College; and also Lawrence Foster (1991–2010), whose winsome conversations about Spurgeon on the Eden Golf Course made my frequent excavations of its bunkers always worth the dig.

When Nigel Wright and Andy Brockbank at Spurgeon's College first contracted with me in 2010 to publish Spurgeon's sermons, I could not have envisioned the scope of this project. Nigel's timely emails over the years are among my most cherished correspondences. Peter Morden, former acting principal of Spurgeon's College, is a Spurgeon scholar of the highest caliber whose friendship I value. I am also indebted to the librarian of the College for many years, Judy Powles, who aided my research in the Heritage Room Archives and, along with Mary Fugill, made arrangements for prolonged research visits.

Roger Standing, Helen Stokley, Annabel Haycraft, the board of governors, and all those who have served in the administration of Spurgeon's College have also garnished my gratitude. Their continued partnership with B&H Academic and

The Spurgeon Library is accomplishing much in keeping Spurgeon's legacy alive for rising generations of scholars, pastors, and students. London-based photographer Chris Gander also deserves special acknowledgment for his indefatigable resolve in photographing every single page of Spurgeon's notebooks.

After I moved from St. Andrews to teach at Oklahoma Baptist University, the project benefited from the leadership of President David Whitlock, Provost Stan Norman, and Dean Mark McClellan. My colleagues in the Herschel H. Hobbs College of Theology and Ministry and in other departments offered helpful feedback in the initial editing and organization of the sermons. I am also grateful for the research assistants who offered their time in assisting me on the original proposal: Cara Cliburn Allen, Justine Kirby Aliff, Kasey Chapman, Raliegh White, and Christina Perry.

During my last semester in Shawnee, Oklahoma, Jim Baird, vice president of B&H Academic, expressed interest in publishing these sermons. Jim's enthusiasm, commitment to Christian publishing, and courage for undertaking a one-million-word project have not escaped me. He and his capable team in Nashville stand in direct continuity with Spurgeon's original London publisher, Passmore & Alabaster, who would have published these sermons in 1857–1858 if Spurgeon had completed his editing process. Special thanks goes to Chris Thompson, Dave Schroeder, Mike Cooper, Barnabas Piper, Audrey Greeson, Jade Novak, Heidi Smith, Steve Reynolds, India Harkless, Debbie Carter, Judi Hayes, Lesley Patterson-Marx, Jason Jones, Ryan Camp, Mandi Cofer, Jennifer Day, Jessi Wallace, Renée Chavez, Kris Bearss, and Alissa McGowan for shaping the project thus far. I am also grateful for Trevin Wax, Chris Martin, and Brandon Smith. I am also deeply thankful for my literary agent, Greg Johnson, a friend and fellow laborer.

A turning point in the project came in 2014 when Jason Allen, president of Midwestern Baptist Theological Seminary, hired me to teach historical theology and serve as curator of The Spurgeon Library. His allocation of resources and excitement for these sermons allowed me to undertake a publication of this scope. I am grateful for his friendship, leadership, initiative, and vision for all that God has in store for this seminary. Connie and Bill Jenkins gave generously for the construction of The Spurgeon Library, and their support has provided a platform on which this project can stand. The opportunity to curate the thousands of volumes Spurgeon owned and often annotated has added innumerable layers of unexpected value to the research. Spurgeon owned some of the books in this collection during the writing of his early sermons.

The faculty, administration, and staff of Midwestern Seminary have been instrumental in creating an environment where scholarship and collegiality excel. I am particularly grateful to Provost Jason Duesing, Deans Thor Madsen and John Mark Yeats, Vice President for Institutional Relations Charles Smith, and all those who work in the Communications Office, seminary library, and bookstore who daily embody the kind providence of God.

I have discovered a lifelong friend in Jared Wilson, director of content strategy and managing editor of "For the Church" (www.ftc.co). Jared is a wordsmith par excellence who won't shut up about grace and whose weekly conversations have sustained me through the editing of these sermons. I am grateful for Jared and the "thinklings" who join our weekly discussions and for all those associated with The Spurgeon Library. I am appreciative of Brian Albert, David Conte, and research assistants Ronni Kurtz, Phillip Ort, Tyler Sykora, Adam Sanders, Devin Schlote, Drake Osborn, Garrett Skrbina, and Savannah Nokes. I am also grateful for the team of Spurgeon scholars who have worked in some capacity on the project: Allyson Todd, Cody Barnhart, Colton Strother, Austin Burgard, Gabriel Pech, Jordan Wade, Jacob Overstreet, Garet Halbert, and Andrew Marks. I am also thankful for Chad McDonald, my pastor at Lenexa Baptist Church, whose sermons rarely suffer from the absence of a poignant Spurgeon quotation.

During my research in Oxford, Cambridge, and London in November and December 2014, the following librarians offered me their expertise:

Emily Burgoyne, library assistant, The Angus Library and Archive, Regent's Park College, University of Oxford;

Yaye Tang, archives assistant, Cambridgeshire Archives and Local Studies, Shire Hall;

Josh E. Acton, Myles Greensmith, Celia Tyler, and Mary Burgess, local studies assistants with the Cambridgeshire Collection, Central Library;

Anne Taylor, head of the Map Department, and Ian Pittock, assistant librarian, Maps Room, Cambridge University Library;

Stephen Southall, Dorrie Parris, Marion Lemmon, and Anne Craig, Waterbeach Independent Lending Library;

John Matthews, archivist, St. Andrew's Street Baptist Church;

The librarians of Cherry Hinton Public Library, Bottisham Community Library Association, and Suffolk County Council Information and Library Service;

The librarians of Dr. Williams's Library and John Harvey Library, London.

I am thankful for the tremendous hospitality of Osvaldo and Kristen Padilla and their son Philip during this season of research in the UK.

I am also grateful for assistance provided by Taylor Rutland, Pam Cole, and Amanda Denton of the New Orleans Baptist Theological Seminary, along with Jeff Griffin, Eric Benoy, and Kyara St. Amant. Numerous individuals also contributed to this project from a distance and deserve acknowledgment: Peter Williams at Tyndale House, Cambridge; Charles Carter, Robert Smith Jr., Gerald Bray, Paul House, Vickie Gaston, and Le-Ann Little at Beeson Divinity School; and David Dockery, Thomas Kidd, Nathan Finn, David Crosby, Fred Luter, and my longtime pilgrim friend, David Riker. I am also grateful for Stephen McCaskell, whose documentary *Through the Eyes of Spurgeon* (www.throughtheeyesofspurgeon.com) remains second to none, and Jeff Landon, who champions Spurgeon through www.missionalwear.com.

This project also found support in those who are historically and even biologically connected with Spurgeon. I am grateful for Darren Newman and Mary McLean, current residents of the Teversham cottage where Spurgeon preached his first sermon; Martin Ensell, pastor of Waterbeach Chapel, and his wife, Angela, for their hospitality; and also Peter Masters, senior pastor of the Metropolitan Tabernacle.

I am humbled to have known Spurgeon's living descendants: David Spurgeon (great-grandson), whom I met shortly before his passing in 2015. His wife, Hilary, and their two children, Susie (along with her husband, Tim, and children, Jonah, Lily, Juliet, and Ezra) and Richard (along with his wife, Karen, and daughter, Hannah), have become family to me.

I would especially like to acknowledge my father, who first inspired me to read Spurgeon on a pilgrimage to England and who continues to model scholarship, preaching, fatherhood, and Christian hospitality at their very best. My mother is one of the best writers I know, and her encouragements along the way have allowed me to better undertake this project. Bayne and Jerry Pounds have been prayer warriors for us from the beginning and would require additional paragraphs to acknowledge all they have done. Hannah and Jerry (and Luke and Caroline) Pounds are family who have become precious friends, and I am also grateful for the friendship of Stephanie and Nic Francis (and Andrew, Ella Grace, and Caleb). I am so thankful for Jane and Jack Hunter and for Dorothy Smith, an editor extraordinaire who worked tirelessly on the sermons during the early stages of editing.

The warmest words of gratitude I reserve for my wife, Rebecca—a writer, editor, and scholar of uncanny ability. Rebecca's companionship has made this road worth walking. When I first encountered the sermons in London, Rebecca was with me.

Since then she has sacrificed greatly in donating hundreds of hours to copyediting, proofreading, researching, brainstorming, and improving every aspect of this project. Were it not for Rebecca's fearless resolve in 2013 during my illness, the *Lost Sermons* would have remained as lost today as when Spurgeon abandoned them in 1857 when his own life circumstances gridlocked the publication. To Rebecca I give full credit, not only for saving the life of this project but also for saving the life of its editor.

When the first copy of his seven-volume commentary on the Psalms, *The Treasury of David*, was bound, Spurgeon "looked at it as fondly as he might have done at a favourite child."[1] The release of this present volume has solicited a similar sentiment in us and in many who have played roles in the stewardship of these sermons. To them, and to all those yet to join our journey, I remain a grateful bondservant.

---

1   Eric Hayden, introduction to *The Treasury of David*, by C. H. Spurgeon (London: Passmore & Alabaster ed.; Pasadena, TX: Pilgrim Publications, 1983), 1:iii.

ABBREVIATIONS

Autobiography	*C. H. Spurgeon's Autobiography. Compiled from His Diary, Letters, and Records, by His Wife, and His Private Secretary.* 4 vols. London: Passmore & Alabaster, 1899–1900. The Spurgeon Library.
Lectures	*Lectures to My Students: A Selection from Addresses Delivered to the Students of the Pastors' College, Metropolitan Tabernacle.* London: Passmore & Alabaster, 1893. The Spurgeon Library.
MTP	*The Metropolitan Tabernacle Pulpit: Sermons Preached and Revised by C. H. Spurgeon.* Vols. 7–63. Pasadena, TX: Pilgrim Publications, 1970–2006.
Notebook	*Spurgeon Sermon Outline Notebooks.* 11 vols. Heritage Room, Spurgeon's College, London. K1/5, U1.02.
NPSP	*The New Park Street Pulpit: Containing Sermons Preached and Revised by the Rev. C. H. Spurgeon, Minister of the Chapel.* 6 vols. Pasadena, TX: Pilgrim Publications, 1970–2006.
ST	*The Sword and the Trowel; A Record of Combat with Sin & Labour for the Lord.* 37 vols. London: Passmore & Alabaster, 1865–1902. The Spurgeon Library.
TD	*The Treasury of David: Containing an Original Exposition of the Book of Psalms; A Collection of Illustrative Extracts from the Whole Range of Literature; A Series of Homiletical Hints Upon Almost Every Verse; And Lists of Writers Upon Each Psalm.* 7 vols. London: Passmore & Alabaster, 1869–1885. The Spurgeon Library.

INTRODUCTION

"BEAR WITNESS, OH PAPER!
OF MY THANKS FOR THESE
INSTANCES OF GRACE."
—*Charles Spurgeon*

(Notebook 3, final page, 1853)

On March 20, 1852, a deacon at Waterbeach Chapel wrote a letter to Charles Spurgeon's father. In it the deacon described the chapel's reception of the teenage pastor:

> Allow me to say that, since his coming, the congregation is very much increased, the aisles and vestry being often full, and many go away for want of room; there are several cases of his being made useful in awakening the careless; and although we have only known him about five months, the attachment is as strong as if we had been acquainted with him as many years; and if he were to leave us just now, it would be the occasion of general "Lamentation, Mourning, and Woe."[1]

Coupled with Charles's third notebook of sermons, this letter presents a higher-resolution snapshot of the spiritual revival that took place in Waterbeach during 1852–53. Before Charles accepted the pastorate, crime, violence, robbery, and alcoholism pervaded the village. The once-dwindling cottage, now overflowing, drew visitors from other towns, and Waterbeach earned a new reputation. "God requires labour of us," Charles told his congregation, "but not success."[2]

Yet success did come. Unprecedented acts of charity were recorded in Waterbeach. On January 24, 1852, "nearly 60 tons of coal were given to the poor of the parish."[3]

---

1   *Autobiography* 1:235.
2   "Who Is Sufficient for These Things?" (Sermon 173).
3   Denis Cheason and Joan Danby, comp., *The Waterbeach Chronicle: Events in the Life of a Fen-Edge Village Between 1779 and 1899, as Reported in the Cambridge Chronicle* (orig. pub.: Stratford, London: Plaistow Press Magazines, Ltd., 1984; repr: Cambridge: Print-Out, 1994), "1852, 24th Jan."

On February 5, 500 bedsheets were distributed to the boys' schoolroom. According to the report, "widows and single persons received single sheets, and if we may judge by the smiling faces which left the school all seemed highly gratified."[4]

Charles claimed no credit for the spiritual awakening affecting his chapel and village. "God doeth good," he wrote, "and all the good herein is every atom his."[5] Throughout his sermons, Charles's humility, dependence on God, and hatred of sin are on display. "Sin must not be endured. Out with the traitor."[6]

Numerous "traitors" had infiltrated Waterbeach Chapel. Not bashful in speaking forcefully and directly, Charles introduced the intruders to his congregation: "Behold the caverns of evil, the floods of sin, of evil affections, desires, imaginations. See our own weakness, proneness to evil, aversion to good, our lust, pride, self love."[7] If Waterbeach Chapel would succeed, her members must renew their commitment to personal holiness and Scripture. "We must learn to submit to God's Word," Charles said, "for one letter of that is worth a volume either of Calvin or Arminius."[8]

Repentance could remedy even the worst sin, but delaying could prove disastrous. "You will repent tomorrow," Charles mused. "Alas! No such thing. The heart hardens every moment."[9] Overcoming temptation was possible by thinking "on thy far off and absent Jesus"[10] and by communing closely with him, for, as Charles observed, "The man who communes much with God will be meek."[11]

In a rare autobiographical reference, Charles even warned *himself* against worshiping the idols that confront those, like him, who possess "clear heads, good voices, lively wit, strong mind, learning, knowledge." Charles added, "We may preach well and be useful. But if we have a vain glory and praise not God, we sin."[12]

Always ready to redirect the sermon back onto himself, Charles confessed that he too needed the comfort Isaiah offered: "Fear not, thou worm Jacob, and ye men of Israel; I will help thee" (Isa 41:14). In this sermon, the third Roman numeral is "Now notice a few cases when we need this indeed" and was followed immediately by Charles's own confession: "I do, when preaching and fearing."[13]

---

4   Ibid., "1852, 5th Feb."
5   Notebook 3, final page.
6   "Do It with Thy Might" (Sermon 162).
7   "God's Binding the Floods" (Sermon 186).
8   "Making Shipwreck of Faith" (Sermon 161), underscore in the original.
9   "Boast Not Thyself of Tomorrow" (Sermon 150).
10 "Remember Jesus" (Sermon 163).
11 "Fear Not, Thou Worm Jacob" (Sermon 170).
12 "Little Children Keep Yourselves from Idols" (Sermon 153).
13 "Fear Not, Thou Worm Jacob" (Sermon 170).

In 1852, Charles had no plans to leave Waterbeach. In fact, he may have even had a ten-year plan for the chapel. In his sermon "The Church of Antioch," he said, "The first preachers were very successful, for it seems about 10 years and the church was firmly established." Then he added, "And why should not ours?"[14]

To be sure, Charles's reputation attracted the attention of nearby chapels, especially those in which he preached as a participant of the Lay Preachers' Association at St. Andrew's Street Baptist Church. But his botched interview with Joseph Angus only months earlier had convinced him to decline the pursuit of a formal education at Stepney College in London. Against his father's wishes he decided to remain a pastor in Waterbeach. Revival was breaking out. Charles would not abandon his flock, who needed shepherding now more than ever.

As in the previous two notebooks, Charles's prayers in Notebook 3 reflect an energetic vitality and spiritual intensity. "God, melt me and you."[15] At times his desperation comes to the surface: "God, help me, a poor thing."[16] "Lord, revive my stupid soul!"[17] He likely even referenced Benjamin Franklin's famous kite experiment of 1752 as a model for prayer: "We must send up our wire on high to attract the heavenly influence."[18]

In his electric sermon "Oh That Thou Wouldest, Etc.," Charles selected Isaiah 64:1–2 as his text, verse 2 of which reads, "As when the melting fire burneth, the fire causeth the waters to boil, to make thy name known to thine adversaries, that the nations may tremble at thy presence!" He yearned that "the fire would burn in our breast. The fire of love and zeal would warm us. Yea, it would be a melting fire, melting our hearts completely. The fire would make our cold hearts boil. No lukewarm water,

---

14 "The Church of Antioch" (Sermon 172).

15 "Jesus['s] Obedience and Self Denial" (Sermon 148).

16 "The Tabernacle of Jacob and Mount Zion Blessed of God" (Sermon 145).

17 "The Meekness of Moses" (Sermon 179). For additional prayers in this notebook, see "God's Dealings with the Antediluvians" (Sermon 138); "Ephraim's Goodness like the Morning Cloud" (Sermon 139); "Put Ye in the Sickle for the Harvest Is Ripe" (Sermon 143); "The Joy of Heaven" (Sermon 147); "The Call of Abraham" (Sermon 152); "Little Children Keep Yourselves from Idols" (Sermon 153); "The Washing of the Disciples' Feet by Jesus" (Sermon 156); "Open Profession Required" (Sermon 158); "If the Footmen Weary Thee, Etc." (Sermon 159); "Making Shipwreck of Faith" (Sermon 161); "Do It with Thy Might" (Sermon 162); "Remember Jesus" (Sermon 163); "I Glory in Infirmities" (Sermon 165); "I Have Gone Astray like a Lost Sheep" (Sermon 166); "The Unclean Spirit Returning" (Sermon 168); "Fear Not, Thou Worm Jacob" (Sermon 170); "Oh That Thou Wouldest, Etc." (Sermon 171); "Who Is Sufficient for These Things?" (Sermon 173); "No Condemnation to Christians" (Sermon 174); "Mary with Jesus in the Garden" (Sermon 175); "Absolute Sovereignty" (Sermon 177); "The Meekness of Moses" (Sermon 179); "More for Us Than Against Us" (Sermon 180); "The Baptism of the Spirit" (Sermon 181); "Profane Esau" (Sermon 182); "Leaning on Jesus['s] Bosom" (Sermon 183); "The Resurrection Body" (Sermon 185); "God's Binding the Floods" (Sermon 186); and "Following Jesus with a Cross on Our Back" (Sermon 187).

18 "Oh That Thou Wouldest, Etc." (Sermon 171).

but boiling hot. The waters of penitence, love, prayer, compassion, and all holy waters would boil."[19]

Charles's visible love for the unconverted and his urgent zeal for winning souls is multiplied in this volume. "Oh! my God," he begged, "stir up me and my hearers to work, for Jesus's sake."[20] "Lord, compel us to come in."[21] "Oh my God, turn them."[22] Charles's desire for conversions manifests in his prayer, "Oh! God, I commit to paper this prayer, that thou wouldst come down now and help me and save sinners through Jesus."[23]

His trademark appeal to the cross—a feature of his preaching that blossoms fully in Charles's later ministry—is not only seeded in these sermons but richly fertilized. The force of the Waterbeach revival is felt in his numerous exhortations. "Let your heart ascend as the flames toward heaven," he pleaded.[24] Charles believed "the conversion of the world will not always go on at snail-pace, and we ought to pray that it may not in this place."[25] Regardless of his audience's age or occupation, Charles preached the gospel to everyone who came to hear his sermons. "Young, old," he said, "the Lord awaken ye. Oh God! Grant it."[26]

19 Ibid.
20 "Do It with Thy Might" (Sermon 162).
21 "The Great Gospel Supper" (Sermon 137).
22 "Boast Not Thyself of To-morrow" (Sermon 150).
23 "Oh That Thou Wouldest, Etc." (Sermon 171).
24 "The Baptism of the Spirit" (Sermon 181). Examples of final exhortations are found in the following sermons: "The Certain Judgment" (Sermon 136); "God's Dealings with the Antediluvians" (Sermon 138); "Ephraim's Goodness like the Morning Cloud" (Sermon 139); "Who Shall the Lord's Elect Condemn?" (Sermon 141); "Put Ye in the Sickle for the Harvest Is Ripe" (Sermon 143); "The Harvest and the Vintage" (Sermon 144); "The Tabernacles of Jacob and Mount Zion Blessed of God" (Sermon 145); "Go Not in Any Other Field" (Sermon 146); "The Joy of Heaven" (Sermon 147); "Jesus['s] Obedience and Self Denial" (Sermon 148); "The Golden Crown of Holiness" (Sermon 149); "Boast Not Thyself of To-morrow" (Sermon 150); "The Call of Abraham" (Sermon 152); "Little Children Keep Yourselves from Idols" (Sermon 153); "Zeal in Religion Commended" (Sermon 154); "Complaint, Prayer, and Answer" (Sermon 155); "The Washing of the Disciples' Feet by Jesus" (Sermon 156); "Open Profession Required" (Sermon 158); "If the Footmen Weary Thee, Etc." (Sermon 159); "The Word Very Precious" (Sermon 160); "Making Shipwreck of Faith" (Sermon 161); "Remember Jesus" (Sermon 163); "Bring My Soul out of Prison" (Sermon 164); "In the World Ye Shall Have Tribulation" (Sermon 167); "The Unclean Spirit Returning" (Sermon 168); "Christ the Power of God" (Sermon 169b); "Oh That Thou Wouldest, Etc." (Sermon 171); "No Condemnation to Christians" (Sermon 174); "Light at Eventide" (Sermon 176); "The Queen of Sheba" (Sermon 178); "The Baptism of the Spirit" (Sermon 181); "Leaning on Jesus['s] Bosom" (Sermon 183); "The Resurrection Body" (Sermon 185); and "God's Binding the Floods" (Sermon 186).
25 "The Church of Antioch" (Sermon 172).
26 "Following Jesus with a Cross on Our Back" (Sermon 187).

As in his first two notebooks, Charles displayed in Notebook 3 a broad evangelical perspective and desire for Christian cooperation.[27] He had only recently adopted the Baptist tradition and frequently interacted with other denominations. In his sermon "The Church of Antioch," Charles studied the apostolic church and noted, "There was much unity among the disciples so that one name would apply to all. Blessed time when this shall return and we shall be gathered in one."[28]

Non-Baptists came to hear Charles preach, and in his controversial and possibly divisive sermon "The Baptism of the Spirit," he acknowledged, "I am not one who often brings this prominent. All know that I endeavor to preach unity: but my warrant for taking this text is the fact that it is the Word of God." After appealing to the doctrine of believer's baptism by immersion, Charles said, "Let us leave the water, the naval combat, and go to where we are agreed." The conclusion of his sermon brought both Baptists and paedo-Baptists under a singular instruction: "All men, be Fire-Baptists even if you will not be Water-Baptists."[29]

One of the more fascinating aspects of Notebook 3 is that for the first time in Charles's earliest ministry, a member from his congregation—an "old sister"—requested Charles to preach from four Scripture passages of her choosing. In the introductory comments of one of these sermons, "Mary with Jesus in the Garden," Charles explained: "This text is one of four which were solemnly committed to me on Wednesday, Oct. 13, 1852, by an old sister in the faith then lying on her bed, which I believe to be the bed of death."[30]

On the final page of the notebook, Charles recorded the four texts she had requested: John 20:16;[31] Zechariah 14:6–7;[32] John 13:23;[33] and Isaiah 41:10.[34] Charles preached sermons on these four texts as requested with one adjustment: instead of preaching on verse 10 of Isaiah 41, Charles preached instead on verse 14, which he deemed was "similar."

---

27 See "Pleasure in the Stones of Zion" (Notebook 1, Sermon 53); "Can Two Walk Together Unless They Are Agreed?" (Notebook 1, Sermon 76); and "David in the Cave of Adullam" (Notebook 2, Sermon 116).
28 "The Church of Antioch" (Sermon 172).
29 "The Baptism of the Spirit" (Sermon 181).
30 "Mary with Jesus in the Garden" (Sermon 175).
31 See "Mary with Jesus in the Garden" (Sermon 175).
32 See "Fear Not, Thou Worm Jacob" (Sermon 170).
33 See "Light at Eventide" (Sermon 176).
34 See "Leaning on Jesus['s] Bosom" (Sermon 183).

Who was this "old sister"? Unfortunately, Charles failed to mention her in his autobiography. Nor can she be traced in his later sermons, writings, letters, or biographies. Why did she select these particular texts? In his sermon "Leaning on Jesus['s] Bosom," Charles hinted at the reason: "She declared that this was the position she ever occupied and that Jesus was her pillow."[35] But for the other three texts, she may have concealed her reasons even from Charles. Beyond similar themes of sympathy, hope, and intimacy with Christ, no obvious commonalities connect these four texts.

Yet the woman hoped that these four sermons would produce spiritual fruit in Charles's ministry. He recorded, "May the God who put them into her mind also hear her prayer and mine that they may become the seed of many souls."[36] It is not clear how long this elderly woman lived, and she likely did not see the thousands of conversions generated after Charles became London's premier pastor in the late 1850s. Nevertheless, Charles preached from her requested texts on numerous occasions at the Metropolitan Tabernacle and throughout his worldwide ministry.

In Notebook 3, Charles continued honing his homiletic. His sermons showcase the gradual development of his textual treatment and highlight the tension that emerged between literal and allegorical interpretations. Charles sought to uncover the original authorial intent in many of his sermons, claiming, "By the help of the Holy Spirit I may be able to speak only what is in the text."[37]

But Charles also saw danger in stifling Scripture. Influenced by John Bunyan's allegory *The Pilgrim's Progress,* which he continued referencing in his sermon illustrations,[38] Charles becomes all the more prone toward spiritualization. "Whilst we like not the torturing scheme which finds a spiritual meaning everywhere," he explained, "we would not cramp a sentence into barely literal meaning when a natural figure appears in it."[39]

---

35 "Leaning on Jesus['s] Bosom" (Sermon 183).
36 "Mary with Jesus in the Garden" (Sermon 175).
37 "The Baptism of the Spirit" (Sermon 181).
38 See "Remember Jesus" (Sermon 163). For previous references to Bunyan, see "The Fight and the Weapons" (Notebook 1, Sermon 37a); "The Fight" (Notebook 1, Sermon 37b); and "David in the Cave of Adullam" (Notebook 2, Sermon 116).
39 "God's Binding the Floods" (Sermon 186).

Stylistically, Charles's handwriting grows larger in comparison to that in his first two notebooks of sermons. For the first time he even illustrated some of his letters for emphasis, like the bolded word "Christian" in his sermon "The Church of Antioch."[40] At the conclusion of this sermon, he sketched a horizontal cross that spans half the length of the page. Other orthographic characteristics include abbreviations,[41] dittography,[42] lines and stippling,[43] strike-throughs,[44] superscripts,[45]

---

40 "The Church of Antioch" (Sermon 172).

41 Examples of abbreviations are found in the following sermons: "The Seven Cries on the Cross" (Sermon 142); "The Call of Abraham" (Sermon 152); "Open Profession Required" (Sermon 158); "Making Shipwreck of Faith" (Sermon 161); "Do It with Thy Might" (Sermon 162); "In the World Ye Shall Have Tribulation" (Sermon 167); "Christ the Power of God" (Sermon 169b); "Mary with Jesus in the Garden" (Sermon 175); and "The Meekness of Moses" (Sermon 179).

42 Examples of dittography are found in the following sermons: "The Joy of Heaven" (Sermon 147); "Little Children Keep Yourselves from Idols" (Sermon 153); "Complaint, Prayer, and Answer" (Sermon 155); and "Mary with Jesus in the Garden" (Sermon 175).

43 Examples of lines and stippling are found in the following sermons: "Calling and Election Sure" (Sermon 135); "God's Dealings with the Antediluvians" (Sermon 138); "The Tower of Babel" (Sermon 140); "Who Shall the Lord's Elect Condemn?" (Sermon 141); "The Harvest and the Vintage" (Sermon 144); "The Joy of Heaven" (Sermon 147); "Jesus['s] Obedience and Self Denial" (Sermon 148); "The Golden Crown of Holiness" (Sermon 149); "Boast Not Thyself of To-morrow" (Sermon 150); "The Call of Abraham" (Sermon 152); "Complaint, Prayer, and Answer" (Sermon 155); "Open Profession Required" (Sermon 158); "Do It with Thy Might" (Sermon 162); "Remember Jesus" (Sermon 163); "The Unclean Spirit Returning" (Sermon 168); "Christ the Power and Wisdom of God" (Sermon 169a); "Christ the Power of God" (Sermon 169b); "Fear Not, Thou Worm Jacob" (Sermon 170); "Oh That Thou Wouldest, Etc." (Sermon 171); "The Church of Antioch" (Sermon 172); "Who Is Sufficient for These Things?" (Sermon 173); "No Condemnation to Christians" (Sermon 174); "Mary with Jesus in the Garden" (Sermon 175); "Light at Eventide" (Sermon 176); "The Meekness of Moses" (Sermon 179); "The Baptism of the Spirit" (Sermon 181); "Profane Esau" (Sermon 182); "Leaning on Jesus['s] Bosom" (Sermon 183); "The Resurrection Body" (Sermon 185); and "God's Binding the Floods" (Sermon 186).

44 Examples of strike-throughs are found in the following sermons: "Calling and Election Sure" (Sermon 135); "Ephraim's Goodness like the Morning Cloud" (Sermon 139); "Jesus['s] Obedience and Self Denial" (Sermon 148); "The Golden Crown of Holiness" (Sermon 149); "The Call of Abraham" (Sermon 152); "Little Children Keep Yourselves from Idols" (Sermon 153); "Zeal in Religion Commended" (Sermon 154); "Complaint, Prayer, and Answer" (Sermon 155); "Open Profession Required" (Sermon 158); "If the Footmen Weary Thee, Etc." (Sermon 159); "Making Shipwreck of Faith" (Sermon 161); "In the World Ye Shall Have Tribulation" (Sermon 167); "The Unclean Spirit Returning" (Sermon 168); "Oh That Thou Wouldest, Etc." (Sermon 171); "Mary with Jesus in the Garden" (Sermon 175); "Light at Eventide" (Sermon 176); "Absolute Sovereignty" (Sermon 177); "The Meekness of Moses" (Sermon 179); "Profane Esau" (Sermon 182); "Leaning on Jesus['s] Bosom" (Sermon 183); "The Resurrection Body" (Sermon 185); and "God's Binding the Floods" (Sermon 186).

45 Examples of superscripted text are found in the following sermons: "God's Dealings with the Antediluvians" (Sermon 138); "The Golden Crown of Holiness" (Sermon 149); "Little Children Keep Yourselves from Idols" (Sermon 153); "Do It with Thy Might" (Sermon 162); "Christ the Power and Wisdom of God" (Sermon 169a); "Light at Eventide" (Sermon 176); "The Meekness of Moses" (Sermon 179); "Leaning on Jesus['s] Bosom" (Sermon 183); and "The Resurrection Body" (Sermon 185).

subscripts,[46] underscores,[47] marginal inscriptions,[48] exclamations,[49] inconsistent numbering,[50] and extraneous notations.[51]

46 Examples of subscripted text are found in the following sermons: "The Certain Judgment" (Sermon 136); "The Tabernacles of Jacob and Mount Zion Blessed of God" (Sermon 145); "I Have Gone Astray like a Lost Sheep" (Sermon 166); and "God's Binding the Floods" (Sermon 186).

47 Examples of underscores are found in the following sermons: "The Great Gospel Supper" (Sermon 137); "God's Dealings with the Antediluvians" (Sermon 138); "Ephraim's Goodness like the Morning Cloud" (Sermon 139); "The Tower of Babel" (Sermon 140); "Who Shall the Lord's Elect Condemn?" (Sermon 141); "The Harvest and the Vintage" (Sermon 144); "Go Not in Any Other Field" (Sermon 146); "The Joy of Heaven" (Sermon 147); "Jesus['s] Obedience and Self Denial" (Sermon 148); "The Golden Crown of Holiness" (Sermon 149); "Boast Not Thyself of To-morrow" (Sermon 150); "Give Us This Day Our Daily Bread" (Sermon 151); "Little Children Keep Yourselves from Idols" (Sermon 153); "Complaint, Prayer, and Answer" (Sermon 155); "The Washing of the Disciples' Feet by Jesus" (Sermon 156); "If the Footmen Weary Thee, Etc." (Sermon 159); "Making Shipwreck of Faith" (Sermon 161); "I Glory in Infirmities" (Sermon 165); "I Have Gone Astray like a Lost Sheep" (Sermon 166); "In the World Ye Shall Have Tribulation" (Sermon 167); "The Unclean Spirit Returning" (Sermon 168); "Fear Not, Thou Worm Jacob" (Sermon 170); "The Church of Antioch" (Sermon 172); "Who Is Sufficient for These Things?" (Sermon 173); "Mary with Jesus in the Garden" (Sermon 175); "Absolute Sovereignty" (Sermon 177); "The Meekness of Moses" (Sermon 179); "More for Us Than Against Us" (Sermon 180); "The Baptism of the Spirit" (Sermon 181); "Profane Esau" (Sermon 182); "Leaning on Jesus['s] Bosom" (Sermon 183); "The Resurrection Body" (Sermon 185); "God's Binding the Floods" (Sermon 186); and "Following Jesus with a Cross on Our Back" (Sermon 187).

48 Examples of marginal notations are found in the following sermons: "The Great Gospel Supper" (Sermon 137); "God's Dealings with the Antediluvians" (Sermon 138); "Ephraim's Goodness like the Morning Cloud" (Sermon 139); "The Tower of Babel" (Sermon 140); "The Seven Cries on the Cross" (Sermon 142); "The Harvest and the Vintage" (Sermon 144); "The Tabernacle of Jacob and Mount Zion Blessed of God" (Sermon 145); "Go Not in Any Other Field" (Sermon 146); "Jesus['s] Obedience and Self Denial" (Sermon 148); "Boast Not Thyself of To-morrow" (Sermon 150); "The Call of Abraham" (Sermon 152); "Complaint, Prayer, and Answer" (Sermon 155); "The Washing of the Disciples' Feet by Jesus" (Sermon 156); "If the Footmen Weary Thee, Etc." (Sermon 159); "The Word Very Precious" (Sermon 160); "Making Shipwreck of Faith" (Sermon 161); "Do It with Thy Might" (Sermon 162); "Remember Jesus" (Sermon 163); "Bring My Soul out of Prison" (Sermon 164); "I Glory in Infirmities" (Sermon 165); "I Have Gone Astray like a Lost Sheep" (Sermon 166); "In the World Ye Shall Have Tribulation" (Sermon 167); "The Unclean Spirit Returning" (Sermon 168); "Christ the Power and Wisdom of God" (Sermon 169a); "Christ the Power of God" (Sermon 169b); "Fear Not, Thou Worm Jacob" (Sermon 170); "Oh That Thou Wouldest, Etc." (Sermon 171); "The Church of Antioch" (Sermon 172); "No Condemnation to Christians" (Sermon 174); "Mary with Jesus in the Garden" (Sermon 175); "Light at Eventide" (Sermon 176); "Absolute Sovereignty" (Sermon 177); "The Queen of Sheba" (Sermon 178); "The Meekness of Moses" (Sermon 179); "The Baptism of the Spirit" (Sermon 181); "Profane Esau" (Sermon 182); "Leaning on Jesus['s] Bosom" (Sermon 183); "By His Stripes We Are Healed" (Sermon 184); "The Resurrection Body" (Sermon 185); and "God's Binding the Floods" (Sermon 186).

49 Examples of exclamations are found in the following sermons: "Ephraim's Goodness like the Morning Cloud" (Sermon 139); "Who Shall the Lord's Elect Condemn?" (Sermon 141); "Put Ye in the Sickle for the Harvest Is Ripe" (Sermon 143); "The Golden Crown of Holiness" (Sermon 149); "Boast Not Thyself of To-morrow" (Sermon 150); "The Call of Abraham" (Sermon 152); "Little Children Keep Yourselves from Idols" (Sermon 153); "The Washing of the Disciples' Feet by Jesus" (Sermon 156); "I Glory in Infirmities" (Sermon 165); "Oh That Thou Wouldest, Etc." (Sermon 171); "The Church of Antioch" (Sermon 172); "Who Is Sufficient for These Things?" (Sermon 173); "No Condemnation to Christians" (Sermon 174); "Mary with Jesus in the Garden" (Sermon 175); "The Queen of Sheba" (Sermon 178); "The Baptism of the Spirit" (Sermon 181); and "God's Binding the Floods" (Sermon 186).

50 For an example of Charles's inconsistent sermon numbering, see "The Washing of the Disciples' Feet by Jesus" (Sermon 156).

51 Examples of extraneous notations are found in the following sermons: "The Tower of Babel" (Sermon 140); "Complaint, Prayer, and Answer" (Sermon 155); "The Washing of the Disciples' Feet

Charles also referenced in these sermons a wide array of religious and nonreligious subjects, including Anglicanism,[52] antinomianism,[53] art,[54] apostacy,[55] Arianism,[56] Arminianism,[57] baptism,[58] Calvinism,[59] formalism,[60] fratricide,[61] hieroglyphics,[62] Judaism,[63] Martin Luther,[64] martyrdom,[65] medicine,[66] moralism,[67] nominalism,[68] philosophy,[69] polygamy,[70] Protestantism,[71] Puseyism,[72] Roman Catholicism,[73] self-mortification,[74] Socinianism,[75] stoicism,[76] Sunday school,[77] and the Trinity.[78]

by Jesus" (Sermon 156); "Oh That Thou Wouldest, Etc." (Sermon 171); "The Church of Antioch" (Sermon 172); "Light at Eventide" (Sermon 176); "Profane Esau" (Sermon 182); "Leaning on Jesus['s] Bosom" (Sermon 183); "The Resurrection Body" (Sermon 185); and "God's Binding the Floods" (Sermon 186).

52 See "Christ the Power of God" (Sermon 169b) and "The Baptism of the Spirit" (Sermon 181).

53 See "Making Shipwreck of Faith" (Sermon 161).

54 See "Jesus['s] Obedience and Self Denial" (Sermon 148).

55 See "Profane Esau" (Sermon 182).

56 See "More for Us Than Against Us" (Sermon 180).

57 See "Making Shipwreck of Faith" (Sermon 161).

58 See "The Baptism of the Spirit" (Sermon 181).

59 See "Making Shipwreck of Faith" (Sermon 161).

60 See "Profane Esau" (Sermon 182).

61 See "God's Dealings with the Antediluvians" (Sermon 138).

62 See "The Golden Crown of Holiness" (Sermon 149).

63 See "Christ the Power of God" (Sermon 169b).

64 See "The Meekness of Moses" (Sermon 179).

65 See "The Joy of Heaven" (Sermon 147); "If the Footmen Weary Thee, Etc." (Sermon 159); "The Church of Antioch" (Sermon 172); and "Profane Esau" (Sermon 182).

66 See "In the World Ye Shall Have Tribulation" (Sermon 167).

67 See "The Certain Judgment" (Sermon 136); "Who Shall the Lord's Elect Condemn?" (Sermon 141); and "Christ the Power of God" (Sermon 169b).

68 See "Open Profession Required" (Sermon 158).

69 See "I Glory in Infirmities" (Sermon 165).

70 See "God's Dealings with the Antediluvians" (Sermon 138).

71 See "Ephraim's Goodness like the Morning Cloud" (Sermon 139); "Little Children Keep Yourselves from Idols" (Sermon 153); "Open Profession Required" (Sermon 158); "Do It with Thy Might" (Sermon 162); "The Unclean Spirit Returning" (Sermon 168); and "Christ the Power of God" (Sermon 169b).

72 See "More for Us Than Against Us" (Sermon 180).

73 See "The Golden Crown of Holiness" (Sermon 149); "Little Children Keep Yourselves from Idols" (Sermon 153); "Open Profession Required" (Sermon 158); "Christ the Power of God" (Sermon 169b); "More for Us Than Against Us" (Sermon 180); and "Leaning on Jesus['s] Bosom" (Sermon 183).

74 See "The Golden Crown of Holiness" (Sermon 149).

75 See "The Certain Judgment" (Sermon 136) and "Open Profession Required" (Sermon 158).

76 See "I Glory in Infirmities" (Sermon 165).

77 See "Do It with Thy Might" (Sermon 162).

78 See "The Tower of Babel" (Sermon 140).

In the fifty-four[79] sermons contained in Notebook 3, Spurgeon wrote twenty-six sermons (48 percent) on Old Testament texts, twenty-seven sermons (50 percent) on New Testament texts, and one sermon (2 percent) without a Scripture text. In his third notebook Spurgeon preached more sermons from Psalms, Isaiah, and Matthew than any other biblical books (five sermons each), followed by the book of John (four sermons).

Of his twenty-six Old Testament sermons in Notebook 3, 20 percent each are from Psalms and Isaiah (five sermons each); 12 percent from Jeremiah (three sermons); 8 percent from Genesis (two sermons); and 4 percent (one sermon) each from Exodus, Numbers, Ruth, 1 Kings, 2 Kings, Job, Proverbs, Ecclesiastes, Hosea, Joel, and Zechariah. Charles preached from fourteen of the thirty-nine books of the Old Testament (36 percent). He did not preach any sermons from the Old Testament books of Leviticus, Deuteronomy, Joshua, Judges, 1 Samuel, 2 Samuel, 1 Chronicles, 2 Chronicles, Ezra, Nehemiah, Esther, Song of Solomon, Lamentations, Ezekiel, Daniel, Amos, Obadiah, Jonah, Micah, Nahum, Habakkuk, Zephaniah, Haggai, or Malachi (62 percent of the Old Testament books).

Of his twenty-seven New Testament sermons,[80] 19 percent are from Matthew (five sermons); 15 percent (four sermons) from John; 11 percent (three sermons) each from 1 Corinthians and 2 Corinthians; 7 percent (two sermons) each from Romans and Hebrews; and 4 percent (one sermon) each from Mark, Luke, Acts, Galatians, 1 Timothy, 2 Peter, 1 John, and Revelation.[81] Spurgeon preached from fourteen of the twenty-seven books of the New Testament (52 percent). He did not preach any sermons from Ephesians, Philippians, Colossians, 1 Thessalonians, 2 Thessalonians, 2 Timothy, Titus, Philemon, James, 1 Peter, 2 John, 3 John, or Jude (48 percent of the New Testament books).

In total, Charles preached from twenty-eight of the sixty-six books of the Bible (42 percent).

In Notebook 1, Charles wrote one-page outlines (or "skeletons" as he called them). In Notebook 2, he expanded his sermon word counts and page lengths. The fifty-four sermons in Notebook 3, however, include both short and long sermons. These sermons range in word count from 104 words ("Go Not in Any Other Field" [Sermon 146]) to 1,201 words ("God's Binding the Floods" [Sermon 186]). These word counts include Roman numerals and other outlining mechanisms for headings and subheadings, but they do not include sermons titles, Scripture references, Scripture texts, references

---

79 In Notebook 3, Charles preached two sermons on 1 Cor 1:24: "Christ the Power and Wisdom of God" (Sermon 169a) and "Christ the Power of God" (Sermon 169b).

80 Charles's sermon "The Seven Cries on the Cross" (Sermon 142) is from the Gospels, but since it does not have a specific scripture text, it has not been included in these calculations.

81 All percentages have been rounded.

to villages or dates, or marginal notations written on the sermon page. Below are the word counts for the sermons in Notebook 3:

Sermon 135 = 262 words
Sermon 136 = 219 words
Sermon 137 = 231 words
Sermon 138 = 525 words
Sermon 139 = 434 words
Sermon 140 = 612 words
Sermon 141 = 346 words
Sermon 142 = 147 words
Sermon 143 = 240 words
Sermon 144 = 455 words
Sermon 145 = 273 words
Sermon 146 = 104 words
Sermon 147 = 494 words
Sermon 148 = 424 words
Sermon 149 = 746 words
Sermon 150 = 624 words
Sermon 151 = 204 words
Sermon 152 = 906 words
Sermon 153 = 796 words
Sermon 154 = 372 words
Sermon 155 = 853 words
Sermon 156 = 947 words
Sermon 157 = 118 words
Sermon 158 = 822 words
Sermon 159 = 527 words
Sermon 160 = 192 words
Sermon 161 = 772 words

Sermon 162 = 432 words
Sermon 163 = 349 words
Sermon 164 = 522 words
Sermon 165 = 618 words
Sermon 166 = 231 words
Sermon 167 = 839 words
Sermon 168 = 775 words
Sermon 169a = 150 words
Sermon 169b = 421 words
Sermon 170 = 618 words
Sermon 171 = 730 words
Sermon 172 = 870 words
Sermon 173 = 481 words
Sermon 174 = 557 words
Sermon 175 = 1,126 words
Sermon 176 = 609 words
Sermon 177 = 703 words
Sermon 178 = 168 words
Sermon 179 = 961 words
Sermon 180 = 177 words
Sermon 181 = 645 words
Sermon 182 = 1,030 words
Sermon 183 = 848 words
Sermon 184 = 149 words
Sermon 185 = 707 words
Sermon 186 = 1,201 words
Sermon 187 = 206 words

The average word count of the sermons in Notebook 3 is 533 words.

WORD COUNT *per* SERMON

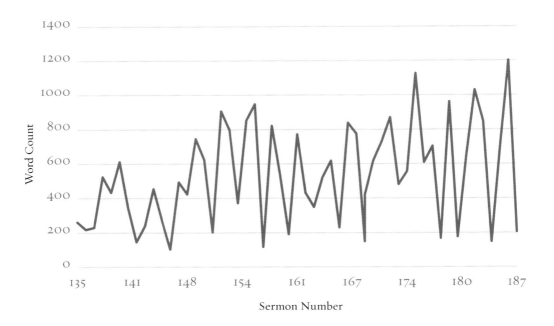

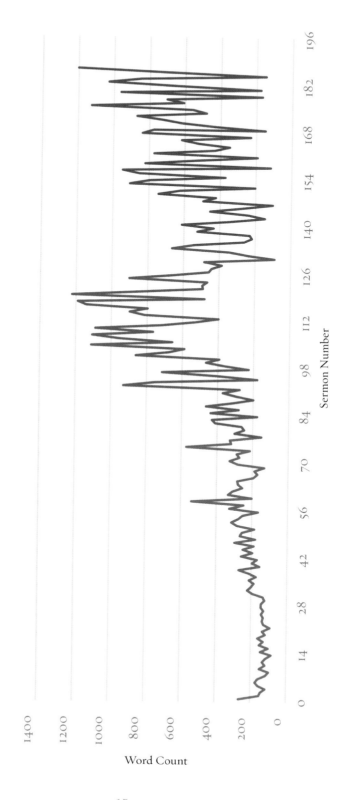

WORD COUNT TREND *for* NOTEBOOKS 1, 2, *and* 3

WORD COUNT DISTRIBUTION *of* SERMONS
in NOTEBOOK 3[82]

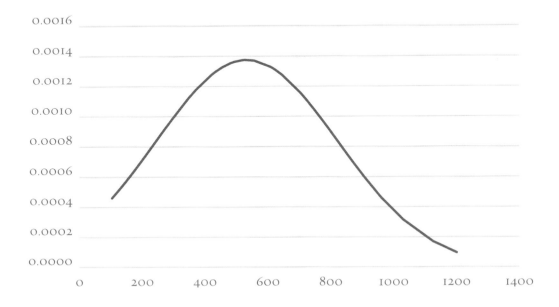

82 Of note to the statistician, the sermon word count in Notebook 3 forms a nearly perfect normal distri-
bution ("bell curve") with a mean of 569 and a standard deviation of 293. This graph was plotted using
Microsoft Excel. The x-axis represents word count and the y-axis represents probability.

16

PERCENTAGE *of* SERMONS
from OLD *and* NEW TESTAMENTS

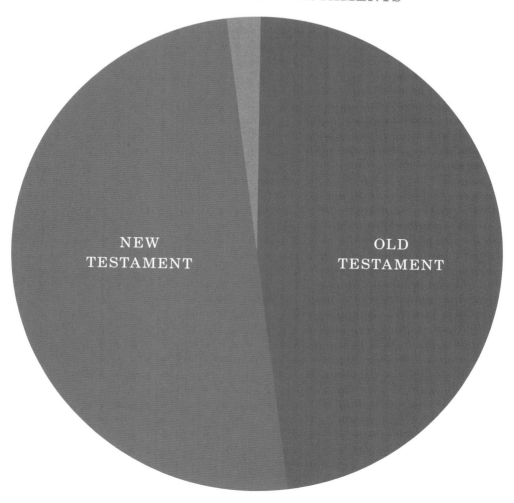

NEW
TESTAMENT

OLD
TESTAMENT

Percentage of Sermons:

Old Testament – 48% (26 sermons)

New Testament – 50% (27 sermons)

No Text – 2% (1 sermon)

Books Most Frequently Preached:

Psalms – 5 times

Isaiah – 5 times

Matthew – 5 times

John – 4 times

Length of Sermons:

Longest Sermon – 1,201 words

Shortest Sermon – 104 words

Average Sermon – 533 words

PERCENTAGE *of* OLD TESTAMENT SERMONS
*Preached from Each Book**

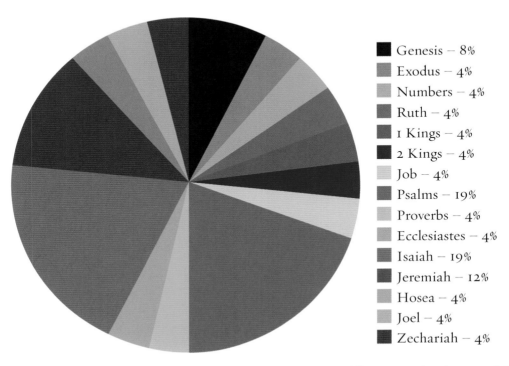

- Genesis – 8%
- Exodus – 4%
- Numbers – 4%
- Ruth – 4%
- 1 Kings – 4%
- 2 Kings – 4%
- Job – 4%
- Psalms – 19%
- Proverbs – 4%
- Ecclesiastes – 4%
- Isaiah – 19%
- Jeremiah – 12%
- Hosea – 4%
- Joel – 4%
- Zechariah – 4%

*All percentages have been rounded.

NUMBER *of* PREACHING OCCASIONS USING
OLD TESTAMENT TEXTS

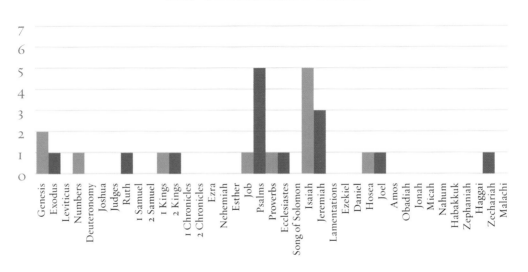

PERCENTAGE *of* NEW TESTAMENT SERMONS
*Preached from Each Book**

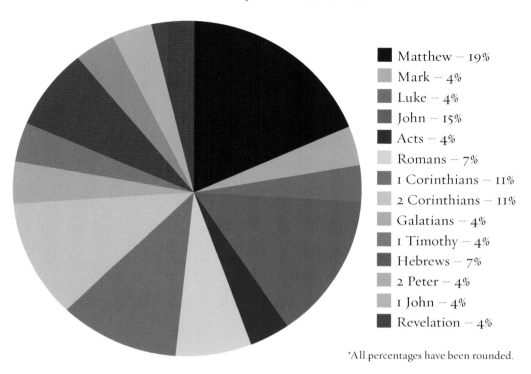

- Matthew – 19%
- Mark – 4%
- Luke – 4%
- John – 15%
- Acts – 4%
- Romans – 7%
- 1 Corinthians – 11%
- 2 Corinthians – 11%
- Galatians – 4%
- 1 Timothy – 4%
- Hebrews – 7%
- 2 Peter – 4%
- 1 John – 4%
- Revelation – 4%

*All percentages have been rounded.

NUMBER *of* PREACHING OCCASIONS USING
NEW TESTAMENT TEXTS

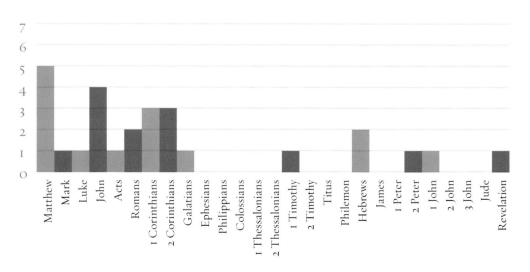

WORD CLOUD *of* TOPICAL FREQUENCY

In this word cloud, the larger the word, the more frequently it appears in Notebook 3.

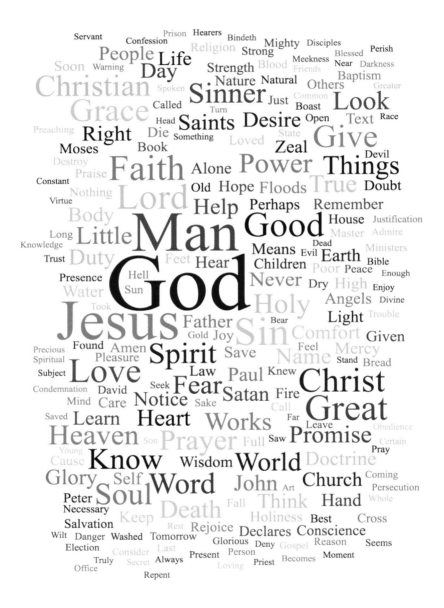

THE SERMONS

NOTEBOOK 3 (SERMONS 135–187)

53^{1}_

1. At first glance the number 53 appears to indicate the date 1853 since the last date Charles provided in Notebook 2 is June 19, 1852. More likely this number reflects Charles's attempt to account for the total number of sermons in Notebook 3. He arrived at this total number by subtracting the first sermon ("Calling and Election Sure," Sermon 135) of this notebook from the final sermon ("Following Jesus with a Cross on Our Back," Sermon 187). However, the correct total number of sermons in this notebook is fifty-four. In his calculation Charles failed to account for Sermon 169, which he included twice (see "Christ the Power and Wisdom of God" [Sermon 169a] and "Christ the Power of God" [Sermon 169b]). This tendency is also demonstrated in Notebook 1 (see "The Fight and the Weapons" [Sermon 37a] and "The Fight" [Sermon 37b]). On the following page Charles corrected the total number of sermons in this notebook by changing 188 to 187. The discoloration of the four corners on this page reflects efforts at taping the interior of the front cover. Structural damage is also evident in the central crack of the cover (compare the cover of this notebook to the half flap on the front cover of Notebook 2). The imprint of the ink from the illustrations on the following page can also be seen in the top right corner.

III[1]

SKELETONS[2] FROM
135 TO 187[3]

1.   The pencil inscription, III, represents the third of nine sermon notebooks. The following inscriptions are found in the front of the notebooks: "A2.6" appears on the inside front cover of the 1849 notebook entitled "Antichrist and Her Brood; or, Popery Unmasked." The front cover of Notebook 2 is partially missing and may have contained a similar inscription. A circled Roman numeral IV appears on the second page of Notebook 4. The Roman numeral V appears on the second page of Notebook 5. A circled Roman numeral VI appears on the second page of Notebook 6. A circled Roman numeral VII appears on the second page of Notebook 7. Two inscriptions are found on the inside front cover of Notebook 8: the Roman numeral VIII in the upper left corner and "Vol. VIII" in the upper right. The front cover of Notebook 9 is partially missing; however, the inscription "VOL IX" appears in the remaining space at the top of the truncated flap. The illustrations on this page were not original to Charles. However, for the first time in his sermon notebooks, Charles did not include his own words, Scripture verses, or additional illustrations (compare this page with the title page of Notebook 2). The horizontal lines on the left side of the page may serve as the beginning of Charles's illustrations; however, their purpose is unclear. The lack of Charles's interaction on this page may reflect the increased demand of ministry on his time. The discolorations on the four corners of this page are imprints of those on the interior of the front cover of this notebook.

2.   The ligatures on the letters "S," "k," "l," "e," "t," and "s" in the word "Skeletons" are Charles's attempt to add distinction to the word. This style of writing can also be seen on the title pages of Notebooks 1, 2, and 3.

3.   Charles originally wrote the number 188 before changing the 8 to 7 to construct the correct sermon total, 187 (see "Following Jesus with a Cross on our Back," Sermon 187).

[blank page][1]

1. The discolorations on the four corners of this page are imprints of those on the interior of the front cover of this notebook. The imprint of the ink from the illustrations on the previous page is also evident.

II Oct. 1. 10. 11. Calling & election sure. —

The Doctrines of grace are eminently practical.

<u>I</u>. There are such things as calling & election.

otherwise how could we make them sure. Election is God's choice of man & the calling is the effectual call of the Spirit. Election precedes calling but is here put after it to shew that our knowledge of our election depends upon our knowledge of calling. — Those persons who reject one deny the other and that because they do not like sovereign grace but they are both true for an host of texts plainly declares them and our experience proves it.

<u>II</u>. That a Christian man may be assured of his calling & election yea & ought to be.

Many good men have attained to assurance - multitudes doubt but they need not. certainty is within reach.

By strong faith we serve God well. the more the better — Some know their calling but doubt their election - this is foolish. we may be assured that we are elect & called.

<u>III</u>. True assurance is only attainable by diligence.

presumption comes on the drowsy but not assurance. — we must give diligence at all times & in all ways. in prayer in searching the word - in watchfulness - in good works particularly those mentioned in ver - 5. 6. 7.

<u>IV</u>. Many advantages attending such assurance

1. Keeping us from falling either foully or finally.

2. Giving us abundant entrance — head of the poll.

best of the four. the far off. the near. the hardly safe. abundant Great joy. Great success. Easy or triumphant death Great glory. 1st class train to heaven — —

199. 204.

CALLING *and* ELECTION SURE
2 Peter 1:10 – 11[1]

"Wherefore the rather, brethren, give diligence to make your calling and election sure: for if ye do these things, ye shall never fall: for so an entrance shall be ministered unto you abundantly into the everlasting kingdom of our Lord and Saviour Jesus Christ."

The Doctrines of grace are eminently practical.

I. THERE ARE SUCH THINGS AS CALLING AND ELECTION.[2]

Otherwise, how could we make them sure? Election is God's choice of man and the calling is the effectual call of the Spirit.[3] Election precedes calling,[4] but is here put after it to shew[5] that our knowledge of our election depends upon our knowledge of calling. Those persons who reject one deny the other, and that because they do not like sovereign grace. But they are both true for an host of texts[6] plainly declares them and our experience proves it.

II. THAT A CHRISTIAN MAN MAY BE ASSURED OF HIS CALLING AND ELECTION, YEA, AND OUGHT TO BE.

Many good men have attained to assurance. Multitudes doubt, but they need not. Certainty [assurance] is within reach.

By strong faith we serve God well. The more, the better. Some know their calling but doubt their election. This is foolish. We may be assured that we are elect and called.[7]

III. TRUE ASSURANCE IS ONLY ATTAINABLE BY DILIGENCE.

Presumption comes on the drowsy, but not assurance. We must give diligence at all times and in all ways. In prayer, in searching the Word, in watchfulness, in good works,[8] particularly those mentioned in ver.[9] 5, 6, 7.[10]

IV. MANY ADVANTAGES ATTENDING SUCH ASSURANCE.

1. Keeping us from falling,[11] either foully or finally.[12]

2. Giving us abundant entrance. Head of the poll.[13] Best of the four.[14] The far off. The near. The hardly safe. Abundant. Great joy.[15] Great success. Easy or triumphant death. Great glory. 1st class train to heaven.[16]

199. 204.

1. On March 22, 1857, Charles preached an additional sermon on 2 Pet 1:10–11 entitled "Particular Election" (*NPSP* 3, Sermon 123). The overlapping content suggests Charles may have had his earlier outline in mind when writing his later sermon, particularly *NPSP* 3:130–32.

2. The doctrine of election was a prominent theme in Charles's early notebooks of sermons. In a letter to his father on April 6, 1852, Charles wrote, "When I have been thinking on the many difficulties in preaching the word, the doctrine of election has been a great comfort to me" (Angus Library and Archive, Regent's Park College, Oxford University, D/SPU 1, Letter 13). See also "Election" (Notebook 1, Sermon 10).

3. "Those who are saved are saved because God chose them to be saved, and are called as the effect of that first choice of God. If any of you dispute this, I stand upon the authority of Holy Scripture; ay, and if it were necessary to appeal to tradition, which I am sure it is not, and no Christian man would ever do it, yet I would take you upon that point; for I can trace this doctrine through the lips of a succession of holy men, from this present moment to the days of Calvin, thence to Augustine, and thence on to Paul himself; and even to the lips of the Lord Jesus Christ. The doctrine is, without doubt, taught in Scripture, and were not men too proud to humble themselves to it, it would universally be believed and received as being no other than manifest truth" (*NPSP* 3:130–31).

4. "It will be asked, however, why is *calling* here put before *election*, seeing election is eternal, and calling takes place in time? I reply, because calling is first to us. The first thing which you and I can know is our calling: we cannot tell whether we are elect until we feel that we are called. We must, first of all, prove our calling, and then our election is sure most certainly" (*NPSP* 3:131, italics in the original).

5. Charles used the word "shew" interchangeably with "show" throughout this sermon. For previous examples of this tendency, see "God, the Guide of His Saints" (Notebook 1, Sermon 62) and "The Effect and Design of the Law" (Notebook 2, Sermon 103).

6. An alternative reading is "a host of texts."

7. "'Make your calling and election sure.' Not towards God, for they are sure to him: make them sure to yourself. Be quite certain of them; be fully satisfied about them" (*NPSP* 3:132).

8. "I like to think in the morning that all things are ready for my pathway through the day, that if I will go out to serve God in my ministry he has prepared some ear into which I am to drop a gracious word, and some heart in the furrows of which I shall sow some blessed seed effectually. Behold all providence with its mighty wheels is co-working with the servant of the living God; only go forward in zeal and confidence, my brother, and thou shalt find that every step of thy way is ready for thee" (*MTP* 23:282).

9. Abbr. "verses."

10. Second Peter 1:5–7, "And beside this, giving all diligence, add to your faith virtue; and to virtue knowledge; and to knowledge temperance; and to temperance patience; and to patience godliness; and to godliness brotherly kindness; and to brotherly kindness charity."

11. Cf. Jude 24.

12. In a letter to his father on September 9, 1852, Charles wrote, "My soul, I am persuaded, is secure. Jesus has entered my name in his book of life and I do not fear a final perishing. But I do fear temporary abandonment. I tremble lest the grieved Spirit should withdraw and leave me to be stripped and beaten by my cruel foes. My jewels are secure, but I fear lest I should lose my [sc]roll by sleep, or my way by negligence" (Angus Library and Archive, Regent's Park College, Oxford University, D/SPU 1, Letter 14).

13. The phrase "head of the poll" was a political expression in Spurgeon's day describing the candidate who received the most votes in an election. In 1852, *Bell's Weekly Messenger* published an article about the political victory of Lord Chelsea: "The election has terminated in a most unexpected manner. Lord Chelsea, the Derby candidate, has been returned at the head of the poll" ("Dover," *Bell's Weekly Messenger*, July 12, 1852).

14. The phrase "best of the four" describes the Victorian card game Whist. A precursor to Bridge or Spades, the game of Whist involved four players. The player who

laid down the best four cards was the winner. Samuel Johnson offers the following definition: "A game at cards, requiring close attention and silence. Vulgarly pronounced *whisk*" (Johnson's *Dictionary*, s.v. "whist," italics in the original).

15. An alternative reading of this line is "Abundantly great joy" or "Abundant, great joy."

16. When set against the backdrop of the development of the railroad industry in mid-nineteenth-century Cambridgeshire, Charles's phrase "1st class train to heaven" acquires added meaning. Approximately seven years prior to the preaching of this sermon, the Great Eastern Railway was laid to connect Cambridge to Norwich. The main line also passed through the village of Waterbeach. A railroad station was constructed in Waterbeach during Charles's first year as pastor at the Baptist chapel ("Waterbeach: Introduction," in *A History of the County of Cambridge and the Isle of Ely: Volume 9, Chesterton, Northstowe, and Papworth Hundreds*, ed. A. P. M. Wright and C. P. Lewis [London, 1989], 237–43. British History Online, http://www.british-history.ac.uk/vch/cambs/vol9/pp237-243, accessed December 16, 2016). In a letter to his father on October 16, 1851, Charles wrote, "There is rail there and back, and it is only six miles (from Cambridge)" (Angus Library and Archive, Regent's Park College, Oxford University, D/SPU 1, Letter 10). Throughout his later ministry as pastor of the Metropolitan Tabernacle and as an itinerate evangelist, Charles often traveled by rail. On one occasion Charles's preference for traveling first class was noticed by a fellow minister: "On a later occasion, Spurgeon stood on the platform of the train station waiting for his train to arrive. When it pulled into the station, the conductor announced the boarding instructions. Spurgeon had been in conversation with a fellow minister. The reverend gentleman said to Charles, 'Well, I am going to the third class section of the train to save the Lord's money.' Spurgeon retorted, 'Well, I am going to the first class section of the train to save the Lord's servant'" (Lewis Drummond, *Spurgeon: Prince of Preachers* [Grand Rapids: Kregel, 1992], 280).

136 II Cor. V. 10.   The Certain Judgment.

The great realities of eternity are spurs to true ministers particularly, the coming judgment.

I. There must be a judgment.

     1 Natural reason & conscience as well as dying groans testify to this
     2 Man's vile & horrid sins demand it
     3. Christ's insults & rejections demand it
     4. So also the sufferings of the righteous

It is consistent with analogy since even in time we have judges

II.   All must appear.

all are sinners. the saints even desire to be judged & although others dread it yet they *must* appear.

No bail. no bribery. "every one" singly in "propria persona".

III. Christ is the judge. —

He is a prince — he was an eyewitness — he is God — he is man — he knows the laws — ergo. he is a good judge. Infidels. blasphemers. pharisees & socinians will be wrong.

IV. Man's deeds are the rule of judgment & the measure of punishment. —

① Done not said — one sin is damning — but punishment is proportionate — guilt will be punished. no acts of pardon — no false witness — divided jury or escape.

     Let us judge ourselves.

If the X⁰ be accused by Satan. yet he shall be acquitted Trial of the moralist & outwardly profane.

     Charge against all

of murder, robbery, treason, false witness. God's name in vain
200. 205. 209. get a counsellor — flee for refuge.

136

THE CERTAIN JUDGMENT
2 Corinthians 5:10[1]

"For we must all appear before the judgment seat of Christ; that every one may receive the things done in his body, according to that he hath done, whether it be good or bad."

The great realities[2] of eternity are spurs to true ministers, particularly the coming judgment.

I. THERE MUST BE A JUDGMENT.

1. Natural reason and conscience as well as dying groans testify to this.

2. Man's vile and horrid sins demand it.[3]

3. Christ's insults and rejections demand it.

4. So also the sufferings of the righteous.

It is consistent with analogy since, even in time, we have judges.

II. ALL MUST APPEAR.[4]

All are sinners.[5] The saints even desire to be judged, and although others dread it yet they <u>must</u> appear.[6] No bail. No bribery. "Every one" singly in "propriâ persona."[7]

III. CHRIST IS THE JUDGE.

He is a prince.[8] He was an eyewitness. He is God. He is man.[9] He knows the laws. Ergo,[10] he is a good judge. Infidels, blasphemer[s], Pharisees,[11] and Socinians[12] will be wrong.

IV. MAN'S DEEDS ARE THE RULE OF JUDGEMENT[13] AND THE MEASURE OF PUNISHMENT.

Done,[14] not said. One sin is damning. But punishment is proportionate. Guilt will be punished. No acts of pardon. No false witness, divided jury, or escape.

Let us judge ourselves.[15]

If the Xn[16] be accused by Satan,[17] yet he shall be acquitted. Trial of the moralist and outwardly profane. Charge against all of murder, robbery, treason, false witness, God's name in vain. Get a counsellor. Flee for refuge.[18]

200. 205. 209.[19]

1. Charles preached two additional sermons on 2 Cor 5:10. On August 25, 1872, he preached "The Great Assize" (*MTP* 18, Sermon 1076) and on July 2, 1876, he preached "The Believer in the Body and out of the Body" (*MTP* 22, Sermon 1303). The scope of the former sermon is exclusively verse 10 while the latter is verses 5–10. There is enough structural similarity and overlapping content in Charles's 1872 sermon to suggest he had in mind his earlier outline when writing this sermon.

2. Charles exaggerated the bowl of the letter "e" in the word "realities." For an additional example of this tendency, see "The Redeemer's Tears over Sinners" (Notebook 2, Sermon 121) and "God's Dealings with the Antediluvians" (Sermon 138).

3. "There is no punishment worse than for a man who is sinfully disposed to gratify his lusts, to satiate his bad propensities, and to multiply and fatten his vices. Only let men grow into what they would be, and then see what they would be like! Take away the policemen in some parts of London, and give the people plenty of money, and let them do just as they like. . . . Why, they would be worse than a herd of tigers. Let them give way to their rage and anger, with nothing to check their passions; let miserly, greedy people for ever go on with their greed. It makes them miserable here, but let these things be indulged in for ever, and what worse hell do you want? Oh, sin is hell and holiness i[s] heaven" (*MTP* 18:588). Cf. Rom 2:6.

4. "'We must *all* appear.' What a vast assembly, what a prodigious gathering, that of the entire human race! It struck me as I was meditating upon this subject, what would be the thoughts of Father Adam, as he stood there with Mother Eve and looked upon his offspring. It will be the first time in which he has ever had the opportunity of seeing all his children met together. What a sight will he then behold,—far stretching, covering all the globe which they inhabit, enough not only to people all earth's plains, but crown her hill-tops, and cover even the waves of the sea, so numberless must the human race have been, if all the generations that have ever lived, or shall ever live, shall at once rise from the dead! Oh, what a sight will that be!" (*MTP* 18:581).

5. Cf. Rom 3:23.

6. "No disguise will be possible. Ye cannot come there dressed in masquerade of profession or attired in robes of state, but we must *appear*; we must be seen through, must be displayed, must be revealed; off will come your garments, and your spirit will be judged of God, not after appearance, but according to the inward heart. Oh, what a day that will be when every man shall see himself, and every man shall see his fellow, and the eyes of angels and the eyes of devils, and the eyes of God upon the throne, shall see us through and through. Let these thoughts dwell in your mind" (*MTP* 18:582–83, italics in the original).

7. Latin, "In one's own person or behalf" (James A. Ballentine, *A Law Dictionary of Words, Terms, Abbreviations and Phrases Which Are Peculiar to the Law of Those Which Have a Peculiar Meaning in the Law Containing Latin Phrases and Maxims with Their Translations and a Table of the Names of the Reports and Their Abbreviations* [Indianapolis: Bobbs-Merrill, 1916], 229). In his 1872 sermon, Charles also referenced this Latin phrase: "Now, the most important thought connected with this to *me*, is that *I* shall be there; to *you* young men, that *you* will be there; to *you*, ye aged of every sort, that *you, in propria personae*—each one shall be there. Are you rich? Your dainty dress shall be put off. Are you poor? Your rags shall not exempt you from attendance at that court. None shall say, 'I am too obscure.' You must come up from that hiding place. None shall say, 'I am too public.' You must come down from that pedestal. Everyone must be there" (*MTP* 18:582, italics in the original).

8. Cf. Isa 9:6; Rev 1:5; "The Prince of Life" (*MTP* 36, Sermon 2139).

9. "Our British law ordains that a man shall be tried by his peers, and there is justice in the statute. Now the Lord God will judge men, but at the same time it will be in the person of Jesus Christ the man. Men shall be judged by a man. He that was once judged by men shall judge men. Jesus knows what man should be;—he has been under the law himself in deep humility, who is ordained to administer the law in high authority. He can hold the scales of justice evenly, for he has stood in man's place and borne and braved man's temptations; he therefore is the most fit judge that could be selected" (*MTP* 18:583).

10. Latin, "therefore." Charles originally wrote the letter "i" beneath the "e" in the word "ergo."

11. Cf. "Pharisees and Sadducees Reproved" (Notebook 1, Sermon 39) and "A Righteousness Better than the Pharisees" (Notebook 5, Sermon 268).

12. Cf. "Pleasure in the Stones of Zion" (Notebook 1, Sermon 53) and "What Think Ye of Christ?" (Notebook 1, Sermon 79).

13. "Not our profession, not our boastings, but our actions will be taken in evidence at the last, and every man shall receive according to what he hath done in the body. That implies that everything done by us in this body will be known. It is all recorded; it will be all brought to light. Hence, in that day every secret sin will be published. What was done in the chamber, what was hidden by the darkness, shall be published as upon the housetop—every secret thing. With great care you have concealed it, most dexterously you have covered it up; but it shall be brought out to your own astonishment to form a part of your judgment. . . . Oh, how fine we can make some things look with the aid of paint and varnish and gilt; but at the last day off will come the varnish and veneer, and the true metal, the real substance, will then be seen" (*MTP* 18:584).

14. "Oh yes, the deeds, the deeds, the deeds of men—not their prating, not their profession, not their talk, but their deeds (though nobody shall be saved by the merits of his deeds)—their deeds shall be the evidence of their grace, or their deeds shall be the evidence of their unbelief; and so, by their works shall they stand before the Lord, or by their works shall they be condemned as evidence and nothing more" (*MTP* 18:587). See also *MTP* 25:308.

15. "The Judge is at the door. Jesus comes to judge you: will you have him now to be your Saviour? If not, his coming will cause you to weep and wail, and that throughout eternity. Remember that word,—ETERNITY" (*MTP* 25:312).

16. Abbr. "Christian."

17. "Good old Martin Luther used to say, 'The devil comes to me, and says, "Martin, thou art an exceeding sinner."' 'I know that very well,' said Martin, 'and I'll cut off thy head with thine own sword; for Christ died for sinners, and the more I feel I am a sinner, the more evidence I have that Christ died for me'" (*Autobiography* 1:337). Cf. Zech 3:1–2; Rev 12:10.

18. "A simple belief in the merit of the Lord Jesus, wrought in us by the Holy Ghost, is the rocky foundation upon which shall be built up, by the same divine hands,

the character which shall evidence that the kingdom was prepared for us from before the foundations of the world. God work in us such a character, for Christ's sake" (*MTP* 18:588).

19. The number 209 is smeared toward the bottom of the page. The cause of the smear was Charles's finger, resulting in the partial print above the numbers 2 and 0.

Luke XIV. 21.   The great gospel supper.   137

A King made a great supper, he was great & the prince of his realm was there so that it was truly great. There was a vastness of provision & an infinity of invitation.

I. Why make the feast. Not to get money by it, nor because the subjects deserved it, nor to gain their good opinions but merely to benefit them & honour his son.

He sends first to the gentry Jews & noble Pharisees but they make silly excuses — 'twas supper time why not see the land tomorrow why try the oxen in the dark & why not bring the wife with him.

II. Why make excuses. Some might doubt the bounty of the provision or the fatness of the bullocks — but the secret was they despised the king & hated him & loved the world better.

The King grows angry & does well. But oh deed of mercy

III. How did his wrath work. He sends for the poor — the maimed by fall & wounds. The halt not halters but the powerless — the blind & cripples sit down with him.

Then there is room remaining & since lanes & allies are swept clean — the messengers go beneath the hedgerows for lepers, gipsies, highway robbers.

Surely in spiritualizing this we can put ourselves among the beggars. Come then for all things are ready

Lord compel us to come in.

207. 208.

137

THE GREAT GOSPEL SUPPER
Luke 14:21[1]

"So that servant came, and shewed his lord these things. Then the master of the house being angry said to his servant, Go out quickly into the streets and lanes of the city, and bring in hither the poor, and the maimed, and the halt, and the blind."

A king made a <u>great</u> supper. He was great and the prince of his realm was there so that it was truly great. There was a vastness of provision and an infinity of invitation.

I. WHY MAKE THE FEAST?

Not to get money by it. Nor because the subjects deserved it. Nor to gain their good opinions. But merely to benefit them and honour his son. He sends first to the gentry Jews and noble Pharisees,[2] but they make silly excuses: T'was supper time. Why not see the Lord tomorrow? Why try the oxen in the dark?[3] And why not bring the wife with him?[4]

II. WHY MAKE EXCUSES?

Some might doubt the bounty of the provision or the fatness of the bullocks. But the secret was they despised the king and hated him and loved the world better.[5] The King grows angry and does well. But oh, deed of mercy.[6]

III. HOW DID HIS WRATH WORK?

He sends for the poor, the maimed[7] by fall and wounds.[8] The halt, not halters, but the powerless.[9] The blind and cripples sit down with him. Then there is room remaining, and since lanes and all[eys][10] are swept clean, the messengers go beneath the hedgerows[11] for lepers, gipsies,[12] highway robbers.[13]

Surely, in spiritualizing this we can put ourselves among the beggars. Come then, for all thing[s] are ready.[14]

Lord, compel us to come in.[15]

207. 208.[16]

1. Charles did not preach any additional sermons on Luke 14:21. However, for additional sermons on the parable of the great banquet, see "Compel Them to Come In" (*NPSP* 5, Sermon 227), "A Bad Excuse Is Worse Than None" (*MTP* 10, Sermon 578), "All Things Are Ready. Come" (*MTP* 23, Sermon 1354), "A Straight Talk" (*MTP* 36, Sermon 2122), "Yet There Is Room" (*MTP* 56, Sermon 3221), "More Room for More People" (*MTP* 62, Sermon 3529). Overlapping content will be noted below.

2. Cf. Luke 14:16. An alternative reading of this line is "He sends first to the gentry Jews and noble Pharisees."

3. Cf. Luke 14:19.

4. Cf. Luke 14:20.

5. Cf. 1 John 2:15.

6. An alternative reading of this line is "But oh, [what a] deed of mercy."

7. "Another class of them were *maimed*, and so were not very comely in appearance: an arm had been lopped off, or an eye had been gouged out. One had lost a nose, and another a leg. They were in all stages and shapes of dismemberment. Sometimes we turn our heads away, and feel that we would rather give anything than look upon beggars who show their wounds, and describe how they were maimed. But it did not matter how badly they were disfigured; they were brought in, and not one of them was repulsed because of the ugly cuts he had received. So, poor soul, however Satan may have torn and lopped thee, and into whatsoever condition he may have brought thee, so that thou feelest ashamed to live, nevertheless this is no unfitness for coming; just as thou art thou mayest come to the table of grace. Moral disfigurements are soon rectified when Jesus takes the character in hand. Come thou to him, however sadly thou art injured by sin" (*MTP* 23:286, italics in the original).

8. By using the phrase "the maimed by fall and wounds," Charles likely had in mind the fall of humanity into sin (Genesis 3) and the wounds caused by sinning.

9. The phrase "The halt, not halters" can also read, "The lame, not those who hesitate but the powerless." Samuel Johnson defined the word "halt" as: "The act of

limping; a limping fait; lameness." Johnson provided three definitions for "halter": "one who halts or limps," "a rope for hanging malefactors," and "a cord for tying or restraining an animal; particularly a cord or sort of bridle for leading or for tying a horse" (Johnson's *Dictionary*, s.v. "halt," "halter"). In other words, Jesus desires the lame and crippled to sit at his banquet table, not those who hesitate or who operate on their own strength (Rom 5:8; 1 Cor 1:27; Eph 2:5).

10. Charles originally wrote the word "allies." However, the context suggests he intended to write the word "alleys."

11. "The series of trees or bushes planted for enclosures" (Johnson's *Dictionary*, s.v. "hedgerow"). Hedgerows were common to Cambridgeshire in Charles's day and still mark property boundaries to this day. "Come our of your hedges, then. I am looking for you. Though you hide yourself away yet God's own Spirit will discover you, and bring you, I trust this very morning, to feed on love divine. Trust Jesus Christ, that is all, just as you are, with all your unfitness and unreadiness" (*MTP* 23:288).

12. See "Imitation of God" (Notebook 1, Sermon 69) and "Justification, Conversion, Sanctification, Glory" (Notebook 2, Sermon 102).

13. Charles may have had in mind the parable of the good Samaritan (Luke 10:30).

14. "It is not what you have not but what you have that keeps many of you from Christ" (*MTP* 23:285).

15. "The shadows lengthen, the sun of the present dispensation is nearing its setting; by nearly nineteen hundred years has its day been shortened since first the Lord sent forth his servants at supper time. The fulness of time for the marriage supper of the Lamb must speedily arrive, and therefore it behoves us to be more than ever earnest in delivering the message to the invited guests" (*MTP* 23:277).

16. The ink imprint on the right side of the page was caused by the number 209 on the opposing page.

138.   Gen <u>II</u>. 12. 13.   God's dealings with the Antediluvians

The deluge is one of the grandest events which ever occurred in the history of man & one more widely known than any other. Traditions of it are found with every nation, written in every language. It is an event which the whole earth has embalmed never to be buried. We however have the only genuine account & this is given us not as a bait for curiosity but as a lesson of instruction. Let us notice.

<u>I</u>. The particulars sins then more rife than usual.

1. Murder even to fratricide in Cain, murder in Lamech — bloody wars & deeds of violence among the giants & men of renown — it was full of violence. warlike music & implements were in full use.

2. Drunkenness — for they were eating & drinking &c how should so good a man as Noah fall unless this sin was common amongst the viler sort.

3. Idolatry had spread fearfully their sins could not allow them to worship the holy, just & true.

4. Uncleanness & all lasciviousness were fearfully common. Lamech was a polygamist. lust had turned even the Sethites aside, & all was corrupt.

<u>II</u>. The particular causes of this corruption.

Of course the grand cause was man's natural depravity but the reasons for this awful developement

138

GOD'S DEALINGS *with* *the* ANTEDILUVIANS

Genesis 6:12–13[1]

"And God looked upon the earth, and, behold, it was corrupt; for all flesh had corrupted his way upon the earth. And God said unto Noah, The end of all flesh is come before me; for the earth is filled with violence through them; and, behold, I will destroy them with the earth."

The deluge is one of the grandest events which ever occurred in the history of man, and one more widely[2] known than any other. Traditions of it are found with every nation, written in every language.[3] It is an event which the whole earth has embalmed, never to be buried. We, however, have the only genuine account, and this is given [to] us not as a bait for curiosity but as a lesson of instruction.   Let us notice:

I. THE PARTICULARS SINS THEN MORE RIFE THAN USUAL.

1. Murder, even[4] to fratricide, in Cain.[5] Murder in Lamech.[6] Bloody wars and deeds of violence among the giants and men of renown. It was full of violence. Warlike music and implements were in full use.

2. Drunkenness. For they were eating and drinking, etc. How should so good a man as Noah fall[7] unless this sin was common amongst the viler sort?

3. Idolatry had spread fearfully. Their sins could not allow them to worship the holy, just, and true.

4. Uncleanness and all lasciviousness were fearfully common. Lamech was a polygamist.[8] Lust had turned even the Sethites aside[9] and all was corrupt.

II. THE PARTICULAR CAUSES OF THIS CORRUPTION.

Of course, the grand cause was man's natural depravity,[10] but the reasons for this awful development at this time were probably. ×) Population was great 10 thousand million this made sin more common.

1. The long age of man. for the distance of death would make men even less serious than they are. Bad example was thus perpetuated and sinful projects were matured and craft grew by long experience backing up depravity.

2. The conformity of professors with the world, the gradual thinning of the hosts of the Lord & the fewness of those who remained faithful to God amid the faithless.

III. The means God used for reforming man before his last resource was tried.

1. He gave man an instance of the effect of sin by driving Adam from Eden. this was fresh in their minds.

2. Cain he made a living warning, bearing the mark of God's displeasure, wherever he went.

3. Enoch was translated as a reward of virtue, no doubt in a conspicuous & glorious manner.

4. Noah preached 120 years. this was a long respite they saw the ark gradually rising - a conspicuous sign of his faith........ But these things failing let us see God's mercy justice & wisdom combined.

IV. The last remedy. the deluge.

Some think the deluge so fattened the soil that the curse of sterility was much removed. but certainly the carcases as they decayed would much enrich the land but -

1. God by the flood gave man once for all a decisive proof of his hatred of sin universally & shut the mouths of those who say "all things continue as they were

at this time were probably: Population was great, 11[11] thousand million. This made sin more common.[12]

1. The long age of man.[13] For the distance of death would make men even less serious than they are. Bad example was thus perpetuated and sinful projects were matured, and craft grew by long experience backing up depravity.

2. The conformity of professors with the world, the gradual thinning of the hosts of the Lord,[14] and the fewness of those who remained faithful to God amid the faithless.[15]

III. THE MEANS GOD USED FOR REFORMING MAN BEFORE HIS LAST RESOURCE WAS TRIED.

1. He gave man an instance of the effect of sin by driving Adam from Eden.[16] This was fresh in their minds.

2. Cain. He made a living warning,[17] bearing the mark of God's displeasure wherever he went.

3. Enoch was translated as a reward of virtue,[18] no doubt in a conspicuous and glorious manner.

4. Noah preached 120 years.[19] This was a long respite. They saw the ark gradually rising, a conspicuous sign of his faith. But these things[20] failing, let us see God's mercy,[21] justice, and wisdom combined in:

IV. THE LAST REMEDY: THE DELUGE.

Some think the deluge so fattened the soil that the curse of sterility was much removed.[22] But certainly, the carcases, as they decayed, would much enrich the land. But:

1. God, by the flood, gave man once for all a decisive proof of his hatred of sin universally, and shut the mouths of those who say, "all things continue as they were."

2. God gave man another start – he removed the old blood and gave morality & holiness a little breathing room.

　　　Let us learn.

1. The great longsuffering of God.

2. His immense **love** of justice.

3. Fear – Oh sinner least his fires devour although the waterfloods be overpast.

210.

　　　　　　　　　　　　God bless me. I pray.

　　　　　　　　　　　　　　　　amen

---

139. Hos VI. 4. Ephraim's goodness like the morning cloud.

The prophet in the commencement of the chapter gives a hearty invitation to them to return – putting himself among them he urges a return, for says he we lose much by our separation, the wounder will be a healer & we shall enjoy many privileges.

　　But yet Ephraim turns not & Judah is stubborn – or if they somewhat relent it is no enduring reformation. – There are many like unto them now. –

I. Let us find out the characters.

1. Hearers a little moved & excited by earnest preaching but forgetting all at the end

2. God gave man another start. He removed the old blood and gave morality and holiness a little breathing room.

> Let us learn:
>
> 1. The great longsuffering of God.[23]
>
> 2. His immense love[24] of justice.[25]
>
> 3. Fear, Oh Sinner, lest[26] his fires devour[27] although the waterfloods be overpast.

God bless me, I pray.

210.[28]

<u>A men</u>

EPHRAIM'S GOODNESS
like the MORNING CLOUD
Hosea 6:4[1]

"O Ephraim, what shall I do unto thee? O Judah, what shall I do unto thee? For your goodness is as a morning cloud, and as the early dew it goeth away."

The prophet, in the commencement of the chapter, gives a hearty invitation to them to return. Putting himself among them, he urges a return.[2] For, says he, we lose much by our separation, the wounder will be a healer, and we shall enjoy many privileges.

But yet, Ephraim turns not and Judah is stubborn. Or if they somewhat relent it is no enduring reformation. There are many like unto them now.

I.   LET US FIND OUT THE CHARACTERS.

1.   Hearers [who are] a little moved and excited by earnest preaching, but forgetting all at the end.

2. Hearers who go home & remember the sermon for a longer time & feel uncomfortable but it wears off.

3. Hearers who pray once or twice, make resolves, read the Scriptures, are under conviction but it goes.

4. Those who make an outward profession by more frequent attendance at weekly meetings, who reform very greatly & even pray in public but it all goes off when some temptation comes.

5. Some go further yet – are baptized, lead an outwardly consistent life but have no root.

6. Many when sick have vowed but forgotten.

7. When we lose friends we often feel serious but it vanishes.

II. Now I have found you let me ask you what made your goodness vanish as the dew.
        Why the sun — — —

    The Sermon is over — silly companions are near – business dries up thought – sickness is gone – the funeral is over – the feast is near —

III. Let me show you your sin. ~~& danger~~.

1. You have sinned against light & knowledge.

2. You have lied to your conscience & your God.

3. You have been ungrateful to your God & your friends.

4. You have disappointed & grieved God's

2. Hearers who go home and remember the sermon for a longer time and feel uncomfortable, but it wears off.

3. Hearers who pray once or twice, make resolves, read the Scriptures, are under conviction, but it goes.

4. Those who make an outward profession by more frequent attendance at weekly meetings, who reform very greatly, and even pray in public, but it all goes off when some temptation comes.

5. Some go further yet, are baptized, lead an outwardly consistent life, but have no root.

6. Many when sick have vowed,[3] but forgotten.

7. When we lose friends, we often feel serious, but it vanishes.

II. NOW I HAVE FOUND YOU, LET ME ASK YOU WHAT MADE YOUR GOODNESS VANISH AS THE DEW?

Why the sun?[4]

The Sermon is over, silly companions are near, business dries up thought, sickness is gone, the funeral is over, the feast is near.[5]

III. LET ME SHOW YOU YOUR SIN. ~~AND DANGERS~~.[6]

1. You have sinned against light and knowledge.

2. You have lied to your conscience and your God.

3. You have been ungrateful to your God and your friends.

4. You have disappointed and grieved God's

people - your minister - & your dearest relatives.

5. You have caused the enemy to blaspheme & have done what you could to slander religion.

6. You are now a rebel against God.

There is mercy for the vilest. But

IV. Listen to your danger.

1. You may be given up. God says what more can I do? I have tried you sick & tried you well.

Beware lest he say "let him alone".

2. You are in danger of an awful hell. God says what is bad enough? what painful enough for thy punishment.

How we deserve the deepest hell
That slight the joys above
What chains of vengeance must ye feel
Who break such cords of love?

Sinners be wise. God. Father! Son! Spirit! make me wise, to show the only way & may the Spirit lead men in it.

211. 401.   For Jesus sake. Amen

people, your minister, and your dearest relatives.

5. You have caused the enemy to blaspheme and have done what you could to slander religion.

6. You are now a rebel against God.

> There is mercy for the vilest. But

IV. LISTEN TO YOUR DANGER.

1. You may be[7] given up. God says, "What more can I do? I have tried you sick and tried you well."[8] Beware, lest he say, "Let him alone."

2. You are in danger of an awful hell. God says, "What is bad enough? What [is] painful enough for thy punishment?"

> How we deserve the deepest hell
>
> That slight the joys above!
>
> What chains of vengeance must ye feel?[9]
>
> Who[10] break such cords of love![11]

Sinners, be wise. God. Father! Son! Spirit! Make me wise to show the only way, and may the Spirit lead men in it.

211. 401.   For Jesus's sake. Amen

1.   This is the only time Charles preached a sermon on Gen 6:12–13.

2.   Charles exaggerated the bowl of the letter "e" in the word "widely." See also "The Certain Judgment" (Sermon 136).

3.   Literature about global flood narratives were common in the commentaries and resources Charles encountered during this season of his ministry. In his commentary on Genesis, John Gill noted: "That there was such a flood of waters brought upon the earth, is confirmed by the testimony of heathen writers of all nations; only instead of *Noah* they put some person of great antiquity in their nation, as the *Chaldeans, Sisitbrus* or *Xisutbrus*; the *Grecians*, and *Romans*, *Prometheus* or *Deucalion*, or *Ogyges. Josephus* says, all writers of the *Barbarian* or heathen history make mention of the flood, and of the ark" (John Gill, *An Exposition of the Old Testament, in Which Are Recorded the Original of Mankind, of the Several Nations of the World, and of the Jewish Nation in Particular: The Lives of the Patriarchs of Israel; the Journey of That People from Egypt Through the Wilderness to the Land of Canaan, and Their Settlement in that Land; Their Laws Moral, Ceremonial, and Judicial; Their Government and State Under Judges and Kings; Their Several Captivities, and Their Sacred Books of Devotion. In the Exposition of Which, It Is Attempted to Give an Account of the Several Books, and the Writers of Them; a Summary of Each Chapter; and the Genuine Sense of Every Verse: And Throughout the Whole, the Original Text, and the Versions of It, Are Inspected and Compared; Interpreters of the Best Note, Both Jewish and Christian, Consulted; Difficult Places at Large Explained; Seeming Contradictions Reconciled; and Various Passages Illustrated and Confirmed by Testimonies of Writers, as Well Gentile as Jewish* [London: printed for the author and sold by George Keith at the Bible and Crown in Grace-church-street, 1763, The Spurgeon Library], 1:47, italics in the original). Matthew Henry's commentary included James Thomas Horne's comment: "Many ancient heathen writers particularly mention one man alone and his family to have been preserved, during a flood, in an ark, with pairs of all creatures" (Matthew Henry and Thomas Scott, *A Commentary upon the Holy Bible: With Numerous Observations and Notes from other Writers; Also Maps of the Countries Mentioned in Scripture, and Various Useful Tables. Genesis to Deuteronomy* [London: The Religious Tract Society, 1834, The Spurgeon Library], 27). In their 1850 commentary notes on Gen 6:17, George D'oyly and Richard Mant wrote, "If we take the circuit of the globe, and inquire of the inhabitants of every climate, we shall find, that the fame of this deluge is gone through the earth; and that in every part of the known world there are certain records and traditions of it" (George D'Oyly and Richard Mant, *The Holy Bible, According to the Authorized Version, with Notes, Explanatory and Practical, Taken Principally*

from the Most Eminent Writers of the United Church of England and Ireland, Together with Appropriate Introductions, Tables, Indexes, and Maps, Vol. 1. Genesis-Job [London: Society for Promoting Christian Knowledge, 1850, The Spurgeon Library], n.p.).

4. A dark yellow stain, likely the result of the aging process of the manuscript, appears above and to the right of the word "even."

5. Cf. Gen 4:8. 6. Cf. Gen 4:23.

7. Cf. Gen 9:21. 8. Cf. Gen 4:19.

9. According to John Gill, the phrase "sons of God" is a reference to the offspring of Seth: "As there were giants before this general defection, so there were at this time, when there was a mixture of the *Cainites* and *Sethites*; which were the offspring of the sons of God, or posterity of Seth, mixing with the daughters of men, or the posterity of Cain" (Gill, *An Exposition of the Old Testament*, 1:43, italics in the original).

10. Cf. Genesis 3.

11. A bolded, illegible number appears after the number 1. If Charles was drawing on John Gill's commentary on Genesis, then the illegible number is 1. Gill wrote, "It is thought it may be easily allowed, that their number amounted to eleven thousand millions; and some have made their number to be eighty thousand millions" (Gill, *An Exposition of the Old Testament*, 1:52).

12. The lines "Population was great, 11 thousand million. This made sin more common" were written in superscript. Charles commonly inserted phrases into his margins and indicated their locations with the letter "x" or an asterisk (see "The Wise Men's Offerings" [Notebook 1, Sermon 58]). However, because there is not a corresponding "x" on the page, the marginal notations in this instance are kept in their original locations.

13. Cf. Gen 5:26–28. 14. Cf. Jude 6.

15. Dark stains, likely the result of the aging process of the manuscript, are smudged above and below the word "faithless." The smudges were imprinted on the opposite page of the notebook over the word "buried."

16. Cf. Gen 3:24.

17. An alternative reading of these lines is "Cain. He made a living [as a] warning, bearing the mark of God's displeasure wherever he went."

18. Cf. Gen 5:24.

19. "It is a well-known truth that God has great longsuffering, but that there is a point beyond which even his longsuffering will not go. It has been so in the great judgments of God in the world. Before the days of Noah, men had revolted from God; but Noah was sent to them as a preacher of righteousness, and he did preach, and the Spirit of God was with him; yet, for all that, the antediluvian world turned not from its sin; and when the 120 years had expired,—but not till then,—God opened the windows of heaven, and down came the deluge which destroyed the whole race with the exception of the eight souls who were preserved in the ark. Those old-world sinners had had 120 years for repentance, and 120 years of earnest, faithful warning from holy Noah; and not till all those years had expired did God's patience come to an end, and his judgments begin" (*MTP* 53:277). Cf. Gen 6:3.

20. Charles originally wrote the word "thing" and likely added the letter "s" after the line had been written.

21. "[God] drowned the antediluvian world, but not till Noah was safely in the ark" (*MTP* 40:541).

22. It is unclear from which resource Charles was drawing. However, the "some" Charles referenced could have been Robert Taylor: "'But was not the curse removed after the Deluge?' To a certain degree. Seed time and harvest; summer and winter; rain and fair weather were granted. And as the Deluge swept over the surface of the whole earth, so it in part re-blended the materials, and gave us fertile vales, dells, and slopes; and thus, the Almighty still working by means or second causes, was the curse to a great degree removed" (Robert Taylor, *Natural History of Religion; or Youth Armed Against Infidelity and Religious Errors* [London: Baldwin and Cradock, 1832], 93). William Worthington also noted: "The Curse was in *Part* removed from the Ground after the Deluge, and that the Earth was in some *Measure* restored to its orig[i]nal Fruitfulness" (William Worthington, *An Essay on the Scheme and Conduct, Procedure and Extent of Man's Redemption Wherein Is Shewn from the Holy Scriptures, that This Great Work Is to Be Accomplished Gradually. To Which Is Annexed,*

A Dissertation on the Design and Argumentation of the Book of Job [London: printed for Edward Cave at St. John's Gate, 1763], 85, italics in the original).

23. Cf. Exod 34:6; Num 14:18; Ps 84:15; Rom 2:4.

24. It is unclear why Charles bolded the letters "ove" in the word "love." He may have intended emphasis, but more likely the reinforcement of the letters was the result of a malfunction of his writing instrument as also displayed in "Sinners Must Be Punished" (Notebook 1, Sermon 9).

25. Cf. Ps 99:4; Isa 30:18; 61:8.

26. Charles originally wrote the word "least" here. This tendency also appears in "The Watchman, His Work, Warning, and Promise" (Notebook 2, Sermon 120); "Christ's Sheep" (Notebook 2, Sermon 132); "By Faith Jericho Fell" (Notebook 2, Sermon 133); "Put Ye in the Sickle for the Harvest Is Ripe" (Sermon 143); and "Complaint, Prayer, and Answer" (Sermon 155).

27. Cf. 2 Pet 3:7.

28. The period at the end of the number 210 was smeared toward the bottom left of the page.

1. Charles preached two additional sermons on Hos 6:4. On January 24, 1869, he preached "Constancy and Inconstancy—a Contrast" (*MTP* 15, Sermon 852) and on March 9, 1890, he preached "The Rough Hewer" (*MTP* 36, Sermon 2134). The lack of structural similarity and overlapping content suggests Charles did not have this early sermon in mind when writing his later two sermons.

2. Hosea 6:1, "Come, and let us return unto the Lord: for he hath torn, and he will heal us; he hath smitten, and he will bind us up."

3. "Brethren, I have to thank God, and I think you may join with me, for many a sharp pang which has gone through the soul, for many a sharp cut which has come from a stinging text of Scripture, when that word of God has searched us through and through, and like a strong corrosive, or sharp acid, has burnt its way into our inmost soul, destroying and maiming in us much that we looked upon as precious and admirable. The faithfulness of God wears not always silken robes, and goeth not always arrayed in scarlet and fine linen, but it puts on steel armour, and comes out to us sword in hand, cutting and wounding, and making us bleed" (*MTP* 15:52).

4. Charles may have had in mind Jas 4:14, "Whereas ye know not what shall be on the morrow. For what is your life? It is even a vapour, that appeareth for a little time, and then vanisheth away."

5. See "The Great Gospel Supper" (Sermon 137).

6. Charles likely struck through the words "and dangers" because he intended to address this topic instead under his fourth Roman numeral on the following page.

7. Charles wrote the word "be" above the line. He indicated its location by inserting a caret between the words "may" and "given."

8. "This I am sure of, if the Lord takes the alternative not of giving you up, but of saving you, if he tries gentle means and they succeed not, he will turn to rougher methods; you shall be beaten with many stripes. The fire shall burn up your comforts, the moth and rust shall consume your treasures, the light of your eyes shall be taken from you at a stroke, your children shall die before your eyes; or, the partner of your bosom shall be laid in the grave, for by any means God will bring you in. He has determined to save you, and he will do it, let it cost what

it may. He spared not his own Son to save you, and he will not spare yours. Nor will he spare your body. You shall be worn with disease and wasted with sickness; you shall have misery of soul and despair of heart, but he will save you if he so resolves upon it; and for this you shall one day bless his name, and kiss the rod by which he chastened you to himself" (*MTP* 15:59–60).

9. Isaac Watts originally wrote, "What chains of vengeance should we feel?" Charles changed Watts's pronoun from "we" to "ye," and he also changed "should" to "must." In doing so, the stanza acquired a heightened sense of urgency and directness.

10. Charles originally wrote the letter "t" beneath "w" in the word "Who." In the original stanza, Isaac Watts began the sentence with the word "That."

11. This stanza was original to Isaac Watts's hymn "Frailty and Folly." Charles owned a copy of this hymn in his personal copy of *Psalms, Hymns, and Spiritual Songs*: 1. How short and hasty is our Life! / How cast our soul's affairs! / Yet senseless mortals vainly strive / To lavish out their years. / 2. Our days run thoughtlessly along, / Without a moment's stay; / Just like a story or a song, / We pass our lives away. / 3. God from on high invites us home, / But we march heedless on, / And ever hast'ning to the tomb, / Stoop downwards as we run. / 4. How we deserve the deepest hell, / That slight the joys above! / What chains of vengeance should we feel, / That break such cords of love! / 5. Draw us, O God, with sov'reign grace, / And lift our thoughts on high, / That we may end this mortal race, / And see salvation nigh" (Isaac Watts, *Psalms, Hymns, and Spiritual Songs, A New Edition, With Copious Indexes Carefully Revised* [London: T. Nelson and Sons, Paternoster Row, 1860], Book II, Hymn 32, 480–81). For additional quotations of this stanza in Charles's later sermons, see also *NPSP* 1:199; *MTP* 20:269; *MTP* 31:359; and *MTP* 59:396.

Gen XI. 6. 7. —   The tower of Babel.   140

After so great a flood, such a clearance of the earth
& such mercy to the remnant — we look on the world
with hope for better days. —————.

I. Let us trace man from the ark to Babel.
God lets Noah out just as he shut him in, — in due time
Noah full of gratitude rears the altar & burns the beast
God is pleased for Jesus' sake & blesses his creatures
anew & bids them multiply. — but even though
   they saw the earth's wreck & shuddered at it
tho' they were all the offspring of a pious parent &
tho' they had now no Cainish race to entrap them yet
   Sin was seen in Noah himself.
   In Canaan & Ham lewdness was conspicuous.
Nimrod was ambitious & insatiable of dominion
see how many cities he had, "hunter against the Lord"
Note. No providences will keep man from sin
   God's Holy Spirit is indispensably necessary.
Now there were again two races Ham & Eber —
   the Hebrews & the race of Ham, opposed to each other
II. Let us come & see the tower. —
   The people left Ararat perhaps for Eden & then
went eastward or however this was the first great
emigration. They wanted a plain extensive enough
for all & for multitudes of cattle such they found
at Shinar. Here all dwelt & fearing least

140

THE TOWER *of* BABEL
Genesis 11:6–7[1]

"And the Lord *said, Behold, the people is one, and they have all one language;
and this they begin to do: and now nothing will be restrained from them,
which they have imagined to do. Go to, let us go down, and there confound
their language, that they may not understand one another's speech."*

After so great a flood, such a clearance of the earth and such mercy to the remnant,
we look on the world with hope for better days.

I. LET US TRACE MAN FROM THE ARK TO BABEL.

God lets Noah out just as he shut him in. In due time,[2] Noah, full of gratitude,
rears the altar and burns the beast.[3] God is pleased for Jesus's sake and blesses
his creatures anew and bids them multiply.[4] But even though they saw the
earth's wreck and shuddered at it, tho'[5] they were all the offspring of a pious
parent and tho' they had now no Cainish race to entrap them, yet:

Sin was seen in Noah himself.[6]

In Canaan and Ham lewdness was conspicuous.

Nimrod was ambitious and insatiable of dominion. See how many cities he
had. "Hunter against the Lord."[7]

Note: No providences will keep man from sin. God's Holy Spirit is
indispensably necessary. Now, there were again two races, Ham and Eber.[8] The
Hebrews and the race of Ham [were] opposed to each other.[9]

II. LET US COME AND SEE THE TOWER.

The people left Ararat[10] perhaps for Eden and then went eastward, or however.
This was the first great emigration.[11] They wanted a plain extensive enough for
all and for multitudes of cattle such [as] they found at Shinar.[12] Here all dwelt
and fearing lest[13]

dispersion should come they thought of building a high tower so as to be seen to a distance & a city at its base — — not to escape the deluge for if so a mountain would be chosen, but

1. In opposition to God's command that they should disperse they desired to live together & this tower would be a landmark & centre point.

2. They, or at least the chieftains — wanted to gain universal dominion, this being the metropolis.

3. They designed it, as a vain glorious frolic of power & a piece of lasting boast of might.

the tower gradually rose — tier on tier & the city was commenced — but now.

III. Let us watch the Lord's movements. He suffers the building to progress so that he might gain the greater & more signal triumph. He did not sweep them away — But the glorious Trinity said "let us go down" for it was a great descent for God to notice this anthill or worm heap. He did not prejudge or rashly condemn. He sees & laughs at their folly — effects three purposes at once by a most simple means.

He confounded their language He stopped their work He dispersed the multitudes dispersion should come they thought of building a high tower so as to be seen to a distance and a city at its base. Not to escape the deluge, for if so a mountain would be chosen. But:

1. In opposition to God's command that they should disperse.[14] They desired to live together and this tower would be a landmark and centre point.

2. They, or at least the chieftains,[15] wanted to gain universal dominion [with] this being the metropolis.

3. They designed it as a vainglorious[16] frolic of power and a piece of lasting boast of might. The tower gradually rose, tier on tier, and the city was commenced. But now:

III. LET US WATCH THE LORD'S MOVEMENTS.

He suffers the building to progress so that he might gain the greater and more signal triumph. He did not sweep them away, but the glorious Trinity said, "Let us go down," for it was a great descent for God to notice this anthill or worm heap. He did not prejudge or rashly condemn. He sees and laughs at their folly [and] effects three purposes at once by a most simple means:

He confounded their language.

He stopped their work.

He dispersed the multitudes.

Here were three birds with one stone as men say.

IV. Now let us notice the Lord's mercy & wisdom.
Mercy - staid wrath from sweeping them away.
Wisdom - chose most excellent means - not a tempest to
destroy the tower it stands a monument of God's triumph
wis-dom - shine when we consider.

1. The one ness of speech made them mighty in sin.
2. Their union in vast numbers would make them vile.
3. Universal slavery would have been the fruit of one evil empire
4. The earth would not have been peopled.

This was a preventive of crime - the flood, a punishing
for sin -

God's policy now is to gather together in one
all his people scattered abroad but Babel prevents
unity as much as once it was designed to aid it,
we do not understand one another in religious
doctrines - words have different meanings.
But as God effected the dispersion so will he
effect the union of his people - despite all
the opposition which a perverse generation will
offer to God - let him do what he may they oppose
but his will & decree are absolutely sure. —

215

Here were three birds with one stone, as men say.[17]

IV. NOW LET US NOTICE THE LORD'S MERCY AND WISDOM.

Mercy staid[18] wrath from sweeping them away.

Wisdom chose most excellent means. Not a tempest to destroy the tower. It stands [as] a monument of God's triumph.[19] Wisdom shines when we consider:

1. The one-ness of speech made them mighty in sin.
2. Their union in vast numbers would make them vile.
3. Universal slavery would have been the fruit of universal[20] empire.
4. The earth would not have been peopled. This was a preventive of crime. The flood, a punishment for sin.

God's policy now is to gather together in one all his people scattered abroad.[21] But Babel prevents unity as much as once it was designed to aid it. We do not understand one another in religious doctrines. Words have different meanings.[22]

But as God effected the dispersion so will he effect the union of his people despite all the opposition which a perverse generation will offer to God.[23] Let him do what he may. They oppose, but his will and decree are absolutely sure.

215

1. This is the only time Charles preached a sermon on Gen 11:6–7.

2. An alternative reading of this line is "God lets Noah out just as he shut him in: in due time."

3. Cf. Gen 8:20.

4. Genesis 9:7, "And you, be ye fruitful, and multiply; bring forth abundantly in the earth, and multiply therein."

5. Contraction, "though."

6. Cf. Gen 9:21.

7. Genesis 10:9, "He was a mighty hunter before the LORD: wherefore it is said, Even as Nimrod the mighty hunter before the LORD."

8. Cf. Gen 10:21.

9. An alternative reading of this sentence is "The Hebrews and the race of Ham opposed each other."

10. Cf. Gen 9:19.

11. An alternative reading of these sentences is "The people left Ararat, perhaps for Eden, and then went eastward. Or however [they went], this was the first great emigration."

12. An alternative reading of this line is "They wanted a plain extensive enough for all and for multitudes of cattle. Such they found at Shinar." Cf. Gen 11:2.

13. Charles originally wrote the word "least." For additional examples of this tendency, see "Ephraim's Goodness like the Morning Cloud" (Sermon 139) and "Put Ye in the Sickle for the Harvest Is Ripe" (Sermon 143).

14. Cf. Gen 9:1.

15. "A leader; a commander" and "the head of a clan" (Johnson's *Dictionary*, s.v. "chieftain").

16. Charles originally separated the word "vain" from "glorious."

17. The expression "kill two birds with one stone" was common in Charles's day. In his personal copy of James Dixon's *Dictionary of Idiomatic English Phrases*, the following definition is offered: "*To kill two birds with one stone*—to effect two results with one expenditure of trouble" (James Main Dixon, *Dictionary of Idiomatic English Phrases* [London: T. Nelson and Sons, 1891, The Spurgeon Library], 32, italics in the original). Later in his life Charles provided an entry for this expression in the second volume of his popular *The Salt-Cellars* and even suggested a way to improve the proverb: "To kill two birds with one stone. Occasionally a person is able to accomplish two objects by one act. One would rather like the proverb to run, 'To feed two birds with one hand,' or 'To move two stones in one barrow'" (C. H. Spurgeon, *The Salt-Cellars: Being a Collection of Proverbs, Together with Homely Notes Thereon, Vol.II.– M-Z* [London: Passmore & Alabaster, 1889, The Spurgeon Library], 272). For additional references to this expression in Charles's sermons, see *MTP* 9:325; *MTP* 11:310; *MTP* 19:53; *MTP* 23:613; *MTP* 27:133; and *MTP* 28:97.

18. An alternative spelling of the word "staid" is "stayed."

19. "Remember Babel, and how God has scattered us and confounded our tongues. It was man's pride which led him to seek for an undivided monarchy that so he might be great. The tower was to be the rallying-point of all the tribes, and would have been the central throne of all human grandeur, but God has scattered us, that pride might not climb to so high a pitch. Pride, thou hast indeed suffered severe strokes from God" (*MTP* 8:25).

20. Due to a shortage of margin space, Charles constructed the underscored word "universal" by separating the letters "univ" from the rest of the word "ersal," which he wrote above the line.

21. "I saw a picture of the Tower of Babel by an eminent painter. All the various races of mankind were represented as going off in different directions,—some to the North, others to the South, to the West, or to the East, all being scattered over the face of the whole earth; it was a painful sight to see the great family broken up, never, as far as we could see, to be reunited again. But, dear friends, hear how this text collects the whole family of mankind into one; and gathers all these scattered ears of corn, and just makes one sheaf of them. 'There is no difference.' All men are fallen through sin, but whosoever out of them all believes in Jesus Christ shall have eternal life. There is one blessed bath of salvation in

which all may be washed, whiter than snow; there is one remedy, and only one, for the disease of sin, and all who apply to the great Physician are healed for ever. I love to see the human race thus reunited' (*MTP* 45:68–69). Cf. Acts 2:5–14; Gal 3:28; Col 3:11; Rev 7:9.

22. "Human language is necessarily imperfect. Since man's fall, and especially since the confusion of tongues at Babel, there has not only been a difference in speech between one nation and another, but also between one individual and another. Probably, we do not all mean exactly the same thing by any one word that we use; there is just a shade of difference between your meaning and mine. The confusion of tongues went much further than we sometimes realize; and so completely did it confuse our language that we do not, on all occasions, mean quite the same thing to ourselves even when we use the same word" (*MTP* 48:494).

23. For additional references to church unity in the context of Charles's ecclesiology, see "Can Two Walk Together Unless They Are Agreed?" (Notebook 1, Sermon 76).

141.   Rom VIII . 33 . 34 .   Who shall the Lord's elect condemn.

Paul seems in a triumphant mood & not without
reason — for he had just been getting by inspiration
an insight into the great doctrines of grace & was
gathering up all his eloquence for an impassioned
boast before earth & hell — & was coming on now
to election in Rom IX & he seems to scent it in
the air & tosses his head gallantly —

I.   He boasts of freedom from guilt.

Not as the Pharisee — nor as the moralist but as
a sinner saved by grace alone. He bases
his hope on election —   & uses that as an argument for justification for if he choose he will
acquit — — —   God's justification is like man's

b. It exempts from punishment. —

2. It does not exempt from the judgment bar.

3. It secures the man all immunities
but God beats man in that

1. He exempts from the guilt itself.

2. He makes acquittal an act of justice.

3. Gives more rights than ever were lost.

Conscience, law, Satan all would lay
something to our charge but God shuts their

141

WHO SHALL *the* LORD'S ELECT CONDEMN?

Romans 8:33–34[1]

"Who shall lay anything to the charge of God's elect? It is God that justifieth.
Who is he that condemneth? It is Christ that died, yea rather, that is risen again,
who is even at the right hand of God, who also maketh intercession for us."

Paul seems [to be] in a triumphant mood and not without reason. For he had just been getting by inspiration an insight into the great doctrines of grace[2] and was gathering up all his eloquence for an impassioned boast before earth and hell[3] and was coming on now to election in Rom IX.[4] And he seems to scent it in the air and tosses his head gallantly.

I. HE BOASTS OF FREEDOM FROM GUILT.[5]

Not as the Pharisee. Nor as the moralist.[6] But as a sinner saved by grace alone.[7] He bases his hope on election and uses that as an argument for justification. For if he choose, he will acquit.[8] God's justification is like man's:[9]

1. It exempts from punishment.

2. It does not exempt from the judgment[10] bar.

3. It secures [for] the man all immunities.[11]

But God beats man in that

1. He exempts from the guilt itself.[12]

2. He makes acquittal[13] an act of justice.

3. Gives more rights than ever were lost.

Conscience, law, Satan[14] all would lay something to our charge. But God shuts their mouths by giving them their demands.

God is the highest court — justified there — all is safe. Up! Up! Up! Christian to the hills! to the hills!! for here is strength rejoice ye righteous. —

II. Here is freedom from condemnation.

For 1. Christ died & the penalty is paid — the price laid down — the covenant sealed & bound with oaths — who shall rob Jesus of his purchase.

2. Christ is risen — he is not dead — he is alive his rising proved his acceptance. God has been satisfied or why loose the surety — who shall condemn?

3. Christ is at God's right hand. So he can keep the devil out. he has regal, God's authority Prince & a Saviour — we are secure.

4. Christ makes intercession — with prayers & with blood & can one perish for whom he intercedes. — — — — — —

Sinners here is the best of religions for you Faith, Faith, Faith get this & this is all. Christian how changed thy conditions, how blessed be grateful be humble, be cheerful —

216

mouths by giving them their demands.

God is the highest court. Justified there. All is safe.[15]

Up! Up! Up![16] Christian, to the hills! To the hills!![17] For here is strength. Rejoice, ye righteous.

II. HERE IS FREEDOM FROM CONDEMNATION.

For 1.[18] Christ died[19] and the penalty is paid, the price laid down,[20] the covenant sealed and bound with oaths. Who shall rob Jesus of his purchase?

2. Christ is risen. He is not dead. He is alive. His rising proved his acceptance. God has been satisfied, or why loose the surety? Who shall condemn?

3. Christ is at God's right hand.[21] So he can keep the devil out.[22] He has regal, God's authority.[23] Prince and a Saviour. We are secure.[24]

4. Christ makes intercession with prayers[25] and with blood, and can one perish for whom he intercedes?

Sinners, here is the best of religions for you.[26]

Faith, Faith, Faith. Get this and this is all.

Christian, how changed [are] thy conditions. How blessed. <u>Be grateful. Be humble. Be cheerful.</u>

216[27]

1. On October 15, 1876, Charles preached an additional sermon on Rom 8:33–34 entitled "False Justification and True" (*MTP* 51, Sermon 2932). In the first portion of the sermon, Charles expounded on Job 9:20; however, in the later portion he addressed Rom 8:33–34. There does not appear to be overlapping content between the early outline and this portion of the later sermon. Charles preached four additional sermons on Rom 8:34: "The Believer's Challenge" (*NPSP* 5, Sermon 256); "Jesus, the Substitute for His People" (*MTP* 21, Sermon 1223); "A Challenge and a Shield" (*MTP* 38, Sermon 2240); and "A Bold Challenge Justified" (*MTP* 53, Sermon 3067). Structural similarity can be noticed only in the second Roman numeral in the sermon above and "Jesus, the Substitute for His People (cf. *MTP* 21:160–63). Overlapping content, however, will be noted below.

2. "We have before us in the text the four marvellous pillars upon which the Christian rests his hope. Any one of them were all-sufficient. Though the sins of the whole world should press on any one of these sacred columns, it would never break nor bend. Yet for our strong consolation, that we may never tremble or fear, God hath been pleased to give us these four eternal rocks, these four immovable foundations upon which our faith may rest and stand secure. . . . It reminds me of what I have sometimes heard of the ropes that are used in mining. It is said that every strand of them would bear the entire tonnage, and consequently, if each strand bears the full weight that will ever be put upon the whole, there is an absolute certainty of safety given to the whole when twisted together" (*NPSP* 5:249–50).

3. "Satan, our arch-enemy, would condemn us if it were in his power. Only fancy him, for a moment, sitting on the judgment-seat. If we had the devil to judge us, he would soon bring to our recollection our many faults, and follies, and failings, and condemn us for them. But, O thou fiend of hell, God has not made thee the judge of his saints! . . . Satan has no right to judge us, and no power to condemn us; so, when he speaks the worst he can about us, we laugh him to scorn, rejoicing that God will bruise him under our feet shortly" (*MTP* 38:566).

4. Charles originally wrote Roman numeral V.

5. "There is in the death of Christ enough and more than enough. There is not only a sea in which to drown our sin, but the very tops of the mountains of our guilt are covered. . . . There is not only enough to put our sins to death, but enough to bury them and hide them out of sight. I say it boldly and without a

figure,—the eternal arm of God now nerved with strength, now released from the bondage in which justice held it, is able to save unto the uttermost them that come unto God by Christ" (*NPSP* 5:250).

6.   "Rest assured, dear hearer, that you will never attain to a well-founded freedom from the fear of condemnation by trying to make your sins appear little" (*MTP* 21:158).

7.   Cf. Eph 2:8.

8.   For clarity, the sentence may also read, "For if [God] chooses, he will acquit."

9.   Due to the lack of space in the margin, it is unclear whether Charles intended singularity or plurality. The word may also be "men's." A comparison between this phrase and "But God beats man" four lines below suggests Charles wrote the word "man."

10.   Charles originally spelled the word "judment."

11.   "But I feel a darkness coming down over my spirit, and in the darkness there is a fiendish voice that says, 'But *you have committed unknown sins*, sins that nobody else knows, and there have been sins which you yourself did not know. Hidden in your heart there is a damning spot which your eyes has not discovered.' . . . My unknown sins are buried in the unknown deeps of [Christ's] almighty sacrifice" (*MTP* 38:47, italics in the original).

12.   "But, Paul, you have broken God's law, so he must punish you. He replies, 'God cannot punish me; he cannot even condemn me.' But, Paul, you helped to put Stephen to death; your hands were red with the blood of the martyrs. You hunted the saints of God, and delighted to put them to death; and yet you say that God cannot condemn you for that, and never will. 'Ay,' says the apostle, 'he never will; he never can.' And why? 'Because Christ died.' But, Paul, what has Christ's death to do with your guilt? His answer is, 'All my sins, however many or however black they may have been, were laid upon Christ, and he stood in my stead in the sight of God, and in my place he suffered that which has rendered full satisfaction to the law of God for all my evil deeds, and thoughts, and words'" (*MTP* 38:569).

13.   Charles originally spelled the word "acquital."

14. "Take care that you do not answer Satan with any other argument than this: 'It is Christ that died'" (*MTP* 38:40).

15. An alternative reading of this line is "God is the highest court. [We are] justified there. All is safe."

16. "It is recorded concerning every believer that he is justified, and that the claim he makes that he is a child of God is a true one, and that all the glorious inheritance in the land of the blessed is his, and he may claim it at once as his own, for it all belongs to him. So up with you, child of God! Up with you, bird of the day! Eagle of God, will you sit, day after day, moping in the dark, when you might soar up into the light and gaze even at the sun? Up with you, son of the morning; up with you, child of light; away from all your gloomy doubts and fears! . . . You are forgiven, man; then live as a forgiven man should" (*MTP* 38:572).

17. Charles used the expression "To the hills!" later in his ministry. With reference to the 1889 flood in Johnstown, Pennsylvania, Charles said, "Let the Word of God be like one who, during the great flood in America, rode on a white horse down the valley, crying out, as he rode along, 'To the hills! To the hills! To the hills!' The waters were following fast behind him, and he would have the people escape to the mountains, lest they should be destroyed" (*MTP* 36:163). Charles also used this expression in the context of Psalm 121 (see *MTP* 42:485 and *MTP* 52:461).

18. The indentation of the number 1 after the word "For" suggests Charles likely did not originally seek to begin a list on this line.

19. "If any confront you with other confidences, still keep you to this almighty plea, 'Christ has died.' If one says, 'I was christened, and confirmed,' answer him by saying, 'Christ has died.' Should another say, 'I was baptized as an adult,' let your confidence remain the same: 'Christ has died.' When another says, 'I am a sound, orthodox Presbyterian,' you stick to this solid ground, 'Christ has died.' And if still another says, 'I am a red-hot Methodist,' answer him, 'Christ has died.' Whatever may be the confidences of others, and whatever may be your own, put them all away, and keep to this one declaration, 'It is Christ that died.' There is enough in that one truth to include all that is excellent in the others, and to answer all the accusations that may be brought against you" (*MTP* 38:38).

20. "Not in one jot or tittle will the intent of Christ's death be frustrated. Jesus shall see of the travail of his soul and be satisfied. That which he meant to do by dying shall be done, and he shall not pour his blood upon the ground in waste in any measure or sense" (*MTP* 21:160).

21. "Suppose you were actually at the right hand of God, would you then have any fear of being condemned? . . . 'No,' say you, 'I should have perfect confidence if I were there.' But you are there in your representation" (*MTP* 21:162). Cf. Mark 16:19; Col 3:1; Heb 8:1.

22. An alternative reading of this line is "Christ is at God's right hand so he can keep the devil out."

23. "Dyed is the wondrous garment that we are to wear, for it has been dipped in his precious blood" (*MTP* 53:571).

24. An alternative reading of these sentences is "[He has] God's authority. [He is a] Prince and a Saviour. We are secure."

25. Cf. Rom 8:34.

26. "Sometimes, when I think of what the Lord has done for me, I feel myself to be like a church steeple that I saw some few months ago. There had been a wedding in the place, and the bells were pealing out a merry chime; and, as they rang, I distinctly saw that steeple reel and rock, and the four pinnacles seemed to be tossing to and fro, and the whole tower seemed as though it must come down as the bells pealed out again and again. And sometimes, when my soul pulls the big bell, 'Jesus loved thee, and gave himself for thee, and thou art accepted in him, thou art God's own child, and on thy way to heaven, and a crown of eternal life is thine,' I feel as if this crazy steeple of my body would rock and reel beneath the excess of joy, and be scarcely able to hold the ecstatic bliss which the love of God creates within my soul" (*MTP* 53:573).

27. The number 216 was smeared toward the left side of the page.

142.   The seven cries on the cross.—

The words of a dying Jesus should be as precious as diamonds to every follower he has; the trifling sayings of great men are treasured, how great then the respect which we owe to dying words of the son of God.

1. Whilst nailing him & fixing the cross. he said "Father forgive them, for they know not what they do."

2. Before the darkness came on he beheld his mother. and said "Woman behold thy son".

3. The instant before the sun was darkened he comforted the expiring thief "This day shalt thou &c

4.   Eli, Eli, lama sabacthani.

5.   I thirst—

6.   It is finished.

7.   Father into thy hands I commit my spirit

No 1. Luke 23. 34.   No 2. John 19. 26.
No 3. Luke 23. 43   No 4. Matt. 27. 46
No 5 - John 19. 28.   No 6 John 19. 30
No 7 Luke 23. 46
              Read XX Psalm.

217.

142

THE SEVEN CRIES
on THE CROSS[1]

The words of a dying Jesus should be as precious as diamonds to every follower he has.[2] The trifling sayings of great men are treasured. How great, then, the respect which we owe to dying words of the son of God?[3]

1. Whilst nailing him and fixing the cross,[4] he said, *"Father forgive them,[5] for they know not what they do."*[6]

2. Before the darkness came on, he beheld his mother and said, *"Woman, behold thy son."*

3. *The instant before the sun was darkened, he comforted the expiring thief. "This day shalt thou, etc."*

4. *"Eli, Eli, lama sabacthani."*[7]

5. *"I thirst."*[8]

6. *"It is finished."*[9]

7. *"Father, into thy hands I commit my spirit."*[10]

No[11] 1. Luke 23.34[12]   No 2. John 19.26[13]

No 3. Luke 23.43[14]   No 4. Matt 27.46[15]

No 5. John 19.28   No 6. John 19.30[16]

No 7. Luke 23.46[17]

Read XX Psalm.[18]

217.

1. Did Charles intend Psalm 20 to be the dominant Scripture text of the sermon? If so, it was uncharacteristic of him to write the Scripture reference at the conclusion of the sermon. The content of the sermon suggests Charles likely intended to write Psalm 22 instead of 20. Either way, the outline follows the exposition of neither text. Charles likely intended to treat his subject topically as he did in "Regeneration" (Notebook 1, Sermon 7), "Creation of Man" (Notebook 8, Sermon 369), "Faith Before Baptism" (Notebook 9, Sermon 396), and "The Day of Vengeance, the Year of Acceptance" (Notebook 9, Sermon 397). Charles preached ten sermons on the subject of the last seven statements of Christ on the cross: "Cries from the Cross" (*MTP* 44, Sermon 2562); "The First Cry from the Cross" (*MTP* 15, Sermon 897); "The Shortest of the Seven Cries" (*MTP* 24, Sermon 1409); "Lama Sabachthani" (*MTP* 36, Sermon 2133); "Christ's Plea for Ignorant Sinners" (*MTP* 38, Sermon 2263); "Our Lord's Last Cry from the Cross" (*MTP* 39, Sermon 2311); "Christ's Dying Word for His Church" (*MTP* 40, Sermon 2344); "The Last Words of Christ on the Cross" (*MTP* 45, Sermon 2644); "The Saddest Cry from the Cross" (*MTP* 48, Sermon 2803); and "Unknown Depths and Heights" (*MTP* 53, Sermon 3068). In the title of this sermon, Charles reverted to writing the "long s" in the word "Cross." The base of the letter "s" was smeared toward the lower left side of the page.

2. "There has been a great deal said about these seven cries from the cross by divers writers; and though I have read what many of them have written, I cannot add anything to what they have said since they have delighted to dwell upon these seven last cries; and here the most ancient of writers, of what would be called the Romish school, are not to be excelled, even by Protestants, in their intense devotion to every letter of our Saviour's dying words; and they sometimes strike out new meanings, richer and more rare than any that have occurred to the far cooler minds of modern critics, who are as a rule greatly blessed with moles' eyes, able to see where there is nothing to be seen, but never able to see when there is anything worth seeing. Modern criticism, like modern theology, if it were put in the Garden of Eden, would not see a flower" (*MTP* 39:266).

3. "It was most fitting that every word of our Lord upon the cross should be gathered up and preserved. As not a bone of him shall be broken, so not a word shall be lost" (*MTP* 24:217).

4. "Not in cold blood did the Saviour pray, after he had forgotten the injury, and could the more easily forgive it, but while the first red drops of blood were spurting on the hands which drove the nails; while yet the hammer was bestained with crimson gore, his blessed mouth poured out the fresh warm prayer, 'Father, forgive them, for they know not what they do'" (*MTP* 15:591).

5. "He does not say, 'Why do ye this? Why pierce the hands that fed you? Why nail the feet that followed after you in mercy? Why mock the Man who loved to bless you?' . . . How often, when men say, 'I forgive you,' is there a kind of selfishness about it! At any rate, self is asserted in the very act of forgiving. Jesus takes the place of a pleader, a pleader for those who were committing murder upon himself" (*MTP* 38:213).

6. "Was not this prayer, 'Father, forgive them,' like a stone cast into a lake, forming at first a narrow circle, and then a wider ring, and soon a larger sphere, until the whole lake is covered with circling waves? Such a prayer as this, cast into the whole world, first created a little ring of Jewish converts and of priests, and then a wider circle of such as were beneath the Roman sway; and to-day its circumference is wide as the globe itself, so that tens of thousands are saved through the prevalence of this one intercession 'Father, forgive them'" (*MTP* 15:595–96). See also "The Saddest Cry from the Cross" (*MTP* 48, Sermon 2803) and "Unknown Depths and Heights" (*MTP* 53, Sermon 3068).

7. "I do not think that the records of time, or even of eternity, contain a sentence more full of anguish" (*MTP* 36:133). "There are seasons when the brightness of our Father's smile is eclipsed by clouds and darkness. But let us remember that God never does really forsake us. It is only a seeming forsaking with us, but in Christ's case it was a real forsaking. . . . In our case, this is the cry of unbelief; in his case, it was the utterance of a fact, for God had really turned away from him for a time" (*MTP* 44:146).

8. "Have *we* not often given him vinegar to drink? . . . Are you so frozen at heart that not a cup of cold water can be melted for Jesus? Are you lukewarm? O brother, if he says, 'I thirst' and you bring him a lukewarm heart, that is worse than vinegar, for he has said, 'I will spue thee out of my mouth.' He can receive vinegar, but not lukewarm love. Come, bring him your warm heart, and let him drink from that purified chalice as much as he wills. Let all your love be his.

I know he loves to receive from you, because he delights even in a cup of cold water that you give to one of his disciples: how much more will he delight in the giving of your whole self to him? Therefore while he thirsts give him to drink this day" (*MTP* 24:224, 226–27, italics in the original).

9. "*The redemption of Christ's Church is perfect.* There is not another penny to be paid for her full release. There is no mortgage upon Christ's inheritance. Those whom he bought with blood are for ever clear of all charges, paid for to the utmost" (*MTP* 40:29, italics in the original).

10. "How instructive to us is this great truth that the Incarnate Word lived on the Inspired Word! It was food to him" (*MTP* 45:495). Cf. Ps 31:5.

11. Abbr., "Number." These abbreviations correspond to the numbers Charles listed above. By drawing comparison between the Old and New Testaments, Charles likely had in mind the fulfillment of prophecy.

12. Luke 23:34, "Then said Jesus, Father, forgive them; for they know not what they do. And they parted his raiment, and cast lots."

13. John 19:26, "When Jesus therefore saw his mother, and the disciple standing by, whom he loved, he saith unto his mother, 'Woman, behold thy son!'"

14. Luke 23:43, "And Jesus said unto him, Verily I say unto thee, Today shalt thou be with me in paradise."

15. Matthew 27:46, "And about the ninth hour Jesus cried with a loud voice, saying, Eli, Eli, lama sabacthani? that is to say, My God, my God, why hast thou forsaken me?"

16. John 19:30, "When Jesus therefore had received the vinegar, he said, It is finished: and he bowed his head, and gave up the ghost."

17. Luke 23:46, "And when Jesus had cried with a loud voice, he said, Father, into thy hands I commend my spirit, and having said thus, he gave up the ghost."

18. The content of this sermon suggests Charles likely intended to write Psalm 22, which, as he noted in his commentary on the Psalms, "*is beyond all* THE PSALM

OF THE CROSS" (*TD* 1:365, italics and capitalization in the original). However, the entirety of Psalm 20 is provided: "The Lord hear thee in the day of trouble; the name of the God of Jacob defend thee; send thee help from the sanctuary, and strengthen thee out of Zion; remember all thy offerings, and accept thy burnt sacrifice; Selah. Grant thee according to thine own heart, and fulfill all thy counsel. We will rejoice in thy salvation, and in the name of our God we will set up our banners: the Lord fulfill all thy petitions. Now know I that the Lord saveth his anointed; he will hear him from his holy heaven with the saving strength of his right hand. Some trust in chariots, and some in horses: but we will remember the name of the Lord our God. They are brought down and fallen: but we are risen, and stand upright. Save, Lord: let the king hear us when we call."

Joel III. 13. "Put ye in the sickle for the harvest is 143 ripe.

Harvest is a joyful time & it should be a time of gratitude men should praise God when loaded with his mercies perhaps we may be helped to maintain true piety in the harvest field if the Spirit unfold this text.

Though perhaps wresting the text. Let us consider it
I. As spoken to ministers. & when God gives us this errand it is delightful — we sow on & on, & reaping is promised in time. When our hearers are attentive, when moist eyes & swelling hearts are seen, when prayer meetings are full — then we hope men are ripening. But we long to put the sickle in & gather them into the church.
II. As spoken to the ungodly who have sown to the flesh for many years. How much harvest have you? What fruit have ye now? Where are your gains? Put in the sickle! reap! Ah ye reap the whirlwind.
III. As spoken to the angels concerning the saints. They are plants of the Lord's right hand planting they are not meant to continue here, they must be gathered in when ripe, but not before.
IV As spoken to the angels concerning the wicked for these are ripening — hardness of heart, puttings away of the Holy Spirit, sin with greediness these are marks of ripening — take care least the angel is on his way with sharpened sickle to cut thee down. Now I invoke the Holy Spirit.
219. 220,

143

PUT YE *in the* SICKLE *for the* HARVEST IS RIPE
Joel 3:13[1]

"Put ye in the sickle, for the harvest is ripe: come, get you down; for the press is full, the fats overflow; for their wickedness is great."

Harvest is a joyful time[2] and it should be a time of gratitude. Men should praise God when loaded with his mercies. Perhaps we may be helped to maintain true piety in the harvest field if the Spirit unfold[s] this text.[3]

Though, perhaps wresting[4] the text, let us consider it:

I. AS SPOKEN TO MINISTERS. AND WHEN GOD GIVES US THIS ERRAND IT IS DELIGHTFUL.

We sow on and on and reaping is promised in time. When our hearers are attentive, when moist eyes and swelling hearts are seen, when prayer meetings are full, then we hope men are ripening. But we long to put the sickle in and gather them into the church.

II. AS SPOKEN TO THE UNGODLY WHO HAVE SOWN TO THE FLESH FOR MANY YEARS.

How much harvest have you? What fruit have ye now? Where are your gains? Put in the sickle! Reap! Ah, ye reap the whirlwind.

III. AS SPOKEN TO THE ANGELS CONCERNING THE SAINTS.

They are plants of the Lord's right hand planting.[5] They are not meant to continue here. They must be gathered in when ripe, but not before.

IV. AS SPOKEN TO THE ANGELS CONCERNING THE WICKED.

For these are ripening: hardness of heart,[6] puttings away of the Holy Spirit,[7] sin with greediness. These are marks of ripening. Take care, lest[8] the angel is on his way with sharpened sickle to cut thee down.

Now I invoke the Holy Spirit.

219. 220.

1. This is the only time Charles preached a sermon on Joel 3:13.

2. Charles originally wrote the letter "n" instead of "m" at the end of the word "time." He corrected the mistake by reinforcing the concluding stem of the "m."

3. An alternative reading of this sentence is "Perhaps we may be helped to maintain true piety in the harvest field if the Spirit [will help us] unfold this text."

4. "To twist by violence; to extort by writhing or force. . . . to distort" (Johnson's *Dictionary*, s.v. "wrest").

5. Cf. Ps 1:3.

6. Cf. Ps 95:8–9; Prov 28:14; Rom 2:5; Eph 4:18; Heb 3:7–9.

7. Cf. Rom 1:24; Eph 4:30.

8. Charles originally wrote the word "least" here. The context, however, suggests that he intended to write the word "lest." See also "The Tower of Babel" (Sermon 140).

144.   Rev. XIV. 14 – 20.   The Harvest & the Vintage.

The Revelation is for the most part confessedly difficult of comprehension but these words do not seem so.

The Harvest & vintage were two occurrences known & noticed by all.   It is formed into majestic imagery to show the judgment of the good & the con--demnation of the wicked. —

I, The Harvest – the ingathering of the good comes before the vintage for the dead in Christ shall rise first. ---- Let us notice –

1. Those reaped – those who died in the Lord, who laboured for him, & have good works following, all saints, all ages, every one that believeth.

2, The time of reaping – when they were ripe, or dry. when affliction had its perfect work, when sanctification is complete. no green corn will be cut down.

3. The reaper. he was a royal one, the man Jesus. He loves his saints so much that he suffers none else to gather them in. A king, a God turns reaper. He comes on a white cloud least he should terrify us – the sickle will cut well – it is sharp.

4. The completeness of the work. He put in his sickle & reaped all at one handful. He left none for the earth was reaped. not one straggler left. the ministers & angels requested him to reap it was welcom

THE HARVEST *and* *the* VINTAGE
Revelation 14:14–20[1]

"And I looked, and behold a white cloud, and upon the cloud one sat like unto the Son of man, having on his head a golden crown, and in his hand a sharp sickle. And another angel came out of the temple, crying with a loud voice to him that sat on the cloud, Thrust in thy sickle, and reap: for the time is come for thee to reap; for the harvest of the earth is ripe. And he that sat on the cloud thrust in his sickle on the earth; and the earth was reaped. And another angel came out of the temple which is in heaven, he also having a sharp sickle. And another angel came out from the altar, which had power over fire; and cried with a loud cry to him that had the sharp sickle, saying, Thrust in thy sharp sickle, and gather the clusters of the vine of the earth; for her grapes are fully ripe. And the angel thrust in his sickle into the earth, and gathered the vine of the earth, and cast it into the great winepress of the wrath of God. And the winepress was trodden without the city, and blood came out of the winepress, even unto the horse bridles, by the space of a thousand and six hundred furlongs."

The Revelation is, for the most part, confessedly difficult of comprehension,[2] but these words do not seem so. The Harvest and Vintage were two occurrences known and noticed by all. It is formed into majestic imagery to show the judgment of the good and the condemnation of the wicked.

I.   THE HARVEST.

The ingathering of the good comes before the vintage, for the dead in Christ shall rise first.[3] Let us notice:

1.   Those reaped. Those who died in the Lord, who laboured for him, and have good works following.[4] All saints, all ages, every one that believeth.

2.   The time of reaping. When they were ripe or dry. When affliction had its perfect work. When sanctification is complete. No green corn will be cut down.

3.   The reaper. He was a royal one, the man Jesus. He loves his saints so much that he suffers none else to gather them in. A king, a God turns reaper.[5] He comes on a white cloud lest[6] he should terrify us. The sickle will cut well. It is sharp.

4.   The completeness of the work. He put in his sickle and reaped all at one handful. He left none, for the earth was reaped. Not one straggler left. The ministers and angels requested him to reap. It was <u>welcome</u>.[7]

II . The Vintage. The ingathering of the wicked will come after the harvest of the righteous. Let us notice
1. Those gathered. All persons left in the harvest. Sinners openly & those who are near the kingdom but not in. they are the clusters of the vine of the earth, not heavenly fruit they are "her grapes" the natural products of the soil.
2. The time of reaping – when they are fully ripe. Corn is ripe when it is dry, grapes are ripe when full of juice, Saints are ripe when free from sin, sinners are ripe when full of it. There is a point to which saints & sinner attain before their final ingatering. –
3. The reaper – was no royal personage, only an angel. the angels requested that the grapes might be gathered in for they longed to clear the world of sin .
4. The completeness of the work, he left not one.
5. The treatment of the grapes. they were not gathered with tender care by Jesus, but the angel cast them into the great wine-press of the wrath of God. They were then pressed, broken, their hearts blood flowed from them – in most awful profusion.
This was not done in heaven but outside of the city.
. . . .
1. How important are our actions, upon which all these tremendous things depend,
2. 'Tis but prudence to seek to God & beg that he would by omnipotence transform you . –
222.

II. THE VINTAGE.

The ingathering of the wicked will come after the harvest of the righteous. Let us notice:

1. Those gathered. All persons left in the harvest. Sinners openly and those who are near the kingdom but not in. They are the clusters of the vine of the earth, not heavenly fruit. They are "her grapes," the natural products of the soil.

2. The time of reaping. When they are fully ripe. Corn is ripe when it is dry. Grapes are ripe when full of juice. Saints are ripe when free from sin. Sinners are ripe when full of it. There is a point to which saints and sinners attain before their final ingathering.

3. The reaper was no royal personage, only an angel. The angels requested that the grapes might be gathered[8] in, for they longed to clear the world of sin.

4. The completeness of the work. He left not one.

5. The treatment of the grapes. They were not gathered with tender care by Jesus, but the angel cast them into the great wine-press of the wrath of God. They were then pressed, broken. Their heart[']s blood flowed from them in most awful profusion. This was not done in heaven but outside of the city.

. . . .

1. How important are our actions upon which all these tremendous things depend.

2. 'Tis but prudence[9] to seek to God and beg that he would by omnipotence transform you.

222.

1. On September 17, 1876, Charles preached an additional sermon on Rev 14:14–20, also entitled "The Harvest and the Vintage" (*MTP* 50, Sermon 2910). There is enough overlapping content to suggest Charles had the above sermon in mind when writing his later sermon. A primary difference is found in the 1876 sermon in which Charles added three observations about the Day of Judgment: "1. '*The Judge's throne*'"; "2. '*his person*'"; and "3. '*his adornments*'" (*MTP* 50:555-557, italics in the original).

2. The vertical stem of an illegible letter can be seen beneath the "o" in the word "comprehension." Charles may have prematurely written the letter "p" or "h."

3. First Thessalonians 4:16, "For the Lord himself shall descend from heaven with a shout, with the voice of the archangel, and with the trump of God: and the dead in Christ shall rise first."

4. Cf. Eph 2:10.

5. Alternative readings of this sentence are: "A king, a God-turn[ed] reaper" or "A king, a God [who] turn[ed the] reaper." The former reading is more likely.

6. As in the previous sermon, Charles wrote the word "least" instead of "lest."

7. Due to a lack of space in the margin, Charles wrote the underscored word "welcome" above the line.

8. A dark yellow stain, likely the result of the aging process of the manuscript, appears beneath the letter "a" in the word "gathered."

9. Charles initially failed to provide the bowl of the letter "e" in the word "prudence." See also the word "realities" in "The Certain Judgment" (Sermon 136), "widely" in "God's Dealings with the Antediluvians" (Sermon 138), and "perceived" in "The Washing of the Disciples' Feet by Jesus" (Sermon 156).

145. Is IV. 5.   The tabernacles of Jacob & Mt Zion blessed of God.

verse 2 contains a promise of the raising up of Jesus.
verse 3. declares that God will reserve a people.
verse 4. declares that God will reform & perfect them
& now this contains a great promise of blessing.
I. The houses of the saints are blessed.
1. With God's care - both by night & by day.
2. With God's guidance in all their steps.
3. With God's covering in distress.
4. With light in darkness.
And every other idea couched in the fiery cloudy pillar.
But they must be on Mount Zion - there must be
family prayer there; thus shall we be blessed.
II. The assemblies of the saints are blessed.
1. Shall enjoy God's presence.
2. Shall enjoy his love & care.
3. Shall have his guidance.
4. Shall be kept in protection from enemies
5. Shall enjoy much comfort.
This is promised to a Church fashioned after
the gospel model. See if it has not been fulfilled
in our history as a Church.
III. Our glory is our defence.
1. God is our greatest glory & so our great defence

145

THE TABERNACLES *of* JACOB *and* MT.[1] ZION BLESSED *of* GOD
Isaiah 4:5[2]

"And the Lord will create upon every dwelling place of mount Zion, and upon her assemblies, a cloud and smoke by day, and the shining of a flaming fire by night: for upon all the glory shall be a defence."

Verse 2[3] contains a promise of the raising up of Jesus.[4]

Verse 3[5] declares that God will reserve a people.[6]

Verse 4[7] declares that God will reform and perfect them. And now this contains a great promise of blessing.

I.   THE HOUSES OF THE SAINTS[8] ARE BLESSED.

1. With God's care, both by night and by day.

2. With God's guidance in all their steps.

3. With God's covering in distress.

4. With light in darkness.

And every other idea couched in the fiery, cloudy pillar. But they[9] must be on Mount Zion. There must be family prayer[10] there. Thus shall we be blessed.

II. THE ASSEMBLIES OF THE SAINTS ARE BLESSED.

1. Shall enjoy God's presence.

2. Shall enjoy his love and care.

3. Shall have his guidance.

4. Shall be kept in protection from enemies.

5. Shall enjoy much comfort.

This is promised to a Church fashioned after the gospel model. See if it has not been fulfilled in our history as a Church.

III. OUR GLORY IS OUR DEFENCE.

1. God is our greatest glory, and so, our great defence.[11]

2. Christ & his cross are our glory & defence.

3. Our practical godliness is our glory & defence.

4. Our sound doctrine is our glory & defence.

5. Our prayers are our glory & defence

By Gods grace, may these things be in us & abound then shall we be strong in God & shall do great things.   Grace in us is our glory & defence

Take heed lest ye relapse into your old courses & become again cold, losing your present fervour,

God help me, a poor thing.

221.

Ruth. II. 22.   Go not in any other field.   146

She had gleaned most plenteously & received truly generous treatment – therefore says Naomi go no where else.

So Christian thou hast been well treated by Jesus though thou art poor he feedeth thee & thou are loaded with blessing therefore go not even for a moment elsewhere

1. Self advantage should keep us to this field for in no other is there good gleaning.

2. Remembrance of thy state when first Jesus received thee should forbid thy running away.

3. Remember how well the man treated thee & go not because thou doest him good but thou wilt enrich thyself

Keep to Jesus Christ.

223.

2. Christ and his cross[12] are our glory and defence.

3. Our practical godliness is our glory and defence.

4. Our sound doctrine[13] is our glory and defence.

5. Our prayers are our glory and defence.

By God's grace, may these things be in us and abound. Then shall we be strong in God and shall do great things. Grace in us is our glory and defence.[14]

Take heed, lest you relapse into your old courses and become again cold,[15] losing your present fervour.

221. God, help me, a poor thing.

GO NOT *in* ANY OTHER FIELD

Ruth 2:22[1]

"And Naomi said unto Ruth her daughter in law, It is good, my daughter, that thou go out with [Boaz's] maidens, that they meet thee not in any other field."

She had gleaned most plenteously and received truly generous treatment.[2] Therefore, says Naomi, go no where else.

So, Christian, thou hast been well treated by Jesus.[3] Though thou art poor he feedeth thee[4] and thou are loaded with blessing. Therefore, go not even for a moment elsewhere.[5]

1. Self advantage should keep us to this field, for in no other is there good gleaning.

2. Remembrance of thy state when first Jesus reced[6] thee should forbid thy running away.

3. Remember how well the man treated thee and go, not because thou doest him good, but thou wilt enrich thyself.[7]

Keep to Jesus Christ.

223.

1. Abbr., "Mount" or "Mountain."

2. This is the only time Charles preached a sermon on Isa 4:5.

3. Charles originally wrote the number 1 instead of 2.

4. Isaiah 4:2, "In that day shall the branch of the Lord be beautiful and glorious, and the fruit of the earth shall be excellent and comely for them that are escaped of Israel."

5. Charles originally wrote 2 instead of 3. Charles corrected his mistake before proceeding to the next line.

6. Isaiah 4:3, "And it shall come to pass, that he that is left in Zion, and he that remaineth in Jerusalem, shall be called holy, even every one that is written among the living in Jerusalem."

7. Isaiah 4:4, "When the Lord shall have washed away the filth of the daughters of Zion, and shall have purged the blood of Jerusalem from the midst thereof by the spirit of judgment, and by the spirit of burning."

8. It is unclear whether Charles intended to emphasize the word "saints." Its bolded letters were likely the result of a malfunction of his writing instrument.

9. A dark brown stain, likely the result of the aging process of the manuscript, appears over the word "they."

10. See C. H. Spurgeon, *C. H. Spurgeon's Prayers. With an Introduction by Dinsdale T. Young* (London: Passmore & Alabaster, 1905, The Spurgeon Library).

11. Alternative readings of this line are: "God is our greatest glory, and so [he is] our great defence" or "[Because] God is our greatest glory, [he is] our great defence."

12. See "Christ Is All" (Notebook 1, Sermon 22).

13. See "Effects of Sound Doctrine" (*NPSP* 6, Sermon 324).

14. The handwriting in the sentence "Grace in us is our glory and defence" differs from that in the surrounding sentence. Charles may have intended this sentence to be the sixth point in his list three lines above.

15. "Are your hearts hard and solid? Has your soul become steeled? Has it become frozen like an iceberg? O sun of righteousness arise, and melt the icy heart" (*NPSP* 4:168).

1.   This is the only time Charles preached a sermon on Ruth 2:22. For additional sermons on Ruth, see "A Sermon for Gleaners" (*MTP* 8, Sermon 464); "Mealtime in the Cornfields" (*MTP* 9, Sermon 522); "Ruth's Reward; or, Cheer for Converts" (*MTP* 31, Sermon 1851), "Spiritual Gleaning" (*MTP* 44, Sermon 2585); "Ruth Deciding for God" (*MTP* 46, Sermon 2680); and "Spiritual Gleaning" (C. H. Spurgeon, *Farm Sermons* [London: Passmore & Alabaster, 1882], 247–62). See also *Morning & Evening*, August 1 AM, August 2 PM, and October 25 PM.

2.   Cf. Ruth 2:2–3.

3.   "It will make thy corn grind all the better, and taste all the sweeter, if you thinkest that it is a proof of love that thy sweet seasons, thy high enjoyments, thy blessed ravishments of spirit, are so many proofs of thy Lord's affection to thee. Boaz allowed Ruth to go and glean among the sheaves because of his love to her; so, beloved, it is God's free grace that lets us go among his sheaves, and that lets us lay hold of doctrinal blessings, promise blessings, or experience blessings. We have no right to be there of ourselves; it is all the Lord's free and sovereign grace that lets us go there. . . . O child of God, never be afraid to glean! All there is in all thy Lord's fields is thine" (*MTP* 44:417).

4.   "Now, I like to scatter the corn on the ground as much as ever I can; I do not mean to hold it up so high that you cannot reach it. One reason is that I cannot; I have not the talent to hold it up where you cannot see it; my ability will only allow me just to throw the corn on the ground, so that the people can pick it up; and if it is thrown on the ground, then all can get it" (*MTP* 44:413).

5.   "Gleaners must not be choosers, and where the Lord sends the gospel, there he calls us to be present" (*Farm Sermons*, 255).

6.   Abbr. "received."

7.   An alternative reading of this line is "Remember how well the man treated thee and go not because thou does him good. But thou wilt enrich thyself."

147   Ps. **XVI** . 11.   The joy of Heaven.

We know but little of other worlds, & heaven is so beyond the power of understanding that we must not think to have all made clear as noonday. Yet Heaven heaven has been the beloved theme of God's sons & will be till time shall end ——— This verse answers 2 questions

I. Where is heaven. "in thy presence", "at thy right hand"

1. Heaven is "in <u>Gods presence</u>",   In one sense the whole earth is in gods presence, in a higher degree his saints are in his presence now, higher yet was his degree of presence in some specially, chosen ones such as Enoch, Abraham, Moses, the prophets.

but these are inferior to that dazzling degree of presence which is seen in heaven. These are the antechambers, Heaven is the secret presence chamber, the Holy of Holies.

2. Heaven is "<u>at god's right hand</u>" Now we are at god's feet sitting there. we are on his footstool earth, some are laid in the lowest conditions of poverty & ~~suffering~~ suffering but we shall - be just where Jesus is. Receive the same honors as he.   Exaltation, dignity, friendship, glory.

II. What is heaven - "fulness of joy", "pleasures for evermore"

1. Heaven is "fulness of joy"; we can scarcely say there is joy on earth for we are born to trouble, — when we do rejoice as we often do greatly, yet we never enjoy the fulness of joy. satiety of bliss, for we want more.

2. Heaven is "pleasure for evermore". Pleasure of a high. & spiritual nature. Pleasure is gained here by good

147

THE JOY *of* HEAVEN
Psalm 16:11[1]

"Thou wilt shew me the path of life: in thy presence is fullness of joy; at thy right hand there are pleasures for evermore."

We know but little of other worlds,[2] and heaven is so beyond the power of understanding that we must not think to have all made clear as noonday. Yet Heaven, heaven[3] has been the beloved theme of God's sons and will be 'till time shall end. This verse answers 2 questions:

I.   WHERE IS HEAVEN? *"In thy presence," "at thy right hand."*

  1. Heaven is "in God's presence."
      In one sense, the whole earth is in God's presence.[4] In a higher degree, his saints are in his presence now. Higher yet was his degree of presence in some specially chosen ones such as Enoch,[5] Abraham,[6] Moses,[7] the prophets.[8] But these are inferior to that dazzling degree of presence which is[9] seen in heaven. These are the antechambers.[10] Heaven is the secret presence chamber, the Holy of Holies.[11]

  2. Heaven is "at God's right hand."[12] Now we are at[13] God's feet. Sitting there, we are on his footstool,[14] earth. Some are laid in the lowest conditions of poverty and suffering,[15] but we shall be just where Jesus is. Receive[16] the same honors as he.[17] Exaltation, dignity, friendship, glory.[18]

II. WHAT IS HEAVEN? *"Fulness of joy," "pleasures forevermore."*

  1. Heaven is "fulness of joy." We can scarcely say there is joy on earth, for we are born to trouble.[19] When we do rejoice as we often do greatly, yet we never enjoy the fulness of joy,[20] satiety[21] of bliss,[22] for we want more.

  2. Heaven is "pleasure forevermore." Pleasure of a high and spiritual nature. Pleasure is gained here by good

state of mind & body, by friendship, by satisfied desires, by sweet communion with Jesus. & heaven will have this in a grand degree. "for evermore" no intervals of pain, no fear of a close of existence, nor of a fall from it ......

<u>III</u>. What makes us think heaven so happy.

1. Gods promise is that we shall have a glorious inheritance & we know not how great that promise is since already we have been suprized at what he has given us, we thought the promise could not mean so much.

2. Those who have come nearest affirm its beauty, Paul, Moses &c could not bear the splendor. Martyrs & dying saints have been ravished by the prospect Have borne their trials patiently & happily —

3. God's presence in our own experience has been most sweet — though that's faint compared with heaven. Surrounded by sin we are happy — how blest to be free. In company with the saints we cannot but be blest. When we shall know all & be like Jesus. we shall be blest

4. The perfect angels must be exquisitely happy & so shall we since we shall enjoy the same.

5. Jesus' groans agonies, death must win a glorious heaven for his people — so great a price must buy a splendid home indeed.

Saint cheer up. Sinner thou art a fool to miss this — Oh Father Help thro' Jesus. —

224

state of mind and body,[23] by friendship, by satisfied desires, by sweet communion with Jesus. And heaven will have this in a grand degree. "For evermore." No intervals of pain. No fear of a close of existence,[24] nor of a fall from it.

III. WHAT MAKES US THINK HEAVEN [IS][25] SO HAPPY?

1. God's promise is that we shall have a glorious inheritance, and we know not how great that promise is since already we have been surprised[26] at what he has given us. We thought the promise could not mean so much.

2. Those who have come nearest affirm its beauty. Paul,[27] Moses,[28] etc., could not bear the splendor. Martyrs and dying saints have been ravished by the prospect. [They] have borne their trials patiently and happily.[29]

3. God's presence in our own experience has been most sweet, though that is faint compared with heaven.

    Surrounded by sin, we are happy. How blest[30] to be free.[31]

    In company with the saints we cannot but be blest.[32]

    When we shall know all and be like Jesus,[33] we shall be blest.

4. The perfect angels must be exquisitely happy, and so shall we [be] since we shall enjoy the same.

5. Jesus's groans, agonies, death must win a glorious heaven for his people.[34] So great a price must buy a splendid home indeed.[35]

    Saint, cheer up. Sinner, thou art a fool to miss this.[36]

    Oh Father, help thro'[37] Jesus.

224

1. On June 10, 1877, Charles preached an additional sermon on Ps 16:11 entitled "Life, and the Path to It" (*MTP* 49, Sermon 2813). Overlapping content is found in Charles's later treatment of heaven as being in God's presence, at God's right hand, and full of enjoyment (*MTP* 49:17–18). Charles likely had in mind his early sermon when writing this part of his later one.

2. Astronomical advances were common during this time in Charles's ministry. "The wonderful extent of that space" was, as Scottish minister Thomas Chalmers wrote, "teeming with unnumbered worlds" (Thomas Chalmers, *A Series of Discourses on the Christian Revelation Viewed in Connection with the Modern Astronomy* [Glasgow: Chalmers and Collins, 1822, The Spurgeon Library], 95). In the 1840s, the eighth planet of the solar system, Neptune, was discovered by French mathematician Urbain Le Verrier. Not long before Charles preached the sermon above, Ormsby Mitchell, writing in 1851, wrote that Neptune was "the most wonderful discovery that ever marked the career of astronomical sciences" (O. M. Mitchell, *The Orbs of Heaven; or, the Planetary and Stellar Worlds. A Popular Exposition of the Great Discoveries and Theories of Modern Astronomy* [London: Office of the National Illustrated Library, 1851, The Spurgeon Library], 146). For a selection of volumes on astronomy in Charles's personal library, see Thomas Milner, *The Heavens and the Earth. A Popular Handbook of Astronomy. A New Edition. With Revision and Additions by Edwin Dunkin* (London: The Religious Tract Society, n.d., The Spurgeon Library); Robert James Mann, *The Planetary and Stellar Universe (A Series of Lectures)* (London: Reeve, Brothers, King William Street, Strand, 1845, The Spurgeon Library); and Mungo Ponton, *The Great Architect; As Manifested in the Material Universe*, 2nd ed. (London: T. Nelson and Sons, 1866, The Spurgeon Library).

3. The repetition of the word "heaven" may be an example of dittography. More likely, however, Charles intended emphasis.

4. Cf. Ps 139:7–12; Prov 15:3; Jer 23:23–24.

5. Cf. Gen 5:24.　　6. Cf. Gen 18:1.

7. Cf. Exodus 3.　　8. Cf. 1 Sam 3:4; Isaiah 6; Dan 3:25.

9. A dark stain, likely the result of the aging process of the manuscript, appears after the word "is."

10. "The chamber that leads to the chief apartment" (Johnson's *Dictionary*, s.v. "antechamber").

11. "Many people ask, 'Where is heaven?' Others enquire, 'Is there such a place at all?' Assuredly, there is such a place, but where it is, I cannot tell. Some have imagined that, possibly, it is in the central star of our solar system, Alcyone in the constellation of the Pleiades. We may dismiss the conjecture as soon as we have heard it, and not be any the better for having heard it. What we do know, however, about heaven is, that it is in the presence of God" (*MTP* 44:17).

12. "God is not going to give his people any left-handed heaven, but they are to dwell at his right hand for evermore" (*MTP* 49:17).

13. A tittle appears above the letter "a" in the word "at." Charles likely wrote the word "in."

14. Cf. Isa 66:1; Matt 5:34–35.

15. The first two letters in the word "suffering" are illegible.

16. Charles originally wrote the word "receve" and then added an "i" between the "e" and "v."

17. An alternative reading of these lines is "Some are laid in the lowest conditions of poverty and suffering. But we shall be just where Jesus is [and] receive the same honors as he [receives]: exaltation, dignity, friendship, [and] glory."

18. "O Christian, treasure up this precious thought! Thou art one with Jesus; and, consequently, much that is said concerning him may also be said concerning thee" (*MTP* 49:13).

19. Job 5:7, "Yet man is born unto trouble, as the sparks fly upward."

20. "In this world, a few drops of joy fall here and there, and there are sometimes showers of blessings; but, up there it is joy, joy, joy for ever, 'pleasures for evermore.' Let these blessed joy-bells ring in your ears and in your heart just now. . . . It may well be described as the fulness of joy because it is infinite. . . . 'Fulness of joy' means that you shall not only have as much joy as you can hold, but that it shall

still keep on running, and then your capacity shall be enlarged, but still you shall be filled with joy, and so it shall continue for ever. . . . You know that, when you are full of anything, you cannot put anything else in; so, where there is fulness of joy at God's right hand, no sorrow will ever be able to enter" (*MTP* 49:18).

21. "Fulness beyond desire or pleasure; more than enough; wearisomeness of plenty; state of being palled or glutted" (Johnson's *Dictionary*, s.v. "satiety").

22. Charles may have pluralized the word "bliss."

23. "Where will my body be then? These limbs, all mouldered back to dust; these eyes vanished from human ken; the whole mortal fabric dissolved, and returned to mother earth. Ah, my Lord! but I shall not have to raise myself from the grave,—I could not work that miracle of resurrection; my bones have not to come together to their fellow bones by their own power. God will teach each atom to come to its fellow, and each individual life will be identified the same as before, yet wondrously changed. . . . Is not this a blessed truth? Then, drink it in; and if you have any fears of death, let them all fly away as you meditate upon this comforting assurance which your Lord himself has so graciously revealed to you" (*MTP* 49:16–17).

24. "Even the last enemy, death himself, will then have been destroyed. . . . Victory blended with security will indeed make glad the spirits of the saints at God's right hand" (*MTP* 49:19).

25. An alternative reading of this line is "What makes us think heaven [to be/will be] so happy?"

26. Charles spelled the word "surprised" with the letter "z" instead of "s."

27. Cf. 2 Cor 12:2.

28. Cf. Exodus 3; 33:19–23.

29. For books on martyrdom in Charles's personal library, see John Foxe, *An Universal History of Christian Martyrdom, Being a Complete and Authentic Account of the Lives, Sufferings, and Triumphant Deaths of the Primitive as Well as Protestant Martyrs, in All Parts of the World, from the Birth of the Blessed Saviour to the Latest Periods of Pagan*

and Catholic Persecution: Together with a Summary of the Doctrines, Prejudices, Blasphemies, and Superstitions of the Modern Church of Rome, with Notes, Commentaries, and Illustrations by the Rev. J. Milner (London: George Routledge, 1845, The Spurgeon Library); Charlotte Elizabeth, *The English Martyrology: Abridged from Foxe in Two Volumes* (London: R. B. Seeley and W. Burnside, 1837, The Spurgeon Library); William Ellis, *The Martyr Church: A Narrative of the Introduction, Progress, and Triumph of Christianity in Madagascar with Notices of Personal Intercourse and Travel in that Island* (London: John Snow and Co., 1870, The Spurgeon Library); and John H. Thomson, *The Martyr Graves of Scotland Being the Travels of a Country Minister in His Own Country* (Edinburgh: Johnson, Hunter, & Co., 1875, The Spurgeon Library).

30. Contraction, "blessed." Charles uses this contraction again in the following two sentences.

31. "There, too, their joy will consist in freedom from every form of evil. No temptation can ever enter there, no carking care, no spiritual weakness. They are eternally clear of all that made them sad in the days of their sinfulness and imperfection. One great part of the joy of the glorified will be the perfection of their characters, for he that is holy must be happy" (*MTP* 49:19). "I am longing for the time when I shall have a heart that will never wander from my Lord; what hallelujahs will I sing to his holy name; and will not you, who love him, do the same? Oh, what shoutings we will together make when, as one complete family before the throne, we shall praise the almighty grace which has brought us safely home" (*MTP* 49:21). An alternative reading of this sentence is "How bless[ed] to be free?"

32. "I have heard some people say that they will not want to have any [fellowship] with his people, but that is both absurd and impossible, because you cannot have fellowship with the Head without having fellowship with the members at the same time" (*MTP* 49:20).

33. First John 3:2, "Beloved, now are we the sons of God, and it doth not yet appear what we shall be: but we know that, when he shall appear, we shall be like him; for we shall see him as he is."

34. "To bring his chosen to eternal happiness was the high ambition which inspired him, and made him wade through a sea of blood" (*TD* 1:222).

35. Cf. John 14:2.

36. "How dreadful this punishment of loss must be, in addition to all the suffering that must be endured in hell for ever! There stand the pearly gates, but what if you should never enter them? Yonder are the streets of gold, but what if you should never stand upon that radiant pavement? There is the face of Jesus, but what if he should say to you, 'I never knew you'? There is the throne of God, but what if it should burn like a devouring fire for you, so that you should be unable to come near to it, and to say, 'Father,' to him who sits thereon? Shut out of heaven! Shut out for ever! In the outer darkness for ever!" (*MTP* 49:22).

37. Contraction, "through." For an additional example of this abbreviation, see "The Tower of Babel" (Sermon 140).

148.   Is 50 .. 5.6 — Jesus' obedience & self denial.

Men stand with wonder & regard a painting or statue
by some eminent artist.   What finish, what proportion
say they —   Jesus now stands before us our
perfect model, let us observe him in his perfect
obedience, remembring it was voluntarily undertaken.

I, Christs clear perception of his duty.

Duties he had as man, & so a creature; as our surety
  as bound by covenant obligations to his father.
His ear was bored as the eternal bondsman of his people,
but better. his ear was opened to know his duty.
He was not as some who say they cannot see their duty.
He was free from prejudice - though no doubt he was
    subject to an educational that would have
    made us prejudiced —
He was not inattentive to slight particulars as men
  are apt to call them for instance baptism.
Your Duty is your Duty, even if you do not see it.
He never cavilled or resisted conscience, or took
up with slight excuses as men now do .—
        His ear was opened.

II Christs ready obedience to his perceptions.
Some refuse to obey when they know their duty.
but he was not rebellious in one solitary instance.
None but he can say that. and none dare gainsay

116

JESUS'[S] OBEDIENCE
and SELF DENIAL
Isaiah 50:5–6[1]

"The Lord God hath opened mine ear, and I was not rebellious, neither turned away back. I gave my back to the smiters, and my cheeks to them that plucked off the hair: I hid not my face from shame and spitting."

Men stand with wonder and regard a painting or statue by some eminent artist.[2] What finish, what proportion, say they.

Jesus now stands before us, our perfect model. Let us observe him in his perfect obedience,[3] remembering it was voluntarily undertaken.

I. CHRIST'S CLEAR PERCEPTION OF HIS DUTY.

Duties he had as man, and so a creature. As our surety,[4] as bound by covenant obligations to his father. His ear was bored as the eternal bondsman of his people. But better, his ear was opened to know his duty.[5] He was not as some who say they cannot see their duty.[6] He was free from prejudice, though no doubt he was subject to an educational that would have made us prejudiced.

He was not inattentive to slight particulars[7] as men are apt to call them. For instance, baptism. Your Duty is your Duty even if you do not see it. He never cavilled[8] or resisted conscience or took up with slight excuses as men now do. His ear was opened.

II. CHRIST'S READY OBEDIENCE TO HIS PERCEPTIONS.

Some refuse to obey when they know their duty, but he was not rebellious in one solitary instance. None but he can say that, and none dare gainsay.

He was more able to rebel than we — none could force him
He could come from the cross — but no — he would not rebel.
"neither did he "turn back" he might have done so
& yet might not have rebelled. but then we should
have been lost. He would not turn back. Love held
him so fast. He did not even look back for an instant
He never kept out of the way of duty as some do. —

III. The self denial of Christ Jesus.

Some keep with duty as far as that lies parallel with
advantage but they should go much further.

He denied himself all his life. Self denial is
a rare but precious virtue. To love another better
than myself is godlike above flesh & blood. —
Jesus gave his back to the smiters — the lash.
He gave his cheek to have the hair plucked off
in wanton insult & cruelty. he gave it, he needed
not to be bound, he would have turned his back.
He did not even hide his face from shame &
mockery & slaps & buffetings & spitting.
Spitting in one's face is awful indeed —

See then Jesus the Model & the Saviour.
1. Imitate him Christians.
2. Behold his love sinner & melt.

God melt me & you. Amen
For Jesus sake.

225

He was more able[9] to rebel than we. None could force him. He could come from the cross.[10] But no, he would not rebel.

Neither did he ~~re~~"turn[11] back." He might have done so, and yet might not have rebelled. But then we should have been lost. He would not turn back. Love held him so fast. He did not even look back for an instant. He never kept out of the way of duty as some do.[12]

III. THE SELF-DENIAL OF CHRIST JESUS.

Some keep with duty as far as that lies parallel with advantage, but they should go much further.

He denied himself all his life.[13] Self denial is a rare but precious virtue. To love another better than myself is godlike,[14] above flesh and blood. Jesus gave his back to the smiters,[15] the lash. He gave his cheek to have the hair plucked off in wanton insult and cruelty.[16] He gave it. He needed not to be bound, He would have turned his back. He did not even hide his face from shame and mockery, and slaps, and buffetings, and spitting.[17] Spitting in one's face is awful[18] indeed.[19]

See, then, Jesus the Model and the Saviour.

1. Imitate him, Christians.

2. Behold his love, sinner, and melt.

God, melt me and you. Amen.

For Jesus['s] sake.

225

1. On July 1, 1877, Charles preached a sermon on Isa 50:5–6 entitled "The Redeemer Described by Himself" (*MTP* 49, Sermon 2827). Overlapping content exists between the above sermon and *MTP* 49:185–89. Charles likely had his early sermon in mind when preaching his 1877 sermon. Two years later, on July 27, 1879, Charles preached a sermon on Isa 50:6 entitled "The Shame and Spitting" (*MTP* 25, Sermon 1486). There is enough overlapping content to suggest Charles had in mind the sermon above when preaching his 1879 sermon.

2. Charles often observed paintings, statues, and architecture in his travels. During this time in his ministry, he visited Trinity College Library in Cambridge and marveled at the artistic design of Lord Byron's statue (*Autobiography* 1:297–98). In his lecture "Posture, Action, Gesture, Etc." at the Pastors' College, he said, "Who, for example, can deny the eloquence of the hands in the Magdalens of Guido; their expression in the cartoons of Raphael, or in the last Supper, by Leonardo da Vinci?" (*Lectures* 2:114). With regard to posture in the pulpit, he also instructed his students, "Observe the statues of the Roman or Greek orators, look at Raphael's picture of Paul, and, without affectation, fall naturally into the graceful and appropriate attitudes there depicted" (*ST* July 1875:302). Charles applauded the statue of Antinous in the Vatican in Rome, saying, "Every feature in that statue is perfect in itself, and in complete harmony with all the rest. You could not find the slightest fault with eye or nose or mouth" (*MTP* 24:663). For books on art in Charles's personal library, see William P. Nimmo, *Art and Artists: Curious Facts and Characteristic Sketches* (Edinburgh: Murray and Gibb, n.d., The Spurgeon Library); R. Donald, *Marvels of Architecture. Translated from the French of M. Lefèbre; to Which Is Added a Chapter on English Architecture* (London: Cassell, Petter, and Galpin, n.d., The Spurgeon Library); Thomas Greenwood, *Museums and Art Galleries* (London: Simpkin, Marshall, and Co., 1888, The Spurgeon Library); Henry Grey, *Trowel Chisel & Brush, a Concise Manual of Architecture Sculpture & Painting, Ancient and Modern* (London: Griffith, Farran, Okeden & Welsh; New York: E. P. Dutton, 1884, The Spurgeon Library); Dionysius Lardner, ed., *The Museum of Science & Art. Illustrated by Engravings on Wood. Vols. I–XII* (London: Walton and Maberly, 1854–56, The Spurgeon Library); and Godfrey Wordsworth Turner, *Homely Scenes from Great Painters. Illustrated by Twenty-four Full-page Photographs by the Woodbury Process* (London: Cassell, Petter & Galpin, n.d., The Spurgeon Library).

3. "Brothers and sisters, there was never another such an ear as Christ had. He heard the faintest whispers of his Father's voice. He never neglected the will of God, nor needed to be reminded of it, or to be pressed and persuaded to do it" (*MTP* 49:185).

4. Hebrews 7:22, "By so much was Jesus made a surety of a better testament."

5. "Oh, beloved, there was never one who had his ear so near the mouth of God as Jesus had. His Father had no need to speak to him in dreams and visions of the night, for when all his faculties were wide awake there was nothing in them to hinder his understanding the mind of God; and therefore every morning when his Father wakened him he spake into his ear" (*MTP* 25:424).

6. "Men do not get character among their fellows by indolence and listlessness, or by pretensions and talk. Action! action!—this is what the world wants; and there is more truth than we have dreamed in Nelson's aphorism, 'England expects every man to do his duty'" (*MTP* 10:647). The Victorian sense of duty is also seen in newspapers such as London's *The Daily News*: "There is in English gentlemen a spirit of chivalry that seeks in foreign lands to experience the gallant habit of personal danger and the proof of martial exercise, by volunteer service in some just and generous cause" ("English Duty Towards the Restoration of Italy," *The Daily News (London)*, January 15, 1859). See also "English Responsibility in Bulgaria," *The Birmingham Daily Post*, September 4, 1876; "English Responsibility for Egypt," *The Huddersfield Daily Chronicle*, January 7, 1884; and "English and French Responsibility at the Present Crisis," *The Daily News (London)*, September 14, 1855.

7. In Victorian England, the phrase "slight particulars" was synonymous with minutiae. Samuel Johnson's fifth definition of "particular" captured this definition: "A minute detail of things singly enumerated" (Johnson's *Dictionary*). Examples of usage around the time of Charles's Waterbeach ministry include an entry in *The Morning Post*: "The Earl of Clarendon mentioned to the Earl of Malmesbury that the Government had received a copy of the manifesto issued by the Emperor of Russia to his subjects, relative to the Turkish question. With the exception of some slight particulars, the published translation of the document was correct" (*The Morning Post*, July 8, 1853). An additional usage of this phrase is found in *The Staffordshire Advertiser* with regard to the differences between witches' Sabbath practices: "The description of the Sabbath given by

the witches differed only in slight particulars of detail, for their examinations were all carried on upon one model and measure" ("The 'Witch's Sabbath,'" *The Staffordshire Advertiser*, May 10, 1851).

8. "To raise captious and frivolous objections" or "to receive or treat with objections" (Johnson's *Dictionary*, s.v. "cavil").

9. Charles originally wrote the name "abel" before inserting the letter "l" before the "e."

10. An alternative reading of this sentence is "He could come [down] from the cross." Cf. Matt 26:53; Mark 15:32.

11. By originally writing the word "return," Charles may have had in mind Christ's return to the Father. Cf. John 16:10, 28; 20:17. He struck through the letters "re" to construct the word "turn."

12. "Oh, splendour of voluntary condescension, and of marvellous love, on the part of him before whom the nations are as a drop in the bucket, who taketh up the isles as a very little thing, and to whom time is but a span compared with his own eternity!" (*MTP* 49:188).

13. Cf. Matt 16:24.   14.   Cf. John 15:13; 1 John 3:16.

15. Cf. Matt 27:16; John 19:1.   16.   Cf. Isa 50:6; Matt 27:30.

17. "Many a martyr has suffered much, but he could not avoid it; for he was bound, and he was not able to smite his foes, or to escape. But here sat One, to be spit upon, who could, if he had willed it, have withered into nothingness all who stood about him. With one glance of that eye of his, had he but grown angry, as he well might have done, he could have burned up their very souls, for it was he who dried up the river, and who clothed the heavens with blackness, who was thus despitefully used. Blessed be the majesty of that omnipotence which controlled omnipotence,—that mighty love which bound the Godhead so that it came not to the rescue of the manhood of the suffering Saviour!" (*MTP* 49:187).

18. An illegible letter appears after the letter "a" in the word "awful." The stem suggests Charles may have originally written the letter "f" before correcting the misspelling by writing the "w."

19. "Spitting was regarded by Orientals, and, I suppose, by all of us, as the most contemptuous thing which one man could do to another; yet the vile soldiers gathered around him, and spat upon him. It is almost too terrible to think of or to speak of; but what must it have been for Jesus to endure it?" (*MTP* 49:188).

149. Ex. XXVIII. 36.37.38. The Golden crown of Holiness.

Children are best instructed by pictures, so in this infancy of Jewish intellect & infancy of their religion it was well to instruct them thus. Egyptian brickkilns are not the places to brighten ones wits, so they were instructed. just as language was once written that is by hieroglyphics. Let us regard this ancient hieroglyphic which tells us something not of old time alone but of the now.

What see we? a priest, with a mitre on his head, not with a high crown but low & wrapt-like a turban. he has on a breastplate & various other articles all deeply significant but we must notice on his forehead connected with the mitre by blue lace. a plate of pure gold. See there is a deep inscription on it, like as of a signet

   Holiness to the Lord.

That is Aaron, the high priest, and these the pontifical attire

  Let us learn. transferring the type —

I. In application to the public servants of God.

1. That it is an honour as well as a service to be devoted to the Lord. His mitre is the turban of a servant but bearing the golden plate it becomes a crown.

2. That one essential requisite for any sacred office is holiness. Holiness of motive in entering upon it. Holiness of aim. of heart, of doctrine & of conduct. How little do those know their sad state who enter this office for a piece of bread & labour only

149

THE GOLDEN CROWN
of HOLINESS
Exodus 28:36—38[1]

"And thou shalt make a plate of pure gold, and grave upon it, like the engravings of a signet, HOLINESS TO THE LORD. And thou shalt put it on a blue lace, that it may be upon the mitre; upon the forefront of the mitre it shall be. And it shall be upon Aaron's forehead, that Aaron may bear the iniquity of the holy things, which the children of Israel shall hallow in all their holy gifts; and it shall be always upon his forehead, that they may be accepted before the LORD."

Children are best instructed by pictures. So, in this infancy of Jewish intellect and infancy of their religion, it was well to instruct them thus. Egyptian brickkilns[2] are not the place to brighten one's[3] wits. So they were instructed just as language was once written, that is, by hieroglyphics.[4] Let us regard this ancient hieroglyphic which tells us something, not of old time alone but of the now.

What see we? A priest with a mitre[5] on his head. Not with a high crown, but low and wrapt[6] like a turban. He has on a breastplate and various other articles. All deeply significant,[7] but we must notice on his forehead connected with the mitre by blue lace a plate of pure gold.

See there is a deep inscription on it like as of a signet:

> Holiness to the Lord.

That is, Aaron, the high priest. And this,[8] the pontifical attire.[9]

Let us learn, translating[10] the type.

I. IN APPLICATION TO THE PUBLIC SERVANTS OF GOD.

1. That it is an honour as well as a service to be devoted to the Lord. His mitre is the turban of a servant, but bearing the golden plate it becomes a crown.

2. That one essential requisite for any sacred office is holiness.[11] Holiness of motive in entering upon it. Holiness of aim, of heart, of doctrine, and of conduct.[12] How little[13] do those know their sad state[14] who enter this office for a piece of bread, and labour only

for preferment.   Take heed lest Abihu & Nadab's fate be their's

3. Again let us learn that he who minister's in the temple must have his holiness on his forehead; letting all clearly see what they mean.   Continually, upon the forefront of the mitre must it be.   Bold holiness is wanted, brazen piety, which is a fear-nought.

II.   Now again let us learn, translating it of Jesus.

1. That Christ in heaven counts his service as our priest to be his crown.   Many crowns he has but this is his finest one.   What he has done for man, is his royal crown.   He is Melchisedek, priest & King.

2. That he is continually reminding his father of his finished work & perfect righteousness, for he wears on his brow, the declaration that he is Holiness unto the Lord.

3. That his righteousness is not in danger of fading for it is engraved deep on a plate of pure gold. Nor can any tear it away for it is fastened to the mitre & he who would deny his righteousness must first destroy his priestly office itself.   Nor can it be washed off. for deeply it is cut in solid gold.

4. This golden righteousness of Jesus. removes all our guilt & make our polluted holy things, pure. For even our holy gifts are impure but this bears them & moreover – through this the good in them is accepted in the beloved.   This ever on Jesus forehead should inspire hope, & in his name our prayer & praise should rise.

for preferment. Take heed, lest Abihu[15] and Nahab's[16] fate[17] be theirs.[18]

3. Again, let us learn that he who ministers[19] in the temple must have his holiness on his forehead[20] letting all clearly see what they mean. Continually upon the forefront of the mitre must it be. Bold holiness is wanted, brazen piety, which is a fear-nought.

II.[21] NOW AGAIN LET US LEARN, TRANSLATING IT OF JESUS.

1. That Christ in heaven counts his service as our priest to be his crowns.[22] Many crowns he has, but this is his finest one. What he has done for man is his royal crown. He is Melchizedek,[23] priest and king.

2. That he is continually reminding his father of his finished work and perfect righteousness,[24] for he wears on his brow the declaration that he is Holiness unto the Lord.

3. That his righteousness is not in danger of fading, for it is engraved deep on a plate of pure gold. Nor can any tear it away, for it is fastened to the mitre and he who would deny his righteousness must first destroy his priestly office[25] itself. Nor can it be washed off, for deeply it is cut in solid gold.

4. This golden righteousness of Jesus removes all our guilt and make[s] our polluted holy things pure.[26] For even our holy gifts are impure. But this bears them, and moreover, through this the good in them is accepted in the beloved.[27] This, ever on Jesus's forehead, should inspire hope and in his name our prayer and praise should rise.

Come soul send not this scene away until thou
canst discern thy high priest, with his golden plate.
Art sick my soul? art full of sin? behold the Man!
Sinner, would that thou wouldst throw thy tin
plated righteousness away, & look at this come!
look & live! He is thy holiness. Sinner! & saint!

III   But now translate this picture
of the priest & kings unto our God even of believers.
     And here let us learn ———— — ——————
1. That the glory of the Christian religion is its holiness
and holiness is a crown to a Christian which becomes
him better than does the diadem befit a Cæsar.
2. That we must take care that our holiness is ever
on us, never take off thy crown. & let it be conspicuous
    let it be thy most observable feature that thou art holy
3. That we must wear only gold. A holiness, the
effect of faith, & the working of the Holy Spirit, sincere
obedience springing from love. . . . . ——— .
4. That our holiness should lie deep, cut as in a
signet, no mere surface paint, . . —— ———

     Brethren, the gold is become dim, the crown is falling
godless living is becoming common even in the church.
we are too carnal, too worldly; where are the martyrs
or where their spirit? Where is self mortification &
holy self denial? Call home these banished graces
     & pray that the Holy Spirit may bring you nearer to Jesus.
227. 404.

Come, soul, send not this[28] scene away until thou canst[29] discern thy high priest with his golden plate.

Art sick, my soul? Art full of sin?[30] Behold the Man! Sinner, would that thou wouldst throw thy tin-plated[31] righteousness away and look at this. Come! Look and live! He is thy holiness, sinner! and saint!

III. BUT NOW TRANSLATE THIS PICTURE OF THE PRIEST AND KINGS UNTO OUR GOD, EVEN OF THE BELIEVERS.

And here let us learn:

1. That the glory of the Christian religion is its holiness, and holiness is a crown to a Christian which becomes him better than does the diadem befit a Caesar.[32]

2. That we must take care that our holiness is ever on us.[33] Never take off thy crown. And let it be conspicuous. Let it be thy most observable feature that thou art holy.

3. That we must wear only gold: a holiness, the effect of faith, and the working of the Holy Spirit, sincere obedience springing from love.[34]

4. That our holiness should lie deep, cut as in a signet. No mere surface paint.[35]

Brethren, the gold is become dim, the crown is falling, godless living is becoming common even in the church. We are too carnal, too worldly. Where are the martyrs, or where [is] their spirit? Where is self-mortification and the holy self[36] denial?[37] Call home these banished graces and pray[38] that the Holy Spirit may bring you nearer to Jesus.

227. 404.

1. On July 6, 1890, Charles preached an additional sermon on Exod 28:36–38 entitled "The Iniquity of Our Holy Things" (*MTP* 36, Sermon 2153). There is enough overlapping content to suggest Charles had his early sermon in mind when preaching his later one.

2. Cf. Exod 5:7.

3. Charles originally wrote the word "ones." The context, however, suggests he intended the word to be possessive, not plural.

4. With the invention of railroads and easier transportation technologies in the nineteenth century, European archaeologists working in Egypt could bring their research into the mainstream. In 1799, Napoleon's soldiers were digging for the foundations of a fort near el-Rashid and discovered a stone later dated to the Ptolemaic Period in 196 BC. In 1802, not long after France was defeated by the English, the "Rosetta" stone, later named for the region where it was discovered, was brought to London where it remains today at the British Museum (displayed at G4/CSE). In 1822, French Egyptologist Jean-François Champollion deciphered the stone, which contained three blocks of text: hieroglyphics, Demotic, and Greek (www.britishmuseum.org/research/collection_online/collection_object_details.aspx?objectId=117631&partId=1, accessed January 7, 2017). Charles later mentioned the Rosetta Stone in the indices of a series of lectures published posthumously by his son Thomas (see C. H. Spurgeon, *What Stones Say; or Studies in Stones* [London: Christian Herald Publishing Co., n.d., The Spurgeon Library], 77–79).

5. "An ornament for the head" and "A kind of episcopal crown" (Johnson's *Dictionary*, s.v. "mitre").

6. Contraction, "wrapped."

7. An alternative reading of this phrase is "All [of them are] deeply significant."

8. Charles originally wrote the word "these" but changed it to "this" by converting the letter "e" to "i." He did not include the tittle before striking through the final "e."

9. In a commentary on Exodus that Charles later owned, the following description was offered for "Priestly garments" described in Exodus 28: "(1) The *persons* who

'serve' are not ordinary citizens of God's kingdom, but officials. (2) The *service* is not in the ordinary course of duties to God and man; they are distinctively priestly, under the two heads of oblation and intercession. (3) The *vestments* make the priest" (James Macgregor, *Exodus, with Introduction, Commentary, and Special Notes, Etc. Part II: The Consecration* [Edinburgh: T. & T. Clark, The Spurgeon Library, 1889], III, italics in the original).

10. Charles originally wrote the word "transferring" but struck through "ferring" before replacing the letters with the superscripted letters "lating." The reason for this change is not obvious; however, it does evidence a recognition that the text needed to be explained, interpreted, rendered, applied, or translated instead of merely being delivered or transferred to the congregation. Charles uses the word "translate" similarly in this notebook (cf. "I Glory in Infirmities" [Sermon 165]. In *Lectures to My Students*, Charles referenced Richard C. Trench's "Introductory Essay" in *Notes on the Parables of Our Lord*. In highlighting the differences between parables, fables, proverbs, myths, and allegories, Trench used the word "transferring" to describe the communication of "properties and qualities and relations of one *to* the other" (*Lectures* 3:95, italics in the original). Charles was also interested in uncovering typological interpretation of Jesus Christ and used the word "translating" in a similar way: "Thus he acted as Mediator, Interpreter, taking the will of God, and translating it to us, letting us know the meaning of that writing of the right hand of God which we could never have deciphered, but which, when Christ looses the seals, is made clear to us" (*MTP* 39:385). In his 1859 sermon "Christ Precious to Believers," Charles quoted a Welsh minister: "I have never yet found a text that had not got a road to Christ in it, and if I ever do find one that has not a road to Christ in it, I will make one; I will go over hedge and ditch but I would get at my Master, for the sermon cannot do any good unless there is a savour of Christ in it" (*NPSP* 5:140).

11. Cf. "The Minister's Self-Watch" (*Lectures* 1:2–17).

12. "One of my brethren behind me said to me one Sabbath morning, 'We come here from business dull and dead; but you seem always to be full of holy life.' I dropped a tear when I got away from him, to think that he should have an opinion of me which I could not pretend to deserve. Alas, beloved! we know what it is to kneel down, and feel as if we could not pray, though we had then

most need to wrestle at the throne. We know what it is to read our Bible, but we might as well have read a newspaper, for all the desire of our heart to the truth of God. Have you never felt almost unwilling to worship God? . . . Do not our spirits need whipping to devotion? Towards the business of the world we can fly like eagles, but in coming to God we creep like snails" (*MTP* 36:376–77).

13. A line of dots written in pencil appears beneath the words "How little." Charles likely intended to draw attention to his point, namely that those who enter into a sacred office for "a piece of bread," or "preferment," are truly in a "sad state."

14. Cf. *MTP* 36:375.

15. An illegible letter, possibly "c," was written beneath the "b" in the word "Abihu."

16. An illegible letter was written beneath the "d" in the word "Nadab's." Charles likely wrote the letter "a" instead of "d."

17. In Leviticus 10, Abihu and Nahab, the eldest sons of Aaron, offered "strange fire" (v. 1) before God, and "there went out fire from the Lord, and devoured them, and they died before the Lord" (v. 2).

18. Charles inserted an unnecessary apostrophe between the letters "r" and "s" in the word "theirs."

19. Charles inserted an unnecessary apostrophe between the letters "r" and "s" in the word "ministers."

20. Cf. Rev 14:1.

21. The Roman numeral II was smeared toward the left side of the page.

22. The strike-through of the "s" in the word "crowns" may have triggered in Charles's mind the topic of the following sentence: "Many crowns he has."

23. Hebrews 6:20, "Whither the forerunner is for us entered, even Jesus, made an high priest for ever after the order of Melchisedec."

24. Cf. Rom 3:24; 1 Cor 1:30; Phil 3:9.

25. See "Our Sympathizing High Priest" (*MTP* 32, Sermon 1927) and "The Tenderness of Jesus" (*MTP* 36, Sermon 2148).

26. "Our God is so gracious as to call his people's love, his people's faith, his people's labour, his people's patience, 'holy things,' because he sees how truly their hearts desire that they should be so. He knows what is holy, and what is not holy; and though there be a defilement about our holy things, yet holy things they are, if sincerely presented, for the Lord God calls them so" (*MTP* 36:375). A modernized reading of this line is "Jesus removes all our guilt and make[s] pure the holy things that are polluted."

27. "*Your* holiness is not always on your brow, but his holiness is always on the forefront of his mitre, and therefore you are always accepted in the beloved. . . . It is not what is upon our forehead, but what is upon his forehead that makes us and our offerings to be accepted" (*MTP* 36:381, italics in the original).

28. It is unclear whether the ink blot over the word "this" was accidental or represents Charles's attempt to strike through the letters "is" to construct the word "the." The latter interpretation is more likely.

29. An older form of "can," the word "canst" means "in constant use as an expression of the potential mood" (Johnson's *Dictionary*, s.v. "canst"). In this notebook Charles used the word "canst" in the following sermon, "Boast Not Thyself of To-morrow" (Sermon 150), and also in "Mary with Jesus in the Garden" (Sermon 175).

30. An alternative reading of these sentences is "Are you sick, my soul? Are you full of sin?"

31. Charles used the phrase "tin-plated" pejoratively to describe a righteousness that only appears legitimate but in reality is less valuable. Samuel Johnson defined "tin" as "thin plates of iron covered with tin" (Johnson's *Dictionary*). In Charles's personal library is a book entitled *The Slang Dictionary* that offers a negative connotation on the word "tin-pot": "'He plays a TIN-POT game' *i.e.* a low or shabby one" (*The Slang Dictionary; or, the Vulgar Words, Street Phrases, and "Fast" Expressions of High and Low Society. Many with Their Etymology, and a Few with Their History Traced* [London: John Camden Hotten, 1864, The Spurgeon Library], 257, capitalization in the original).

32. See Albert Harris Tolman, ed., *Julius Caesar by William Shakespeare*, English Classics-Star Series (New York: World Book Company, 1913), 126.

33. "Oh, that we could tether our thoughts to the cross, and never allow them to go further than where they can constantly have him in view!" (*MTP* 36:377).

34. Similar to the conclusion of his fourth point, Charles included eight periods after the word "love."

35. Charles later purchased a book for his personal library entitled *Horticultural Buildings* in which the author gave instructions for how a greenhouse should be painted: "To paint a house periodically is a bare necessity. It is true economy to protect the materials from the exceptionally trying atmospheric influences which surround horticultural buildings. If they have three to five coats when erected, they should have one coat outside within at least a year; after this say two coats outside and in, every three years" (F. A. Fawkes, *Horticultural Buildings: Their Construction, Heating, Interior Fittings, Etc., with Remarks on Some of the Principles Involved and Their Application (123 Illustrations)* [London: B. T. Batsford, Journal of Horticulture, 1881], 112). Charles's point was that holiness should go to the core of a Christian and not merely reside on the surface for others to see.

36. Charles struck through the descender of the letter "l" in the word "self," likely because he prematurely wrote the "f."

37. Cf. Matt 16:24; Luke 9:23.

38. "If God wanted to surprise his people, all he would have to do would be to answer certain of their prayers; for these are offered as a matter of course, with no idea of their being heard!" (*MTP* 36:378).

150. Prov. XXVII. 1. "Boast not thyself of to-morrow"

The words of a venerable, learned & experienced preacher
should find a ready admittance into our minds.
They come too from the mouth of the adorable Jesus
in the shape of a parable of the rich fool.
James too sounds the same alarm "Go to now" &c.
The pulpit perpetually sounds the truth, nor that
alone. Your corn-fields ruined by the rain cry out the same.
the sigh of him who youthful falls a prey to disease.
the wail of parents over loved ones torn suddenly
from their embrace. The toll of the bell, the
report of sudden death all utter the same words.

Lift up hell's cover, listen & you hear the
damned millions say the same, while insatiable
death, & fallen Lucifer join their chorus.
—— But you say how do I boast of tomorrow,
1 You do who think you shall be happier when
you arrive at a future time. You want
but one or two steps & then you will be happy.
The apprentice, a journeyman, married master.
Perhaps a wedding day is your summum of happiness.
2. You do who think your present happiness
will continue, you fancy you are above gunshot.
your nest well feathered & you safe.

150^1

BOAST NOT THYSELF
of TO-MORROW
Proverbs 27:1[2]

"Boast not thyself of tomorrow; for thou knowest not what a day may bring forth."

The words of a venerable, learned, and experienced preacher should find a ready admittance into our minds. They come too from the mouth of the adorable Jesus in the shape of[3] a parable of the rich fool.[4]

James, too, sounds the same alarm. "Go to now,"[5] etc. The pulpit perpetually sounds the truth. Nor that alone. You[r][6] cornfields, ruined by the rain, cry out the same.[7] The sigh of him who [is] youthful falls a prey to disease. The wail of parents over loved ones torn suddenly from their embrace. The toll of the bell,[8] the report of sudden death, all utter the same words.

Lift up hell's cover. Listen and you hear the damned millions say the same, while insatiable death and fallen Lucifer join their chorus.

———BUT[9] YOU SAY, HOW[10] DO I BOAST OF TOMORROW?

1.[11] You do who think you shall be happier when you arrive at a future time. You want but one or two steps and then you will be happy. The apprentice, a journeyman, married master.[12] Perhaps a wedding day is your summon of happiness.

2. You do who think your present happiness will continue. You fancy you are above gunshot. Your nest [is] well-feathered and you [are] safe.

3. Some of you boast of tomorrow, when you make vows of future amendment and purpose to repent and be converted at a future time.

4. You Christians do who say I will profess Jesus soon, when I am more grown in grace.

5. You who postpone holy duties put off visiting the sick &c — Whatsoever thy hand &c.. do it with &c.

———— But why may I not boast of tomorrow?

1. Because it may never come, the judgment may sit & time may be no more ere to morrow dawn

2. But if not are you sure you may be alive

3. You hope for pleasure; you may never gain it hopes have been blasted so may yours.

4. If gained you may find it is not worth the having as many have done before you.

5. You will repent to-morrow alas! no such thing, the heart hardens every moment.

6. You will do good my brother soon, do't rather now, lest the person or thyself be gone.

— But may I never look forward.

Yes to provide but not to presume Set thine house in order, but not think to live in it for ever — prepare to meet thy God by a daily practise of death.

3. Some of you boast of tomorrow when you make vows of future amendment and purpose to repent and be converted at a future time.

4. You Christians do who say, I will profess Jesus soon when I am more grown in grace.[13]

5. You who postpone holy duties, put off visiting the sick, etc. Whatsoever thy hand, etc., do it with etc.[14]

———BUT WHY MAY I NOT BOAST OF TOMORROW?

1. Because it may never come. The judgment may sit[15] and time may be no more, 'ere[16] tomorrow['s] dawn.

2. But if not, are you sure you may be alive?[17]

3. You hope for pleasure. You may never gain it. Hopes have been blasted.[18] So may yours.

4. If gained, you may find it is not worth the having, as many have done before you.

5. You will repent tomorrow. Alas! No such thing. The heart hardens every moment.

6. You will do good, my brother, soon.[19] Do it rather now lest the person, or thyself, be gone.

———BUT MAY I NEVER LOOK FORWARD?

Yes, to provide, but not to presume. Set thine house in order,[20] but [do] not think to live in it for ever. Prepare to meet thy God by a daily practise of death.[21]

— But may I never look forward with hope & expect pleasure — why you make my pleasures less.

Yes you may take this look when you have looked three other ways.

1. A look back on your old courses.
2. A look of penitence & faith to Calvary.
3. A look of trust to God & the Mediator

Then look for as much happiness as you like.

& now let me ask thee.

— How can you boast of tomorrow.

1. You are no prophet but you act as if you knew.
2. You had not much to boast of yesterday why to morrow

— In the name of God. How dare you boast of tomorrow

1. Know you not you are a rebel & a sinner
2. Know you not you are at enmity with God that he can do as he will with you
3. & that before tomorrow he may give thee up to hardness of soul or blast thee & send thee to hell. See thou can'st not escape.

Come friend hear me why prate of to morrow the devils cry ha! ha! hell yells in triumph. angels all but weep — 'Tis all fools day the day of besotted madmen

Oh my God turn them

228

Through Jesus, Amen, Amen, Amen

Hear me, thou God of Israel.

———BUT MAY I NEVER LOOK FORWARD WITH HOPE
AND EXPECT PLEASURE? WHY [DO] YOU MAKE MY
PLEASURE LESS?

Yes, you may take this look when you have looked three other ways:

1. A look back on your old courses.

2. A look of penitence and faith to Calvary.

3. A look of trust to God and the Mediator.

Then look for as much happiness as you like, and now, let me ask thee:

———HOW <u>CAN</u> YOU BOAST OF TOMORROW?

1. You are no prophet, but you act as if you knew.[22]

2. You had not much to boast of yesterday. Why tomorrow?

———IN THE NAME OF GOD. HOW <u>DARE</u> YOU BOAST OF
TOMORROW?

1. Know you not [that] you are a rebel and a sinner.[23]

2. Know you not [that] you are at enmity with God, that he can do as he
will with you.

3. And that before tomorrow he may give thee up to hardness of soul or
blast thee and send thee to hell. See, thou canst not escape.

Come, friend, hear me. Why prate[24] of tomorrow? The devils cry, ha! ha!
Hell yells in triumph. Angels all but weep. Tis all fools['] day,[25] the day of
besotted[26] madmen.

Oh my God, turn them.
Through Jesus. Amen, Amen, Amen.
Hear me, thou God of Israel.[27]

228

1. Charles originally wrote the number 7 beneath the 0 in the number 150.

2. On August 25, 1856, Charles preached an additional sermon on Prov 27:1 entitled "To-morrow" (*NPSP* 2, Sermon 94). There is enough overlapping content to suggest Charles had in mind his early sermon when preaching his later one. Charles also preached a sermon on Prov 27:1b entitled "Cheer for Despondency" (*MTP* 56, Sermon 3183); however, there is little overlapping content.

3. A series of faint dots appears beneath the words "shape of a parable." Charles may have intended to break his introduction after this line. For a more pronounced example of this literary tendency, see "Mary with Jesus in the Garden" (Sermon 175).

4. Cf. Luke 12:13–21.

5. James 4:13, "Go to now, ye that say, To day or to morrow we will go into such a city, and continue there a year, and buy and sell, and get gain."

6. An illegible letter appears beneath the "u." It is unclear whether Charles intended the word to be "you" or "your." The latter interpretation is more likely.

7. On Saturday, November 20, 1852, *The Cambridge Chronicle and Journal* reported, "The immense fall of rain which has taken place has caused serious floods in many parts of the country, and great destruction of property. That such a continuance of wet is calculated to do more or less injury to the seed committed to the round in the early part of the autumn can scarcely admit of doubt, and the seed time thus far must be regarded as decidedly unfavourable. All kinds of out-door labour have for weeks past been completely suspended; and should the rain be followed by frost, the land would probably be rendered unfit to be worked until the spring" ("Market Chronicle. Review of the Corn Trade," *The Cambridge Chronicle and University Journal, Else of Ely Herald, and Huntingdonshire Gazette*, November 20, 1852).

8. For a discussion of Charles's use of the phrase "toll of the bell," see "Let Thine House Be in Order" (Notebook 2, Sermon 134).

9. The line preceding the word "But" signals hypothetical objections to which Charles supplied answers. Each objection in this sermon is distinguished with a similar line.

10. An illegible letter, possibly an "n," appears beneath the letter "h" in the word "how." Charles may have initially written the word "now" before correcting it. Cf. Prov 27:1.

11. Charles likely did not originally intend to write the number 1 before the word "You."

12. "You are apprentices: well, you are not going to carry them out till you get to be journeymen. You are journeymen: well, you cannot carry them out till you get to be master" (*NPSP* 2:325). An advertisement for a "Married Master" for the Blackpool Scriptural Schools is found in 1852 in an Irish newspaper ("Wanted," *The Constitution; or, Cork Advertiser*, August 10, 1852).

13. "Possibly you dream that on a future day repentance will be more agreeable to your feelings. But how can you suppose that a few hours will make it more pleasant? If it be vinegar to your taste now, it shall be so then; and if ye love your sins now, ye will love them better then; for the force of habit will have confirmed you in your course" (*NPSP* 2:324).

14. Ecclesiastes 9:10, "Whatsoever thy hand findeth to do, do it with thy might; for there is no work, nor device, nor knowledge, nor wisdom, in the grave, whither thou goest."

15. Cf. Matt 25:31.

16. Contraction, "before."

17. "You think you will have space for repentance, and it may be that sudden doom will devour you: or, perhaps, even while you are sitting there in the pew, your last moment is running out. There is your hour-glass. See! it is running. I marked another grain just then, and then another fell; it fell so noiselessly, yet methought I heard it fall. Yes! there it is! The clock's tick is the fall of that grain of dust down from your hour-glass. Life is getting shorter every moment" (*NPSP* 2:325).

18. "Boast not thyself of to-morrow; it is the frailest and most brittle thing thou canst imagine. Not glass were half so easily broken as thy to-morrow's joys and thy to-morrow's hopes; a puff of wind shall crush them" (*NPSP* 2:322).

19. An alternative reading of this line is "You will do good, my brother, [to repent] soon."

20. See "Set Thine House in Order" (Notebook 2, Sermon 134).

21. "Yea, more, a Christian may rightly look forward to his to-morrows, not simply with resignation, but also with joy. To-morrow to a Christian is a happy thing, it is one stage nearer glory. To-morrow! It is one step nearer heaven to a believer; it is just one knot more that he has sailed across the dangerous sea of life, and he is so much the nearer to his eternal port—his blissful heaven" (*NPSP* 3:327). Cf. 1 Cor 15:31.

22. "Take care of to-morrows. Many Christians go tumbling on without a bit of thought; and then, on a sudden, they tumble down and make a mighty mess of their profession. If they would only look sharp after the to-morrows—if they would only watch their paths instead of star-gazing and boasting about them, their feet would be a great deal surer" (*NPSP* 2:326).

23. It is not clear whether Charles intended these sentences to continue his line of questioning or instead be declarative statements. His third point suggests that the latter interpretation is correct.

24. "To talk carelessly and without weight; to chatter; to tattle; to be loquacious; to prattle" (Johnson's *Dictionary*, s.v. "prate").

25. The phrase "all fools['] day" may suggest Charles preached the sermon above in April. Approximately two years prior, a newspaper reported the following attitude toward the holiday: "Many of our old customs are 'more honoured in the breach than in the observance,' and this is particularly the case with the practice of making April fools, which is more evidently, than any other, the relic of a barbarous age" (*The Western Flying Post, Sherborne and Yeovil Mercury, and General Advertiser for Dorset, Somerset, Devon, and Cornwall*, April 2, 1850).

26. "To infatuate; to stupify; to dull; to take away the senses" (Johnson's *Dictionary*, s.v. "besot").

27. The word "Israel" was smeared toward the lower right side of the page.

151. Matt 6. 11. "Give us this day our daily bread"
'Tis too true, we value mercies most when we lose
them — we think not of bread till famine comes.
Many a lip will pray in a storm, or sickness,
or distress & then that tongue is dumb again.
　　Let us notice the prayer, word by word.
1. Bread we pray for, in temporals ever let us ask
but littles, this is the promise, we are taught temp-
-erance & contentment.　　Jesus once said we
live not by bread alone, Spiritual bread we want too
2. Daily bread; this shows us dependance on Providence
Jesus once lacked even this. Elijah had no more,
nor the Israelites in the wilderness.
3. our daily bread. Let it be profitable to us.
may we eat the fruit of our labour & not anothers
bread, we must not forbear labour.
4. this day, we ought to ask every day, prayer
should be with the family daily
5. us. give us — here we are not selfish but we
pray for our friends, for the poor for all.
6. give us, not pay us as wages, nor lend me
to be repaid anon. But give of thy free grace.
　　Language wonderfully simple, no finery,
229 Hungry starving souls put up the same prayer.
696

"GIVE US THIS DAY OUR DAILY BREAD"

Matthew 6:11[1]

"Give us this day our daily bread."

'Tis too true, we value mercies most when we lose them. We think not of bread till famine comes. Many a lip will pray in a storm, or sickness, or distress, and then that tongue is dumb again.

Let us notice the prayer, word by word.[2]

1. <u>Bread</u> we pray for. In temporals, ever let us ask but littles. This is the promise. We are taugh[t] temperance and contentment.[3] Jesus once said we live not by bread alone.[4] Spiritual bread we want, too.

2. <u>Daily</u> bread. This shows us dependence on Providence.[5] Jesus once lacked even this.[6] Elijah had no more.[7] Nor the Israelites in the wilderness.[8]

3. <u>Our</u> daily bread. Let it be profitable to us. May we eat the fruit of our labour[9] and not another[']s bread. We must not forbear labour.

4. <u>This day</u>.[10] We ought to ask every day. Prayer should be with the family daily.

5. <u>Us</u>. Give us. Here we are not selfish, but we pray for our friends, for the poor, for all.

6. <u>Give</u> us. Not pay us as wages, nor lend me to be repaid anon.[11] But give of thy free grace.

    Language [is] wonderfully simple. No finery.

229
696   Hungry, starving souls put up the same prayer.[12]

1. This is the only time Charles preached a sermon on Matt 6:11. For instances in which Charles referenced this Scripture verse, see *NPSP* 3:196; *NPSP* 6:38; *MTP* 7:450; *MTP* 8:13; *MTP* 9:265; *MTP* 10:442; *MTP* 12:590; *MTP* 13:435; *MTP* 17:662; *MTP* 18:142; *MTP* 21:536; *MTP* 24:133; *MTP* 27:321; *MTP* 28:669; *MTP* 29:172; *MTP* 30:245; *MTP* 33:530; *MTP* 35:110; *MTP* 57:399; and *MTP* 60:417.

2. In this sermon Charles uses the literary technique "copia" in which amplified meaning is found in the analysis of each word. Charles later explained, "One word of God is like a piece of gold, and the Christian is the gold-beater, and he can hammer that promise out for whole weeks" (*MTP* 44:100).

3. An alternative reading of these sentences is "But littles, this is the promise we are taught: temperance and contentment."

4. Matthew 4:4, "But he answered and said, It is written, Man shall not live by bread alone, but by every word that proceedeth out of the mouth of God."

5. An alternative reading of this sentence is "This shows [our] dependence on providence."

6. Charles is likely thinking of Matt 4:1–2 and Luke 4:2.

7. Cf. 1 Kgs 19:1–8.

8. Cf. Exod 16:3.

9. Cf. Ps 128:2.

10. Charles underscored both words "this" and "day." However, in keeping with his tendency to emphasize one word, the context suggests the underscore be reserved only for the word "this."

11. "Quickly; soon; in a short time" or "sometimes; now and then; at other times" (Johnson's *Dictionary*, s.v. "anon").

12. An alternative reading of this line is "Hungry, starving souls, [you] put up the same prayer."

Heb. XI. 8.9.10.   The call of Abraham.   152.

The next important event after the stopping of Babel was the call of Abram.   This derives interest from the fact that his posterity engross nearly all the space given to history in the Scriptures & are interwoven with all that concerns our holy religion.   The founder of so great an empire must be renowned.   The parent of a race existing from the most ancient times & now known every where should receive some attention.
    Let us look & try to learn.

I. God's reasons & designs in calling Abram.
— What was God's design in choosing any one?

    1. To insure their salvation, he knew they would never seek unless he sought them, & remaining where they were all would perish.

    2. He desired in this morning of the world to give his grace so eminently to the chosen person, that he might in after ages be a pattern to others & a trophy of the power of faith as well as a monument of rich grace

    3. But perhaps the main reason was that he designed to commit the conservation of the truth to some tribe that they by tradition might preserve it.   God also intended to develope his plans by a picture & took these to be actors in it, he used this nation as an experiment
— But why did God choose Abram more than another.
Not for his merit at the time — for with his parents he served other gods.   see Josh XXIV. 2...
    Nor for his merit foreseen for this was God's absolute gift
Should I take a beggar & make him rich, who will

THE CALL *of* ABRAHAM

Hebrews 11:8–10[1]

"By faith Abraham, when he was called to go out into a place which he should after receive for an inheritance, obeyed; and he went out, not knowing whither he went. By faith he sojourned in the land of promise, as in a strange country, dwelling in tabernacles with Isaac and Jacob, the heirs with him of the same promise: For he looked for a city which hath foundations, whose builder and maker is God."

The next important event after the stopping of Babel was the call of Abram. This derives interest from the fact that his posterity engross[2] nearly all the space given to history in the Scriptures and are interwoven with all that[3] concerns our holy religion. The founder of so great an empire must be renowned. The parent of a race,[4] existing from the most ancient times and now known every where, should receive some attention.

Let us look and try to learn.

I. GOD'S REASONS AND DESIGNS IN CALLING ABRAM.[5]

———What[6] was God's design in choosing any one?

1. To insure their salvation. He knew they would never seek unless he sought them.[7] And remaining where they were, all would perish.

2. He desired in this morning of the world to give his grace so eminently to the chosen person that he might in after ages be a pattern to others and a trophy of the power of faith as well as a monument of rich grace.

3. But perhaps the main reason was that he designed to commit the conservation of the truth to some tribe that they by tradition might preserve it. God also intended to develope his plans by a picture and took these to be actors in it. He used this nation as an experiment.

———But why did God choose Abram more than another?

Not for his merit at the time, for with his parents he served other gods. See Josh XXIV.2.[8]

Nor for his merit foreseen, for this was God's absolute gift. Should I take a beggar and make him rich? Who will be so foolish as to say that I took him from his fellows because I foresaw I should make him rich.

No, God did it after the counsel of his own will & thus showed the sovereignty of his grace.

II. The call itself. "We read it in full in Gen XII. He had to leave the country of his birth, the home where he was nurtured & the friends who loved him and whom he loved too. Leaving all he must go but he knew not where & seek another country. — Now why did God require this of him?

1. Because this prepared him for future trials this strengthened his faith. The arm gets more sinewy by exercise, It tested his sincerity

2. It took him away from a really greater trial the persecution of the idolaters. & their bad society.

3. It was the means of keeping up the distinction between his family & others. which was one of God's purposes.

III. Abram's obedience — was immediate, & bold he left his country & his friends went with him but only for a distance, they staid in Haran, he received a second call & on he went again. — Now what made him obey so readily?

Ans His strong faith — Do you doubt its strength He left all — He suffered contempt no doubt, He went from a certain livelyhood to an uncertain one. He went to dwell in a tent & leave his house. To be a wanderer. To a strange country, which was to belong to a seed then unborn & apparently be so foolish as to say that I took him from his fellows because I foresaw[9] I should make him rich.

No, God did it[10] after the counsel of his own will, and thus showed the sovereignty of his grace.

II. THE CALL ITSELF.

We[11] read it in full in Gen XII. He had to leave the country of his birth,[12] the home where he was nurtured, and the friends who loved him and whom he loved too. Leaving all, he must go, but he knew not where, and seek another country.[13]

————Now why did God require this of him?

1. Because this prepared him for future trials. This strengthened his faith. The arm gets more sinewy by exercise. It tested his sincerity.

2. It took him away from a really greater trial, the persecution of the idolaters and their bad society.

3. It was the means of keeping up the distinction between his family and others, which[14] was one of God's purposes.

III. ABRAM'S OBEDIENCE[15] WAS IMMEDIATE[16] AND BOLD.

He left his country and his friends went with him, but only for a distance. They staid[17] in Haran.[18] He receives a second call and on he went again.

————Now what made him obey so readily?

Ansr.[19] His strong faith. Do you doubt its strength? He left all. He suffered contempt, no doubt. He went from a certain livelyhood[20] to an uncertain one.[21] He went to dwell in a tent and leave his house to be a wanderer to a strange country,[22] which was to belong to a seed then unborn, and apparently

unlikely ever to come forth. This land was full of enemies
No quiet & repose, — the Canaanite was there.
This was strong faith & from this sprung strong obedience
— Our work of salvation resembles this in various points
& how many there are who go with us to Haran but not to Canaan.

IV. The prop & pillar of this faith.

1. God's call — this was quite sufficient, when God
calls, said he, he will guide — faith only wants to know
its duty & it will be done — the bare call sufficed

2. God's promise. This is the food of faith. God gave
him a fine extensive one —

He was to be a great nation, so he is as the father of the Jews
    but especially of believers. —— he would say then I am safe
"I will bless thee" & for this faith would endure curses & losses.
"Make thy name great". it was now little, how great he knew not —
"Thou shalt be a blessing" — the good man desires to be of use.
Blessings attend those blessing him & vice-versa. Ah cries faith then
    I am secure. "them" in blessing "him" in cursing to show
that many would bless & few curse.
"in thee shall all — be blessed, — this he would regard as the crown
& doubtless would see Christ in it & for Christ faith
would even choose to die

3. The glory of heaven he saw through the promise, he
knew that it had a deeper meaning than to be only temporal.
Living in tents he looked for a city with foundations.
He tents would not provoke the hostility of the natives.
& by them he expressed his faith. He held the
earthly Canaan to be but a faint emblem of the
heavenly. He spiritualized & looked within the vail

unlikely ever to come forth. This land was full of enemies. No quiet and repose. The Canaanite was there. This was strong faith and from this sprung strong obedience.[23]

Our work of salvation resembles this in various points, and how many there are who go with us to Haran but not to Canaan?

IV. THE PROP AND PILLAR OF THIS FAITH.

1. God's call. This was quite sufficient. When God calls, said he, he will guide. Faith only wants to know its duty, and it will be done. The bare call sufficed.

2. God's promise. This is the food of faith. God gave him a fine, extensive one:

    He was to be a great nation.[24] So he is as the father of the Jews, but especially of believers. He would say, then, I am safe. "I will bless thee."[25] And for this faith, [I] would endure curses and losses. "Make thy name great."[26] It was now little. How great he knew not. "Thou shalt be a blessing."[27] The good man desires to be of use. Blessings[28] attend those blessing him, and vice-versa. Ah, cries faith, then I am secure. "Then" in blessing "him," in cursing to show that many would bless and few curse. "In thee shall all be blessed."[29] This, he would regard as the crown,[30] and doubtless would see Christ in it, and for Christ, faith would even choose to die.

3. The glory of heaven. He saw through the promise.[31] He knew that it had a deeper meaning than to be only temporal. Living in tents,[32] he looked for a city[33] with foundations. The tents[34] would not provoke the hostility of the natives, and by them he expressed his faith. He held the earthy Canaan to be but a faint emblem of the heavenly. He spiritualized and looked within the vail.[35]

how Abram does but serve as a picture of
what we must be if we would be saved we must be

1. Called of God by effectual grace.
2. We must leave everything.
3. We must traverse untried lands.
4. We must live as strangers & foreigners.
5. & this by faith of joys to come.

230   O giver of faith! give it to us thy servants.
yea & to the vilest of sinners,

---

153.   1 John V. 21. Little children keep yourselves from idols.
Idolatry is one of the sins most common in this degraded
world. Men do not love a God whom they cannot
see & therefore attempt to make representations
of him contrary to the will & command of the Lord.
There would be some occasion for John to address
this caution to the young Gentile converts surrounded
by the heathens & so effectual by God's grace
was this warning joined with others that but
very few ever apostatized although every conceivable
& one would have thought inconceivable torture
was practised on them. The Jews needed
not to be warned of the open sin of idol worship
for after the Babylonish captivity they never
did nor could be forced to worship idols
Yet was this necessary even to them & so also

Now, Abram does but serve as a picture of what we must be if we would be saved. We must be:

1. Called of God by effectual grace.[36]

2. We must leave everything.[37]

3. We must traverse untried lands.

4. We must live as strangers and foreigners.[38]

5. And this, by faith of joys to come and given of faith!

Give it to us, thy servants.

Yea, and to the vilest of sinners.[39]

230

LITTLE CHILDREN KEEP YOURSELVES *from* IDOLS
1 John 5:21[1]

"Little children, keep yourselves from idols. Amen."

Idolatry is one of the sins most common in this degraded world. Men do not love a God whom they cannot see and therefore attempt to make representations of him contrary to the will and command of the Lord.[2]

There would be some occasion for John to address this caution to the young Gentile converts surrounded by the heathens. And so effectual by God's grace was this warning joined with others that but very few ever apostatized.[3] Although every conceivable and one[4] would have thought inconceivable, torture was practiced on them.[5] The Jews needed not to be warned of the open sin of idol worship, for after the Babylonish[6] captivity they never did, nor could, be forced to worship idols.[7] Yet was this necessary even to them, and so also to us though we may think we are in no danger. If hoary headed John could rise from his grave & see the Catholics engaged in their worship of the pyx, the Virgin, relics, crucifix &c how would he thunder out as well as sweetness would allow "Keep yourselves from idols" & I feel equally sure should he behold our Protestant Christian assemblies he would not blush to conclude his discourse with these same words. Allow him then to speak. Hear him. he addresses –

I. Characters – whom he calls "little children" the children of God should have the best of our sermons, the best warning, the best comforts not that the ungodly are to be neglected far from it but this one is to God's children, to those who are alive & to others the word is Repent ye!

They are little children, though this term sometimes means even the newborn babes & ex-presses the first stage of spiritual life yet here it applies to all believers of all growths, for they are little children

1. In knowledge – the wisest is but a child, learning the very rudiments & elements of religion.

2. In spiritual strength, the strongest is a babe & would stumble at a straw.

3. In dependance, we are even more helpless

to us, though we may think we are in no danger.

If hoary-headed John could rise from his grave and see the Catholics engaged in their worship of the pope, the Virgin, relics, crucifix,[8] etc., how would he thunder out as well as sweetness would allow,[9] "Keep yourselves from idols."

And I feel equally sure should he behold our Protestant Christian assemblies, he would not blush to conclude his discourse with these same words. Allow him, then, to speak. Hear him. He addresses:

I.   CHARACTERS WHOM HE CALLS "LITTLE CHILDREN."

The children of God should have the best of our sermons, the best warning, the best comforts. Not that the ungodly are to be neglected. Far from it. But this one is to God's children, to those who are alive.[10] To others, the word is, Repent ye![11]

They are little children, though this term sometimes means even the newborn babes[12] and expresses the first stage of spiritual life. Yet here it applies to all believers of all growths, for they are little children:

1. In knowledge. The wisest is but a child learning the very rudiments and elements of religion.[13]

2. In spiritual strength.[14] The strongest is a babe and would stumble at a straw.

3. In dependence. We are even more helpless

than the babe - like that we cannot speak, move,
n find ourselves food. Sometimes we are weaker still

But yet though little children we are God's
little children + and as such
4. We are full of simplicity or ought to be believing God.
5. We love God + trust him as little ones the Father.
John calls them little children because he saw
these marks in them + perhaps they were his spiritual sons.

Now then Beloved little ones Hear again
your danger is from. -
II. Idols ....   You may not worship
any that are set up by other and you must
not turn image makers but avoid them
Make not an idol .
1. Of your business. pursue it diligently but be
also fervent in spirit, do not follow it anxiously,
nor at times, which are God's property do it is sin.
2. Of your property .. - your money + goods. if you
have but little if you love it too much you are
committing sin.   You all have something - you
may worship - your wife, husband, children, friends, or lovers.
3. Of our dress. we should be neat but beyond
this we may not go.   Rank in society, may give
some a right to better garments than other but he
who boasts and glories in this is an idolater
4. Of your person. It is a misfortune to be handsome
to be fine in figure &c more so even than to be

than the babe like that we cannot speak, move, or find ourselves food. Sometimes, we are weaker still.

But yet, though little children, we are God's little children.[15] And[16] as such,

4. We are full of simplicity, or ought to be believing God.

5. We love God and trust him as little ones [trust] the Father.[17] John calls them little children because he saw these marks in them and perhaps they were his spiritual sons.

Now then, Beloved little ones, hear again your danger is from

II. IDOLS.

You may not worship any that are set up by other[s],[18] and you must not turn [into] image-makers, but avoid them.

Make not an idol.

1. Of your business. Pursue it diligently, but be also fervent in spirit. Do not follow it anxiously, nor at times which are God's property.[19] If you[20] do, it is sin.

2. Of your property, your money,[21] and goods. If you have but little: if you love it too much you are committing sin. You all have something you may worship: your wife, husband, children, friends, or lovers.[22]

3. Of our dress. We should be neat, but beyond this we may not go. Rank in society may give some a right to better garments than other[s],[23] but he who boasts and glories in this is an idolater.

4. Of your person. It is a misfortune to be handsome, to be fine in figure, etc. More[24] so even than to be

deformed — let those who are handsome take care they do not idolize themselves — Or others pamper, nurse & feed this vile body & so make it viler still.

5. Of your respectability. for some may not be touched may not be slighted, they must have every punctilio attended to & sniff for ever the fumes of sacrafice

6. Of our endowments. Clear heads, good voices, lively wit, strong mind, learning, knowledge &c or we may preach well & be useful but if we have a vary glory & praise not God we sin. —
Now children hear again. what you are to do.

<u>III</u>. <u>Keep yourselves from these idols</u>. How you Say, can little children do it? Yet you must do it.

1. Seek strength from the Holy Spirit, he renewed thee and he will do this for thee.

2. Look much at Immanuel in his person & in his sufferings & loving him thou wilt dash idols away

3. Pray God to make you willing to resign all for his sake. practise self denial — be sure that God only can suffice you. & remember

1. How abominable idolatry is in God's sight
2. How it debases you,
3. How it tends to ruin you
        Oh Lord keep me from idols — by Jesus.

deformed. Let those who are handsome take care they do not idolize themselves.[25] Or others pamper, nurse, and feed this vile body and so make it viler still.

5. Of your respectability. For some may not be touched, may not be slighted. They must have every punctilio[26] attended to and sniff for ever the fumes of sacrafice.

6. Of our endowments. Clear heads, good voices, lively wit, strong mind, learning, knowledge, etc. Or we may preach well and be useful.[27] But if we have a vain glory and praise not God, we sin.

Now children, hear again what you are to do.

III. KEEP YOURSELVES FROM THESE IDOLS.

How, you say, can little children do it? Yet, you must do it.

1. Seek strength from the Holy Spirit. He renewed thee[28] and he will do this for thee.

2. Look much at Immanuel in his person and in his suffering, and loving him thou wilt dash idols away.

3. Pray God to make you willing[29] to resign all for his sake. Practise self denial.[30] Be sure that God only can suffice you and remember:

   1. How abominable idolatry is in God's sight.

   2. How it debases you.

   3. How it tends to ruin you.

   Oh Lord, keep me from idols, by Jesus.

1. Charles preached three additional sermons on Heb 11:8–10. On July 10, 1859, he preached a sermon entitled "The Call of Abraham" (*NPSP* 5, Sermon 261). On June 27, 1875, he preached a sermon entitled "Abraham's Prompt Obedience to the Call of God" (*MTP* 21, Sermon 1242). On August 21, 1890, he preached a sermon entitled "The Obedience of Faith" (*MTP* 37, Sermon 2195). Charles also preached an undated sermon on Heb 11:9–10 entitled "Abraham, a Pattern to Believers" (*MTP* 39, Sermon 2292). Overlapping content is found in all of these sermons; however, there is not enough structural similarity to suggest Charles had his early sermon in mind when writing these later sermons.

2. Alternative possible words are "engross[ed]" or "engross[es]."

3. Charles originally wrote the word "the" before changing it to "that."

4. "Abraham's faith was of the most eminent order, for he is called the Father of the Faithful" (*NPSP* 5:289).

5. An alternative reading of these two lines is "Let us look and try to learn [about] God's reasons and designs in calling Abram."

6. As in the former sermon, "Boast Not Thyself of Tomorrow" (Sermon 150), Charles again incorporated the use of lines to draw distinction to the objections/questions he anticipated. In this sermon, however, the lines do not replace Roman numerals but instead fall under the primary points.

7. Cf. 1 John 4:19.

8. Joshua 24:2, "And Joshua said unto all the people, Thus saith the Lord God of Israel, Your fathers dwelt on the other side of the flood in old time, even Terah, the father of Abraham, and the father of Nachor: and they served other gods."

9. In his autobiography Charles later recounted the episode in John Newton's life when he said, "Ah, sir, the Lord must have loved me before I was born, or else He would not have seen anything in me to love afterwards." Charles added, "I am sure it is true in my case; I believe the doctrine of election, because I am quite certain that, if God had not chosen me, I should never have chosen Him; and I am sure He chose me before I was born, or else He never would have chosen me afterwards; and he must have elected me for reasons unknown to me, for I never

could find any reason in myself why He should have looked upon me with special love. So I am forced to accept that great Biblical doctrine" (*Autobiography* 1:170). In his sermon "God's Foreknowledge of Man's Sin," Charles later said in 1867, "Some, who know no better, harp upon the foreknowledge of our repentance and faith, and say that, 'Election is according to the foreknowledge of God;' a very scriptural statement, but they make a very unscriptural interpretation of it. Advancing by slow degrees, they next assert that God foreknow the faith and the good works of his people. Undoubtedly true, since he foreknew everything; but then comes their groundless inference, namely, that therefore the Lord chose his people because he foreknew them to be believers" (*MTP* 13:621).

10. Charles struck through the descender of the letter "f" and thus converted it into a "t."

11. Since the opening quotation mark Charles inserted before the word "We" does not close, he may have intended to quote from Genesis 12.

12. Cf. Gen 12:1, 4.

13. "How often have I told you how quickly my horses go home! They seem to know when their heads are turned homewards, and away they go. They pull up even the highest of Norwood's hills with all their might because they are going home. They do not go so fast when they are coming here, and I do not blame them. They know where there is good feed for them, and a place to lie down in; and even a horse goes best with his head towards home. Come, beloved, our heads are towards home, as many of us as believe in Jesus! We do not want to be lashed as we go up the everlasting hills. We will pull against the collar with all our might to get home as soon as we can" (*MTP* 39:45).

14. A dark stain, likely the result of the aging process of the manuscript, appears beneath the letter "h" in the word "which."

15. "If all the world would obey the Lord, what a heaven on earth there would be! Perfect obedience to God would mean love among men, justice to all classes, and peace in every land. Our will brings envy, malice, war; but the Lord's will would bring us love, joy, rest, and bliss" (*MTP* 37:157). See "The Obedience of Faith" (*MTP* 37, Sermon 2195).

16. "Delayed obedience is disobedience" (*MTP* 37:162). "Some one asked Alexander to what he owed his conquests, and he said, 'I have conquered because I never delayed'" (*MTP* 21:382).

17. A modern spelling of the word "staid" is "stayed."

18. Cf. Gen 11:31.

19. Contraction, "Answer."

20. A modern spelling of the word "livelyhood" is "livelihood."

21. "Our greatest risk is over when we obey" (*MTP* 37:166).

22. "And shall *we* doubt for the future? No; mariner, hoist the sail; loose the rudder bands; drag up the anchor; once again to sea we go, with the flag of faith at the masthead, with Jehovah at the helm, to a sure port the vessel shall be guided, though the storm may howl, and hell beneath shall be stirred; for God is with us, and the God of Abraham is our refuge. God give to every one of you the firmest trust in his providence, that you may go forth not knowing whither you go" (*NPSP* 5:296, italics in the original).

23. "Obedience is heaven in us, and it is the preface of our being in heaven. Obedient faith is the way to eternal life—nay, it is eternal life revealing itself" (*MTP* 37:167).

24. Cf. Gen 12:2a.   25. Cf. Gen 12:2b.

26. Cf. Gen 12:2c.   27. Cf. Gen 12:2d.

28. Charles originally inserted opening quotation marks before the word "Blessings" before striking through them with a single diagonal stroke.

29. Charles did not insert closing quotation marks at the end of the phrase, "In thee shall all be blessed." He may have intended to paraphrase Gen 22:18, "And in thy seed shall all the nations of the earth be blessed; because thou hast obeyed my voice."

30. See "The Golden Crown of Holiness" (Sermon 149).

31. An alternative reading of this line is "The glory of heaven he saw through the promise."

32. "I cannot tell you the strange joy I felt after the earthquake at Mentone. I had been to see many of the houses that had been shaken down, and the two churches that were greatly injured, and I was full of the earthquake. I had quite realized its terrors and its power; and when I went up the stairs of my hotel, I thought, 'Well, at any moment this may all come down with a run. When I go to bed, it may all slip away;' and I felt a great delight in thinking that I actually realized, not in a dream, but as a matter of fact, the shakiness of this poor earthquaky world, and how everything in it is without foundation, but is just a mere tent which might come down at any moment. . . . Let not your roots strike into this accursed soil. Live here as those who are soon to live there" (*MTP* 39:41).

33. "We are looking for a city. We think all this so-called city of London to be but a dissolving view. We count this great country of England to be but like a pack of cards which will soon be knocked over. We reckon the whole world to be but a dream. There is a city, and we are looking for it" (*MTP* 39:44).

34. An illegible letter is written beneath "n" in the word "tents." Charles may have originally written the word "texts."

35. Cf. Heb 6:19.

36. Cf. *MTP* 21:375; Eph 1:19; 3:7.

37. Cf. Matt 19:29; Mark 10:29–30; Luke 18:29.

38. "Christian people, if you were what you should be, men would know that you did not belong to this ungodly race. You have been redeemed from among men; you have been endowed with a new life to which they are strangers; and it ought to be apparent in your daily walk and conversation that you seek another country. This world is not your country, and never can be" (*MTP* 39:39). Cf. 1 Pet 2:11.

39. Cf. 1 Tim 1:15.

1. Charles preached two additional sermons on 1 John 5:21: On September 6, 1874, he preached a sermon entitled "Idolatry Condemned" (*MTP* 53:613), and on February 6, 1887, he preached a sermon entitled "Eternal Life!" (*MTP* 41:25). There is enough overlapping content and structural similarity between the 1874 sermon and the one above to suggest the latter is an expansion of the former. Charles's 1887 sermon shares no noticeable structural similarity to the sermon above.

2. Cf. Exodus 32.

3. "To forsake one's profession; it is commonly used of one who departs from his religion" (Johnson's *Dictionary*, s.v. "apostatize").

4. Three diagonal strokes appear in pen above the letter "e" in the word "one."

5. In their commentary on Heb 11:32–38, which Charles later owned in his personal library, Matthew Henry and Thomas Scott noted, "These believers endured much by faith. They bore torture, and would not accept of deliverance upon the terms of becoming apostates; that which animated them thus to suffer, was, their hope of obtaining a better resurrection, and deliverance upon more honourable terms. They were persecuted in their reputation by mockings, cruel to a well-disposed mind; in their persons by scourging, the punishment of slaves; in their liberty by bonds and imprisonment" (Matthew Henry and Thomas Scott, *A Commentary upon the Holy Bible: With Numerous Observations and Notes from Other Writers, Also Maps of the Countries Mentioned in Scripture, and Various Useful Tables. Romans to Revelation* [London: The Religious Tract Society, n.d., The Spurgeon Library], 452).

6. In his sermon "By Faith Jericho Fell" (Notebook 2, Sermon 133), Charles compared Babylon with Roman Catholicism. Charles added to this comparison on the following page.

7. Cf. Dan 3:13–15.

8. See "Salvation in God Only" (Notebook 1, Sermon 34).

9. This sentence may also be interrogative: "how would he thunder out, as well as sweetness would allow?"

10. Cf. Eph 2:5; Col 2:13.   11.   Cf. Matt 3:2; Mark 1:15; Acts 3:19.

12. Charles is likely drawing on John Gill's commentary on 1 John 2:1: "The Apostle may address the saints under this character, on account of their regeneration by the Spirit and grace of God, in which they were as new-born babes; and on account of his being the instrument of their conversion, and so was their spiritual father, and therefore calls them his own children" (John Gill, *An Exposition of the New Testament, in Three Volumes, in Which the Sense of the Sacred Text Is Given; Doctrinal and Practical Truths Are Set in a Plain and Easy Light, Difficult Places Explained, Seeming Contradictions Reconciled; and Whatever Is Material in the Various Readings, and the Several Oriental Versions, Is Observed. The Whole Illustrated with Notes Taken from the Most Ancient Jewish Writings, Vol. 3* [London: printed for the author and sold by Aaron Ward at the King's-Arms in Little-Britain, 1748, The Spurgeon Library], 584).

13. "Know all you can that is really worth knowing; but, with your knowledge, mind that you have the childlike spirit without which all your knowledge will be of little service to you. After all, there is not much difference between those who are called wise men and those who know but little, for the wisest of men really know but little; and if they are truly wise, they know that they know but little" (*MTP* 53:615).

14. "Growing Christians reckon themselves to be nothing, but full-grown Christians count themselves less than nothing; and when we feel ourselves to be 'less than the least of all the saints,' then we are indeed making good progress in the divine life. To grow less and less in your own esteem is the right kind of growth. Naturally, we grow up from childhood to manhood; but, spiritually, we grow down from manhood to childhood" (*MTP* 53:615).

15. The emphasis of this sentence is on the word "God's," which may be read, "But yet, though little children, we are *God's* little children."

16. Charles struck through the ampersand and wrote the word "and" after it.

17. An alternative reading of this line is "We love God and trust him as little ones [of] the Father."

18. An alternative reading of this phrase is "You may not worship any that are set up by [an]other."

19. Charles is likely referring to observing the Sabbath (Cf. Exod 20:8).

20. Charles wrote the words "if you" in superscript above the word "do" and indicated its location by a bolded caret beneath the line.

21. "Remember, dear friends, that it will be only a little while ere you must leave all that you have. What is the use of your having it at all unless you really enjoy it, and how can you so truly enjoy it as by laying it at your Saviour's feet, and using it for his glory?" (*MTP* 53:619).

22. "I remember reading a story of a good man who seemed as if he could never forgive God for taking away his child. He sat in a Quakers' meeting, bowed down, and sorrowful, and his time of deliverance came when a sister rose, uttered these words, 'Verily, I perceive that children are idols,' and then resumed her seat. Such a message as that is often needed; yet it is a pity that it should be. Make no idol of your child, of your wife, or your husband; for, by putting them into Christ's place, you really provoke him to take them from you. Love them as much as you please;—I would that some loved their children, their husbands, or their wives more than they do;—but always love them in such a fashion that Christ shall have the first place in your hearts" (*MTP* 53:619).

23. The differences between the upper and lower classes would have been pronounced during this season in Charles's ministry. The clothes, for instance, of his agricultural congregation in Waterbeach would have contrasted sharply with those of the academics studying in Cambridge where he lived. According to Joan Nunn, "During the 1850s and early 1860s coloured shirts might be worn by working-class men, but gentlemen usually wore white" (Joan Nunn, *Fashion in Costume: 1200–2000* [2nd ed.; Chicago: New Amsterdam Books, 2000], 140). Women of lower class usually sewed their own dresses and "generally wore secondhand garments that fitted badly, or they ignored styles and made themselves looser bodices in which they could comfortably do physical labor" (Sally Mitchell, *Daily Life in Victorian England* in Daily Life Through History Series [Westport, CT; London: Greenwood Press, 1996], 138–39). In a letter to his father on December 31, 1851, Charles shed light on how he spent his finances: "Mr. Leeding has given me a five-pound note, which I shall not touch except for clothes. I mean to keep that money only for clothes; what I earn on Sundays is my own for books, expenses, etc." (Angus Library and Archive, Regent's Park

College, Oxford University, D/SPU 1, Letter 11). The style of clothes Charles wore while pastor at Waterbeach came under critique from Susannah after he moved to London to pastor New Park Street Chapel. In contrast to the "dapper" deacon James Smith who "wore the silk stockings and knee-breeches dear to a former generation," Charles received a lesser commendation from his future wife: "For, if the whole truth be told, I was not at all fascinated by the young orator's eloquence, while his countrified manner and speech excited more regret than reverence. . . . [T]he huge black satin stock, the long, badly-trimmed hair, and the blue pocket-handkerchief with white spots, which he himself has so graphically described,—these attracted most of my attention, and, I fear, awakened some feelings of amusement" (*Autobiography* 2:5). On October 16, 1881, Charles said, "I heard one say the other day that he could not attend a place of worship because he had not clothes that were fit to come in. I wonder what sort of garments the Lord Jesus would object to in a coming sinner! I am afraid if he were to see some of you he would hardly think that you are dressed fit for public worship, for you are too smart by half: but I do not believe that he ever rejected a man or woman because of their patched or unfashionable garments. What cared he for court dress, and full dress, and all that nonsense?" (*MTP* 27:586).

24. An illegible letter is written under the first stem of the letter "m" in the word "more." It is possibly the beginning of a "t."

25. In his commentary on the proverb, "Prettiness makes no porridge," Charles later wrote, "That is to say, the handsomeness of the wife will not feed the family. In a woman domestic ability is needed even more than personal beauty. Still there is no proof that ugly women cook better than handsome ones do. Prettiness spoils no porridge" (C. H. Spurgeon, *The Salt-Cellars. Being a Collection of Proverbs, Together with Homely Notes Thereon. Vol. II.—M to Z* [Pasadena, TX: Pilgrim Publications, 1975], 104).

26. "A small nicety of behavior; a nice point of exactness" (Johnson's *Dictionary*, s.v. "punctilio").

27. Charles was aware of his strengths and weaknesses during this season of his ministry. In this section he was likely speaking autobiographically. In a letter to his father on February 24, 1852, he wrote, "Providence has thrown me into a great sphere of *usefulness.*" In the same letter Charles offered as one reason for

not enrolling as a student of Stepney College in London: "I am not uneducated" (Angus Library and Archive, Regent's Park College, Oxford University, D/SPU 1, Letter 12, italics added). With regard to the powers of Charles's mind, he once confessed, "[W]hen but a child, I could have discussed many a knotty point of controversial theology" (*Autobiography* 1:70). He also said, "I was, by my tutor's own expressed verdict, considered to be sufficiently proficient in my studies to have taken a good place on the list had the way been open. 'You could win in a canter,' said he to me" (*Autobiography* 1:204). In 1892, Charles was described by Wayland Hoyt as "a man of the most singular ability of self-marshaling and self-control. . . . He seemed to be absolutely sure of himself for any moment for any occasion. At once his powers would gather themselves in exact order, and he could call on this or that at will, as it was needed ("Charles Haddon Spurgeon," *The Christian Union: A Family Paper*, February 6, 1892). Charles's humor was, as Lewis Drummond described it, "winsomely contagious" (Lewis Drummond, *Spurgeon: Prince of Preachers* [Grand Rapids, MI: Kregel, 1992], 27). William Williams, Charles's friend, once "confessed to having laughed more in Spurgeon's company than in the entire rest of life besides" (Tom Nettles, *Living by Revealed Truth: The Life and Pastoral Theology of Charles Haddon Spurgeon* [Fern, Ross-shire, Scotland: Christian Focus Publications, 2013], 15). John Stevenson testified to Charles's demeanor and character during his Waterbeach ministry, saying, "Mr. Spurgeon's character and conduct were as amiable as his talents were attractive" (John Stevenson, *Sketch of the Life and Ministry of the Rev. C. H. Spurgeon. From Original Documents. Including Anecdotes and Incidents of Travel; Biographical Notices of Former Pastors; Historical Sketch of Park-Street Chapel; and an Outline of Mr. Spurgeon's Articles of Faith* [New York: Sheldon, Blakeman & Co.; Chicago: S. C. Griggs, 1857], 52).

28. Cf. Eph 4:23; Titus 3:5.

29. A modernized reading of this sentence is "Pray that God would make you willing to resign all for his sake."

30. Cf. Matt 16:24.

154   Gal. II. 18   Zeal in Religion commended

Paul had seen the error into which the Galatians
had fallen, he had reproved them for it, & now
he warns them of the teachers who were secretly
the cause of all the mischief. Though zealous
says he they have sinister motives & their zeal
is of no value.   As a by-blow he puts in
"but think not I object to zeal, I would have
it rightly directed & then it is an invaluable
thing.

I. The zeal of the apostle. which he recommends was what he practised. It is a genuine
fruit of true faith, though it often cools.
It consists in great love to religion & action
somewhat at least commensurate. It is the
true blood-heat of religion. It must be
1 Constant. not effervescing, or yearly as Missin-
or rash & then finished. but always.
2. Not to be seen of men but of God, the fewer
see us the more reward.
That is not zeal — which is now called
charity, a carelessness for the great doctrines
this is utterly inconsistent with zeal.
Moderation, meekness are false names for
lukewarmness. Want of zeal is the want of

~~THE~~ ZEAL *in* RELIGION COMMENDED

Galatians 4:18[1]

*"But it is good to be zealously affected always in a good thing,
and not only when I am present with you."*

Paul had seen the error into which the Galatians had fallen. He had reproved them for it[2] and now he warns them of the teachers who were secretly the cause of all the mischief.[3] Though zealous, says he, they have sinister motives and their zeal is of no value. As a by-blow,[4] he puts in, "but think not I object to zeal. I would have it rightly directed and then it is an invaluable thing.["][5]

I. THE ZEAL OF THE APOSTLE WHICH HE RECOMMENDS WAS[6] WHAT HE PRACTISED.

It is a genuine fruit of true faith, though it often cools. It consists in great love to religion and action somewhat, at least as commensurate.[7] It is the true blood-heat of religion. It must be:

1. Constant. Not effervescing,[8] or yearly as mission,[9] or rash and then finished. But always.

2. Not to be seen of men but of God.[10] The fewer see us, the more reward. That is not zeal which is now called charity,[11] a carelessness for the great doctrines. This is utterly inconsistent with zeal. Moderation, meekness are false names for lukewarmness. Want of zeal is the want of

the times, men love not self-denial, sickbeds un-
-visited, prayer-meetings neglected, private prayer
formally offerred, preachings not sustained. —
Some are warmer blooded that other & they must
do more & must study caution.
But the slow & drowsy, must learn zeal too.

II. The causes of want of zeal.
1. Too much care for the world.
2. Forgetfulness of first love.
3. Neglect of meditation.
4. Looking to past things & not to the beyond.

III. The benefits of Religious zeal.
1. Success is only to be expected in proportion
to our zeal. Zeal has done mighty things.
See the Crusades, Cromwell's Commonwealth,
Churches, Chapels, Schoolrooms, have all been
the fruits of zeal. Miss foc. all its children.
The most zealous ministers are most successful
2. It is admired even by the worldly.
3. It brings comfort & happiness to ones-
self.
4. It preserves from many falls.

IV. Some incentives to it.
1. The cloud of witnesses.

the times.[12] Men love not self-denial. Sickbeds unvisited, prayer-meetings neglected, private prayer formally offered, preachings not sustained. Some are warmer-blooded tha[n][13] other[s] and they must do more and must study caution. But the slow and drowsy must learn zeal too.

II. THE CAUSES OF WANT OF ZEAL.

1. Too much care for the world.[14]

2. Forgetfulness of first love.[15]

3. Neglect of meditation.[16]

4. Looking to past things and not to the beyond.

III. THE BENEFITS OF RELIGIOUS ZEAL.

1. Success is only to be expected in proportion to our zeal. Zeal has done mighty things. See the Crusades,[17] Cromwell's Commonwealth,[18] Churches, Chapels, Schoolrooms, have all been the fruits of zeal. Miss Socs all its children. The most zealous ministers are most successful.[19]

2. It is admired even by the worldly.

3. It brings comfort and happiness to one[']s self.

4. It preserves from many falls.

IV. SOME INCENTIVES TO IT.

1. The cloud of witnesses.[20]

2. God the judge beholds.

3. See thy perfect pattern.

4. Remember thy vows.

Sinners behold, the saints bestir for you
why not bestir yourself.

233. 393.

---

155.   Ps. 119. – 25. 26. Complaint, Prayer & Answer.

The human race is not altered in size of body, nor
in the main features of their organization: Nor have they
altered much in their spiritual feelings or in the way whereby
the Lord our God led them. Study the anatomy of an
ancient skeleton and you can tell the bones of present
man — to examine David & you behold yourself if
you are a Christian. This whole Psalm is beautiful

These two verses give us an account of the progress
of a sinner to salvation — or of a downcast saint
to the liftings up we sometimes enjoy.

I. A discovery of the sin common to man, causing
a grievous complaint on its account. is the first
stage of gracious life. Discovery of sin & lament over it.

The sin grieved over is "cleaving unto the dust", a sin in
which the whole world by nature is plunged. It
consists in   Love to earthly things.
                Love to sinful things.
                Love of ease & indolence
                Forgetfulness of God.

2. God, the judge, beholds.

3. See thy perfect pattern.

4. Remember thy vows.

Sinners behold, the saints bestir[21] for you. Why not bestir[22] yourself?

233. 393.

COMPLAINT, PRAYER, *and* ANSWER
Psalm 119:25–26[1]

"My soul cleaveth unto the dust: quicken thou me according to thy word.
I have declared my ways, and thou heardest me: teach me thy statutes."

The human race is not altered in size of body, nor in the main features of their organization.[2] Nor have they altered much in their[3] spiritual feelings or in[4] the way whereby the Lord our God led them. Study the anatomy of an ancient skeleton and you can tell the bones of present man. So examine David and you behold yourself if you are a Christian. This whole Psalm is beautiful.

These two verses give us an account of the progress of a sinner to salvation or of a downcast saint to the liftings up we sometimes enjoy.

I. A DISCOVERY OF THE SIN COMMON TO MAN CAUSING A GRIEVOUS COMPLAINT ON ITS ACCOUNT IS THE FIRST STAGE OF GRACIOUS LIFE.

Discovery of sin[5] and lament over it. The[6] sin grieved over is "cleaving unto the dust," a sin in which the whole world by nature is plunged. It consists in:

> Love to earthly things.[7]
> Love to sinful things.
> Love to ease and indolence.
> Forgetfulness of God.

In this the elect as well as others have delighted & even after believing to salvation - the same complaint must be often uttered. The newly convinced sinner feels a want of power in holy exercises, a want of delight in the word, the draggings back of Satan, the enticements of the world.

But he hates all this & grieves much over it. The Christian too finds, want of love, worldliness, coldness &c but he hates it — A feeling & hating of this is one of Jesus' marks on us. Indifference is the devil's mark.

"Prone to wander" all can say.

"Lord I feel it " is more, than a tenth of the world dare say At certain times David used this with emphasis as some of the Psalms testify "My soul cleaveth unto the dust" See 77, 42. 38. &c - so was Paul & who among us is not subject to the same, wherefore be of good cheer. Oh stripling for behold the fathers endure this same distress.

II. The resort of the soul in this hour of need. To the throne of God .... Not to pleasure to shake off their melancholy but to God — Not to man, minister, or book but to prayer & the book of books — The soul feels that here alone is peace — It knows its dependance on God & cries.

1. "Quicken thou me", I know I must be born again. or if that it is done already I want more of the same life-giving spirit which first did it — This is the prayer of prayers.

2. " According to thy word", With his hand on the Bible the poor soul says — whatever thy way may be I desire to go in that way & be saved according to thine own plan.

3. Then searching he finds the promise & returns again — "according to thy word" of promise quicken me.

We may only ask for what is promised; it is good

In this the elect, as well as others, have delighted.[8] And even after believing to salvation the same complaint must be often uttered. The newly convinced sinner feels a want of power in holy exercises, a want of delight in the Word, the dragging back of Satan, the enticements of the world. But he hates all this and grieves much over it.[9]

The Christian too finds want of love, worldliness, coldness, etc., but he hates it. A feeling and hating of this is one of Jesus's marks on us. Indifference is the devil's mark.

"Prone to wander," all can say.

"Lord, I feel it"[10] is more than a tenth of the world dare say.

At certain times, David used this with emphasis, as some of the Psalms testify. "My soul cleaveth unto the dust." See 77,[11] 42,[12] 38,[13] etc. So was Paul,[14] and who among us is not subject to the same? Wherefore, be of good cheer, oh stripling,[15] for behold, the fathers endure[d] this same distress.

II. THE RESORT OF THE SOUL IN THIS HOUR OF NEED.

To the throne of God. Not to pleasure to shake off their melancholy, but to God. Not to man, minister, or book, but to prayer and the [B]ook[16] of books. The soul feels that here alone is peace. It knows its dependence on God and cries.

1. "Quicken thou me."[17] I know I must be born again,[18] or if that is done already I want more of the same life-giving Spirit which first did it. This is the prayer of prayers.[19]

2. "According to thy Word."[20] With his hand on the Bible, the poor soul says, ["]Whatever thy way may be, I desire to go in that way and be saved according to thine own plan.["]

3. Then searching, he finds the promise and returns again. "According to thy Word" of promise, quicken me.[21] We may only ask for[22] what is promised. It is good

to plead God's promise & lay our finger on the place

Thus can we distinguish real concern of soul. It leads to prayer ~ Some complain of want of power, of coldness, & deadness. but this is idle wind unless it blows upwards & leads to real, earnest, continued seeking.

III. The souls' obedience to the heavenly direction is followed with success. — The Bible points this.

IV. { Believe on the Lord Jesus, Repent, Confess. in so doing thou shalt by grace be saved.

The sinner or fallen saint obeys & declares his ways to God ... Pours out his wants & burdens. Recounts his sins & hides not one single whit. He tells every thing in a humble, penitential manner. This is a necessary prelude to relief. Confession of all unburdens the mind. And why fear it. All is known already — God promises & he who performs will soon say "thou heardest me". None but the sincere will declare their ways & such God hears.

We need not fear that our unworthiness, weakness, coldness or deadness unfit us for confession — nay they render it all the more necessary. Prayer is heard. Though in God's way & time — But oh Joy, Joy, Joy. when we can say "thou hast heard me." —

IV. The souls' desire after the way of goodness.

When salvation is thus secured by grace; gratitude leads the saved person to desire to please God. He is impatient to obey & only longs to know his duty for now he stands prepared to do anything.

to plead God's promise and lay one finger on the place. Thus can we distinguish real concern of soul. It leads to prayer. Some complain of want of power, of coldness, and deadness,[23] but this is idle wind unless it blows upwards and leads to real, earnest, continued seeking.

III. THE SOUL'S OBEDIENCE TO THE HEAVENLY DIRECTION IS FOLLOWED WITH SUCCESS. THE BIBLE POINTS THUS,

{Believe[24] on the Lord Jesus. Repent. Confess. In so doing thou shalt by grace be saved.[25]

The sinner or fallen saint obeys and declares his ways to God, pours out his wants and burdens,[26] recounts his sins, and hides not one single whit.[27] He tells every thing in a humble, penitential manner. This is a necessary prelude to relief. Confession of all unburdens the mind. And why fear it? All is known already.[28] God promises, and he who performs will soon say, "[T]hou heardest me." None but the sincere will declare their ways, and such God hears.

We need not fear that our unworthiness, weakness,[29] coldness, or deadness, [will] unfit us for confession.[30] Nay, they render it all the more necessary. Prayer is heard, though in God's way and time. But oh, Joy, Joy, Joy when we can say, "[T]hou hast heard me."

IV. THE SOUL'S DESIRE AFTER THE WAY OF GOODNESS.

When salvation is thus secured by grace, gratitude leads the saved person to desire to please God. He is impatient to obey and only longs to know his duty. For now, he stands prepared to do anything.

He knows his ignorance & fears least he should by this go wrong; he therefore earnestly desires teaching.

Now I say - you must say all this prayer.

Take it as it comes or leave it alone & perish eternally.

Here mark the steps of grace it gives.

1. A longing to be delivered from sin.
2. A spirit of prayer for deliverance.
3. A humble confession & obedience to Christ.
4. A desire after sanctification.

This is the pilgrim's progress from Destruction to Salvation — & also from Backsliding distance from God to the True Restoration.

May the Lord lead me & all who hear me in this good old path.

234.

He knows his ignorance and fears lest[31] he should by this go wrong. He therefore earnestly desires teaching.

Now, I say, you must say all this prayer.[32] Take it as it comes or leave it alone and perish eternally.

Here marks the steps of grace. It gives:

    1. A [l]onging to be delivered from sin.

    2. A spirit of prayer for deliverance.

    3. A humble confession and obedience to Christ.

    4. A desire after sanctification.

This is the pilgrim's progress from Destruction to Salvation[33] and also from Backsliding distance from God to the true Restoration.

May the Lord lead me and all who hear me in this good old path.

234.[34]

1. This is the only time Charles preached a sermon on Gal 4:18.

2. Cf. Gal 4:9–11.

3. Cf. Gal 1:6–7.

4. "An accidental encounter" (Worcester's *Dictionary*, s.v. "by-blow").

5. Charles did not insert a closing quotation mark around the sentences "but think not I object to zeal. I would have it rightly directed and then it is an invaluable thing." However, the context suggests the quotation mark should close after the word "thing."

6. An illegible letter, likely an "h," appears beneath the letter "a" in the word "was." Charles may have intended to write the word "what" before changing it to "was."

7. The word "commensurate" is here used to mean "in proportion to." Charles rephrased this thought on the following page: "Success is only to be expected in proportion to our zeal."

8. "To generate heat by intestine motion" (Johnson's *Dictionary*, s.v. "effervesce").

9. Charles may have had in mind the Baptist Missionary Society. Originally titled "Particular Baptist Society for the Propagation of the Gospel Amongst the Heathen," the Baptist Missionary Society was founded on October 2, 1792, by William Carey and thirteen others, including Andrew Fuller. Charles may have been familiar with the account of the origins of the Baptist Missionary Society in Francis Augustus Cox, *History of the English Baptist Society, 1792 to 1842* (Boston: Isaac Tompkins, 1844). Charles addressed the Baptist Missionary Society on numerous occasions throughout his ministry, including on April 28, 1858, when he preached a sermon entitled "The Desolations of the Lord, the Consolations of His Saints" (*NPSP* 4, Sermon 190). See also "Gospel Missions" (*NPSP* 2, Sermon 76) and "The Model Home Mission and the Model Home Missionary" (*MTP* 15, Sermon 929).

10. Cf. Matt 6:1.

11. Samuel Johnson offered five definitions for the word "charity": 1. Tenderness; kindness; love. 2. Goodwill; benevolence; disposition to think well of others.

3. The theological virtue of universal love. 4. Liberality to the poor. 5. Alms; relief given to the poor (Johnson's *Dictionary*). Charles may have been speaking about the word in the general sense. If not, it is unclear which organized or unorganized charity he had in mind. See also "Do It with Thy Might" (Sermon 162).

12. A modernized reading of this line is "A lack of zeal is a lack of the times."

13. The context suggests Charles likely intended to write the word "than."

14. Cf. 1 John 2:15.   15. Cf. Jer 2:2; Rev 2:4.

16. Cf. Josh 1:8; Pss 63:6; 104:34; 119:15–16.

17. For additional references to the Crusades in Charles's sermons, see *NPSP* 5:8 and *MTP* 13:432. For an academic treatment, see Jonathan Riley-Smith, ed., *The Oxford History of the Crusades* (Oxford: Oxford University Press, 2002).

18. The phrase "Cromwell's Commonwealth" refers to the period in English history after the execution of Charles I when England functioned as a republic and Oliver Cromwell served as the lord protector. For an academic treatment, see Sean Kelsey, *Inventing a Republic: The Political Culture of the English Commonwealth, 1649–1653* (Stanford, CA: Stanford University Press, 1997). Charles owned multiple biographies of Cromwell in his personal library, including Thomas Carlyle, *Oliver Cromwell's Letters and Speeches: with Elucidations. In Four Volumes. Vol. III* (London: Chapman and Hall, 1850, The Spurgeon Library). With regard to Cromwell, Charles said, "I may almost venture to say that the war against the tyrant, Charles I., was a consecrated fight. The people of God had been hunted like partridges upon the mountains, in the reigns of Elizabeth, and James, and Charles. At last their lion-like spirits turned at bay, and their enemies were driven back before their gallant fury; when Cromwell, the Christian hero, mounted his charger, and bade his saintly warriors, with the sword in one hand and the Bible in the other, fight for England's liberty" (*MTP* 7:410).

19. Abbr., "Missionary Societies." An alternative reading of this line is "Missionary societies [and] all [her] children."

20. Hebrews 12:1, "Wherefore seeing we also are compassed about with so great a cloud of witnesses, let us lay aside every weight, and the sin which doth so easily beset us, and let us run with patience the race that is set before us."

21. "To put into vigorous action" (Johnson's *Dictionary*, s.v. "bestir").

22. Charles originally wrote "bestr" before changing the letter "r" into an "i." This literary tendency also appears in "Ephraim's Goodness like the Morning Cloud" (Sermon 139); "Bring My Soul out of Prison" (Sermon 164); and "The Unclean Spirit Returning" (Sermon 168).

1. Charles preached two additional sermons on Ps 119:25–26. He preached on verse 25 in his sermon "Enlivening and Invigorating" (*MTP* 23, Sermon 1350) and on verse 26 in his sermon "A Man of God Alone With God" (*MTP* 48, Sermon 2796). Overlapping content is found in both sermons; however, it is unlikely Charles had his early sermon in mind when writing the later two sermons.

2. In the United Kingdom today, the word "organisation" is spelled with the letter "s." However, Samuel Johnson and Joseph Worcester both spelled the word "organization" with the letter "z," as did Charles in this sermon. See also Charles's spelling of the word "civilization" in "Christ the Power of God" (Sermon 169b).

3. Charles originally wrote the word "the."

4. Charles originally wrote the word "is."

5. "I question whether you can read a newspaper and scan the story of a murder or a robbery, or survey with more distant glance in any book of history the sin of your fellow men, without being in a degree injured therewith" (*MTP* 23:231).

6. An illegible number or letter appears before the word "The." Charles struck through the illegible number or letter several times.

7. "You cannot think much of treasure laid up in heaven if you think a great deal of this world's goods. Riches are often a dangerous incumbrance to those who seek after righteousness; they steal the heart away from God" (*MTP* 23:231).

8. "The whole world is full of God to him who believes in God, and he has intercourse with God wherever he goes" (*MTP* 48:433).

9. "There was a tendency in his soul to cling to earth which he greatly bewailed. Whatever was the cause of his complaint, it was no surface evil, but an affair of his inmost spirit; his *soul* cleaved to the dust; and it was not a casual and accidental falling into the dust, but a continuous and powerful tendency, or *cleaving* to the earth" (*TD* 6:69, italics in the original).

10. Charles is referencing the hymn "Come, Thou Fount of Every Blessing" by Baptist hymnist Robert Robinson (1735–1790). The original hymn contains subtle differences from many modern renditions and is presented in its entirety: "Come,

thou fount of every blessing, / Tune my heart to sing thy grace: / Streams of mercy, never ceasing, / Call for songs of loudest praise. / Teach me some celestial measure, / Sung by ransomed hosts above; / Oh, the vast, the boundless treasure / Of my Lord's unchanging love! / Here I raise my Ebenezer; / Hither, by thy help I'm come; / And I hope, by thy good pleasure, / Safely to arrive at home. / Jesus sought me when a stranger,/ Wandering from the fold of God; / He, to save my soul from danger, / Interposed his precious blood. / Oh! to grace how great a debtor, / Daily I'm constrained to be; / Let that grace, Lord, like a fetter,/ Bind my wandering heart to Thee. / Prone to wander; Lord, I feel it; / Prone to leave the God I love; / Here's my heart, Lord, take and seal it, / Seal it from thy courts above" (S. W. Christophers, *Hymn-Writers and Their Hymns* [London: S. W. Partridge, 9, Paternoster Row, 1866, The Spurgeon Library], 293). In Charles's personal copy of this book, his signature is written in the front cover.

11. Psalm 77:1–2, "I cried unto God with my voice, even unto God with my voice; and he gave ear unto me. In the day of my trouble I sought the Lord: my sore ran in the night, and ceased not: my soul refused to be comforted."

12. Psalm 42:3, "My tears have been my meat day and night, while they continually say unto me, Where is thy God?"

13. Psalm 38:6, "I am troubled; I am bowed down greatly; I go mourning all the day long."

14. "The text very accurately describes such a state of things as that which exists when a patient relates his symptoms to the physician, and then the physician prescribes for him; for, in addition to sin being a great evil in the sight of God, it is also a disease to which we are all prone, and from which only the great Physician can cure us. We cry out against it, and our better self fights against it, yet the old man is within us, 'the body of this death,' as Paul calls it, fights against the new nature, and we should be overcome were it not for divine grace" (*MTP* 48:436). Cf. Rom 7:14–25; 2 Cor 11:23–29.

15. "A youth; one in the state of adolescence" (Johnson's *Dictionary*, s.v. "stripling").

16. The word "book" has been capitalized to indicate Charles was referring to the Holy Bible.

17. "There is no such thing as dead holiness, it must be living holiness, and you must be made alive in order to be obedient, for there is no such thing as dead obedience" (*MTP* 23:235).

18. Cf. John 3:3.

19. "The word of God shows us that he who first made us must keep us alive, and it tells us of the Spirit of God who through the ordinances pours fresh life into our souls; we beg the Lord to act toward us in this his own regular method of grace" (*TD* 6:70).

20. "If we preach frequently and earnestly the precepts of our Lord there are hearers who will complain and say, 'The minister is getting legal.' Nay, brethren, it is you that are getting dead, for when you are alive you will love God's precepts, and those precepts will quicken you" (*MTP* 23:237).

21. An alternative reading of this line is "Then, searching, he finds the promise and returns again [to say,] 'According to thy word of promise,' quicken me."

22. The words "ask for" are bolded, likely the result of the aging process of the manuscript and not emphasis.

23. "When you are numbed, you know that is next door to being dead; but when that numbed flesh of yours begins to come to life again,—you have felt it, you must have felt it—when the blood begins to circulate by the rubbing, a sharp pain is excited in the part that was numbed and painless before. Be thankful for the pain that is an index of life" (*MTP* 23:237).

24. Before the curly bracket on the left, Charles illustrated a right hand pointing to the following sentence. A comparison of similar drawings of hands in the margins of Charles's personal books in his library reveals he continued drawing these illustrations throughout his later ministry. For an example, see William Gurnall, *The Christian in Compleat Armour; or, a Treatise of the Saints['] War Against the Devil, Wherein a Discovery Is Made of That Grand Enemy of God and His People, in His Policies, Power, Seat of His Empire, Wickednesse, and Chief Design He Hath Against the Saints, A Magazin open'd: from Whence the Christian Is Furnished with Spiritual Armes for the Battel, Help't on with His Armour, and Taught the Use of His Weapon, Together with the Happy Issue of the Whole Warre. The First Part* [London: printed for Ralph Smith at the Bible in

Cornhill near the Royal Exchange, 1655, The Spurgeon Library], 4, 7, 11, 32). See also the Spurgeon collection of Puritan books at the John T. Christian Library, New Orleans Baptist Theological Seminary, New Orleans, Louisiana.

25. Cf. Acts 16:30–31.

26. "You ought to think that you will be more welcome at the house of God when you are in trouble than you ever were before" (*MTP* 23:233).

27. "A point; a jot" (Johnson's *Dictionary*, s.v. "whit"). A modernized reading of this phrase is "hides not one single point."

28. Cf. Ps 139:4.

29. An illegible letter is written beneath the "w" in the word "weakness."

30. An alternative reading of this phrase is "[makes us] unfit for confession."

31. The context suggests that Charles intended to write the word "lest" instead of "least." For more examples of this tendency, see "Ephraim's Goodness like the Morning Cloud" (Sermon 139).

32. Depending on where the comma is placed, an alternative reading of this line is "Now I say, you must say all this prayer."

33. Charles is referencing Christian's pilgrimage from the City of Destruction to the Celestial City in John Bunyan's *The Pilgrim's Progress* (John Bunyan, *The Pilgrim's Progress from This World to That Which Is to Come. Delivered Under the Similitude of a Dream. Wherein Is Discovered, the Manner of His Setting Out; His Dangerous Journey, and Safe Arrival at the Desired Country.* [London: J. Haddon, Castle Street, Finsbury, 1847]). See also "The Fight and the Weapons" (Notebook 1, Sermon 37a) and "The Fight" (Notebook 1, Sermon 37b).

34. The number 234 is smeared toward the left side of the page.

156.　　　　John XIII. 4. 5.　　The washing of the disciples feet by Jesus.

It may be useful to give some account of the passover.

1. The males in the house, met, reclined, took a cup of wine & then ate the pascal lamb, each must eat to the size of an olive.

2. They washed their feet, reclined & ate bitter herbs & a sauce in which Jesus dipped the sop — this reminded them of the mud of the bricks since it was of the same consistency. Another cup of wine & one half the bread was consumed.

3. Then the rest of the bread, some one asked the meaning & another cup was drank --

4. The fourth cup & the singing of the 113 to 118 psalms. This was the Hallelujah. So Jesus reclining took one cup & gave to them to drink not tasting it himself — see Luke. XXII. 15. the lamb was eaten & so the first course was concluded

2. Jesus going round washes the feet of all, made allusion to Judas " not all" — cautioned all & especially Peter then gave Judas the sop — wine &c consumed.

3. Jesus took the reserved portion of bread & the cup of wine & celebrated his own supper.

4. The Hymn or psalms were sung.

Now one great act in this was the washing of feet which followed the eating of the lamb.

Let us admire two things & learn two things.

I. Admire. Jesus constant love.

Here was the constancy of his love. He loved to the end. In this last hour, when moments were as pearls he was found washing their feet. He remembered

156

THE WASHING *of the* DISCIPLES' FEET *by* JESUS
John 13:4–5[1]

"He riseth from supper, and laid aside his garments; and took a towel, and girded himself. After that he poureth water into a bason, and began to wash the disciples' feet, and to wipe them with the towel wherewith he was girded."

It may be useful to give some account of the passover.[2]

I.[3] The males in the house met, reclined, took a cup of wine, and then ate the pascal lamb. Each must eat to –– the size of an olive.

|2|. They washed their feet, reclined, and ate bitter herbs and a sauce in which Jesus dipped the sop. This reminded them of the mud of the bricks since it was of the same consistency.[4] Another cup of wine and one half [of] the bread was consumed.[5]

③ Then the rest of the bread. Someone asked the meaning and another cup was drank.

4. The fourth cup and the singing of the 113 to 118 Psalms. This was the Hallelujah.[6]

I. So Jesus, reclining, took one cup and gave [it] to them to drink, not tasting it himself. See Luke –– XXII.15.[7] The lamb was eaten, and so the first course was concluded.

|2|. Jesus, going round, washes the feet of all. Made allusion to Judas, "not all,"[8] cautioned all, and especially Peter,[9] then gave Judas the sop.[10] Wine, etc., [was] consumed.

③ Jesus took the reserved portion of bread and the cup of wine and celebrated his own supper.

4. The Hymn or Psalms were sung.

Now, one great act in this was the washing of feet which followed the eating of the lamb. Let us admire two[11] things and learn two things:

I. ADMIRE JESUS'S CONSTANT LOVE.

Here was the constancy of his love. He loved to the end.[12] In this last hour when moments were as pearls,[13] he was found washing their feet. He remembered their ignorance, unbelief, & sin, he perceived their desire of preeminence, he foresaw their cowardice, in some apostacy & fall but yet he loved them even so as to wash their feet. They once found fault of the precious ointment on his head & had not washed his feet as Magdalen but see he washes them ah! constant love. See too the intensity of love that he could stoop to anything for them. He foresaw his death & agonies, he had need of rest but he rested not. Admire ye now. He washed their feet.

II. Admire. Jesus' condescension.

The Master washed his disciples feet. The Holy washed the vile. The Maker washed the created. His upper garbs all cast aside, (to teach us to lay aside every weight), he girds the menial towel on him, goes through all the operations. Like Peter we feel all astonishment. The more we reverence the more we admire.

But what is this to his greater humiliation when rising from the bosom of his father, he cast his robes of glory away & begirt himself with our poor garment, the servants towel of our nature. Pierced his own veins to find a liquid to wash our filthy feet with, the feet of sinners of the vilest dye.

Admire when you remember.

1. That among the Jews none but the meanest servants did it.
2. That he washed the feet of those who should have washed his.
3. That he put on a servants' garb to do it in.
4. He left supper to do it, though he would not leave off preaching to please either father, mother, or brethren.

Admire! Admire!! Jesus the servant of servants.

their ignorance, unbelief, and sin. He perceived[14] their desire of preeminence.[15] He foresaw their cowardice. In some, apostasy and fall.[16] But yet, he loved them even so as to wash their feet.

They once found fault of the precious ointment on his head and had not washed his feet as Magdalene.[17] But see, he washes them. Ah! Constant love.[18] See too the intensity of love that he could stoop to anything for them. He foresaw his death and agonies. He had need of rest, but he rested not. Admire ye, now. He washed their feet.

II. ADMIRE JESUS'S CONDESCENSION.

The Master washed his disciples' feet. The Holy washed the vile. The Maker washed the created. His upper garbs all cast aside (to teach us to lay aside every weight),[19] he girds the menial[20] towel on him, goes through all the operations. Like Peter, we feel all astonishment.[21] The more we reverence, the more we admire.[22]

But what is this to his greater humiliation? When rising from the bosom of his father, he cast his robes of glory away and begirt[23] himself with our poor garment, the servant's towel of our nature.[24] [He] pierced his own veins to find a liquid to wash our filthy feet with,[25] the feet of sinners of the vilest dye.

Admire when you remember:

1. That among the Jews, none[26] but the meanest servants did it.[27]

2. That he washed the feet[28] of those who should have washed his.[29]

3. That he put on a servant's garb to do it in.

4. He left supper to do it, though he would not leave off preaching to please either father, mother, or brethren.

Admire! Admire!! Jesus, the servant of servants.

Now God the Holy Spirit help us to learn two thing
I. Learn. That we have need of washing.
This was a sign of the inward washing, the sign
itself did not save for Judas perished, — but yet the
sign must not be omitted said Jesus to Peter.
Let us notice Peter.
1. He is surprised & so are we all at Jesus first actions of love.
2. Jesus tells him he would understand one day.
3. Peter now sets up for wiser than his master & again
refuses, let us not by mock humility lose real benefits.
4. Jesus deigns to reason with him & tells him that
"If I wash thee not thou hast no part in me". Peter's soul must
be truly washed or else he must perish.
5. Peter changes his mind & cuts "never" out — & now
desires complete sanctification all at once — pure
doctrine, unalloyed faith & good conduct.
6. Jesus tells him "you have once bathed in my
blood & you are clean you are perfectly justified
but walking but a little way defiles your feet & you
want to have them often washed, Daily pardon
goes with complete justification
Ah we may well learn this — we want washing
bad enough. Lord ! wash us all —
II. Learn. That we should be very humble.
We must imitate him in spirit, though the form is
not needed — 1 Humble condescension is taught
us, our stoops are nothing — we are not high enough
to call our stoop anything. Humility is rare though
let us cultivate it & try to bow for that is to rise,

Now, God the Holy Spirit, help us to learn two thing[s]:

I. LEARN THAT WE HAVE NEED OF WASHING.

This was a sign of the inward washing. The sign itself did not save, for Judas perished. But yet, the sign must not be omitted, said Jesus to Peter.

Let us notice Peter.

1. He is surprised,[30] and so are we all at Jesus's first actions of love.[31]

2. Jesus tells him he would understand one day.[32]

3. Peter now sets up for wiser than his master,[33] and again refuses. Let us not by mock humility lose real benefits.

4. Jesus deigns to reason with him and tells him that "If I wash thee not, thou[34] hast no part in me."[35] Peter's soul must be truly washed or else he must perish.

5. Peter changes his mind and cuts "never" out and now desires complete sanctification all at once, pure doctrine, unalloyed faith, and good conduct.

6. Jesus tells him, "You have once bathed[36] in my blood and you are clean. You are perfectly justified. But walking but a little way defiles your feet and you want to have them often washed.["] Daily pardon goes with complete justification.

Ah, we may well learn this. We want washing bad enough. Lord! Wash us all.

II. LEARN THAT WE SHOULD BE VERY HUMBLE.

We must imitate him in spirit, though the form is not needed.

1. Humble condescension is taught [to] us. Our stoops are nothing. We are not high enough to call our stoop anything. Humility is rare, though let us cultivate it and try to bow, for that is to rise.

2 . Our condescn should be for some end & ~~service~~. Love to the saints & desire to do them service should be our aim . Each bow to each . For there is no authority among us **All we are brethren .**

3 . We should humbly seek the sanctification of our brethren this should be our constant aim .

Is this hard for thee to do brother? why? Is it not because thy proud heart rebels? Go tell thy Lord & 'ere thou come to his table, resolve to wash thy brothers feet, or do anything however lowly.

We invite none to enter our fellowship who desire preeminence, or who will not wash feet On the other hand we desire to do the same for him

God wash us & give us part in his Son.

235.

---

157 . Mark . VII . 37 . He hath done all things well.

What the disciples & bystanders said of Jesus when they saw his miracles . we too may say reviewing all his acts —

1 . When he covenanted with his Father - it was well.

2 . When he lived & went about doing good, it was well

3 . When he made full atonement by his death - all is well.

4 . Now he sits to intercede - all is well.

5 . When he regenerates a soul. It is well.

6 . When he causes it to persevere. It is well.

7 . When all shall meet in heaven & the Father, man, the angels - God shall all be reconciled & all satisfied all will be well. God bless his Kingdom & may he work on us.

236

2. Our condescension[37] should be for some end and service.[38] Love to the saints and desire to do them service should be our aim.[39] Each bow[s] to each.[40] For there is no authority among us.[41] **All we are brethren.**

3. We should[42] humbly seek the sanctification of our brethren. This should be our constant aim.[43]

Is this hard for thee to do, brother? Why? Is it not because thy proud heart rebels? Go tell thy Lord and 'ere[44] thou come to his table, resolve to wash thy brothers['][45] feet or do anything, however lowly.[46]

We invite none to enter our fellowship who desire preeminence or who will not wash feet. On the other hand, we desire to do the same for him.

God, wash us and give us part in his son.[47]

Amen

235.

HE HATH DONE ALL THINGS WELL

Mark[1] *7:37*[2]

"And were beyond measure astonished, saying, He hath done all things well: he maketh both the deaf to hear, and the dumb to speak."

What the disciples and bystanders said of Jesus when they saw his miracles, we too may say, reviewing all his acts.

1. When he covenanted with his Father. It was well.
2. When he lived and went about doing good. It was well.
3. When he made full atonement by his death.[3] All is well.
4. Now he sits to intercede.[4] All is well.
5. When he regenerates a soul.[5] It is well.
6. When he causes it to persevere.[6] It is well.
7. When all shall meet in heaven and the Father, man, the angels, [and] God shall all be reconciled and all satisfied. All will be well. God bless his Kingdom and may he work on us.

236

1. On October 12, 1879, Charles preached a sermon on John 13:3–5 entitled "The Teaching of the Foot-Washing" (*MTP* 25, Sermon 1499). On January 29, 1865, he preached a sermon on the following verse, John 13:6, entitled "Jesus Washing His Disciples' Feet" (*MTP* 11, Sermon 612). Overlapping content is found in both sermons; however, Charles likely had the sermon in this notebook in mind when writing his 1865 sermon.

2. Charles's summary of the Passover meal was commonly known throughout the nineteenth century. See Philip Schaff, *The Oldest Church Manual Called the Teaching of the Twelve Apostles: The Didache and Kindred Documents in the Original with Translations and Discussions of Post-Apostolic Teaching, Baptism, Worship, and Discipline, and with Illustrations and Fac-similes of the Jerusalem Manuscript* (New York: Funk & Wagnalls, 1885, The Spurgeon Library), 58–59. See also C. and A. De Rothschild, *The History and Literature of the Israelites According to the Old Testament and the Apocrypha. Volume I. The Historical Books. With a Map of Palestine, and a Map Showing the Journeys of the Hebrews in the Desert. Second Edition* (London: Longmans, Green, and Co., 1871), 136–39.

3. Charles's unusual structuring of this page reflects his attempt at drawing a parallel between the events of Passover and John 13:4–5. The enclosed alphanumerics in the first four points (1. horizontal lines, 2. vertical lines, 3. encircled, and 4. horizontal lines) correspond to Jesus's actions in the following four points.

4. Cf. Exodus 5.

5. An illegible letter was written beneath the letter "o" in the word "consumed."

6. The handwriting of the sentence "This was the Hallelujah" differs from that in the body of the sermon and was likely added afterward.

7. Luke 22:15, "And he said unto them, With desire I have desired to eat this passover with you before I suffer."

8. John 13:18, "I speak not of you all: I know whom I have chosen: but that the scripture may be fulfilled, He that eateth bread with me hath lifted up his heel against me."

9. John 13:21, "When Jesus had thus said, he was troubled in spirit, and testified, and said, Verily, verily, I say unto you, that one of you shall betray me."

10. John 13:26, "Jesus answered, He it is, to whom I shall give a sop, when I have dipped it. And when he had dipped the sop, he gave it to Judas Iscariot, the son of Simon."

11. A partial fingerprint can be seen above the letter "o" in the word "two." The color of the partial fingerprint is identical in color and appearance to the ink on the page and likely belonged to Charles.

12. Cf. John 14:1–2.

13. "But behold your Lord and Master! It is eventide of the same night in which he was betrayed; he foreknows that the bloody sweat within an hour or two will crimson all his flesh; he is well aware that he who is eating bread with him will that night betray him; he foresees that he must feel the Roman scourge, and be the victim of Jewish slander; he knows right well that he must bear all the wrath of God on the behalf of his people; and yet he sits at supper, he feasts as if no unusual cloud were lowering; and when the supper is over, his inventive mind is fully at work with admirable plans of instruction for his disciples, and among the rest he takes off his upper garment, he wraps himself about the loins with a towel, he goes to them as they are reclining at full length around the table, and coming behind them he begins to wash the feet of first one and then another. What blessed calmness! What hallowed serenity of spirit! O that our hearts were equally fixed on God in our days of trial and grief!" (*MTP* 11:61).

14. Charles originally did not include the bowl of the letter "e" in the word "perceived." For similar occurrences of this tendency in this notebook, see "The Harvest and the Vintage" (Sermon 144).

15. Cf. Luke 22:24.   16. Cf. Luke 22:54–62; John 18:15–18.

17. Cf. Luke 7:37–38; John 11:2.

18. Cf. *MTP* 25:579–85.   19. Cf. Heb 12:1–2.

20. An illegible letter is written beneath the "m" in the word "menial."

21. Cf. John 13:8.

22. Given the lack of space in the margin, Charles wrote the final letters "re" beneath the word "admire."

23. "1. To bind with a girdle. 2. To surround; to encircle; to encompass. 3. To shut in with a siege; to beleaguer; to block up" (Johnson's *Dictionary*, s.v. "begirt").

24. Cf. Phil 2:7.

25. "He *has* washed all believers, once for all, in his most precious blood. . . . Cleansing, as before the bar of justice, is completely accomplished for ever for all the chosen by the great blood-shedding upon Calvary" (*MTP* 11:62, italics in the original).

26. Charles originally wrote the word "not" before adding the letters "ne" to construct the word "none."

27. "The foot of the meanest servant of Christ is more honourable than the head of the greatest emporer that ever wore a diadem" (*MTP* 25:588).

28. "Lord, dost thou wash my *feet*? To wash my head, Lord, is very gracious; to purge my mind from evil thoughts is very loving; to wash my hands, to take my heart and make that clean is very condescending; but dost thou absolutely do a slave's work, and wash my *feet*? Lord, wilt thou take the meanest part of me, and wash *that?*" (*MTP* 11:67, italics in the original).

29. "The Lord Jesus loves his people so, that every day he is washing their feet. Their poorest action he accepts; their deepest sorrow he feels; their slenderest wish he hears, and their greatest sin he forgives. He is still their servant as well as their friend; still he takes the basin; still he wears the towel" (*MTP* 11:65). Cf. Rom 8:34; Heb 7:25.

30. "He might have left them to wash one another's feet, might he not? Surely he had but to suggest it and they would have cheerfully waited on each other. Peter, at any rate, would have been first to obey, and to his Lord's command he would have replied, 'Wash them? That I will, with delight.' But no; the Lord laid aside his own garments and took a towel, and himself performed the kindly deed for them" (*MTP* 25:580).

31. "He must first wash our feet before we can wash one another's feet. I think I see the Well-beloved now as he pours the pure water on their ancles! Mark how he

takes their feet into his kind and tender hands, and washes them clean, and then wipes them with the towel! He continues to do this to us even now in a spiritual sense. It is his own dear love that takes away sin from the conscience, so that it does not linger there to foul and mar it" (*MTP* 25:585).

32. Cf. John 21:18.

33. An alternative reading of this phrase is "Peter now sets up [to be] wiser than his [M]aster." Cf. John 13:16.

34. Charles struck through the final illegible letter after the "o" in the word "thou." He may have accidently begun writing the word "though."

35. John 13:8, "Peter saith unto him, Thou shalt never wash my feet. Jesus answered him, If I wash thee not, thou hast no part with me."

36. A dark yellow stain, likely the result of the aging process of the manuscript, appears beneath the word "bathed."

37. Charles originally spelled the word "condescion."

38. Charles reinforced the letters "rv" in the word "service." Either he misspelled the word or wrote another word beneath it. The former interpretation is more likely.

39. "In the world they criticise; this is the business of the public press, and it is very much the business of private circles. Hear how gossips say, 'Do you see that spot? What a terrible walk that man must have had this morning: look at his feet! He has been very much in the mire you can see, for there are the traces upon him.' That is the world's way. Christ's way is very different. He says nothing, but takes the basin and begins to wash away the stain" (*MTP* 25:586).

40. An alternative reading of this sentence is "Each [must] bow to each."

41. Cf. Rom 13:1.

42. Charles originally spelled the word "shoud" before inserting the letter "l" above to construct the word "should." Charles indicated the position of the letter "l" with a caret beneath and between the letters "u" and "d."

43. "Let us be always on bended knee with the basin and the towel near at hand; let us be willing to relieve those who are in need, to restore those who stumble, to reclaim those who wander, and to edify and perfect all the body of Christ as far as our ability will permit. . . . You say it is the pastor's business to look after the church. I know it is, but the true pastor's wisdom is to set the members of the church looking after one another" (*MTP* 25:588).

44. The word "'ere" means "before." For an additional use of this word in this note-book, see "Boast Not Thyself of To-morrow" (Sermon 150).

45. As in the word "Disciples" in the title of this sermon, Charles did not include an apostrophe at the end of the word "brothers" to indicate possession. Did he intend singular or plural possession? The biblical text suggests the latter inter-pretation is correct.

46. "Let us be also ready to perform any office for our brethren, however lowly. If there is a position in the church where the worker will have to toil hard and get no thanks for it, take it, and be pleased with it. If you can perform a service which few will ever seek to do themselves, or appreciate when performed by others, yet occupy it with holy delight. Covet humble work, and when you get it be content to continue in it. There is no great rush after the lowest places, you will rob no one by seeking them" (*MTP* 25:587).

47. The use of the pronoun "his" and not "your" suggests, unlike as in many of his ser-mons, Charles was not offering a prayer at the end of this sermon. An alternative translation of this line is "God [will] wash us and give us part in his son."

1. A dark stain, likely the result of the aging process of the manuscript, appears above the letter "M" in the word "Mark."

2. This is the only time Charles preached a sermon on Mark 7:37.

3. Cf. Rom 3:25.

4. It appears Charles added the letter "s" to the end of the word "intercede" before striking through it. Cf. Rom 8:34; Heb 7:25; 1 John 2:1.

5. Cf. John 3:3; Col 2:13.

6. See "Final Perseverance Certain" (Notebook 2, Sermon 82).

158. Matt X. 32. 33. Open profession required

In this chapter our Saviour before sending out the twelve gave them information as to what they must expect from the world & what he expected of them.

They would receive hatred & persecution, but yet ever must they show, zeal, boldness & an open confession.

May God help me to note & explain.

I. The great duty of open confession.

II. The great sin of denying Christ.

In these words we say that Christ teaches & promises a reward those who practise the great duty.

I The Great duty of open profession.

1 How is this to be done? In Christ's day the disciples were surrounded by idolaters — & by ceasing to frequent the temples, by meeting on the first day of the week, by uniting with the Christians & going even to prison they would make a very clear profession of faith.

In heathen & Catholic countries it is to be done in a somewhat similar manner. But a few years since, the simple entering of a conventicle, absence from Church & rigid piety was true confession

Now we are surrounded by formalists & nominal Protestant Christians — we must come out in some way.

By siding ever with religion, by joining a Christian Church, submission to the ordinances & by a bold avowal of the name of Christ ......

2. Is it certainly a duty — Is it not taught now in the text. is it not in Rom. 10. 9. 10 — In those days

210

158

OPEN PROFESSION REQUIRED
Matthew 10:32–33[1]

"Whosoever therefore shall confess me before men, him will I confess also before my Father which is in heaven. But whosoever shall deny me before men, him will I also deny before my Father which is in heaven."

In this chapter, our Saviour, before sending out the twelve, gave them information as to what they must expect from the world and what he expected of them. They would receive hatred and persecution,[2] but yet ever must they show zeal, boldness, and an open confession.

May God help me to note and explain:

I.   THE GREAT DUTY OF OPEN CONFESSION.

II. THE GREAT SIN OF DENYING CHRIST.

In these words, we say that Christ teaches and promises a reward [to] those who practise ~~the great duty~~.[3]

I.   THE GREAT DUTY OF OPEN PROFESSION.

1.[4] How is this to be done? In Christ's day, the disciples were surrounded by idolaters. And by ceasing to frequent the temples, by meeting on the first day of the week, by uniting with the Christians and going even to prison, they would make a very clear profession of faith.

In heathen and Catholic countries, it is to be done in a somewhat similar manner. But a few years since, the simple entering of a conventicle,[5] absence from Church, and rigid piety was true confession.

Now we are surrounded by formalists[6] and nominal Protestant Christians. We must come out in some way. By siding ever with religion, by joining a Christian Church, submission to the ordinances,[7] and by a bold avowal of the name of Christ.[8]

2. Is it certainly a duty? Is it not taught now in the text? Is it not in Rom. 10.9.10?[9] In those days,

as soon as a man professed it. He lost his position in society, the love of his friends & the protection of the laws and became the object of hatred, persecution, suffering contempt & death — Surely unless this were a very important thing Jesus would have exempted his servants at that time & since he did not — it is far more our duty. It is certainly every man's duty.

3. Why did Jesus command this? Man should not get into a habit of enquiring the "why" & "wherefore" of a plain and positive command — let them rather obey but yet God condescends to let us look & we see.

1. Jesus did not intend his dominion to be secret. it is light & works by open declaration: his empire should be seen.

2. Jesus wants none but those who love with their whole hearts & whosoever does not confess — loves but little.

3. Jesus is worthy of all our faith & by this he tries whether we dare trust ourselves with him.

4. Jesus loves to comfort his church & ministers by letting them see an increase & therefore it is public.

4. What good does an open profession bring?

1. Admission to the ordinances.
2. The more confident intercourse of saints.
3. It often acts as a gracious restraint from sin.
4. It acts as an holy incentive to virtue.

— I hope now to answer a few objections.

1. I am not fit — but what do you mean by this. Are you no Christian? — then sad is your lot. But if you love Christ. then you must come at once.

as soon as a man professed it he lost his position in society, the love of his friends, and the protection of the laws and became the object of hatred, persecution, suffering, contempt, and death. Surely, unless this were a very important thing Jesus would have exempted his servants at that time. And since he did not, it is far more our duty. It is certainly every man's duty.

3. Why did Jesus command this? Man should not get into a habit of enquiring the "why" and "wherefore" of a plain and positive command. Let them rather obey. But yet, God condescends to let us look and we see:

   1. Jesus did not intend his dominion to be secret. It is light[10] and works by open declaration. His empire should be seen.[11]

   2. Jesus wants none but those who love with their whole hearts[12] and whosoever does not confess, loves but little.

   3. Jesus is worthy of all our faith and by this he tries whether we dare trust ourselves with him.

   4. Jesus loves to comfort his church and ministers by letting them see an increase, and therefore it is public.

4. What good does an open profession bring?

   1. Admission to the ordinances.[13]

   2. The more confident intercourse of saints.[14]

   3. It often acts as a gracious restraint from sin.[15]

   4. It acts as an holy incentive to virtue.

—I HOPE NOW TO ANSWER A FEW OBJECTIONS.[16]

   1. I am not fit. But what do you mean by this? Are you no Christian? Then sad is your lot. But if you love Christ then you must come at once.

2. I fear I shall fall.   And can you not fall now?
Are you more safe in disobeying God than in obeying
his divine law. Can you not trust his grace &
care — this fear is good but not if it keeps you from duty.
3. I shall be so much watched by the world. Well
so much the better — they watch you now, — you must
walk so as not to be ashamed or afraid — thus
it will do you good to be watched.

     Now I will guess at a few reasons why you hold back.
1. You may be unbelieving & distrust God's power.
2. You may be cowardly & afraid of man
3. You have pride & think you know better than God.
4. You are worldly & afraid we shall reject you.
5. You do many wrong things which a confession
    would compel you to renounce.
Look at the reward which is all of grace
    Christ will confess our name at last.
     Now let us notice
II. The great sin of denying Christ
which may be done.
1. Orally when men renounced Christ by words
from fear of death — when men declare in company
that they are no Christians.
2. Doctrinally — when by erroneous views we
reject the true gospel. Socinians do so.

2. I fear I shall fall. And can you not fall now? Are you more safe in disobeying God than in obeying his divine law? Can you not trust his grace and care? This fear is good, but not if it keeps you from duty.

3. I shall be so much watched by the world. Well, so much the better. They watch you now. You must walk so as not to be ashamed[17] or afraid. Thus it will do you good to be watched.

Now I will guess at a few reasons why you hold back.

1. You may be unbelieving and distrust God's power.[18]

2. You may be cowardly and afraid of man.[19]

3. You have pride and think you know better than God.

4. You[20] are worldly and afraid we shall reject you.

5. You do many wrong things which a confession would compel you to renounce.

Look at the reward which is all of grace.[21] Christ will confess our name at last.

Now let us notice:

II. THE GREAT SIN OF DENYING CHRIST, WHICH MAY BE DONE:

1. Orally, when men renounced Christ by words from fear of death when men declare in company that they are no Christians.

2. Doctrinally, when by erroneous views we reject the true gospel. Socinians[22] do so.

We must be careful that in nothing we deny any one
of the great doctrines of grace – lest wrath come on us.
3. vitally – by a licentious & ungodly life – for this
is one of the worst ways of denying him & if we
do this no open profession in any other way will
be of the least value in God's sight.
Repent, believe, & confess Christ then will
he confess thee — but if thou refuse & thus
deny him, he will also deny thee.

238   God my Father help me I entreat thee

Jer. XII. 5 — If the footmen weary thee &c.   159
Jeremiah had received a message from God to the men
of Anathoth where he lived & though he knew a prophet
could gain no honour in his own country, off he went.
     The men of Anathoth, told him to hold his tongue
or it would be worse for him & he should die.
He as a true prophet goes to tell his master. He
confesses that God is just, but wonders at the prosperity
of the wicked & laments the continual barrenness
of the land. There was in this a slight tinge
of self & peevishness & therefore our blessed God
gives him a little stir by informing him that
he had greater work to do yet. I have chosen
you to be a perpetual monitor of this people

We must be careful that in nothing we deny any one of the great doctrines of grace[23] lest wrath come on us.

3. Vitally, by a licentious and ungodly life. For this is one of the worst ways of denying him, and if we do this no open profession in any other way will be of the least value in God's sight.

Repent, believe, and confess Christ. Then will he confess thee. But if thou refuse and thus deny him, he will also deny thee.[24]

God, my Father, help me, I entreat thee.

238

IF *the* FOOTMEN
WEARY THEE, ETC.
Jeremiah 12:5[1]

"If thou hast run with the footmen, and they have wearied thee, then how canst thou contend with horses? and if in the land of peace, wherein thou trustedst, they wearied thee, then how wilt thou do in the swelling of Jordan?"

Jeremiah had received a message from God to the men of Anathoth[2] where he lived, and though he knew a prophet could gain no honour in his own country, off he went.

The men of Anathoth told him to hold his tongue or it would be worse for him and he should die.[3] He, as a true prophet, goes to tell his master. He confesses that God is just,[4] but wonders at the prosperity of the wicked and laments the continual barrenness of the land.[5] There was in this a slight tinge of self and peevishness, and therefore our blessed God gives him[6] a little stir by informing him that he had greater work to do yet. "I have chosen you to be a perpetual monitor of this people.

why then are you weary at all past repulses.
I shall use the words & by ministerial license
apply them to purposes more wide than their original
aim . I shall address & may God help me.

I. The people of God.

1. As they are engaged in duty. in endeavouring
to do good . Do you find men's hearts hard?
Are your children obstinate? Your hearers careless?
Are you dispirited? Why? — Did not Jesus
bear even more than you? Your works are little
Insignificant. At them again with fresh heart.

Are you but little improving your talents
Do not expect more. If you cannot keep pace
with footmen ask not for horses. You will not
do for a Missionary, or martyr, or even minister.

2. As they are subject to ~~trials~~ Conflicts.

From the world — Laughs & jeers come on us but
what are these to the sufferings of the early saints.
From Satan's attack. We fear even little brushes
what shall we do in close conflict.
From our evil hearts. Some young ones are
terrified at a little cart-rut — what do you think
of rivers. You will have worse conflicts
Go at these minor ones — so shall you gain
strength for the greater.

Why, then, are you weary at all past repulses?["]

I shall use the words and by ministerial license apply them to purposes more wide than their original aim. I shall address, and may God help me,

I.   THE PEOPLE OF GOD.

1. As they are engaged in duty in endeavouring to do good. Do you find men's hearts hard? Are your children obstinate? Your hearers careless? Are you dispirited? Why? Did not Jesus bear even more than you? Your works are little, insignificant. At them again with fresh heart.[7]

    Are you but little improving your talents?[8] Do not expect more. If you cannot keep pace with footmen, ask not for horses. You will not do for a Missionary, or martyr, or even minister.

2. As they are subject to ~~trials~~ conflicts:

    From the world. Laughs and jeers come on us.[9] But what are these [compared] to the sufferings of the early saints?

    From Satan's attack. We fear even little brushes. What shall we do in close conflict?

    From our evil hearts. Some young ones are terrified at a little cart rut.[10] What do you think of rivers? You will have worse conflicts.

    Go at these minor ones. So shall you gain strength for the greater.

3 . As they endure sufferings .

we expect troubles & shall not be disappointed but we must not cower at trifles — for ours are light compared with those of many — & very little compared with those we must suffer at death . Therefore endure to the end . For suffering is the path to glory .

II . To the ungodly .

1 . Some of you have a hope of heaven — a false one you have some fears now — what! It will not stand even times of peace, what? will you do at death.

2 . Some of you find that the pleasure of this world is imperfect — You are not happy now what will you be soon? and at death .

3 . Some of you are fearful & a little thought a minister's words, a poor creatures reproof terrifies you — how will you stand God?

4 . Some of you have many troubles even now what will you do at Jordan's swelling

5 . You cannot keep yourself one day — how can you work your salvation by your own arm.

How wilt thou do in the swelling of Jordan.

It must come . Oh poor soul . prepare .

Awake . God help thee & me —

amen

239

3. As they endure sufferings. We expect troubles[11] and shall not be disappointed. But we must not cower at trifles, for ours are light compared with those of many and very little compared with those we must suffer at death.[12] Therefore, endure to the end,[13] for suffering is the path to glory.[14]

II. TO THE UNGODLY.

1. Some of you have a hope of heaven, a false one. You have some fears now. What! It will not stand even [in] times of peace. What will you do at death?

2. Some of you find that the pleasure of this world is imperfect. You are not happy now. What will you be soon? And at death.[15]

3. Some of you are fearful and a little thought [of] a minister's words, a poor creature's reproof terrifies you. How will you stand God?[16]

4. Some of you have many troubles even now. What will you do at Jordan's swellings?[17]

5. You cannot keep yourself one day. How can you work your salvation by your own arm?

How[18] wilt thou do in the swelling of Jordan?

It must come.[19] Oh poor soul, prepare.

Awake. God help thee and me.[20]

<u>Amen</u>

239

1. On March 21, 1868, Charles preached an additional sermon on Matt 10:32–33 entitled "Confession to Christ" (*MTP* 60, Sermon 3405). There is enough overlapping content between the two sermons to suggest Charles may have had his early sermon in mind when preaching his 1868 sermon.

2. Cf. Matt 10:16–18.

3. Charles struck through the words "the great duty" likely because he intended to include this content in his first primary division instead.

4. Given its location in the margin, Charles likely wrote the number 1 after penning the following line.

5. "1. An assembly; a meeting. 2. An assembly for worship, generally used in an ill sense, including heresy or schism. 3. A secret assembly; an assembly where conspiracies are formed. 4. An assembly, in contempt" (Johnson's *Dictionary*, s.v. "conventicle").

6. See "The Wrong Roads" (Notebook 1, Sermon 32).

7. See "God's Estimation of Men" (Notebook 1, Sermon 41).

8. Charles inserted seven periods after the word "Christ."

9. Romans 10:9–10, "That if thou shalt confess with thy mouth the Lord Jesus, and shalt believe in thine heart that God hath raised him from the dead, thou shalt be saved. For with the heart man believeth unto righteousness; and with the mouth confession is made unto salvation."

10. Cf. *MTP* 60:223; Matt 5:14–16.

11. "Our religion is not a thing of churches, and Sundays, and Good Fridays, and Easters, and Christmasses, and I do not know what besides. It is a thing of everyday life, for the kitchen and the parlour, the office and factory, the court of justice, the Houses of Parliament. It intertwists itself with all the rootlets of our inner nature, and comes out in all our actions of outward behavior and conversation. Hence, to hide it is impossible" (*MTP* 60:223).

12. Cf. Matt 22:37; Mark 12:30; Luke 10:27.

13. "If you do not love him, he has never washed you from your sins; if he is not your Saviour, if you have never been born again, if you are not truly his servant in the name of God, do not touch baptism, or his Supper; never come to the Communion Table if you have no right there; profess not to be a Christian if you are not; and say not, 'Our Father who art in heaven,' for your Father is not in heaven; you have no part or lot in this matter, you are in the gall of bitterness and bond of iniquity; and, harsh as the words may sound, these words are true, 'Repent, and be converted' that ye may obtain these blessings. Fly to Christ, and trust in him, for until you do you have no right to the ordinances of God's house" (*MTP* 60:225–26).

14. "Unite yourselves with God's people wherever you may find them. Cast in your lot with the lovers of Jesus in whatever Christian denomination you may happen to meet with them" (*MTP* 60:228).

15. "If grace does not make you to differ from your own surroundings, is it really grace at all? Where there is not a thorough separation from the world, there is cause to fear there is no close union to Christ. The best part of our confession to Christ lies in the practically giving up everything which Christ would not sanction, and the following out of whatever Christ would ordain" (*MTP* 60:221).

16. As in his sermons "Boast Not Thyself of To-morrow" (Sermon 150) and "The Call of Abraham" (Sermon 152), Charles inserts a marginal line to begin objections to his argument.

17. "To be ashamed to own yourself a Christian, ah! then Christianity may well be ashamed of you" (*MTP* 60:222).

18. Cf. Mark 12:24.   19.   Cf. Matt 10:28.

20. An accidental stippling of ink appears before the word "You."

21. See "Wise Men and Fools" (Notebook 2, Sermon 111).

22. For a previous reference to Socinians in this notebook, see "Zeal in Religion Commended" (Sermon 154).

23. See "Expositions of the Doctrines of Grace" (*MTP* 7, Sermon 385).

24. Matthew 10:33, "But whosoever shall deny me before men, him will I also deny before my Father which is in heaven."

1. Charles preached an additional sermon on Jer 12:5 entitled "Are You Prepared to Die?" (*MTP* 11, Sermon 635). There is not enough overlapping content to suggest Charles had in mind his early sermon in the preaching of his later one.

2. Anathoth, the Levite city in the tribe of Benjamin, was the hometown of Jeremiah. Cf. Josh 21:18; 1 Chr 6:60; Jer 1:1.

3. Cf. Jer 11:18–21.   4.   Cf. Jer 12:1.

5. Cf. Jer 12:2–4.

6. Charles originally wrote the first three letters of the word "lit" before changing it to the word "him." He was likely spelling the word "little," as he did two words later.

7. An alternative reading of this line is "[Get] at them again with fresh heart."

8. Cf. Matt 25:14–30; Luke 19:12–28.

9. "I do not believe that any preacher will be long in his pulpit without having the temptation to be afraid of some man or another; and if he doth not stand very firmly upon his integrity he will find some of the best of his friends getting the upper hand with him. And this will never do with God's minister. He must deal out God's Word impartially to rich or poor, to good or bad; and he must determine to have no master except his Master who is in heaven; no bit nor bridle for his mouth, except that of prudence and discretion, which God himself shall put there. For if we are afraid of a man that shall die, and the son of man that is crushed before the moth, how fearful shall we be when we have to talk with the grim king of terrors! If we are afraid of puny man, how shall we be able to face it out before the dread ordeal of the day of judgment? Yet I know some Christians that are very much abashed by the world's opinion, by the opinion of their family circle, or of the workshop" (*MTP* 11:340).

10. In rural Cambridgeshire, ruts were formed in the roads by the wheels of horse-drawn carts and buggies as they "made regular trips hauling goods to market and parcels back" (Sally Mitchell, *Daily Life in Victorian England* in Daily Life Through History Series [Westport, CT; London: Greenwood Press, 1996], 129–30). Often, deep road ruts were frozen in winter, as Michelle Higgs posits: "There

is a different hazard for horses during harsh winters as there are deep, frozen ruts made by the wheels of carts, carriages and omnibuses which scar the roads, rendering them dangerous and often impassable" (Michelle Higgs, *A Visitor's Guide to Victorian England* [Barnsley, South Yorkshire, UK: Pen & Sword Books Ltd, 2014], 9). In 1851, only months before Charles preached the sermon above, a one-year-old named Elizabeth Calah was sitting in a rut on the road and was run over by a passing cart ("Inquest at the General Hospital," *Nottingham Review and General Advertiser for the Midland Counties*, March 14, 1851).

11. Cf. John 16:33; Acts 14:22.

12. "Well, then, as I cannot tell in what physical state I may be when I come to die, I just tried to think again, how shall I do in the swelling of Jordan? I hope I shall do as others have done before me, who have built on the same rock, and had the same promises to be their succour. They cried, 'Victory!' So shall I, and after that die quietly and in peace. If the same transporting scene may not be mine, I will at least lay my head upon my Saviour's bosom, and breathe my life out gently there" (*MTP* 11:344). With his wife by his side, Charles died at the Hotel Beau Rivage in Menton, France, at 11:05 PM on Sunday, January 31, 1892, at the age of fifty-seven after falling asleep (*Autobiography* 4:371).

13. Cf. Matt 24:13.   14.   Cf. Phil 3:10.

15. Charles may have intended the phrase "And at death?" to be a question.

16. A modern translation of these lines is "Some of you are fearful. [It only takes] a little thought [of] a minister's words—a poor creature's reproof—[to terrify] you. How will you stand [before] God?"

17. "We all come into the world one by one, and will go out of it also alone" (*MTP* 11:338). Cf. Joshua 3.

18. Charles originally wrote the first two strokes of Roman numeral III before converting the II to the letter "H."

19. "In a little while, there will be a great concourse of people in the streets. Methinks I hear someone enquiring, 'What are all these people waiting for?' 'Do you not know? He is to be buried to-day.' 'And who is that?' 'It is Spurgeon.' 'What!

the man that preached at the Tabernacle?' 'Yes; he is to be buried to-day.' That will happen very soon; and when you see my coffin carried to the silent grave, I should like every one of you, whether converted or not, to be constrained to say, 'He did earnestly urge us, in plain and simple language, not to put off the consideration of eternal things. He did entreat us to look at Christ,'" (*MTP* 49:600).

20. A scribble appears after the word "me" and above "amen." The significance of this scribble is unclear.

160.   Ps. 119. 72 .   The word very precious .

David in common with all holy men much loved
the Bible & wrote this long Psalm upon it.
Probably it was the only book extant.

I. The bible is intrinsically precious.
    as a book.
    1. It is the most ancient book.
    2. It is the only perfect book
    3. It is the most understandable of books.

As   God's book.
    1. It is the only revalation.
    2. It contains a perfect code of law.
    3. The grand secret even Salvation .

II. The Bible is much more precious than gold.
    1. For gold has but a value in certain circumstances
    2. Gold may leave us or we must leave it.
    3. Gold cannot calm the conscience, or lead to Jesus
    4. Gold never satisfies .

III, It should be precious to us, personally.
    David tried gold & the bible too & in his
experience, the Bible was the best.
    It showed him his sin. led him to Jesus.
helped him to fight & conquer. relieved him in
distress — pardoned his guilt. Kept him to the end
    Love the Bible — tis the field of hidden pearls.
count out its thousands & remember Christ is its
    substance.
                — 242 —

160

THE WORD VERY PRECIOUS
Psalm 119:72[1]

"The law of thy mouth is better unto me than thousands of gold and silver."

David, in common with all holy men, much loved the Bible and wrote this long Psalm upon it.

Probably, it was the only book extant.

I. THE BIBLE IS INTRINSICALLY PRECIOUS.

As a book:

1. It is the most ancient book.

2. It is the only perfect book.

3. It is the most understandable of books.

As God's book:

1. It is the only revelation.[2]

2. It contains a perfect code of law.

3. The grand secret, even salvation.[3]

II. THE BIBLE IS MUCH MORE PRECIOUS THAN GOLD.[4]

1. For gold has but a value in certain circumstances.

2. Gold may leave us[5] or we must leave it.

3. Gold cannot calm the conscience or lead to Jesus.

4. Gold never satisfies.

III. IT SHOULD BE PRECIOUS TO US PERSONALLY.

David tried gold and the Bible too. And in his experience, the Bible was the best.

It showed him his sin, led him to Jesus, helped him to fight and conquer, relieved him in distress, pardoned his guilt, kept him to the end.

Love the Bible—[']tis the field of hidden pearls.[6] Count out its thousands and remember Christ is its substance.[7]

242.

1. This is the only time Charles preached a sermon on Ps 119:72. However, overlapping content is found in his commentary on this text in *The Treasury of David*, which is presented at length: "If a poor man had said this, the world's witlings would have hinted that the grapes are sour, and that men who have no wealth are the first to despise it; but this is the verdict of a man who owned his thousands, and could judge by actual experience of the value of money and the value of truth. He speaks of great riches, he heaps it up by thousands, he mentions the varieties of its forms,——'gold and silver'; and then he sets the word of God before it all, as better *to him*, even if others did not think it better to them. Wealth is good in some respects, but obedience is better in all respects. It is well to keep the treasures of this life; but far more commendable to keep the law of the Lord. The law is better than gold or silver, for these may be stolen from us, but not the word; these take to themselves wings, but the word of God remains; these are useless in the hour of death, but then it is that the promise is more dear. Instructed Christians recognize the value of the Lord's word, and warmly express it, not only in their testimony to their fellow-men, but in their devotions to God. It is a sure sign of a heart which has learned God's statutes when it prizes them above all earthly possessions; and it is an equally certain mark of grace when the precepts of Scripture are as precious as its promises. The Lord cause us thus to prize the law of his mouth" (*TD* 6:166, italics in the original).

2. Charles originally misspelled this word "revalation." The letter "e" was written in pencil above "a." The redaction was likely in the hand of Charles.

3. Cf. Eph 3:3; Col 1:26.

4. For a reference to the gold in India, see "Condescending Love of Jesus" (Notebook 1, Sermon 5).

5. An illegible pencil marking appears beneath the word "us." It has the same appearance as the letter "e" five lines above.

6. "All God's words in Scripture are pearls" (*MTP* 18:649). "Precious is this book, but its main preciousness lies in its revealing Jesus himself, it is the field which contains the pearl of great price, the casket which encloses heaven's brightest jewel" (*MTP* 23:690). "Now is the law of God indeed glorious, for it rules by love. It was terrible when written on those tablets of stone which Moses dashed

to pieces; but its radiance is like that of a pearl most precious, when it gently influences our manhood from the central throne of the heart" (*MTP* 34:62).

7. "Jesus Christ is the sum and substance of holy scripture" (*MTP* 31:583). The woman who anointed Christ's feet "may not have known much about the Bible, but she knew him who is the very sum and substance of the Bible" (*MTP* 48:126).

I. Tim. 1. 19. 20.   Making shipwreck of faith.   161

This verse has been often advanced by Arminians against the doctrine of final perseverance. — Some who love to take things for granted might slur their objection by forgetting that such a text existed — but this is far from being wise for then our opponents think that their argument is unanswerable, & we by neglecting to study the word begin to lean more on man's teaching than on God's word. We must learn to submit to God's word for one letter of that, is worth a volume either of Calvin or Arminius. Let us in coming to this verse regard it candidly. It is quite certain that it does not contradict other portions of the word of God. Now beyond all doubt I can prove final perseverance from many passages & if this should seem to lean against it — there are so many clearly for it — that I would think at once that I did not rightly understand it & look for a meaning agreeable with the rest of Scripture. But now let us come & the book being unsealed by the Spirit we notice the occasion Paul was giving a charge to young Timothy concerning strict adhesion to sound doctrine & also concerning certain upstart teachers who were loose in life & erroneous in doctrine. In this charge we see

$$161$$

MAKING[1] SHIPWRECK
of FAITH
1 Timothy 1:19–20[2]

"Holding faith, and a good conscience; which some having put away, concerning faith have made shipwreck: Of whom is Hymenæus and Alexander; whom I have delivered unto Satan, that they may learn not to blaspheme."

This verse has been often advanced by Arminians against the doctrines of final perseverance.[3] Some who love to take things for granted might slur their objection by forgetting that such a text existed. But this is far from being wise, for then our opponents think that their argument is unanswerable, and we, by neglecting to study the Word, begin to lean more on man's teaching than on God's Word.

We must learn to submit to God's Word,[4] for one letter of <u>that</u> is worth a volume either of Calvin or Arminius.[5] Let us in coming to this verse regard it candidly. It is quite certain that it does not contradict other portions of the Word of God.

Now, beyond all doubt, I can prove final perseverance from many passages[6] and if this should seem to lean against it, there are so many clearly for it that I would think at once that[7] I did not rightly understand it and look for a meaning agreeable with the rest of Scripture.

But now, let us come and the book being unsealed by the Spirit we notice the occasion. Paul was giving a charge to young Timothy concerning strict[8] adhesion to sound doctrine and also concerning certain upstart teachers who were loose in life and erroneous in doctrine.

In this charge we see

I. The necessity of a good conscience as the attendant of true faith.

There were in Paul's time as in ours, some who held a good conscience & good works in such estimation that they trusted to be saved by them & ignored faith — Paul therefore charges Timothy to preach first Faith and then a good conscience.

On the other hand there were then, as now some who while professing to trust wholly on faith — denied that a good conscience was necessary to salvation & so held that faith — which James says is dead — even faith not producing works. Of such were Hymeneus & Alexander who put away a good conscience.

But we must learn to hold faith & a good conscience — the one the parent — the other the offspring.

1. For if it be not maintained that true faith produces works, then it may be truly said that our teaching is licentious.

2. It is certain that those who have always relied on faith have been eminently holy & that too in proportion to their faith ∴ faith does produce works.

3. Though faith gets justification, works are necessary for our comfort, & without a good conscience we could not enter heaven.

4. If faith does not make my life good — where is its boasted power & how is Christ the Saviour of his people from their sin.

I. THE NECESSITY OF A GOOD CONSCIENCE AS THE ATTENDANT OF TRUE FAITH.

There were in Paul's time as in ours some who held a good conscience and good works in such estimation that they trusted to be saved by them and ignored faith. Paul, therefore, charges Timothy to preach first Faith and then a good conscience.

On the other hand, there were then as now some who while professing to trust wholly on faith, denied that a good conscience was necessary to salvation and so held <u>that faith</u> which James said is dead, even faith not producing works.[9] Of such were Hymenæus and Alexander who put away a good conscience.

But we must learn to hold faith and a good conscience, the one the parent, the other the offspring.

1. For if it be not maintained that true faith produces works, then it may be truly said that our teaching is licentious.

2. It is certain that those who have always relied on faith have been eminently holy, and that too in proportion to their faith. Faith does produce works.

3. Though faith gets justification,[10] works are necessary for our comfort, and without a good conscience we could not enter heaven.

4. If faith does not make my life good, where is its boasted power and how is Christ the Saviour of his people from their sin[?]

II. When men boast of faith & have not a good conscience, their faith will soon go too.

Hymeneus & Alexander threw a good life away & took up faith alone, but they soon made shipwreck of faith also.   Men make shipwreck of faith.

1. Either by broaching erroneous sentiments.
2. Or by openly denying even the profession they had made

   The reasons of this are

1. The world laughs at the idea that a wicked man may be saved without any change, they see the hollowness & this laugh drives the man to give the idea up.

2. The people of God avoid a man of such character & treat him as an heathen man, he gets disgusted & renounces his empty boast.

3. The man's own common sense & reason cries out against his own faith — his lip is contradicted by his fears & he is afraid to avow what he once did. When a man comes to this state, he will even turn blasphemer or go to any length.

III. We learn here how to treat Antinomians.

Paul gave these men over to Satan, who would afflict them in body & person & Paul hoped that thus though Satan desired it not — they might learn better.

We who have no apostolic gifts may as D.r Gill once did expell them from our communion & tell them plainly that we doubt their sincerity, & believe them to be sons of Satan. — They can be none other —. Some say in objection to this explanation how could they "put away" what they

II. WHEN MEN BOAST OF FAITH AND HAVE NOT A GOOD CONSCIENCE, THEIR FAITH WILL SOON GO TOO.

Hymenæus and Alexander threw a good life away and took up faith alone, but they soon made shipwreck of faith also.

Men make shipwreck of faith

1. Either by broaching erroneous sentiments.

2. Or by openly denying even the profession they had made.

The reasons of this are:

1. The world laughs at the idea that a wicked man may be saved without any change. They see the hollowness and this laugh drives the man to give the idea up.

2. The people of God avoid a man of such character and treat him as an heathen man. He gets disgusted and renounces his empty boast.

3. The man's own common sense and reason cries out against his own faith. His life is contradicted by his fears and he is afraid to avow what he once did. When a man comes to this state he will even turn blasphemer[11] or go to any length.

III. WE LEARN HERE HOW TO TREAT ANTINOMIANS.[12]

Paul gave these men over to Satan who would afflict them in body and person. And Paul hoped that thus, though Satan desired it not, they might learn better. We who have no apostolic gifts may as Dr. Gill once did[13] expell them from our communion and tell them plainly that we doubt their sincerity and believe them to be sons of Satan. They can be none other.[14]

Some say, in objection to this explanation, ["]How could they 'put away' what they

never had — we answer that a preacher who is
vile in character, if he should preach Anti —
— nomian sentiments might be said to put
away good works in his preaching, & yet
he never had them ——

1. Admire the harmony of Scripture
2. Seek to be found rich in good works.
3. Avoid all transgressors as sons of Satan.

     Lord help me again.

243.

---

162 Eccles. IX. 10. Do it with thy might.

The Bible is not wanting in comfort nor in
exhortation in fact the best comfort that can
be given to some men is to find them something
to do & get them warm in it.

This verse is a lump of practical wisdom.

I. Every man may find something to do.

There is certainly work enough for all of us
as long as we live. We all have a little
strength at least — there is no such thing as an
untalented servant all have some power.
If not without us, we may find more than
enough within us. — We must not wait
for work to find us — we must find it,

never had?["] We answer that[15] a preacher who is vile in character, if he should preach Antinomian sentiments, might be said to put away good works in his preaching. And yet, he never had them.

1. Admire[16] the harmony of Scripture.

2. Seek to be found rich in good works.[17]

3. Avoid all transgressors as sons of Satan.

Lord, help me again.

243.

162

DO IT *with* THY MIGHT
Ecclesiastes 9:10[1]

"Whatsoever thy hand findeth to do, do it with thy might; for there is no work, nor device, nor knowledge, nor wisdom, in the grave, whither thou goest."

The Bible is not wanting in comfort, nor in exhortation. In fact, the best comfort that can be given to some men is to find them something to do and get them warm in it.

This verse is a lump[2] of practical wisdom.

I. EVERY MAN MAY FIND SOMETHING TO DO.

There is certainly work enough for all of us as long as we live.[3] We all have a little strength at least.[4] There is no such thing as an untalented servant. All have some power. If not without us, we may find more than enough within us. We must not wait for work to find us. We must find it.

If you cannot find work by your eye, let your hand
of prayer find it. Feel for something with your hand.

II. We should do all we can find.

We should not help one alone, or use one means, or
at one time - but in the morning &c. beside all waters.
We should not shun any part, however humiliating.
We should not shun the inner work, self reform,
not fear to cut off any sin, or practise any virtue.
All things are great if done for Jesus Christ.

III. All we do, we should do at once. *no proof*

Time is more precious than money. Christian
charity & service must not be postponed. ——
In reforming any wrong habits, no time is like
the present, sin grows stronger by age. Do it
now says he & backs it with the fear of death.
Sin must not be endured, out with the traitor.

IV. All we do, must be done in earnest.

With all our might ~ we should not keep a reserve
but spend all now - since God gives strength for to-
-morrow.   In all holy engagements earnestness
is necessary to success. S. School, preaching - prayer -
reformation. Half reformers are useless. God
tells us here the measure of his requirements - as
far as our strength goes - And the will may be
received for the deed. Have we done it with
all our might? Have we used every device?
Have we put all our knowledge & wisdom to
work to do good? If not. Ah. surely we are sinners

If you cannot find work by your eye, let your hand of prayer find it. Feel for something with your hand.

II. WE SHOULD DO ALL WE CAN FIND.

We should not help one alone, or use one means, or at one time. But in the morning,[5] etc. Beside all waters.[6] We should not shun any part, however humiliating. We should not shun the inner work, self-reform. Not fear to cut off any sin[7] or practise, any virtue. All things are great if done for Jesus Christ.[8] No frown.[9]

III. ALL WE DO WE SHOULD DO AT ONCE.

Time is more precious than money. Christian charity and service must not be postponed.[10] In reforming any wrong habits, no time is like the present. Sin grows stronger by age. Do it now, says he, and backs it with fear of death.[11] Sin must not be endured. Out with the traitor.

IV.[12] ALL WE DO MUST BE DONE IN EARNEST.

With all our[13] might. We should not keep a reserve but spend all now since God gives strength for tomorrow.[14] In all holy engagements earnestness is necessary to success. S. School,[15] preaching, prayer, reformation.[16] Half reformers are useless. God tells us here the measure of his requirements as far as our strength goes. And the will may be received for the deed.

Have we done it with all our might? Have we used every device? Have we put all our knowledge and wisdom to work to do good? If not, Ah, surely we are sinners.

V. Approaching death should give us speed.

1. The time of doing good is short.

2. We cannot get a respite after death.

3. Neglected duty will pain us on our sick bed.

4. Judgment will reveal our conduct.

5. Souls are all going so that if we survive they perish. Haste. Haste. we cry —

Oh! my God stir up me & my hearers to work, for Jesus' sake —

245

---

163.   Jer. 51. 50.   Remember Jesus.

As there is so much in the world to draw us away from Jesus & such temptations at certain seasons it is our duty to exhort one another to be stedfast in the faith & remember Jesus.

I. Notice the character addressed.

"Ye that have escaped the 'sword.'"

1. The sword of conscience.

2. The sword of Satan.

3. The sword of vindictive justice now

4. The sword of eternal wrath.

All believers have done this they have fled from the city of Destruction and are safe.

V. APPROACHING DEATH SHOULD GIVE US SPEED.[17]

    1. The time of doing good is short.[18]

    2. We cannot get a respite after death.[19]

    3. Neglected duty will pain us on our sickbed.

    4. Judgment will reveal our conduct.

    5. Souls are all going so that if we survive, they perish. Haste, haste, we cry.

    Oh! my God, stir up me and my hearers to work, for Jesus' sake.[20]

245[21]

163

REMEMBER JESUS
Jeremiah 51:50[1]

*"Ye that have escaped the sword, go away, stand not still: remember
the* Lord *afar off, and let Jerusalem come into your mind."*

As there is so much in the world to draw us away from Jesus and such temptations at certain seasons, it is our duty to exhort one another to be stedfast in the faith and remember Jesus.

I. NOTICE THE CHARACTER ADDRESSED. *"Ye that have escaped the sword."*

    1. The sword of conscience.

    2. The sword of Satan.

    3. The sword of vindictive justice now.

    4. The sword of eternal wrath.

All believers have done this. They have fled from the city of Destruction[2] and are safe.

II. Notice their duty. "go away, stand not still".
Leave Babylon. The Babylon of false doctrine,
The Babel called vanity fair, The pleasures & sins
of this evil world. Go far away. Keep out of it.
Remain not in your present degree of grace
but press onward. Do not sit still & lose your
soul, nor stand still, But flee for thy life.

III. Notice another exhortation.
"remember the Lord afar off & let Jerusalem come into
your mind." When tempted to sin
think on thy far off & absent Jesus, think of the
church & of heaven — Thus thinking we should
be preserved from sin — but we forget.
1. All men forget — through natural depravity
2. Good men forget — through sudden temptation
3. Good ———————— through worldliness.
4. Our Lord is absent & we see him not but

IV. The means of helping our memory.
1. All nature may help us if we are right,
the sun. the morning star, a rose, a lily,
a door, a sheep. vine. branch. rock. —
2. Frequent the places where he walks
in secret — even his house of prayer —
3. Look at his likeness, in the Scriptures.
see him living, dying, reigning
4. Be in company with the Lord's brethren.

II. NOTICE THEIR DUTY. *"Go away, stand not still."*

Leave Babylon.[3] The Babylon of false doctrine, the Babel called Vanity Fair,[4] the pleasures and sins of this evil world. Go far away. Keep out of it.

Remain not in your present degree of grace but press onward. Do not sit still and lose your soul. Nor stand still. But flee for thy life.

III. NOTICE ANOTHER EXHORTATION. *"Remember the Lord afar off and let Jerusalem come into your mind."*

When tempted to sin, think on thy far off and absent Jesus. Think of the church[5] and of heaven. Thus thinking, we should[6] be preserved from sin. But we forget.

1. All men forget through natural depravity.[7]

2. Good men forget through sudden temptation.[8]

3. Good [men forget][9] through worldliness.

4. Our Lord is absent and we see him not.[10] But

IV. THE MEANS OF HELPING OUR MEMORY.

1. All nature may help us if we are right: the sun,[11] the morning star,[12] a rose,[13] a lily,[14] a door,[15] a sheep,[16] vine,[17] branch,[18] rock.[19]

2. Frequent the places where he walks in secret, even his house of prayer.

3. Look at his likeness in the Scriptures.[20] See him living, dying, reigning.

4. Be in company with the Lord's brethren.

5, Take out thy white stone, the witness in thyself.
Look at thy robe & every thing he has done for thee
6, Scan the heavens by faith with the telescope.
7, Meet him at the mercy seat.
8, Be at his table, break bread & thus
remember thy Lord —

             Lord remember me. Amen.

244. 246

---

164   Ps. CXLII. 7.   Bring my soul out of prison.
David was now in the cave Adullam, whither
he fled from the malice of Saul. In this beautiful
psalm he acquaints God with his state and
asks his deliverance.

I. "Bring my soul out of prison"
The cave was David's prison since he could
not go out without fear of being captured & slain.
His doubts, fears, anxieties & absence from the
house of the Lord all tended to make it a
prison. & were indeed the true prison of his soul.
The poor sinner who has been here knows it.
1. A comfortless state. cold, damp, dark as
night, perhaps like Jeremiah's pit without
sound bottom — Terrible beyond compare.

5. Take out thy white stone,[21] the witness in thyself. Look at thy robe[22] and every thing he has done for thee.

6. Scan the heavens by faith with the telescope.[23]

7. Meet him at the mercy seat.[24]

8.[25] Be at his table, break bread, and thus remember thy Lord.[26]

Lord, remember me.[27] Amen.

244. 246.

164

BRING MY SOUL
out of PRISON
Psalm 142:7[1]

> *"Bring my soul out of prison, that I may praise thy name: the righteous shall compass me about; for thou shalt deal bountifully with me."*

David was now in the cave Adullam whither he fled from the malice of Saul.[2] In this beautiful psalm he acquaints God with his state and asks his deliverance.

I.   "BRING MY SOUL OUT OF PRISON."

The Cave was David's prison since he could not go out without fear of being captured and slain. His doubts, fears, anxieties, and absence from the house of the Lord all tended to make it a prison and were, indeed, the true prison of his soul.

The poor sinner who has been here knows it.

1. A comfortless state. Cold, damp, dark as night.[3] Perhaps like Jeremiah's pit[4] without sound bottom. Terrible beyond compare.

2. An apparently hopeless state. Walls massive, bolts for ever barred — all impossible in any human way.

3. A slavish state. no liberty - either in sin or holiness bound up fast. the thing I would not, that I do.

4. A state of dread of execution - it seems the first step to death & shame. The antepast of hell

In this distress, we must tell the Lord & cry aloud unto him " Bring my soul out of prison.

II "That I may praise thy name."

This was the one object of David's life & this he uses as an argument in prayer - we may argue with God. He desired not so much ease for himself as glory for God The man whom God delivers will praise him

1. With his lip in prayer & praise in public.

2. With his heart in private devotion.

3. With his life, serving, honouring & seeking his Lord No praise to self, he has given all that to the winds - God does the work, he should be praised for it

III. "The righteous shall compass me about."

David argues that if God set him free, God's people would be served, since he as captain would be with them - & they would give thanks exceedingly.

1. As companions - the sinner desires the godly to go with him & prays that they may.

2. As being thankful - the soul knows that they desire his welfare & will be very glad of it.

3. As his guard, for the godly guard one another by example and precept.

2. An apparently hopeless state. Walls massive, bolts forever barred. All impossible in any human way.

3. A slavish state. No liberty, either in sin or holiness. Bound up fast. The thing I would not, that I do.[5]

4. A state of dread of execution. It seems the first step to death and shame. The antepast[6] of hell.

In this distress, we must tell the Lord and cry aloud unto him, "Bring my soul out of prison."

II. "THAT I MAY PRAISE THY NAME."

This was the one object of David's life and this he uses as an argument in prayer. We may argue with God. He desired not so much ease for himself as glory for God.[7]

The man whom God delivers will praise him:

1. With his lip in prayer and praise in public.[8]

2. With his heart in private devotion.

3. With his life, serving, honouring, and seeking his Lord.

No praise to self. He has given all that to the winds.[9] God does the work. He should be praised for it.

III. "THE RIGHTEOUS SHALL COMPASS ME ABOUT."

David argues that if God set him free, God's people would be served since he, as captain, would be with them.[10] And they would give thanks exceedingly:

1. As companions. The sinner desires the godly to go with him and prays that they may.

2. As being thankful. The soul knows that they desire his welfare and will be very glad of it.

3. As his guard.[11] For the godly guard[12] one another by example and precept.

4. As being much amazed at God's grace to so great a sinner they crowd to see the saved one.

__IV__ Thou shalt deal bountifully with me.

The soul sees the value of mercy & prizes it much If ever I am pardoned, justified, adopted that will be a most bountiful gift from God.

The soul is content with anything & grumbles at nothing — No desire for great things in the church, or any respect or rank, If the righteous so compass me as to conceal me from view so much the better, Anywhere is all — but too good for one so unworthy. A deep sense of sin, gives a high value to grace. God brings us low to make us prize his grace the more.

1 Let convinced sinners do as David did.
2. Let the saints compass the young ones about,
3. Let the ungodly learn their sad state "in prison

248.

4. As being much amazed at God's grace to so great a sinner.[13] They crowd to see the saved one.[14]

IV. THOU SHALT DEAL BOUNTIFULLY WITH ME.

The soul sees the value of mercy and prizes it much. If ever I am pardoned,[15] justified,[16] adopted,[17] that will be a most bountiful gift from God. The soul is content with anything and grumbles at nothing.[18] No desire for great things in the church, or any respect or rank.[19] If the righteous so compass me as to conceal me from view, so much the better. Anywhere is all but too good for one so unworthy. A deep sense of sin gives a high value to grace. God brings us low[20] to make us prize his grace the more.

1. Let convinced sinners do as David did.

2. Let the saints compass the young ones about.[21]

3. Let the ungodly learn their sad state, "in prison."[22]

248.

1. A dark ink blot, likely accidental, appears over the letter "k" in the word "Making."

2. This is the only time Charles preached a sermon on 1 Tim 1:19–20.

3. Charles may have been thinking of John Wesley, who in his commentary on 1 Tim 1:19 wrote, "Indeed none can make Shipwreck of Faith who never had it. These, therefore, were once true Believers. Yet they fell not only foully, but finally. For Ships once wrecked, cannot be afterwards saved" (John Wesley, *Explanatory Notes upon the New Testament. The Second Edition* [London: W. Bowyer, 1757], 565, capitalization in the original). Charles may have also been familiar with Methodist commentator Adam Clarke, who states in his commentary on 1 Tim 1:20 that Hymenaeus and Alexander "*had* the *faith* but *thrust it away*; who *had a good conscience* through believing, but made *shipwreck* of it. Hence we find that all this was not only *possible*, but did *actually* take place, though some have endeavoured to maintain the contrary; who, confounding eternity with a state of probation, have supposed that, if a man once enter into the grace of God in this life, he must necessarily continue in it to all eternity. Thousands of texts and thousands of facts refute this doctrine" (Adam Clarke, *Holy Bible, Containing the Old and New Testaments: The Text Carefully Printed from the Most Correct Copies of the Present Authorised Translation, Including the Marginal Readings and Parallel Texts. With a Commentary and Critical Notes; Designed as a Help to a Better Understanding of the Sacred Writings; A New Edition, With the Author's Final Corrections. In Six Volumes. Volume VI. 1 Corinthians to Revelation* [London: William Tegg and Co., 1854, The Spurgeon Library], 1 Tim 1:20, italics in the original). On the title page of this volume, Charles struck through the subtitle "*Designed as a Help to a Better Understanding of the Sacred Writings*" and wrote above it, "Adapted to blind the eye and prevent the truth in Jesus from shining upon the soul." Additionally, Charles struck through Adam Clarke's credentials, "L.L.D., F.A.S.," and wrote in the margin, "Arminian Twister of the Word." For a discussion of Charles's views on Arminianism, see "Election" (Notebook 1, Sermon 10) and "Pleasure in the Stones of Zion" (Notebook 1, Sermon 53).

4. Given that Charles used the word "Word" to refer to the Holy Bible, it has been capitalized here and throughout this sermon.

5. "If I am a Christian, I am not to be following Calvin, or Arminius, or any other earthly leader, I am to mould my doctrinal opinions, and my thoughts, and

words, and character, and acts, after the model of Christ's" (*MTP* 53:447). "At this day, my brethren, we have no Master but Christ; we submit ourselves to no vicar of God; we bow down ourselves before no great leader of a sect, neither to Calvin, nor to Arminius, to Wesley, or Whitefield" (*MTP* 16:201).

6. Cf. "Final Perseverance" (Notebook 1, Sermon 8); "Final Perseverance Certain" (Notebook 2, Sermon 82).

7. A check mark, likely in the hand of Charles, was written in pencil between the words "that" and "I."

8. Stippling appears beneath the letter "s" in the word "strict."

9. James 2:17, "Even so faith, if it hath not works, is dead, being alone."

10. Cf. Acts 13:39; Rom 3:23; Eph 2:8–9.

11. An alternative reading of this phrase is "He will even turn [into a] blasphemer."

12. Cf. "Pleasures in the Stones of Zion" (Notebook 1, Sermon 53).

13. Charles was referencing an episode in John Gill's ministry when he disciplined members in his congregation for ascribing to antinomianism. After inheriting Gill's pastorate at New Park Street Chapel in 1854, Charles recounted the episode: "In the days of my venerable predecessor, Dr. Gill, who was in the opinion even of ultra-Calvinists, sound to the core, this pernicious evil broke out in our Church. There were some who believed in what was called 'Imputed Sanctification,' and denied the work of the blessed Spirit. I was reading last night in our old Church-book a note written there in the doctor's own hand-writing, as the deliberate opinion of this Church.—'Agreed: That to deny the internal sanctification of the Spirit, as a principle of grace and holiness wrought in the heart, or as consisting of grace communicated to and implanted in the soul, which, though but a begun work, and as yet incomplete, is an abiding work of grace, and will abide, notwithstanding all corruptions, temptations, and snares, and be performed by the Author of it until the day of Christ, when it will be the saints' meetness for eternal glory; is a greivous [*sic*] error, which highly reflects dishonour on the blessed Spirit and his operations of grace on the heart, is subversive of true religion and powerful godliness, and renders persons unfit for Church communion.

Wherefore, it is further agreed, that such persons who appear to have embraced this error be not admitted to the communion of this Church; and should any such who are members of it appear to have received it and continued in it, that they be forthwith excluded from it.' Two members then present declaring themselves to be of the opinion condemned in the above resolution, and also a third person who was absent, but who was well known to have been under this awful delusion, were consequently excluded that evening. Nay, more, a person of another Church who held the opinion thus condemned was forbidden to commune at the table, and his pastor at Kettering was written to upon the subject, warning him not to allow so great an errorist to remain in fellowship. So that the doctor thought the error to be so deadly, that he used the pruning knife at once; he did not stop till it spread, but he cut off the very twigs; and this is one of the benefits of Church discipline when we are enabled to carry it out under God, that it does nip error in the very bud, and thus those who as yet are not infected are kept from it by the blessed providence of God through the instrumentality of the Church. We have always held, and still hold and teach, that the work of the Spirit in us, whereby we are conformed unto Christ's image, is as absolutely necessary for our salvation, as is the work of Jesus Christ, by which he cleanses us from our sins" (*MTP* 8:93-94). See also Joseph Ivimey, *A History of the English Baptists: Comprising the Principal Events of the History of Protestant Dissenters, from the Revolution in 1668 Till 1760; and of the London Baptist Churches, During that Period. Vol. III* (London: printed for B. J. Holdsworth, 1823), 442–43.

14. To indicate a break in his thought, Charles inserted two lines after the word "other."

15. Charles originally wrote the word "they" before converting the letter "e" into an "a" and striking through the letter "y" to construct the "t." If he had retained the word "they," the line might have read, "We answer, they who are vile in character."

16. An illegible letter is written beneath "A" in the word "Admire."

17. First Timothy 6:18, "That they do good, that they be rich in good works, ready to distribute, willing to communicate."

1. Charles preached two additional sermons on Eccl 9:10: "A Home Mission Sermon" (*NPSP* 5, Sermon 259), and "The Spur" (*MTP* 19, Sermon 1119). There is enough overlapping content in both sermons to suggest Charles had in mind the sermon in this notebook when writing his later sermon.

2. Charles originally did not write the letter "m" in the word "lump" and instead wrote "lup."

3. "If God had willed it we might each one of us have entered heaven at the moment of our conversion. . . . Why then are they here? Does God delight to tantalise his people by keeping them in a wilderness when they might be in Canaan? Will he shut them up in prison when he might give them instant liberty. . . . Why are God's ships still at sea? One breath of his wind might waft them to the haven. Why are his children still wandering hither and thither through a maze, when a solitary word from his lips would bring them into the centre of their hopes in heaven? The answer is; they are here that they may glorify God, and that they may bring others to know his love. We are not here in vain, dear brethren" (*NPSP* 5:273).

4. "It is a great pity when we cannot do anything for Christ; are there any Christians who are in that sad condition? Are they without hands,—without feet,—without eyes,— without tongues,—without hearts? Well, then, I do not think they can do much if that is the case. . . . If you cannot preach, you can pray. If you cannot pray aloud, you can plead with God in secret. There are many who cannot preach, but who can give; and there are others, who cannot give, who, nevertheless, can speak a word here and there for the Lord Jesus Christ. There are plenty of weapons waiting for you if you have a mind to wield them" (*MTP* 45:545).

5. Charles was likely referencing Eccl 11:6, "In the morning sow thy seed, and in the evening withhold not thine hand: for thou knowest not whether shall prosper, either this or that, or whether they both shall be alike good."

6. Charles was likely referencing Eccl 11:1, "Cast thy bread upon the waters: for thou shalt find it after many days."

7. Cf. Matt 5:30; Mark 9:43.   8.   Cf. Col 3:17, 23.

9. Charles wrote the words "No frown" below "all things are great." His intended

location for these words is unclear. The context permits its placement in either the line above or below.

10. Charles wrote an illegible marking to the right of the word "postponed" and also below the word "Christian" in the line above.

11. An alternative reading of this line is "'Do it now,' says he, and [then he] backs it with the fear of death."

12. Charles originally began writing Roman numeral III instead of IV before correcting the numbering.

13. The word "our" is smeared. The directionality of the smear cannot be ascertained; however, it likely resulted from the same gesture that smeared the word "reformation" four lines below.

14. Cf. Ps 118:14; Isa 40:29, 31; 41:10; Phil 4:13.

15. Abbr. "Sunday School." "Serve him in your immediate situation, where you now are. Can you not distribute tracts? 'Oh yes,' you say, 'but I was thinking of doing something else.' Yes, but God put you there to do that. Could you not teach an infant class in the Sunday School? 'I was thinking of being the superintendent of the Sunday School.' Were you, indeed? but your hand has not found out how to get there. Do what thy hand has found: it has found an infant class to teach" (*NPSP* 5:274).

16. The word "reformation" is smeared toward the lower left side of the page, likely from the same gesture that smeared the word "our" four lines above.

17. See also "If the Footmen Weary Thee, Etc." (Sermon 159).

18. "Remember solemnly that while we have been speaking in this Tabernacle we have been spending a part of our allotted time. Every time the clock ticks our time grows less, and less, and less. I have a great love for old-fashioned hourglasses, because they make you see the time go, as the sands run. I remember in the Milan Cathedral seeing the sun travel along the ecliptic line on the floor of the cathedral, and I realised time's ceaseless motion. Every minute our life-candles are shorter; every pulse makes the number of pulses less. Quick,

then, man; quick! quick! quick! Death is behind thee. . . . Anything you have to do for the glory of God, get it done at once, for you will not be able to return. I fancy for a moment how I should preach to you if I should die to-night, and should be allowed to come back to preach to you once more. I know how you would listen. It would be a very strange sermon, but you would catch every word, I am sure. I know how I should preach; I should say, 'Blessed be God for letting me come back to have one more trial with my unconverted hearers, for perhaps they may yet be led to Jesus'" (*MTP* 19:369).

19. "While we live let us live. There are no two lives accorded us on earth. If we build not now, the fabric can never be built. If now we spin not, the garment will never be woven. Work while ye live, and live while ye work" (*NPSP* 5:278).

20. "I feel very often like the chicken in the shell, which has chipped its shell a little, and begun to see that there is a great world outside. We have not as yet begun to serve God as he ought to be served. . . . May God set us free, and raise us up to the highest standard of a consecrated life, and his shall be the praise for evermore" (*MTP* 19:372).

21. Charles originally wrote the number 244 but converted the final 4 into a 5 to form the number 245.

1. On July 9, 1882, Charles preached an additional sermon on Jer 51:50 entitled "Sacred Memories" (*MTP* 45, Sermon 2648). In his later sermon, Charles focuses exclusively on verse 50b, "Remember the LORD afar off, and let Jerusalem come into mind," and there is enough overlap to suggest that for this point particularly, Charles had in mind the sermon in this notebook.

2. This is the second instance in this notebook in which Charles references the City of Destruction in John Bunyan's *The Pilgrim's Progress.* See also "Complaint, Prayer, and Answer" (Sermon 155).

3. In addition to the context of Jer 51:50, Charles may have also had in mind Roman Catholicism. See also "By Faith Jericho Fell" (Notebook 2, Sermon 133) and "Little Children Keep Yourselves from Idols" (Sermon 153).

4. "Vanity Fair" was the name of the town fair through which John Bunyan's characters Christian and Faithful passed as they departed the Valley of the Shadow of Death. "Then I saw in my Dream, that when they were got out of the Wilderness, they presently saw a Town before them, and the name of that Town is *Vanity*; and at the Town there is a *Fair* kept, called *Vanity-Fair.* It is kept all the Year long, it beareth the name of *Vanity-Fair,* because the Town where tis kept, *is lighter th[a]n* Vanity; and also, because all that is there sold, or that cometh thither, is *Vanity.* As is the saying of the wise, *All that cometh is Vanity*" (John Bunyan, *The Pilgrim's Progress from This World to That Which Is to Come. Delivered Under the Similitude of a Dream. Wherein Is Discovered, The Manner of His Setting Out; His Dangerous Journey, and Safe Arrival at the Desired Country* [London: J. Haddon, Castle Street, Finsbury, 1847, The Spurgeon Library], 102, italics in the original). For additional references to Bunyan's allegory, see "The Fight and the Weapons" (Notebook 1, Sermon 37a) and "The Fight" (Notebook 1, Sermon 37b).

5. "Does not God deserve at least some part of their time, and his Church some little effort for her extension? There are some people who are busy, here and there, and rightly so, in all sorts of philanthropic movements; but they seem to forget that the greatest philanthropic organization on the face of the earth is the Church of the living God; and that there is nothing which can so bless the world as Christ in the midst of his own people" (*MTP* 45:544).

6. An inkblot, likely accidental, appears over the letter "o" in the word "should."

7. Cf. Rom 3:23.

8. Though unusual in his penmanship, Charles's crossbar spanned the distance of all three letter "t's" in the word "temptation." Cf. Judges 16; 1 Samuel 11.

9. Charles wrote dashes after the word "Good" as a dittography device to represent the repetition of the words "Good men" from the line above.

10. "I believe that most of God's children do get down in the dumps sometimes. There is a coal cellar to God's house as well as a banqueting hall; and, although I should like always to live in the banqueting hall, I have many a time been down in the coal cellar, and I have learnt more there than I have learnt upstairs" (*MTP* 45:549).

11. Cf. Gen 1:16; Ps 113:13.   12. Cf. Rev 22:16.

13. Cf. Song 2:1.   14. Cf. Hos 14:5.

15. Cf. John 10:9.   16. Cf. John 10:11, 14.

17. Cf. John 15:1.   18. Cf. John 15:5.

19. Cf. Deut 32:18; Pss 18:2, 46; 144:1.

20. Cf. Luke 24:27.

21. In the context of the "robe" in the following sentence, the "white stone" could be a reference to a clean and purified heart. Cf. Rev 3:4, "Thou hast a few names even in Sardis which have not defiled their garments; and they shall walk with me in white: for they are worthy."

22. Cf. Isa 61:10; Rev 3:4.

23. Charles lived not far from the Cambridge Observatory, which regularly published astronomical reports in the *Cambridge Chronicle and University Journal*. Around the time Charles preached this sermon, the journal reported, "The courses of observations carried on in the present year is a continuation of that commenced at the beginning of 1850, consisting of meridian observations of the Sun, the Moon, and Moon-culminating Stars, the recently discovered Planets and Zodiacal Stars,

and Equatorial observations of the recently discovered Planets and Comets" ("University Journal: Report of the Observatory Syndicate," *Cambridge Chronicle and University Journal, Isle of Ely Herald, and Huntingdonshire Gazette*, July 17, 1852). In Spurgeon's day the most well-known telescope was Airy's Transit Circle at the Greenwich Observatory, officially commissioned in the year Charles began his preaching ministry in Cambridgeshire, 1851. About this telescope, royal astronomer George Biddell Airy said, "[N]o other existing meridional instrument can be compared with it" (Wilfred Airy, ed., *Autobiography of Sir George Biddell Airy, Honorary Fellow of Trinity College, Cambridge, Astronomer Royal from 1836 to 1881* [Cambridge: University Press, 1896], 205). With regard to his own sermons (introduction, primary divisions and subdivisions, and final exhortation), Charles was familiar with *Essay on the Composition of a Sermon* by Jean Claude (1619–1687), pastor of the French Reformed Church at Charenton, near Paris, who emphasized that "a sermon should be like a telescope," and primary divisions are like lenses that "bring the subject of your text nearer" (Hugh Evans Hopkins, *Charles Simeon of Cambridge* [Hodder and Stoughton, 1977; repr., Eugene, OR: Wipf & Stock, 2012], 59). Not only is the believer in Christ exhorted here to "scan the heavens by faith with the telescope," but Charles later reversed the directionality of the telescope by saying, "With the telescope of his prescience, [Christ] foresaw our existence, and he loved us when we had no being. Then he struck hands with the great Father, and entered into covenant on our behalf, and engaged that he would stand sponsor for us, and redeem us from the ruin of our sin" (*MTP* 39:65). See also "God the Father of Lights" (Notebook 2, Sermon 95) and "The Father of Light" (Notebook 8, Sermon 351).

24. Cf. Exod 25:22; 30:6; Heb 9:5.

25. Charles began writing an illegible number before converting it to 8.

26. Cf. Luke 22:19; 1 Cor 11:24.

27. Cf. "The Dying Thief in a New Light" (*MTP* 32, Sermon 1881) and Luke 23:42.

1. This is the only time Charles preached a sermon on Ps 142:7; however, an exposition of this text is found in Charles's later commentary on the Psalms, *The Treasury of David*. The exposition is offered here in its entirety: "That God may be glorified is another notable plea for a suppliant. Escaped prisoners are sure to speak well of those who give them liberty. Soul-emancipation is the noblest form of liberation, and calls for the loudest praise: he who is delivered from the dungeons of despair is sure to magnify the name of the Lord. We are in such a prison that only God himself can bring us out of it, and when he does so he will put a new song into our mouths. The cave was not half such a dungeon to David's body as persecution and temptation made for his soul. To be exiled from the godly is worse than imprisonment, hence David makes it one point of his release that he would be restored to church fellowship—'*The righteous shall compass me about.*' Saints gather around a child of God when his Father smiles upon him; they come to hear his joyful testimony, to rejoice with him, and to have their own faith encouraged. All the true believers in the twelve tribes were glad to rally to David's banner when the Lord enlarged his spirit; they glorified God for him and with him and through him. They congratulated him, consorted with him, crowned him, and championed him. This was a sweet experience for righteous David, who had for awhile come under the censure of the upright. He bore their smiting with patience, and now he welcomes their sanction with gratitude. '*For thou shalt deal bountifully with me.*' God's bountiful dealing is sure to bring with it the sympathy and alliance of all the favourites of the Great King. What a change from looking for a friend and finding none to this enthusiastic concourse of allies around the man after God's own heart! When we can begin a psalm with crying, we may hope to close it with singing. The voice of prayer soon awakens the voice of praise" (*TD* 7:313–14, italics in the original). See also "The Lord,—the Liberator" (*MTP* 8, Sermon 484).

2. Cf. 1 Sam 22:1–2.

3. Charles may have been thinking also of his great-grandfather's grandfather, Job Spurgeon, a Quaker from Dedham who was imprisoned for almost four months in a prison in the winter for not paying a fine for attending a nonconformist meeting (*Autobiography* 1:8).

4. Cf. Jer 38:6.

5.   Charles was drawing an analogy from David's cave to the prison-like state in which the apostle Paul found himself in Rom 7:15, "For that which I do I allow not: for what I would, that do I not; but what I hate, that do I." Cf. Rom 7:24.

6.   For additional instances in which Charles used the word "antepast," see "Inventory and Title of Our Treasures" (Notebook 2, Sermon 92) and "The Best Feast" (Notebook 2, Sermon 125).

7.   The word "God" was smudged, likely by accident.

8.   Depending on where Charles intended the comma to be located, this sentence may also read "With his lip in prayer, and [with his] praise in public."

9.   Cf. "Complaint, Prayer, and Answer" (Sermon 155).

10. "I, the preacher of this hour, beg to bear my witness that the worst days I have ever had have turned out to be my best days, and when God has seemed most cruel to me, he has then been most kind. If there is anything in this world for which I would bless him more than for anything else, it is for pain and affliction. I am sure that in these things the richest, tenderest love has been manifested to me. Our Father's wagons rumble most heavily when they are bringing us the richest freight of the bullion of his grace. Love letters from heaven are often sent in black-edged envelopes. The cloud that is black with horror is big with mercy. Fear not the storm, it brings healing in its wings, and when Jesus is with you in the vessel the tempest only hastens the ship to its desired haven" (*MTP* 27:373).

11. Charles wrote the word "gaard" before converting the first "a" into a "u" to construct the word "guard."

12. For the second time in this sermon Charles at first misspelled the word "guard" by not including the "u" after the "g."

13. See John Bunyan, *Bunyan's Grace Abounding to the Chief of Sinners; Heart's Ease in Heart Trouble; The World to Come, or Visions of Heaven and Hell; and the Barren Fig-Tree* (Philadelphia: J. J. Woodward, 1828).

14. An alternative reading of these lines is "As being much amazed at God's grace to so great a sinner, they crowd to see the saved one."

15. Cf. Mark 11:25; 1 John 1:9.

16. Cf. Rom 5:1; "The Saints' Justification and Glory" (Notebook 1, Sermon 68); "Justification, Conversion, Sanctification, Glory" (Notebook 2, Sermon 102).

17. Cf. Eph 1:5; "Adoption" (Notebook 1, Sermon 1).

18. Cf. Phil 2:14.

19. "Pride is yet my darling sin, I cannot shake it off" (*Autobiography* 1:146). "The way to be very great is to be very little" (*Lectures* 2:19). "I would not advise any of you to *try* to be humble, but to *be* humble" (*MTP* 39:474, italics in the original). "God will not fill us until we are emptied of self" (*NPSP* 6:35).

20. "In the true Church of Christ, the way to the top is downstairs; sink yourself into the highest place" (*MTP* 39:474). "A man never lowers himself more than when he tries to lift himself up" (*MTP* 60:148).

21. Cf. Titus 2:3-5; 1 Pet 5:1-5.

22. The phrase "in prison" was smeared toward the bottom of the page.

165.   II Cor XII.9.10.   I glory in infirmities.

Paul was forced to glory in his own defence & show the signs of his apostleship — He glories in active service, in patient suffering, in heavenly revelations & now in infirmity

I, Let us learn what "infirmities" Paul boasts of.

Not of the sins of his life before or after conversion. Not of an experience of backsliding, lowness &c —

Not of his proneness to fall or his evil heart these are good grounds for sorrow not for glory.

1. Liability to suffer is an "infirmity" of frail nature, the Stoics called any care for it, "infirmity" — but Paul boasts & is happy that he can suffer & may suffer for Jesus. In his trials he rejoices.

2. The philosophers declared their power to find out God by reason, & despised Paul because he was able to follow implicitly the word of God. He glories in that simple faith which they despised as an infirmity

3. Some thought him mad for preaching so foolish a doctrine. The Jew despised him for following the Carpenter's Son & the Greek called it foolishness

But in this Paul rejoices & glories much.

4. Paul was an excitable man some said & set it down to infirmity, Perhaps the glories of heaven had loosened his nerves. He would weep much for sinners. He loved Christ intensely. He was hot for the honour of his Master. This the

165

I GLORY *in* INFIRMITIES

2 Corinthians 12:9–10[1]

"And he said unto me, My grace is sufficient for thee: for my strength is made perfect in weakness. Most gladly therefore will I rather glory in my infirmities, that the power of Christ may rest upon me. Therefore I take pleasure in infirmities, in reproaches, in necessities, in persecutions, in distresses for Christ's sake: for when I am weak, then am I strong."

Paul was forced to glory in his own defence and show the signs of his apostleship. He glories in active service, in patient suffering, in heavenly revelations,[2] and now in infirmity.

I. LET US LEARN WHAT "INFIRMITIES" PAUL BOASTS OF.

Not of the sins of his life before or after conversion.
Not of an experience of backsliding, lowness, etc.
Not of his proneness to fall or his evil heart.

These are good grounds for sorrow, not for glory.

1. Liability to suffer in an "infirmity" of frail nature. The Stoics called any care for it, "infirmity."[3] But Paul boasts and is happy that he can suffer and may suffer for Jesus.[4] In his trials he rejoices.

2. The philosophers declared their power to find out God[5] by reason and despised Paul because he was able to follow implicitly the Word of God. He gloried in that simple faith which they despised as an infirmity.

3. Some thought him mad for preaching so foolish a doctrine. The Jew despised him for following the Carpenter's Son and the Greek called it foolishness.[6] But in this, Paul rejoices[7] and glories much.

4. Paul was an excitable man, some said, and set it down to infirmity. Perhaps the glories of heaven had loosened his nerves. He would weep much for sinners. He loved Christ intensely. He was hot[8] for the honour of his Master.[9] This, the

cool and worldly set down for weakness but alas how mistaken. I glory in this says Paul.

5. Paul had no self-sufficiency - he learned his own weakness & need of constant help & owned it yea gloried to think that thus it became more and more of grace. to the praise of Jesus,

II. Let us learn our best conduct under trial. "To glory in them", to rejoice & "take pleasure in them" He had the "infirmities" we have noticed "Reproaches", from friend & foe. All met on him. "Necessities", were his companions, though nursed in affluence & lofty rank. working with his hands, he lacked "Persecutions" of the bloodiest kind he endured. "Distresses" or straits causing great anxiety these being for "Christ's sake" he rejoiced in them. He rejoiced because he knew:

1. It was his Master's will that he should endure
2. It magnified the grace of God in sustaining
3. It checked his pride that might have arisen
4. It encreased his glory in heaven

Tis much to endure with but slight complaint. To be all resigned and patient is more — but To rejoice & be exceeding glad cometh only from so exalted as soul as Paul's & the like of him — High! Heavenly!

cool and worldly set down for weakness, but alas, how mistaken. I glory in this, says Paul.

5. Paul had no self-sufficiency.[10] He learned his own weakness[11] and need of constant help and owned it, yea, gloried to think that.[12] Thus it became more and more of grace to the praise of Jesus.

II. LET US LEARN OUR BEST CONDUCT UNDER TRIAL.

"To glory in them," to rejoice and "take pleasure in them." He had the "infirmities."[13] We have noticed "Reproaches" from friend and foe. All met on him. "Necessities" were his companions, though nursed in affluence and lofty rank. Working with his hands he lacked. "Persecutions" of the bloodiest kind he endured.[14] "Distresses," or straits, causing great anxiety.[15] These being for "Christ's sake," he rejoiced in them.

He rejoiced because he knew:

1. It was his Master's will that he should endure.

2. It magnified the grace of God in sustaining.[16]

3. It checked his pride that might have arisen.[17]

4. It increased[18] his glory in heaven.

[']Tis much to endure with, but slight complaint. To be all resigned and patient is more. But to rejoice and be exceeding[ly] glad cometh only from so exalted a[19] soul as Paul's and the like of him.[20]

High! Heavenly!

III. Let us try to translate the believer's riddle.
"When I am weak, then I am strong"

1. Often when suffering, comfort the more abounds. when struggling & warring, there has been peace. When unable to do duty we have done all the better.

2. A Christian's strength lies in a knowledge of his weakness provided that drives him to seek Christ's power. Self sufficiency weakens. Self-emptiness strengthens. Self sufficiency brings on carelessness, sloth, pride &c but trusting in Christ never does.

This is the A.B.C of the young Christian. Out of self, on to Christ. Be weak. Confess that thou art so. Then Christ will help thee. If you can do it — Christ need not help & he will not — he will be somewhere else helping those who are helpless. How absurd to hope to save men by preaching up man's native power. — instead of knocking all down and directing him to look to the Holy Spirit, the Son, the Father.

"I glory in mine infirmities."
"When I am weak, then I am strong"
Lord help thy weakling.

247

III. LET US TRY TO TRANSLATE[21] THE BELIEVER'S RIDDLE.
"When I am weak, then I am strong."

1. Often when suffering, comfort the more abounds. When struggling and warring, there has been peace. When unable to do duty we have done all the better.

2. A Christian's strength lies in a knowledge of his weakness provided that [it] drives him to seek Christ's power. Self-sufficiency[22] weakens. Self-emptiness strengthens. Self-sufficiency brings on carelessness, sloth, pride, etc. But trusting in Christ never does.[23]

This is the A. B. C. of the young[24] Christian. Out of self, on to Christ. Be weak. Confess that thou art so.[25] Then Christ will help thee. If you can do it, Christ need not help and he will not. He will be somewhere else[26] helping those who are helpless.

How absurd to hope to save men by preaching up man's native power[27] instead of knocking all down and directing him to look to the Holy Spirit, the Son, the Father.

"I glory in mine infirmities."

"When I am weak,[28] then I am strong."[29]

Lord, help thy weakling.

247

1. Charles preached two additional sermons on 2 Cor 12:9. In 1863 he preached a sermon entitled "A Wafer of Honey" (*MTP* 52, Sermon 2974) and on April 2, 1876, he preached a sermon entitled "Strengthening Words from the Saviour's Lips" (*MTP* 22, Sermon 1287). There is enough overlapping content to suggest Charles had in mind the sermon in this notebook when writing these two later sermons. In 1886, Charles preached a sermon on 2 Cor 12:10 entitled "A Paradox" (*MTP* 34, Sermon 2050). There is also enough overlapping content to suggest Charles had the sermon in this notebook in mind.

2. Charles wrote the word "revalations" before converting the first letter "a" into an "e" to construct the word "revelations." This is the second time in this notebook he has misspelled this word. See also "The Word Very Precious" (Sermon 160). Cf. 2 Cor 12:1–4.

3. In the eyes of a Stoic, Paul's boasting in infirmity was tantamount to boasting about being ill and weak. The Greek Stoic Zeno wrote, "By infirmity is meant disease accompanied by weakness; and by disease is meant a fond imagining of something that seems desirable. And as in the body there are tendencies to certain maladies such as colds and diarrhoea, so it is with the soul, there are tendencies like enviousness, pitifulness, quarrelsomeness, and the like. . . . The wise man is passionless, because he is not prone to fall into such infirmity" (R. D. Hicks, *Diogenes Laertius: Lives of Eminent Philosophers, in Two Volumes. II* [London: William Heinemann; New York: G. P. Putnam's Sons, 1925], 221).

4. An alternative reading of this line is "But Paul boasts and is happy that he *can* suffer and *may* suffer for Jesus."

5. The letter "o" in the word "God" is bolded throughout, likely by accident and not for emphasis.

6. Cf. 1 Cor 1:23, "But we preach Christ crucified, unto the Jews a stumbling block, and unto the Greeks foolishness."

7. Cf. Matt 5:12; Luke 6:23; 1 Pet 4:13.

8. "That is what you must do with your sermons, make them red-hot; never mind if men do say you are too enthusiastic, or even too fanatical, give them a red-hot shot. . . .We do not go out snow-balling on Sundays, we go fire-balling; we ought

to hurl grenades into the enemy's ranks" (C. H. Spurgeon, *The Soul-Winner; or, How to Lead Sinners to the Saviour* [New York: Fleming H. Revell, 1895], 69). Charles also said, "A pulpit may be a refrigerator, but it ought to be a furnace, or rather it should be the fireplace in the house to which all the family turn for warmth" (*ST* February 1880:58).

9. The word "Master" was smeared toward the bottom of the page, along with the preceding word "his" and the tittle in the word "Christ" in the line above.

10. "It is a mark of fitness for heaven when self is dead and grace alone reigns. The strength of God is never perfected till our weakness is perfected. When our weakness is consciously and thoroughly felt, then the strength of God has done its work in us" (*MTP* 22:200).

11. "I do not wonder when strong men say strong things, but I have often marvelled when I have heard such heroic sentences from the weak and trembling. . . . God's strength is perfectly revealed in the trials of the weak. . . . Great tribulation brings out the great strength of God" (*MTP* 22:199).

12. "If God has given you the great sail and the prosperous wind, he will also give you the heavy ballast to keep your keel deep in the stream" (*MTP* 52:73).

13. "I talked about my weakness from this platform five-and-twenty years ago; but I stand here and tremble under it now to a far greater degree than I did in my younger and more vigorous time. I knew it three-and-thirty years ago, when I first spoke to you, but did not know it as I know it now. I was then weak, and I owned it: but I am now weak, and groan about it almost involuntarily" (*MTP* 34:596).

14. Depending on where the punctuation is located in these previous two sentences, an alternative reading is "Working with his hands, he lacked 'Persecutions' of the bloodiest kind. He endured 'Distresses' or straits, causing great anxiety." A more likely reading is "Working with his hands, he lacked [nothing.] 'Persecutions' of the bloodiest kind he endured. 'Distresses,' or straits, causing great anxiety."

15. "Grace is given to keep us from sin, which is a great blessing; but what is the good of grace except it is in the time when the trial comes? Certainly, the grace that will not stand in the hour of temptation or affliction, is a very spurious sort of grace; and we had better get rid of it, if we have it. When a godly woman's child

dies, the infidel husband sees the mother's faith. When the ship goes down, and is lost in the sea, the ungodly merchant understands the resignation of his fellow-man. When pangs shoot through our body, and ghastly death appears in view, people see the patience of the dying Christian. Our infirmities become the black velvet on which the diamond of God's love glitters all the more brightly" (*MTP* 52:80).

16. An alternative reading of this line is "It magnified the grace of God in sustaining [him]." "Believer, it is *now* that grace is sufficient; even at this moment it *is* enough for thee. Do not say this is a new trouble, or if you do say it remember the grace of God is always new. Do not complain that some strange thing has happened unto you, or if you do, remember blessings are provided in the grace of God to meet your strange difficulties. Tremble not because the thorn in the flesh is so mysterious, for grace is mysterious too, and so mystery shall be met by mystery" (*MTP* 22:196, italics in the original).

17. Cf. 2 Cor 12:7.

18. Charles originally wrote the word "encreased." There is no evidence to suggest Charles attempted to correct this misspelling. For an additional instance in this notebook in which he misspelled this word, see "Absolute Sovereignty" (Sermon 177).

19. For modernization, the word "as" has been changed to "a."

20. "I have seen the smallest Christians in the best places, and the best Christians in the worst positions. I have seen, in the midst of the haunts of the harlot, grace shining in all the purity and chastity of lovely womanhood; and in the haunt of the thief and of the burglar, God has been pleased to have some choice saint, that, for honesty, integrity, and holy living, might have been worthy to have walked in a bishop's palace, or to have adorned the best Evangelical drawing-room in England. Brethren, it is not the position that is the main thing; the best of men may grow in the worst places, and some of the meekest of believers may be found where there ought to have been the bravest" (*MTP* 52:78).

21. Charles uses the word "translate" similarly in "The Golden Crown of Holiness" (Sermon 149).

22. Charles did not originally hyphenate the term "self-sufficiency." It has been hyphenated here and in the line below for consistency.

23. The "s" in the word "does" is smudged.

24. Charles added the letter "l" at the end of the word "young." He may have intended to spell the word "younglings."

25. Cf. 1 John 1:9.

26. The letter "s" in the word "else" is smudged, likely the result of the malfunction of the writing instrument.

27. "Tremble when you see a poor, weak preacher made useful in converting souls: then all the papers and magazines begin to blaze his name abroad, and silly Christians—for there are plenty of them—begin to talk him up as if he were a demigod, and say such great things about him, and describe him as wise, and eloquent, and great. Thus they do all they can to ruin the good brother. . . . The best of men are flesh and blood, and they have no power except as God lends them power, and he will make them know and feel this. Therefore, neither exalt others nor exalt yourselves, but beseech the Lord to make and keep you weakness itself, that in you his power may be displayed" (*MTP* 22:204).

28. The word "weak" is smeared toward the lower left side of the page. There is also a slight smear in the words "I am" preceding it, and in the word "Lord" in the line below.

29. "Very well, then, let us pick up our tools and go to our work rejoicing, feeling—Well, I may be weaker, or I may be stronger in myself, but my strength is in my God. If I should ever become stronger, then I must pray for a deeper sense of weakness, lest I become weak through my strength. And if I should ever become weaker than I am, then I must hope and believe that I am really becoming stronger in the Lord" (*MTP* 34:600).

166.　　　Ps. 119. 176. I have gone astray like a lost sheep.

How plainly David speaks. how fresh from the heart is every word — this is his last verse & is a fit conclusion to so beautiful a psalm. It contains a confession, a prayer, & an argument.

I. A confession — such as all men should make for it is true of all. but such as only a good man can make truly. vain confession is grievous sin. David. applied to himself all that is said of our race "I love".

1. The sheep often wanders & would always unless prevented.

2. The sheep foolishly wanders from good to bad.

3. The sheep ungratefully wanders from a kind & good shepherd.

4. The sheep often leads others with it. so we wander.

5. The sheep wanders long & returns not.

II. A prayer — such as we need often to put up.

This implies

1. That he hated his wanderings.

2. That he felt unable to return.

3. That he believed Christ would seek him.

4. That he was willing to be a servant.

III. An argument. not on account of merit but as a pledge of past love.

I should have forgotten all if left to myself.

1. Here he urges God's past teachings.

2. He urges God's present mercies.

3. He urges that if when dead he was loved, how much more now made alive from the dead

　　　　　Lord be with me.

250. 253. 254. 308. 578.

166

I HAVE GONE ASTRAY
like a LOST SHEEP
Psalm 119:176[1]

"I have gone astray like a lost sheep; seek thy servant; for I do not forget thy commandments."

How plainly David speaks. How fresh from the heart is every word. This is his last verse and is a fit conclusion to so beautiful a Psalm. It contains a confession, a prayer, and an argument.

I. A CONFESSION such as all men should make, for it is true of all but such as only a good man can make truly.

Vain confession is grievous sin.[2]

David applied to himself all that is said of our race. "I have."

1. The sheep often wanders and would always unless prevented.
2. The sheep foolishly wanders from good to bad.[3]
3. The sheep ungratefully wanders from a kind and good shepherd.[4]
4. The sheep often leads others with it. So we wander.
5. The sheep wanders long and returns not.

II. A PRAYER such as we need often to put up.

This implies:

1. That he hated his wanderings.
2. That he felt unable to return.
3. That he believed Christ would seek him.[5]
4. That he was willing to be a servant.[6]

III. AN ARGUMENT, not on account of merit but as a pledge of past love.[7]

I should have forgotten all if left to myself.

1. Here he urges God's past teachings.
2. He urges God's present mercies.
3. He urges that if when dead he was loved,[8] how much more now made alive from the dead?[9]

Lord, be with me.

250. 253. 254. 308.[10] 508.

1. On October 29, 1882, Charles preached an additional sermon on Ps 119:168, 176 entitled "A Sincere Summary, and a Searching Scrutiny" (*MTP* 46, Sermon 2671). There is not enough structural similarity to suggest Charles had in mind his early sermon when writing his later one. More overlapping content, however, is found in his commentary on Psalm 119:176 in *The Treasury of David*, which is offered here in its entirety: "This is the *finale*, the conclusion of the whole matter: '*I have gone astray like a lost sheep*'—often, wilfully, wantonly, and even hopelessly, but for thine interposing grace. In times gone by, before I was afflicted, and before thou hadst fully taught me thy statutes, I went astray. 'I went astray' from the practical precepts, from the instructive doctrines, and from the heavenly experiences which thou hadst set before me. I lost my road, and I lost myself. Even now I am apt to wander, and, in fact, have roamed already; therefore, Lord, restore me. '*Seek thy servant.*' He was not like a dog, that somehow or other can find its way back; but he was like a lost sheep, which goes further and further away from home; yet still he was a sheep, and the Lord's sheep, his property, and precious in his sight, and therefore he hoped to be sought in order to be restored. However far he might have wandered he was still not only a sheep, but God's 'servant,' and therefore he desired to be in his Master's house again, and once more honoured with commissions for his Lord. Had he been only a lost sheep he would not have prayed to be sought; but being also a 'servant' he had the power to pray. He cries, 'Seek thy servant,' and he hopes to be not only sought, but forgiven, accepted, and taken into work again by his gracious Master. Notice this confession; many times in the psalm David has defended his own innocence against foul-mouthed accusers, but when he comes into the presence of the Lord his God he is ready enough to confess his transgressions. He here sums up, not only his past, but even his present life, under the image of a sheep which has broken from its pasture, forsaken the flock, left the shepherd, and brought itself into the wild wilderness, where it has become as a lost thing. The sheep bleats, and David prays, 'Seek thy servant.' His argument is a forcible one,—'*for I do not forget thy commandments.*' I know the right, I approve and admire the right, what is more, I love the right, and long for it. I cannot be satisfied to continue in sin, I must be restored to the ways of righteousness. I have a home-sickness after my God, I pine after the ways of peace; I do not and I cannot forget thy commandments, nor cease to know that I am always happiest and safest when I scrupulously obey them, and find all my joy in doing so. Now, if the grace of God enables us it will surely yet restore us to practical holiness. That man cannot be utterly lost whose heart is still with God. If he be gone astray in

many respects, yet still, if he be true in his soul's inmost desires, he will be found again, and fully restored. Yet let the reader remember the first verse of the psalm while he reads the last: the major blessedness lies not in being restored from wandering, but in being upheld in a blameless way even to the end. Be it ours to keep the crown of the causeway, never leaving the King's highway for By-path Meadow, or any other flowery path of sin. May the Lord uphold us even to the end. Yet even then we shall not be able to boast with the Pharisee, but shall still pray with the publican, 'God be merciful to me a sinner;' and with the Psalmist, 'Seek thy servant'" (*TD* 6:346–47, italics in the original).

2. "Suppose you take a needle, one of the very best that has ever been made. . . . They are bright, untarnished, sharp, smooth, all that they should be, quite perfect needles. But just put one of them under a microscope,—I have done so,—and then see what it is like. Why, now, it is a bar of steel,—rough and ugly-looking, tending towards a point at one end, but certainly very blunt. That is just the difference between the microscopic examination and the ordinary observation of our poor eyes. So, the life of a believer may be like that of Job, 'perfect and upright,' but when it comes under the scrutiny of an eye that is illuminated by the Spirit of God, and touched with the heavenly eye-salve, quite another verdict is given; and, tremblingly, with many tears, the confession is poured into the ear of God, 'I have gone astray like a lost sheep.' . . . Keep that microscope close at hand, and it need not have very strong lenses either" (*MTP* 46:185–87).

3. "Has it not struck you, dear friends, as a very wonderful thing that good men— some of the best of men who have ever lived—have nevertheless been guilty of things which, at the present moment, we regard as heinous crimes? Mr. Whitefield had a strong objection to slavery, but still it did not seem to him to be wrong to have a number of negroes at the orphan house at Savannah, and to speak of them as his goods and chattels. That was a matter about which the conscience of the good man was not then enlightened. We do ill if we condemn men too strongly for things about which no enlightenment has come to them; but are they not themselves guilty in the sight of God? Of course, they are" (*MTP* 46:187).

4. Cf. John 10:11,14.   5.   Cf. Luke 15:1–7.

6. Cf. Phil 2:7.

7. "In like manner, may we be kept, by the grace of God, clear of all trusting in our works; but, at the same time, may we abound in good works to the glory of God, and both in thought and in life, may we be clear in the sight of God. Oh! how I have envied that first Quaker, George Fox, who, with all the eccentricities of his life, could honestly say, on his death-bed, 'I am clear, I am clear, I am clear of the blood of all men.' This is the highest ambition that a minister's heart may indulge,—that he should be able to say that at the last, as other men of God have been able to do" (*MTP* 46:184).

8. Cf. Rom 5:8.

9. An alternative reading of this line is "He urges that if when dead he was loved, how much more [is he loved] now [that he has been] made alive from the dead?"

10. The numbers 308 and 508 were written in a different color of ink. The number 308 was smeared, likely because Charles closed the notebook before allowing the ink to dry. For an imprint of the number 308 on the opposite page, see the following sermon, "In the World Ye Shall Have Tribulation" (Sermon 167).

John. XVI. 33. In the world ye shall have tribulation 167.

There is something godlike in this parting discourse of Jesus. there is in it so much self-forgetting love, & all-absorbing care for his flock. We have heard of the dying keeper of the lighthouse who when seized with death, vainly strove to trim his lamp & finished his mortal race by exhorting his companion to take care of the lamp. We have heard of the wounded mother who for a moment staunched her mortal wound, that she might spend her last moment in giving suck to her babe. Such is the scene — not the death of an Augustus crying "Clap me" — nor the bedside of even a Christian saying "Have pity upon me &c" but of the Lord Jesus who instead of receiving comfort - gave it.

I Let us look at the things he had said for their comfort.

II. Let us notice the true design of these things.

III. Let us observe his warning. &

IV Rejoice at his encouragement.

I. Notice the things he had spoken of. We shall as it were - be examining a recipe given by a most eminent physician for curing the heartache - & may perhaps find it useful very often.

1. Jesus spoke to them of heaven. — John XIV. 1. this has ever been an excellent means of reviving one's spirits. The mansion in reversion makes the cottage blest.

2. Jesus spoke to them. ver. 10 of his godhead & union with the Father - which must comfort

167

IN *the* WORLD YE SHALL HAVE TRIBULATION
John 16:33[1]

"These things I have spoken unto you, that in me ye might have peace. In the world ye shall have tribulation: but be of good cheer; I have overcome the world."

There is something God-like[2] in this parting discourse of Jesus.[3] There is in it so much self-forgetting love and all-absorbing care for his flock. We have heard of the dying keeper of the lighthouse who, when seized with death, vainly strove to trim his lamp and finished his mortal race by exhorting his companion to take care of the lamp.[4] We have heard of the wounded mother who for a moment staunched her mortal wound that she might spend her last moment in giving suck to her babe.

Such is the scene. Not the death of an Augustus[5] crying, "Clap me," nor the bedside of even a Christian saying, "Have pity upon me, etc.,"[6] but of the Lord Jesus who instead of receiving comfort, gave it.

I.[7] LET US LOOK AT THE THINGS HE HAD SAID FOR THEIR COMFORT.
II. LET US NOTICE THE TRUE DESIGN OF THESE THINGS.
III. LET US OBSERVE HIS WARNING AND
IV. REJOICE AT HIS ENCOURAGEMENT.

I. NOTICE THE THINGS HE HAD SPOKEN OF.

We shall, as it were, be examining a recipe given by a most eminent physician for curing the heartache and may perhaps find it useful very often.[8]

1. Jesus spoke to them of heaven. John XIV.1.[9] This has ever been an excellent means of reviving one's spirits. The mansion in reversion[10] makes the cottage blest.

2. Jesus spoke to them [in] Ver[11] 10 of his Godhead and union with the Father[12] which[13] must comfort

them while he was absent - since then God was forever theirs.
Reflections on the Godhead of Jesus tend much to comfort.

3. Jesus gave them an absolute promise that he would
hear their prayers. ver. 13 - Surely here is comfort.

4. Jesus spake of the Comforter. ver. 26 - who by his
divine workings will do for us what we cannot do.

5. Jesus spoke of their Union with himself. as the
branches in the vine — & consequently of his sympathy.

6. Jesus spoke of their Election. XV. 16 - which is indeed
a lordly dish to the real Christian.

7. Jesus reminded them that persecution & trouble
for Jesus sake are marks of the heirs of heaven.

8. Jesus spake of his second coming - which
ever should cheer our waiting souls.

Notice well beloved. This recipe of the most
eminent of physicians for the cure of heart-ache.

II. The true design of the things spoken. or.
How the recipe was to act.

"To give them peace in him."
Peace with God was the purchase of his blood, &
peace of conscience, heart & affections was the
design of this discourse.. "In me" or by me
as the phrase often means, since only by Jesus can
we get real peace — "In me". that is not in the
world, not in your country, not in sin but in me.
This peace is possessed in a variety of degrees.

them while he was absent. Since then, God was forever theirs. Reflections on the Godhead of Jesus lend much to comfort.

3. Jesus gave them an absolute promise that he would hear their prayers. Ver.[14] 13.[15] Surely here is comfort.

4. Jesus spake of the Comforter [in] Ver.[16] 26,[17] who by his divine workings will do for us what we cannot do.

5. Jesus spoke of their Union with himself as the branches in the vine[18] and consequently of his sympathy.

6. Jesus spoke of their Election [in] XV.16,[19] which is indeed a lordly[20] dish to the real Christian.

7. Jesus reminded them that persecution and trouble for Jesus's[21] sake are marks of the heirs of heaven.[22]

8. Jesus spake of his second coming,[23] which ever should cheer our waiting souls.

Notice well, beloved, this recipe of the most eminent of physicians for the cure of heartache.

II. THE TRUE DESIGN OF THE THINGS SPOKEN. OR, HOW THE RECIPE WAS TO ACT. *"To give them peace in him."*

Peace with God was the purchase of his blood, and peace of conscience, heart, and affections was the design of this discourse. "In me," or by me, as the phrase often means,[24] since only by Jesus can we get real peace.[25] "In me." That is, not in the world, not in your country, not in sin, but in me. This peace is possessed in a variety of degrees.

Its real state is that of settled rest & quiet — its extra state is that of ecstatic & joy, or oftener full assurance.

The recipe was designed to give peace in Jesus & truly it answers well — but the Christian is like the sea while peace is at bottom there are often storms above. Take examples of quiet rest in Jesus. — Stephen, Paul — Habbakuk — Sick or dying Christian. —

III Notice. The warning

or What the recipe was not intended to cure
In the world ye shall have tribulation. This is unaltered the medecine cures the disease but it does not confine the wind.
1. It is the natural lot of man.
2. It is the lot of Christian to be troubled by worldlings.
3. It is Satan's design at all times to worry us.
If we swim against the tide — we shall feel its force.
In the world ye shall have tribulation
& It is good for you to take off your heart from it, to make you love me, & desire heaven.. — this is as much a promise as any in the Bible.

IV. Notice the encouragement.
Or another remedy Or something which though not a remedy to remove, is a strengthening draught to help us to bear it.
I have overcome the world.
1. Remember that his merit has removed all the sting.
2. Remember his example seeing he triumphed
He joins himself with them & tells how he endured all suffering — the frown of the world.
How he overcame her soft bewitcheries & escaped

Its real state is that of settled rest and quiet. Its extra[26] state is that of extatic ~~or~~ joy, or oftener full assurance.

The recipe was designed to give peace in Jesus, and truly it answers well. But the Christian is like the sea. While peace is at bottom, there are often storms above.[27] Take examples of quiet rest in Jesus.[28] Stephen,[29] Paul,[30] Habbakuk,[31] sick or dying Christian.

III. NOTICE THE WARNING, OR WHAT THE RECIPE WAS NOT INTENDED TO CURE.

In the world ye shall have tribulation. This is unaltered. The medicine cures the disease, but it does not confine the winds.

1. It is the natural lot of man.

2. It is the lot of Christians to be troubled by worldlings.

3. It is Satan's design at all times to worry us.

If we swim against the tide, we shall feel its force. In the world, ye <u>shall</u> have tribulation.[32] And it is good for you to take off your heart from it to make you love me and desire heaven. This is as much a promise as any in the Bible.

IV. NOTICE THE ENCOURAGEMENT. ~~OR ANOTHER REMEDY.~~ OR SOMETHING WHICH, THOUGH NOT A REMEDY TO REMOVE, IS A STRENGTHENING DRAUGHT TO HELP US TO BEAR IT.[33] *"I have overcome the world."*[34]

1. Remember that his merit has removed all the sting.[35]

2. Remember his example, seeing he triumphed. He joins himself with them and tells how he endured all suffering,[36] the frown of the world. How he overcame her soft bewitcheries and escaped

her smiles & her applause. He wrestled with Satan &
was a victor - and now as our captain. He cries
fear not a foe whom I worsted in one combat.
fear not an enemy broken & exhausted already.
I like the men on the palace crying

    Come in Come in
    Eternal glory thou shalt win.

He says I have gained the summit & vanquished
mightier foes than will attack thee.
I fought the unwounded dragon - thou contendest
with a monster whose head is crushed ~
  Let us lay aside all hope of rest or ease here
  Let us dismiss every cowardly fear &
   Be of good cheer. —

252. 275

---

168. Matt ~~Acts~~ XII. 43. 44. 45. The unclean Spirit returning.
This verse often caused distress to desponding
souls, when there was no need for it. They fancied
that the "he" referred to the sinner - that he
sought rest & found none & therefore returned
but the "he" means Satan.
When Jesus spake this, he intended it of the
Jews whom he laboured to benefit & did for
a time chase Satan away. He went among
the Gentiles, those dry places, but he found

her smiles and her applause. He wrestled with Satan and was a victor. And now as our captain,[37] he cries, "[F]ear not a foe whom I worsted in one combat. Fear not an enemy, broken and exhausted already."[38] And like the men on the palace, crying,

> Come in, Come in.
> Eternal glory thou shalt win,[39]

he says, "I have gained the summit and vanquished mightier foes than will attack thee. I fought the unwounded dragon. Thou contendest with a monster whose head is crushed."[40]

> Let us lay aside all hope of rest or ease here.
> Let us dismiss every cowardly fear and
> Be of good cheer.

252. 275

168

THE UNCLEAN SPIRIT RETURNING
Matthew ~~Acts~~ 12:43–45[1]

"When the unclean spirit is gone out of a man, he walketh through dry places, seeking rest, and findeth none. Then he saith, I will return into my house from whence I came out; and when he is come, he findeth it empty, swept, and garnished. Then goeth he, and taketh with himself seven other spirits more wicked than himself, and they enter in and dwell there: and the last state of that man is worse than the first. Even so shall it be also unto this wicked generation."

This verse often caused distress to desponding souls when there was no need for it. They fancied[2] that the "<u>he</u>" referred to the sinner, that he sought rest and found none and therefore returned. But the "he" means Satan. When Jesus spake this, he intended it of the Jews whom he laboured to benefit and did for a time chase Satan away. He went among the Gentiles, those dry places. But he found

no rest there & therefore returned to the Jews & even
now reigns in them with sevenfold might.

I. Satan is the inhabitant of every man's soul by
nature. —

Once man in Adam was upright, but Satan drove
purity away, & sat in God's throne within us.

He has poisoned the heart's best fountains, he
has left a vice-gerent within us. even sin.

And Satan, the prince of darkness. dwells
there sometimes in person. — for ~~three~~ purposes

To prompt to evil; to defeat all good, to watch.

The heart of man is a fit palace it is very dark,
very filthy, very hard. very high & proud.
The heart & unclean & the devil unclean, no wonder
that man becomes vile indeed. This should
cause some thought & fear among the wicked.

II. Satan sometimes withdraws from man
& there is a partial reformation.

When Satan is forced out by Jesus, he will never
get in again, though he will always try.

But sometimes he leaves a man through
the man's fear of hell, or temporary conviction

he leaves not because he must but because
he is full of craft & knows how to destroy.

He goes & for a while no devil is seen as before
the house is empty — the man is not a temple
of the Lord Jesus, but still the old Master is

no rest there and therefore returned to the Jews, and even now reigns in them[3] with sevenfold might.

I. SATAN IS THE INHABITANT OF EVERY MAN'S SOUL BY NATURE.

Once, man in Adam was upright.[4] But Satan drove purity away and sat in God's throne within us. He has poisoned the heart's best fountains. He has left a vice-gerent[5] within us, even sin. And Satan, the prince of darkness, dwells there sometimes in person for three[6] purposes:

> To prompt to evil.
> To defeat all good.
> To watch.

The heart of a man is a fit palace. It is very dark, very filthy, very hard, very high and proud. The heart [is] unclean[7] and the devil [is] unclean. No wonder that man becomes vile indeed. This should cause some thought and fear among the wicked.

II. SATAN SOMETIMES WITHDRAWS FROM MAN AND THERE IS A PARTIAL REFORMATION.

When Satan is forced out by Jesus, he will never get in again, though he will always try. But sometimes he leaves a man through the man's fear of hell or temporary conviction. He leaves, not because he must but because he is full of craft and knows how to destroy. He goes and for a while no devil is seen as before. The house is empty. The man is not a temple of the Lord Jesus, but still the old Master is gone out. Now how may we tell whether the devil is gone out himself or whether he has been turned out.

1. If turned out there has been a great fight, & every thing within is upside down.

2. If he has been turned out you will find every door & window locked & barred inside. When he goes out he puts the key in his pocket.

3. If he has been turned out the house will not only be swept & garnished but inhabited by Jesus who turned him out.

III. Satan is not asleep while he is gone but he walks through dry places.

He is a restless spirit & all the mischief he can do does not satisfy him - he finds no rest.

He knows he can enter the deserted house whenever he likes & therefore he sees after others

He wandering goes on to

1. Dry Christians, whose piety & grace are but little, the tears few, & the affection slight.

2. Dry persons who feel no care for the Sabbath.

3. Dry drunkards he leads to the devil's ditch.

4. All persons openly irreligious. dry of goodness

5. Dry hypocrites, dry Pharisees, dry doctrinals & all who have no true gospel dew.

gone out. Now, how may we tell whether the devil is gone out himself or whether he has been turned out?

1. If turned out, there has been a great fight and every thing within is upside down.

2. If he has been turned out, you will find every door and window locked and barred inside. When he goes out, he puts the key in his pocket.

3. If he has been turned out, the house will not only be swept and garnished but inhabited by Jesus who turned him out.

III. SATAN IS NOT ASLEEP WHILE HE IS GONE, BUT HE WALKS THROUGH DRY PLACES.

He is a restless spirit[8] and all the mischief he can do does not satisfy him. He finds[9] no rest. He knows he can enter the deserted house whenever he likes and therefore he sees after others.[10]

He, wandering, goes on to:

1. Dry Christians, whose piety and grace are but little. The tears few and the affection slight.[11]

2. Dry persons who feel no care for the Sabbath.

3. Dry drunkards he leads to the devil's ditch.[12]

4. All persons openly irreligious, dry of goodness.

5. Dry hypocrites, dry Pharisees, dry doctrinals, and all who have no true gospel dew.

IV. Satan at the time he thinks most fit returns to his house.

He went out with this very intention. He left it that he might keep stronger hold the next time. He says I will return to "my house" it was his still, though he left it temporarily. — When he comes he finds no opposition for it is empty —

Empty – no true religion, no Spirit, no Jesus.

Swept – of many of the more gross & open sins.

Garnished with some outward duties & performances.

Take heed that we be not empty, for if any man fall by Satan it is because he forgot to keep the guard there & the house was empty.

They who go into evil company do sweep & garnish their heart to make a devil's parlour of it.

V. Satan most commonly comes attended.

The one devil becomes 8 & the seven new ones are gigantic ones. Thus it becomes worse than before . . . .

1. Backsliders often are outwardly worse than before

2. They become much more hardened against the truth.

3. They usually perish without remedy.

Now we can apply it.

1. To the dry Christian. thou art Satan's parade & promenade. Get moisture from above.

IV. SATAN, AT THE TIME HE THINKS MOST FIT, RETURNS TO HIS HOUSE.

He went out with this very intention. He left it that he might keep stronger hold the next time. He says, I will return to "my house." It was his still, though he left it temporarily. When he comes, he finds no opposition, for it is empty.

Empty.[13] No true religion. No Spirit. No Jesus.
Swept of many of the more gross and open sins.
Garnished with some outward duties and performances.

Take heed that we be not empty, for if any man fall by Satan it is because he forgot to keep the guard[14] there and the house was empty. They who go into evil company[15] do sweep and garnish their heart to make a devil's parlour of it.

V. SATAN MOST COMMONLY COMES ATTENDED.

The one devil becomes 8, and the seven news ones are gigantic ones. Thus, it becomes worse than before.

1.   Backsliders often are outwardly worse than before.

2.   They become much more hardened against the truth.

3.   They usually perish without remedy.

Now, we can apply it:

1.   To the dry Christian, thou art Satan's parade and promenade. Get moisture from above.

2. To the reformed but not converted, Take care lest Satan return with 7 others.

3. To the backslider tremble lest this is thy case. & thou wilt be worse than fold.

4. Poor penitent — go to the strong for strength — he can turn the 8 out — Go & sin no more, lest a worse thing come unto thee.

Great Father, do good. by me
/Amen

255

---

169   1 Cor. 1. 24. Christ the power & wisdom of God.

This text may be understood as referring either to Christ personally or to the doctrine of Christ. Now if it be understood of Christ personally he is & has indeed   both the power & wisdom of God

Power
1. He made the world & therefore shows his power.

2. He bore the sins of the human race & therefore must have been a God.

3. He taketh Saints to heaven & so must

4. He worked miracles, &c — he is the power of God.

Wisdom — —
1. He displays wisdom in creation, in providence

2. He displayed wisdom in his conduct as man

3. He displayed wisdom in planning the way.

4. He displays wisdom in bringing sons to glory

2. To the reformed but not converted, take care lest Satan return with 7 others.

3. To the backslider, tremble lest this is thy case and thou wilt be worse than of old.

4. Poor penitent, go to the strong for strength.[16] He can turn the 8 out. Go and sin no more lest a worse thing come unto thee.

Great Father, do good by me.

Amen

255

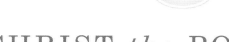

CHRIST *the* POWER *and* WISDOM *of* GOD
1 Corinthians 1:24[2]

*"But unto them which are called, both Jews and Greeks, Christ
the power of God, and the wisdom of God."*

This text may be understood as referring either to Christ personally or to the doctrine of Christ.[3] Now, if it be understood of Christ personally, he is and has[4] indeed both the power and wisdom of God.

POWER:[5]

1. He made the world[6] and therefore shows his power.

2. He bore the sins of the human race[7] and therefore must have been God.

3. He taketh Saints to heaven and so must.[8]

4. He worked miracles, etc. He is the power of God.

WISDOM:

1.[9] He displays wisdom in creation, in providence.[10]

2. He displayed wisdom in his conduct as man.

3. He displayed wisdom in planning the way.

4. He displays wisdom in bringing sons to glory.[11]

But understanding it of the doctrine of Christ crucified the Saviour of men it is equally true

Finding too much matter I leave one part & go on with the other.

---

169. 1. Cor. 1.24. Christ the power of God. 169

In thinking on this verse I am so much enlarged that I do as it were overflow & am constrained to take but one part — & read it thus

"Christ the power of God."

& this I understand both of his person & of his doctrine —

I. Christ personal is the power of God.

In the prophecy of him in Isa. IX. 6. He is called the Mighty God. & undoubtedly he is God.

1 He is the power of God since by him the worlds were made. Colos. 1.16. John 1.

2. He is the God of providence. Heb. 1. 3 & in the management of his vast empire truly he displays the power of none less than God.

3 His miracles demonstrate this. raising the dead stilling seas & walking on them, feeding thousands, bursting the grave &c —

4. He bore alone the weight that must have crused the world to hell, thy myriad sins, oh soul was he not the power of God!

But understanding it of the doctrine of Christ crucified, the Saviour of men, it is equally true.

Finding too much matter, I leave one part and go on with the other.

169b[1]

CHRIST *the* POWER *of* GOD
1 Corinthians 1:24[2]

"But unto them which are called, both Jews and Greeks, Christ the power of God, and the wisdom of God."

In thinking on this verse, I am so much enlarged that I do, as it were, overflow and am constrained to take but one part and read it thus,

"Christ the power of God."

And this I understand both of his person and of his doctrine.

I. CHRIST PERSONAL IS THE POWER OF GOD.

In the prophecy of him in Isa. IX.6.[3] He is called the Mighty God, and undoubtedly, he is God.

1.[4] He is the power of God since by him the worlds[5] were made.[6] Coloss. 1.16.[7] John 1.[8]

2. He is the God of providence. Heb. 1.3.[9] And in the management of his vast empire, truly he displays the power of none less than God.

3. His miracles demonstrate this: raising the dead,[10] stilling seas[11] and walking on them,[12] feeding thousands,[13] bursting the grave,[14] etc.

4. He bore alone the weight that must have cursed[15] the world to hell, thy myriad sins. Oh soul, was he not the power of God?[16]

Let the saint rejoice in a Saviour of immense power, even the power of God.

Let the sinner fly to the arm of this Mighty one.

II. Christ — that is his doctrine is the power of God. —

& this may be proved.

1. From its very existence amid so much to destroy it from without & from within.

From without. The Jewish, Romish, Catholic & Church of England persecutions.

From within. Worldliness. Heresies, Coldness

Beside infidel attacks & other trials.

2. From the civilizing & moralizing effects it produces. See how far Protestant countries overtop others in civilization.

Witness the holiness & morality of Christians.

3. From the objects it benefits — The most depraved, uncivilized, debauched —

4. From its helping men to endure so much trouble & sickness & to work so zealously.

5. From its sustaining its professors at the hour of death & even amid painful death.

III. What makes Christ in the gospel so powerful.

Let the saint rejoice in a Saviour of immense power, even the power of God.

Let the sinner fly to the arm of this Mighty one.

II. CHRIST. THAT IS, HIS DOCTRINE IS THE POWER OF GOD, AND MAY BE PROVED:

1. From its very existence amid so much to destroy it from without and from within.

    From without: The Jewish, Romish,[17] Catholic and Church of England persecutions.[18]

    From within: Worldliness. Heresies. Coldness. Beside infidel attacks, and other trials.

2. From the civilizing and moralizing effects it produces. See how far Protestant countries overtop others in civilization. Witness the holiness and morality of Christians.[19]

3. From[20] the objects it benefits. The most depraved, uncivilized, debauched.

4. From its helping men to endure so much trouble and sickness and to work so zealously.

5. From its sustaining its professors at the hour of death and even amid painful death.

III. WHAT MAKES CHRIST IN THE GOSPEL SO POWERFUL?

Some things in the doctrine itself.
1. It is not at all inconsistent with reason.
2. It appeals to man's conscience
3. It speaks to man's fears & man's hopes.
4. It bears the omnipotence of love in it.
Some things accompanying the doctrine.
1. The preaching of it by earnest & pious men.
2. The influence of the Holy Spirit. —

Christian tremble not for the cause it is
the power of God & cannot fall.
Enemy boast not though thou lead some
astray & think to injure us. The cause of
God is mightier than thou & shall prevail.
256 & 257.

Isa. XLI. 14. Fear not, thou worm Jacob. 170.
The prudent husband provideth not alone for every
days necessities but lays up a store for future wants
The careful parent anticipates for his child the
time of anxiety & care on which he must enter.
& by prudent advice and comfort fortifies his
yet unbeaten breast. So also our God gives
comfort to his people beforehand. — In this case
he foresaw the troubles about to come on
Israel in the Babylonish captivity & gives them
now, what soon they shall need. —

Some things in the doctrine itself:

    1. It is not at all inconsistent with reason.[21]

    2. It appeals to man's conscience.

    3. It speaks to man's fears and man's hopes.

    4. It bears the omnipotence of love in it.

Some things accompanying the doctrine:

    1. The preaching of it by earnest and pious men.

    2. The influence of the Holy Spirit.

Christian, tremble not for the cause. It is the power of God and cannot fall.

Enemy, boast not, though thou lead some astray and think to injure us.[22] The cause of God is mightier than thou and shall prevail.

.256[23] and 257.

170[1]

FEAR NOT, THOU WORM JACOB

Isaiah 41:14[2]

"Fear not, thou worm Jacob, and ye men of Israel; I will help thee,
saith the LORD, and thy redeemer, the Holy One of Israel."

The prudent husband[3] provideth not alone for every day's[4] necessities but lays up a store for future wants. The careful parent anticipates for his child the time of anxiety and care on which he must enter and by prudent advice and comfort fortifies his yet unbeaten breast.

So also our God gives comfort to his people beforehand. In this case he foresaw[5] the troubles about to come on Israel in the Babylonish captivity[6] and gives them now what soon they shall need.

I. Notice how he addresses them. with what a name "Thou worm Jacob, & ye men of Israel." Had he given them a grander title they would have said it was not meant for them but now he gives them the name their enemies called them in scorn and which they felt to be true.

We are worms in our enemies esteem, their mind and intellect are of a grander conformation we are in their eyes. The lowest grade of men deluded enthusiasts, wanting the powers of free thinking and unbridled reason of which they boast.

But we are worms in our own esteem.

1 In Earthliness. By nature born in sin, we grow up in it and should continue in it. This same love of earth, care for earth & carnality dwelleth in us & maketh us groan out as worms. A worm is a fitter emblem than the moth or any creature.

2. In Insignificance. We are less than nothing. our own consequence appears great when we are in sin — little indeed under conviction — less when we believe & smaller as we grow in grace.

3. In our exposure to danger. There is the devil hopping to pick us up, the plough of trouble may turn up our nest. we fear lest the spade of the husbandman should cut us in sunder. We are in a world of dangers. &

4. Amid our exposure - we are <u>weak</u> & defenceless. The ungodly think they can defend themselves but we know we cannot. We <s>have</s> no natural

I. NOTICE HOW HE ADDRESSES THEM WITH WHAT A NAME, *"Thou worm Jacob and ye men of Israel."*

Had he given them a grander title, they would have said it was not meant for them. But now he gives them the name their enemies called them in scorn and which they felt to be true.

We are worms in our enemy's[7] esteem. Their mind and intellect[8] are of a grander conformation. We are in their eyes the lowest grade of men, deluded enthusiasts wanting the powers of free thinking and unbridled reason of which they boast.

But we are worms in our own esteem:

1.[9] In Earthliness. By nature, born in sin. We grow up in it and should continue in it. This same love of earth, care for earth and carnality, dwelleth in us and maketh us groan out as worms. A worm is a fitter emblem than the moth or any creature.

2. In Insignificance. We are less than nothing.[10] Our own consequence appears[11] great when we are in sin. Little,[12] indeed, under conviction, less when we believe, and smaller as we grow in grace.[13]

3. In our exposure to danger. There is the devil, hoping[14] to pick us up. The plough of trouble may turn up our nest.[15] We fear lest the spade of her husbandman should cut us in sunder. We are in a world of dangers, and

4. Amid our exposure, we are <u>weak</u> and defenseless.[16] The ungodly think they can defend themselves, but we know we cannot. We have no natural[17]

armour, no innate strength — we are worms.

But though worms we are men of Israel.

1. Men of prayer - prayer makes the worm a man.

2. Men loving faith - loving the temple - loving the great high priest; men in the wilderness_._._

II. Now let us notice the Lords comfort.—

He does not deny their weakness or remove it for them but says "I will help thee ——.

He bids them dismiss their fear.

1. For fear is needless, there is no necessity for it.

2. Fear is dangerous & tormenting to the Christian

3. It is sinful and dishonouring to God. It seems to imply a doubt of his love, or faithfulness, or power or wisdom & these doubts are vile indeed.

"I will help thee." & this will be quite sufficient Remember what others have done by the help of the Lord. Samson, Moses, David, Daniel, 3 in Babylon & then least the glories of the Lord should dazzle the Saviour says he too will be there.

"thy Redeemer," "the Holy one of Israel" he who died to redeem would die again rather than lose us.

III. Now notice a few cases when we need this indeed.

1. I do when preaching & fearing.

2. In the matter of justification, we often fear because of our sins, but God's help settles this at once.

armour, no innate strength.[18] We are worms.

But though worms, we are men of Israel:

1. Men of prayer. Prayer makes the worm a man.

2. Men loving faith, loving the temple, loving the great high priest, men in the wilderness.

II. NOW LET US NOTICE THE LORD'S COMFORT.

He does not deny their weakness or remove it for them, but says, "I will help thee."[19]

He bids them dismiss their fear.

1. For fear is needless. There is no necessity for it.[20]

2. Fear is dangerous and tormenting to the Christian.

3. It is sinful and dishonouring to God.[21] It seems to imply a doubt of his love, or faithfulness, or power, or wisdom,[22] and these doubts are vile indeed. "I will help thee," and this will be quite sufficient.[23]

   Remember what others have done by the help of the Lord. Samson, Moses, David, Daniel, 3 in Babylon.[24] And then, least[25] the glories of the Lord should dazzle, the Saviour says he too will be there. "Thy Redeemer," "the Holy one of Israel," he who died to redeem would die again rather than lose us.

III. NOW NOTICE A FEW CASES WHEN WE NEED THIS INDEED.

1. I do when preaching and fearing.[26]

2. In the matter of justification, we often fear because of[27] our sins,[28] but God's help settles this at once.

3. In the matter of sanctification – we fear lest we should turn back, or not progress, or fail.

4. In trouble from loss of friends, adverse circumstances, fear for temporal provision.

5. In death or the dread of it, at judgment.

Still the voice cries:

"Fear not I am with thee".

Be with me, Lord —

260. 261. 309. 344. 371. 565.

---

171.   Isa. 64. 1. 2. Oh that thou wouldest &c.

There is nothing the church so much bemoans as an absent God — The sins of Israel had driven away her God & now when in captivity & distress she bitterly laments his absence & desires that he would come again: even if his coming were attended with demonstrations of the most tremendous power.

The prophet has the coming of Sinai in view, & desires that he may come, even if it be in as great & awful a manner.

There are several ways in which this ancient prayer becomes still the language

3. In the matter of sanctification, we fear lest we should turn back or not progress, or fail.

4. In trouble from loss of friends, adverse circumstances, fear for temporal provision.

5. In death, or the dread of it, at judgment.

Still the voice cries,

"Fear not I am with thee."

Be with me, Lord.

260. 261. 309. 344. 371. 565.

OH *that* THOU WOULDEST, ETC.

Isaiah 64:1–2[1]

"Oh that thou wouldest rend the heavens, that thou wouldest come down, that the mountains might flow down at thy presence. As when the melting fire burneth, the fire causeth the waters to boil, to make thy name known to thine adversaries, that the nations may tremble at thy presence!"

There is nothing the church so much bemoans as an absent God. The sins of Israel had driven away her God and now when in captivity and distress[2] she bitterly laments his absence and desires that he would come again, even if his coming were attended with demonstrations of the most tremendous power.

The prophet has the coming of Sinai in view and desires that he may come, even if it be in as great and awful a manner.

There are several ways in which this ancient prayer becomes still the language of the saints.

1. In relation to the Second coming of Christ —
This we know from divers Scriptures will come
& indeed it is the mark of a true Christian that
he looks for & hastens unto that day —

When he comes it will be in a terrific manner,
The blue sky rent in twain, the melting mountains
the extinguished sun, the blushing moon, the
sea boiling & earth dissolving — shall but usher
in the scene — Then comes the great white
throne — the wail of myriads — the vengeance of
a God — the conquest of the earth —

Yet come dread day, I long for thee.
The true Christian fears not to cry out, Come
quickly — Ah! amid the sorrows, persecutions
distresses & afflictions of the godly, how oft has
this been the burthen of their groans. At the
view of earth o'erun by violence & horrid crime
or cursed hypocrisy — how often with a tear
do we cry, Oh Lord how long tarriest thou.
We have all to hope & nothing to fear.
but how will he indeed "make his name known
among his enemies & cause the nations
to tremble."

of the saints:

1. IN RELATION TO THE SECOND COMING OF CHRIST.

This we know from divers[3] Scriptures[4] will come, and indeed, it is the mark of a true Christian that he looks for and hastens unto that day.

When he comes, it will be in a terrific manner.[5] The blue sky rent in twain, the melting mountains,[6] the extinguished sun,[7] the blushing moon,[8] the sea boiling[9] and earth dissolving[10] shall but usher in the scene. Then comes the great white throne,[11] the wail of myriads,[12] the vengeance of a God,[13] the conquest of the earth.[14]

Yet come dread day, I long for thee. The true Christian fears not to cry out, "Come quickly." Ah! Amid the sorrows, persecutions, distresses and afflictions of the godly, how oft has this been the burthen[15] of their groans. At the view of earth o'erun[16] by violence and horrid[17] crime or cursed hypocrisy, how often with a tear do we cry, "Oh Lord, how long tarriest thou?" We have all to hope and nothing to fear. But how will he indeed "make his name known among his enemies and cause the nations to tremble?"

2. To his coming into his people's breasts.

God is an absent God to many of us ; our sins,
ours ingratitude, our unbelief & carnal security
have driven him away & now we mourn him.
If we feel aright we are not for making terms
upon which we would desire his presence ; but
we say "come, anyhow Lord!" Only do speak
& say anything thou wilt — The heaven now
is calm & peaceful but he may rend it with
tribulation if he will but come.   When he
comes the mountainous duty will be done easily
      the mountain of our pride would melt
      & all the mountains of our sin would depart
The fire would burn in our breast, the fire
of love & zeal would warm us, —   yea it would
be a melting fire melting our hearts completely.
The fire would make our cold hearts boil,
no lukewarm water but boiling hot. —
The waters of penitence, love, prayer, com-
-passion & all holy waters would boil.
Then indeed we should make the enemy
afraid & the foes of our religion would
see the presence of the Lord.

2. TO HIS COMING INTO HIS PEOPLE'S BREASTS.

God is an absent God to many of us. Our sins, our[18] ingratitude, our unbelief and carnal security have driven him away and now we mourn him. If we feel aright, we are not for making terms upon which we would desire his presence. But we say, "Come anyhow, Lord!" Only do speak and say anything thou wilt. The heaven now is calm and peaceful, but he may rend it with tribulation if he will but come. When he comes:

> the mountainous duty will be done easily.
> The mountain of our pride would melt,
> and all the mountains of our sin would depart.

The fire would burn in our breast. The fire of love and zeal would warm us. Yea, it would be a melting fire, melting our hearts completely. The fire would make our cold hearts boil. No lukewarm water,[19] but boiling hot. The waters of penitence, love, prayer, compassion, and all holy waters would boil. Then, indeed, we should make the enemy afraid, and the foes of our religion would see the presence of the Lord.

3. In relation to his coming in grace to the con-
-gregations in his house. —

This the one want of our times — we want this more
than money, labourers, hearers or professors.
In vain all learning or eloquence without this. —
We want some rending manifestations, not our
old ordinary course but something remarkable.
Oh would he come — the sinners who now stand
as mountains would melt & victory should be his.
God has two comings in his house.
— His Sinai comings — in the terror of his broken law.
He melts & makes stony heart flow down.
They are sore distressed as by a melting fire &
their breasts are as if they boiled with grief.
— His Calvary comings. in grace & mercy
& these are more mighty still through Jesus
The Cross seems to rend the vail of the heavens.
God in peace & joyfulness dwells with man.
The mountains of our sins flow away.
Our soul burns with love & boils with gratitude
Our enemies seem to have vanished & all
is a changed scene.
Oh! God I commit to paper this prayer
that — thou wouldst come down now —
& help me & save sinners through Jesus.

3. IN RELATIONS[20] TO HIS COMING IN GRACE TO THE CONGREGATIONS IN HIS HOUSE.

This [is] the one want of our times.[21] We want this more than money, labourers, hearers, or professors.[22] In vain [is] all learning or eloquence without this. We want some rending manifestations. Not our old, ordinary course, but something remarkable. Oh, would he come. The sinners who now stand as mountains would melt and victory should be his.

God has two comings in his house:

—His Sinai comings in the terror of his broken law. He melts and makes stony heart[s][23] flow down.[24]

They are sore distressed as by a melting fire and their breasts are as if they boiled with grief.

—His Calvary comings in grace and mercy. And these are more mighty still through Jesus. The Cross seems to rend the vail of the heavens. God in peace and joyfulness dwells with man. The mountains of our sins flow away. Our soul burns with love and boils with gratitude. Our enemies seem to have vanished and all is a changed scene.

Oh! God, I commit to paper this prayer, that thou wouldst come down now and help me and save sinners through Jesus.

Now learn how to obtain his presence.
If we want him to rend heaven we must rend
it too by our constant prayers. ⸺ ⸺
We must send up our wire on high to attract
the heavenly influence. We must count
mountains molehills & go zealously to work
by faith & prayer with constant endeavour
& you will soon see complete success.
    Amen. Even so. Come Lord Jesus.

263.268

---

172.   Acts XI. 26. The Church at Antioch.
 Kings are wont to chronicle their wars; mighty
men expect to be made to live after death in
the historic page ,⸺ but though these have
interest what is it compared with the interest
attaching to this book of Acts. The History
of England is not so important as this.
It is a "book of Martyrs". Stephen, Paul ⸺
It is a "book of voyages & travels" of thrilling interest
It is vol I of "The Christian times," It is a book
of debates, speeches, addresses, sermons &c.
 The Church of Antioch has a history so
interesting that I only pray that I may be

Now learn how to obtain his presence. If we want him to rend heaven, we must rend it too by our constant prayers.

We must send up our wire[25] on high to attract the heavenly influence. We must count mountains [as] molehills[26] and go zealously to work by faith and prayer with constant endeavour and you will soon see complete success.

Amen. Even so. Come, Lord Jesus.[27]

263. 268

172

THE CHURCH *at* ANTIOCH
Acts 11:26[1]

"And when he had found him, he brought him unto Antioch. And it came to pass, that a whole year they assembled themselves with the church, and taught much people. And the disciples were called Christians first in Antioch."

Kings are wont[2] to chronicle their wars. Mighty men expect to be made to live after death in the historic page. But though these have interest, what is it[3] compared with the interest attaching[4] to this book of Acts?

The History of England[5] is not so important as this.

It is a "book of Martyrs."[6] Stephen, Paul.[7]
It is a "book of voyages and travels"[8] of thrilling interest.
It is Vol. I of "The Christian times."[9]
It is a book of debates, speeches, addresses, sermons, etc.

The Church of Antioch has a history so interesting that I only pray that I may be helped to make it so. —

I. A Brief sketch of the history of the church in Antioch

Certain saints driven by persecution from Jerusalem
fled to Antioch & commenced their labours of love.
Their names are unmentioned — but God knoweth
them & they now receive their reward. Let my name
perish & let Christ's name last for ever.

The Lord's hand helped them & many believed
unto the Lord — these were so pious that the
Church in Jerusalem heard of it — & for their
further edification sent down Barnabas to labour
among them — He was full of faith & the Holy
Ghost & under him the church grew so great
that he went after Paul to assist him. They
were a liberal people & by God's grace continuing
to increase they soon had 5 pastors, & the
Holy Ghost put it into their minds to send
out 2 as missionaries elsewhere, who became
eminently successful & thus Antioch was a
mother church — to many surrounding parts.

Paul & Barnabas used to return there after
their laborious tours & there anchored in a haven.

1. Let us note — that the gospel is not of
necessity a slowly progressing affair. The first
preachers were very successful for it seems
about 10 years & the church was firmly established
In the next one — the church grew amazingly,
& why should not ours? & why not all others?

helped to make it so.

I. A BRIEF SKETCH OF THE HISTORY OF THE CHURCH IN ANTIOCH.

Certain saints, driven by persecution from Jerusalem, fled to Antioch and commenced their labours of love. Their names are unmentioned, but God knoweth them and they now receive their reward. Let my name perish and let Christ's name last for ever.[10]

The Lord's hand helped them and many believed unto the Lord. These were so pious that the Church in Jerusalem heard of it and for their further edification sent down Barnabas to labour among them.[11]

He was full of faith and the Holy Ghost, and under him the church grew so great that he went after Saul to assist him.[12] They were a liberal people and, by God's grace continuing to increase, they soon had 5 pastors.[13] And the Holy Ghost put it into their minds to send out 2 as missionaries elsewhere[14] who became eminently successful. And thus, Antioch was[15] a mother church to many surrounding parts.

Paul and Barnabas used to return there after their laborious tours, and there anchored in a haven.

1. Let us note that the gospel is not of necessity a slowly progressing affair. The first preachers were very successful, for it seems about 10 years and the Church was firmly established. In the next one, the Church grew amazingly. And why should not ours? And why not all others?

The conversion of the world will not always go on at snail-pace & we ought to pray that it may not in this place. Oh God! grant it.

2. Let us notice the principal elements of success in this case, believing them to be the same in all. There were things from God — the Ministers, the People.

God — In Providence shielded this Gentile Jerusalem from persecution & gave them peace. He sent them ministers enough. & a congregation. He sent his Spirit with these ministers.

the Ministers: — they preached the Lord Jesus. Barnabas was a good, kind, faithful man. He had a fulness faith & the Holy Ghost.

the people. — Must have much grace — a close cleaving to God & to one another. Liberality & readiness to any work of faith. & abundance of that jewel called "all prayer"

II. A few remarks upon the title first gained by this church at Antioch. "Christians." Perhaps the name was given as a designation by the Gentiles — gladly adopted by the disciples. — & sanctioned by divine authority. They had hitherto styled themselves "disciples" "the faithful", "the elect", "brethren." The Jews called them Nazarenes, Galileans &c & the sect was so small that doubtless among the masses of the heathen it was nondescript.

The conversion of the world will not always go on at snail-pace, and we ought to pray that it may not in this place.[16] Oh God! grant it.

2. Let us notice the principal elements of success in this case, believing them to be the same in all.

There were things from God, the Ministers, the people.

> **God**, in Providence, shielded this Gentile Jerusalem from persecution and gave them peace.
>
> He sent them ministers enough and a congregation.[17] He sent his Spirit with those ministers.
>
> **The Ministers**. They preached the Lord Jesus. Barnabas was a good, kind, faithful man. He had a fulness [of] faith and the Holy Ghost.[18]
>
> **The people** must have much grace, a close cleaving to God and to one another, Liberality and readiness to any work of faith, and abundance of that jewel called "all prayer."[19]

II. A FEW REMARKS UPON THE TITLE FIRST GAINED BY THIS CHURCH AT ANTIOCH, *"Christians."*

Perhaps the name was given as a designation by the Gentiles, gladly adopted by the disciples, and sanctioned by divine authority. They had hitherto styled[20] themselves "disciples," "the faithful," "the elect," "brethren."

The Jews called them Nazarenes, Galileans, etc. And the sect was so small that, doubtless among the masses of the heathen, it was nondescript.

But now in Antioch — the talent, the zeal, the number, influence & (even in some cases) wealth of the members of the new sect made it needful that it should have a name. & that is a good one

— Christians —

1. This intimates that there was much unity among the disciples so that one name would apply to all — Blessed time when this shall return & we shall be gathered in one.

2. This shows that the conversation, singing, worship, preaching of these men must have been much about Christ or how would the common people know their name.

3. This shows that their life & conduct must have been much like Christ — otherwise the more knowing class of the community would have denied their right to the title.

But I am called a Christian. How honourable a name! Manaen the foster-brother of Herod was more honoured in bearing this name than by his connection with a prince. Saul, the learned doctor in the Pharisaic school owess this as his greatest title & surely tis a title which an angel might be envious of. But what does it show.

1. That I am a believer in the divine mission of Jesus. — a believer in his official name "Christ" let me then take care to trust in him, most implicitly, & never by my doubts dishonour him.

But now in Antioch, the talent, the zeal, the number, influence, and (even in some cases) wealth of the members of the new sect made it needful that it should have a name. And that is a good one.

— C h r i s t i a n s —

1. This intimates that there was much unity among the disciples so that one name would apply to all. Blessed time when this shall return and we shall be gathered in one.[21]

2. This shows that the conversation, singing, worship, preaching, etc. of these men must have been much about Christ. Or how would the common people know their name?

3. This shows that their life and conduct must have been much like Christ. Otherwise, the more knowing class of the community would have denied their right to the title.

But I am called a Christian.[22]

How honourable a name! Manaen, the foster-brother of Herod,[23] was more honoured in bearing this name than by his connection with a prince. Saul, the learned doctor in the Pharisaic school, owns[24] this as his greatest title. And surely, [']tis a title which an angel might be envious of.

But what does it show?

1. That I am a believer in the divine Mission of Jesus, a believer in his official name, "Christ." Let me then take care to trust in him most implicitly and never by my doubts dishonour him.

2. That I am a professed imitator of the holy
harmless. undefiled, loving, generous Jesus.
let me then be so in all things.
3. I am a lover of Jesus, then let my
conversation & talk & meditation be of him.
4. A Christian — An anointed one to be a
priest unto God to offer continual prayer
& praise on the High Altar.

Bearing the one name — which the glorious
army of martyrs — the great apostles & the
saints have borne — Oh — may we honour
the name + on our shoulder
bear the cross of Jesus —

264 & 265

---

173. II Cor. 2. 16. "Who is sufficient for these things?"
The words immediately before the text contain
much comfort to all faithful ministers
We have a great contest but we are not defeated
Yea rather we always triumph or more correctly
are led in triumph as instances of the grace &
mercy of God. Though driven from many cities
by the violence of persecution, he did not count
himself beaten, but counted even that a
triumph in Christ. The saviour of his

2. That I am a professed imitator of the holy, harmless, undefiled, loving, generous Jesus. Let me then be so in all things.

3. I am a lover of Jesus. Then let my conversation and talk and meditation be of him.

4. A Christian. An anointed one to be a priest unto God, to offer continual prayer and praise on the High Altar.

Bearing the one name which the glorious army of martyrs, the great apostles, and the saints have borne.

Oh, may we honour the name, and on our shoulder bear the cross of Jesus.

264 and[25] 265

173

WHO IS SUFFICIENT
for THESE THINGS?
2 Corinthians 2:16[1]

"To the one we are the savour of death unto death; and to the other the savour of life unto life. And who is sufficient for these things?"

The words immediately before the text contain much comfort to all faithful ministers.[2] We have a great contest, but we are not defeated. Yea, rather we always triumph, or more correctly, are led in triumph as instances of the grace and mercy of God.

Though driven from many cities by the violence of persecution, he[3] did not count himself beaten, but counted even that a triumph in Christ.[4] The savour of his

preaching was the same as to sweetness, whether men were saved or no :— God rode along as the mighty conqueror & his gospel is the sweet odour cast on the triumphal procession, which was the same, though it fell on those condemned to die or on the soldiers who fought for their King. God requires labour of us, but not success —
On the remembrance of the work of the ministry Paul utters the exclamation before us.

This shall be enforced by noticing

I. The ministerial office as a whole.

1. Where is one worthy to fill the office - to stand & declare in God's name his own gospel. Why even an angel is unworthy to take the office.

2. Consider the glory of the office - It was glorious to be a priest, a minister of the Mosaic ritual but to preach the gospel of light & life :—

3. Consider the importance of the office. In us instrumentally lies the hope of the world. We are its guards, its police — & through divine help its preservers.

4. Consider the danger, to which popularity, or the contrary exposes us. The keen eye on us.

5. Consider the perseverance required, not a flash but a steady fire & blaze.

II. Now let us notice the ministerial office in its various parts & thus enforce it more. —

preaching was the same as to sweetness whether men were saved or no[t].[5] God rode along as the mighty conqueror and his gospel is the sweet odour cast on the triumphal procession, which was the same, though it fell on these[6] condemned to die or on the soldiers who fought for their king.

God requires labour of us, but not success.[7]

On the remembrance of the work of the ministry, Paul utters the exclamation before us. This shall be enforced by noticing:

I.   THE MINISTERIAL OFFICE AS A WHOLE.

1. Where is one worthy to fill[8] the office, to stand and declare in God's name his own gospel? Why, even an angel is unworthy to[9] take the office.[10]

2. Consider the glory of the office. It was glorious to be a priest, a minister of the Mosaic ritual. But to preach the gospel of light and life.[11]

3. Consider the importance of the office.[12] In us instrumentally lies the hope of the world.[13] We are its guards, its police, and through divine help, its preservers.

4. Consider the danger to which popularity,[14] or the contrary, exposes us. The keen eye [is] on us.

5. Consider the perseverance required. Not a flash, but a steady fire and blaze.[15]

II. NOW LET US NOTICE THE MINISTERIAL OFFICE IN ITS VARIOUS PARTS, AND THUS ENFORCE IT MORE.

1. To maintain the true doctrines of the gospel – How difficult so to do – amid the thousand mazes of error. To avoid the extremes & the by-paths.

2. To comfort God's children – to stir them up to diligence – to promote love – to avoid offence. to keep them from wandering by the word.

3. To call backsliders home – neither comforting nor killing – giving no room for presumption or despair.

4. To wake up God's enemies by warning them of sin – by drawing to Jesus &c &c – what hearts!

Out of the pulpit –

1. To lead a consistent life.

2. To manifest no partiality.

3. To visit the sick.

4. To speak faithfully to individuals.

III. What does this lead us to think. –

1. That we have need of all grace & therefore of all the prayers of the people

2. That you must not expect us to be perfect seeing none is sufficient.

3. That if good is done, the glory must all be given to the Lord our God.

4. That the help received demands a song of grateful praise –

O God help – Amen by Jesus.

267

1. To maintain the true doctrines of the gospel. How difficult so to do amid the thousand mazes of error. To avoid the extremes and the by-paths.

2. To comfort God's children, to stir them up to diligence, to promote love, to avoid offence, to keep them from wandering by the Word.

3. To call backsliders home, neither comforting nor killing, giving no room for presumption or despair.[16]

4. To wake up God's enemies by warning them of sin by drawing to Jesus, etc., etc. What hearts!

   Out of the pulpit:

   1. To lead a consistent life.

   2. To manifest no partiality.

   3. To visit the sick.[17]

   4. To speak faithfully to individuals.

III. WHAT DOES THIS LEAD US TO THINK?

1. That we have need of all grace, and therefore, of all the prayers of the people.[18]

2. That you must not expect us to be perfect, seeing none is sufficient.

3. That if good is done, the glory must all be given to the Lord our God.

4. That the help received demands a song of grateful praise.

Oh God, help. Amen by Jesus.

267

1. Charles preached three additional sermons on John 16:33. On December 3, 1876, he preached a sermon entitled "Christ, the Overcomer of the World" (*MTP* 22, Sermon 1327). On December 4, 1887, he preached a sermon entitled "Sweet Peace for Tried Believers" (*MTP* 33, Sermon 1994). And he also preached a sermon published after his death on January 18, 1912, entitled "Good Cheer from Christ's Victory over the World" (*MTP* 58, Sermon 3285). Overlapping content exists among the sermons; however, there is not enough structural similarity to suggest Charles had in mind his early sermon when writing his later three sermons.

2. Charles did not originally hyphenate the word "God-like." It has been hyphenated for consistency.

3. "This farewell discourse may occupy but a short space in Scripture, but the thoughts suggested by it are so many that I suppose that the world itself might hardly contain the books that might fairly be written upon it. It took our Lord but a moment to speak some of its sentences; it will take us a lifetime fully to understand them" (*MTP* 33:649).

4. In his personal library Charles owned a book entitled *The Story of our Lighthouses and Lightships* in which the following excerpt is found: "The first article of the instructions which every light-keeper is bound to obey—and to obey as implicitly as a soldier obeys the laws of military discipline—run thus: 'You are to light the lamps every evening at sun-setting, and keep them constantly burning, bright and clear, till sun-rising.' This is the primary condition of a light-keeper's duty; for this he lives, toils, and watches, in order that the warning light, which has been the salvation of so many tall ships and their gallant crews, may burn with uninterrupted and steadfast rays through the hours of darkness. 'Whatever else happens,' says a graphic writer, 'he is to do this. He may be isolated through the long night-watches, twenty miles from land, fifty or a hundred feet below the level of the sea, with the winds and waves howling around him, and the sea-birds dashing themselves to death against the gleaming lantern, like giant moths against a candle'" (W. H. Davenport Adams, *The Story of our Lighthouses and Lightships: Descriptive and Historical* [London: Thomas Nelson, 1891, The Spurgeon Library], 375–76).

5. Roman historian Suetonius recorded the death of Octavian Augustus: "Upon the day of his death, he now and then enquired, if there was any disturbance in the

town on his account; and calling for a mirror, he ordered his hair to be combed, and his shrunk cheeks to be adjusted. Then asking his friends who were admitted into the room, 'Do ye think that I have acted my part on the stage of life well?' he immediately subjoined . . . 'If all be right, with joy your voices raise, in loud applauses to the actor's praise'" (Alexander Thomson, trans., T. Forester, revised, *The Lives of the Twelve Caesars by C. Suetonius Tranquillus: To Which Are Added His Lives of the Grammarians, Rhetoricians, and Poets* [London: George Bell & Sons, 1896], 144).

6. The words "Have pity upon me" may suggest Charles had Luke 16:24 in mind. In the parable, however, the rich man had already died.

7. This is the second time in this notebook that Charles deductively outlined the major divisions of his sermon after his introduction (see also "Open Profession Required" [Sermon 158]). Given the lack of margin space and punctuation allocated for Roman numeral I, Charles likely added the Roman numeral after writing the sentence.

8. "Doth he not herein teach us that there is no balm for the heart like himself. . . . So then, beloved, in all times of depression of spirit hasten away to the Lord Jesus Christ; whenever the cares of this life burden you, and your way seems hard for your weary feet, fly to your Lord. There may be, and there are, other sources of consolation, but they will not at all times serve your turn; but in Him there dwelleth such a fulness of comfort, that whether it be in summer or in winter the streams of comfort are always flowing. In your high estate or in your low estate, and from whatever quarter your trouble may arise, you can resort at once to him and you shall find that he strengthens the hands that hang down and confirms the feeble knees" (*MTP* 22:673).

9. John 14:1–2, "Let not your heart be troubled: ye believe in God, believe also in me. In my Father's house are many mansions: if it were not so, I would have told you. I go to prepare a place for you." See also "Heaven's Preparations" (Notebook 1, Sermon 28).

10. "Reversion, in the law of England, has two significations; the one of which is, an estate left, which continues during a particular state in being; and the other is the returning of the land, after the particular estate is ended; and is further said to be an interest in lands when the possession of it fails, or where the estate, which was

for a time parted with, returns to the granters or their heirs. But according to the usual definition of a reversion, it is the residue of an estate left in the granter, after a particular estate granted away ceases, continuing in the granter of such an estate" (*The Encyclopædia Britannica; or, Dictionary of Arts, Sciences, and General Literature. Eighth Edition. With Extensive Improvements and Additions; and Numerous Engravings*, Volume 19 [Edinburgh: Adam and Charles Black, 1859]). Not long after moving to London, Charles preached, "I ask no royal pomp or fame now; I am prepared to wait, I have an interest in reversion. I want not a pitiful estate here—I will tarry till I get my domains in heaven, those broad and beautiful domains that God has provided for them that love him. Well content will I be to fold my arms and sit me down in the cottage, for I shall have a mansion of God, 'a house not made with hands, eternal in the heavens.' Do any of you know what it is to live on the future—to live on expectation—to live on what you are to have in the next world—to live upon the manna of expectation which falls in the wilderness, and to drink that stream of nectar which gushes from the throne of God?" (*NPSP* 1:190–91). See also *MTP* 18:172; *MTP* 26:239; and *MTP* 45:92.

11. Abbr. "verse."

12. Because both passages refer to Christ's "Godhead and union with the Father," it is unclear whether Charles was alluding to John's fourteenth or sixteenth chapter. John 14:10, "Believest thou not that I am in the Father, and the Father in me? the words that I speak unto you I speak not of myself: but the Father that dwelleth in me, he doeth the works." John 16:10, "Of righteousness, because I go to my Father, and ye see me no more." In the previous point Charles referenced John 14, which may suggest the former interpretation is more likely.

13. A series of dots and reversed numbers appear on and around the word "which." These ink markings were the result of the imprinting of the number 308 on the opposite page. The periods for numbers 250, 253, 254, and 508 are also evident. The smudges of the numbers on the opposite page, along with these imprints, suggest Charles closed the notebook before the ink dried.

14. Abbr., "verse."

15. John 14:13, "And whatsoever ye shall ask in my name, that will I do, that the Father may be glorified in the Son."

16. Abbr., "verse."

17. John 14:26, "But the Comforter, which is the Holy Ghost, whom the Father will send in my name, he shall teach you all things, and bring all things to your remembrance, whatsoever I have said unto you."

18. John 15:5, "I am the vine, ye are the branches: He that abideth in me, and I in him, the same bringeth forth much fruit: for without me ye can do nothing."

19. John 15:16, "Ye have not chosen me, but I have chosen you, and ordained you, that ye should go and bring forth fruit, and *that* your fruit should remain: that whatsoever ye shall ask of the Father in my name, he may give it you."

20. "Befitting a lord." Charles here did not intend Samuel Johnson's second definition, "Proud; haughty; imperious; insolent" (Johnson's *Dictionary*, s.v. "lordly").

21. Charles did not include an apostrophe or the letter "s" to make the word "Jesus" possessive. They have been added for consistency.

22. Cf. John 15:18–20.

23. John 16:5, "But now I go my way to him that sent me; and none of you asketh me, Whither goest thou?"

24. Charles likely intended to draw attention to the word "by." The sentence may read, "'In me,' or *by* me, as the phrase often means."

25. "O friends, Christ has peace enough and to spare. He is himself, personally, the deep well-spring of an endless peace, and therefore we can understand why we always find peace in him. . . . His infinite peace breathes peace into our vacillating spirits. We rest because we see how he rests" (*MTP* 33:651).

26. An illegible superscript, likely the number 2, appears above the word "extra." By contrasting "real" with "extra," Charles may have been thinking of the differences between internal and external states.

27. "Oh, that we could learn from Christ the art of peace! He desires that we should have it. Then we should not be so often up and so speedily down, to-day so brimming over and to-morrow so empty, one moment so fast and another so

slow, unduly exhilarated at one moment and at the next so needlessly depressed. We ought not to be movable as waves, but fixed as stars. We ought not to be as thistle-down, the sport of every wind, but as yonder granite peak, which defies the storms of the ages" (*MTP* 33:652).

28. Cf. Matt 8:23–27; Mark 4:25–41.

29. Cf. Acts 7:54–59.

30. Cf. Acts 16:26–28; 2 Cor 4:8–9.

31. Charles misspelled the name of the prophet Habakkuk by adding an extra "b" and not including an additional letter "k." Cf. Hab 3:17–18.

32. "Now the world can go no further in persecuting his people than he permits it. Not a martyr can burn, nor a confessor be imprisoned without the permit of Jesus Christ who is the Lord of all; for the government is upon his shoulders and his kingdom ruleth over all" (*MTP* 22:682).

33. "We are quite certain that our Lord Jesus Christ does not desire his disciples to be depressed. . . . The Saviour does not wish his disciples to go through the world as through a twilight of sadness, whispering in fear because of judgments to come, and suppressing all joy because of the evils with which they are surrounded. No, brethren, Jesus wishes us all to be happy in himself, with a quiet peacefulness like his own" (*MTP* 33:652).

34. Quotation marks have been added around this verse for consistency.

35. Cf. 1 Cor 15:55.

36. "The cross is the best piece of furniture in your house, though you have sometimes wished it was not there. . . . It is a bitter tree, apparently, but it is a healthful medicine. Take it, child of God; plant it, and let it grow, and its fruit shall be sweet. We are not guarded from tribulation, but we are promised it, and we are benefited by it" (*MTP* 33:656).

37. Cf. Heb 2:10; see also "Christ About His Father's Business" (Notebook 1, Sermon 15).

38. Quotation marks have been added here and in the lines below to indicate the words of Jesus.

39. The following quotation comes from Charles's personal copy of John Bunyan's *The Pilgrim's Progress*: "Then the *Interpreter* took him, and led him up toward the door of the Palace; and behold, at the door stood a great Company of men, as desirous to go in, but durst not. There also sat a Man, at a little distance from the door, at a Table-side, with a Book, and his Inkhorn before him, to take the Name of him that should enter therein; He saw also that in the door-way, stood many Men in Armour to keep it; being resolved to do to the Man that would enter, what hurt and mischief they could. Now was *Christian* somewhat in a muse: at last, when every Man started back for fear of the Armed Men; *Christian* saw a Man of a very stout countenance come up to the Man that sat there to write; saying, Set down my name, Sir, the which when he had done, he saw the Man draw his Sword, and put an Helmut upon his Head, and rush toward the door upon the Armed Men, who laid upon him with deadly force; but the Man, not at all discouraged, fell to cutting and hacking most fiercely; so, after he had received and given many wounds to those that attempted to keep him out, he cut his way through them all, and pressed forward into the Palace; at which there was a pleasant voice heard from those that were within, even of the Three that walked upon the top of the Palace, 'saying,' *Come in, Come in; Eternal Glory thou shalt win.* So he went in, and was cloathed [*sic*] with such Garments as they. Then Christian smiled, and said, I think verily I know the meaning of this" (John Bunyan, *The Pilgrim's Progress: From This World to That Which Is to Come. Delivered Under the Similitude of a Dream. Wherein Is Discovered, the Manner of His Setting Out; His Dangerous Journey, and Safe Arrival at the Desired Country. Accurately Printed from the First Edition, with Notices of All the Subsequent Additions and Alterations Made by the Author Himself. Edited for The Hanserd Knollys Society, with an Introduction by George Offor* [London: J. Haddon, 1847, The Spurgeon Library], 32–33, italics in the original). Charles first discovered *The Pilgrim's Progress* as a child in his grandfather's attic in Stambourne (see *Autobiography* 1:22–23). Bunyan's allegory became Charles's favorite book. During his courtship with Susannah, he gave her a copy of this book with the inscription "Miss Thompson[,] with desires for her progress in the blessed pilgrimage. From C. H. Spurgeon. April 20, 1854" (*Autobiography* 2:7). With regard to Bunyan's use of allegory, Charles said, "Mr. Bunyan is the chief, and head, and lord of all allegorists, and is not to be

followed by us into the deep places of typical and symbolical utterance. He was a swimmer, we are but mere waders, and must not go beyond our depth" (*Lectures* 1:114). In his final early-sermon notebook, Charles wrote, "No Book has been more honoured of God than the Pilgrim's Progress" ("Deaf Cured" [Notebook 9, Sermon 368]). For additional references to Bunyan's allegory in Charles's early notebooks, see "The Fight and the Weapons" (Notebook 1, Sermon 37a); "The Fight" (Notebook 1, Sermon 37b); and "David in the Cave of Adullam" (Notebook 2, Sermon 116).

40. Cf. Gen 3:15; Rom 16:20.

1. This is the only time Charles preached a sermon on Matt 12:43–45.

2. For additional uses of the word "fancied," see "The Men Possessed of the Devils" (Notebook 1, Sermon 70) and "Inventory and Title of Our Treasures" (Notebook 2, Sermon 92).

3. Charles first wrote the word "the" before adding the letters "i" and "m" to construct "them" or "their." Charles may have intended to write "their hearts."

4. Cf. Gen 2:7–3:6.

5. This is the first instance in this notebook in which Charles misspelled a word by reversing its letters. In this case the letters "ger" should be ordered "reg" to construct the word "vice-regent." A second instance of this occurrence may be found in the reversal of the letters "ru" in the word "cursed" in "Christ the Power of God" (Sermon 169b). For other uses of the word "vice-regent," see "The Improvement of Our Talents" (Notebook 1, Sermon 61) and "Oh That Men Would Praise the Lord" (Notebook 2, Sermon 105).

6. Charles wrote the word "two" before changing it to "three."

7. The ampersand between the words "heart" and "unclean" has been changed to "is." If retained, the sentence would read "The heart and unclean and the devil unclean."

8. Cf. 1 Pet 5:8.

9. The word "find" was smeared toward the bottom of the page, along with the words "deserted," "sees," "and grace," "affection," "care," "the devil's," and "religious" below it and "mischief" above it. The smear was likely caused by one singular gesture.

10. Charles first wrote the word "the" before adding the letters "o" and "rs" to construct the word "others."

11. An alternative reading of this line is "The tears [are] few and the affection slight."

12. The Devil's Ditch (also called the Devil's Dyke) is an eight-mile-long ditch in Newmarket, not far from Newmarket Academy where Charles received his

teenage education. The ditch is approximately fifteen feet deep and acquired its name from mythical origins. "According to myth, Devil's Dyke was not dug at all, but was the work of the devil. When he discovered that he had not been invited to a local wedding, the devil rushed angrily across East Anglia, flicking his tail and so etching the ditch onto the landscape" (Stephanie Boyd, *The Story of Cambridge* [Cambridge: Cambridge University Press, 2005], 15). "It commences abruptly at the river side at Brandon, not being discoverable on the south side of the fen, and towards the north it terminates at the fenny district of the Stoke River, near Cranwick: this is the southern part called *Foss* or *Devil's Dyke*. The northern part, also called *Devil's Dyke*, appears similarly to cross a dry district between fens. It probably commenced at Beachamwell by the fen side, not at Oxburg, which lies to the south of this fen district, and extended to Narburgh on the fens by the side of the River Nar" (Charles Cardale Babington, *Ancient Cambridgeshire; or, an Attempt to Trace Roman and Other Ancient Roads That Passed Through the County of Cambridge; with a Record of the Places Where Roman Coins and Other Remains Have Been Found. Second edition, Much Enlarged* [Cambridge: printed for the Cambridge Antiquarian Society, sold by Deighton, Bell & Co.; and Macmillan & Co.; London: George Bell & Sons, 1883], 105, italics in the original). In 1923, archaeologists believed the dyke was constructed in the first century. Cyril Fox noted, "Consideration of its scale and character justifies the view that it must date from a time when the energies of a large part of the population of Norfolk and N. W. Suffolk were controlled from a single centre" (Cyril Fox, *The Archaeology of the Cambridge Region: A Topographical Study of the Bronze, Early Iron, Roman and Anglo-Saxon Ages, with an Introduction Note on the Neolithic Age* [Cambridge: Cambridge University Press, 1923], 131). Later excavations suggested a post-Roman date of origin. According to Peter Blair, the ditch, along with others in the area, were "not likely to be as late as the seventh century since they are not in accord with what is known as the political geography of that or any later century." He added, "It may be conjectured that they represent defences erected by invaders who had been compelled to abandon the upper Thames valley in the face of defeat at the hands of the British and to seek security within the natural protection afforded by the Fens on the one hand and the sea on the others" (Peter Hunter Blair, *An Introduction to Anglo-Saxon England. Third Edition, with a New Introduction by Simon Keynes* [3rd ed.; Cambridge: Cambridge University Press, originally pub. 1956, 2003], 32). The Devil's Dyke was commonly referenced in literature and popular newspapers throughout Cambridgeshire. In 1882, a potentially fatal shooting occurred near the ditch (see "Serious Affray with Poachers,"

The Citizen: A Daily Newspaper for Gloucestershire and the Surrounding Districts, February 4, 1882). For an additional reference to the Devil's Ditch in Charles's later ministry, see *TD* 3:220.

13. As on the previous page, a noticeable downward smear can be seen over the words "Empty," "Swept," "Garnished," "Take," and "man." This smear was likely the result of one singular gesture.

14. Charles originally wrote the word "gaard" before converting the first "a" into a "u" to construct the word "guard." This is the third instance in which Charles misspelled this word (see also "Bring My Soul out of Prison" [Sermon 164]).

15. Cf. Ps 26:4–5; Prov 14:7; 1 Cor 15:33.

16. An alternative reading of this line is "Poor penitent, go to the strong [One] for strength."

1. This is the second instance thus far in his early notebooks in which Charles preached two sermons on the same text, one after the other (see also "The Fight and the Weapons" [Notebook 1, Sermon 37a] and "The Fight" [Notebook 1, Sermon 37b]). Charles assigned the sermon number 169 to both this sermon and the following one (see "Christ the Power of God"). For this reason this sermon will be labeled 169a. A pattern may be detected in that the second sermon in this notebook and also in Notebook 1 are delimited more narrowly in their titles. Charles offered a reason for the second sermon on 1 Cor 1:24 at the conclusion of this sermon: "Finding too much matter, I leave one part and go on with the other."

2. On May 17, 1857, Charles preached an additional sermon on 1 Cor 1:24 entitled "Christ—the Power and Wisdom of God" (*NPSP* 3, Sermon 132). As in the following sermon, there is enough overlapping content and structural similarity to suggest Charles's 1857 sermon was an expansion of the sermons in this notebook.

3. "Christ considered as God and man, the Son of God equal with his Father, and yet the man, born of the Virgin Mary" (*NPSP* 3:201).

4. Charles wrote the words "and has" above and between the words "is" and "indeed."

5. The lack of margin space suggests the division in this sermon of the word "Power" was an afterthought. He likely inserted it after writing the four points in his list below.

6. Cf. Col 1:16.   7.   Cf. 1 Pet 2:24.

8. An alternative reading of this line is "He taketh Saints to heaven and so must [have been God]."

9. Charles originally wrote the number 2 before correcting it by writing the number 1.

10. "The great things he did *before all worlds* were proofs of his wisdom. He planned the way of salvation; he devised the system of atonement and substitution; he laid the foundations of the great plan of salvation. There was wisdom. But he built

the heavens by wisdom, and he laid the pillars of light, whereon the firmament is balanced, by his skill and wisdom. Mark the world; and learn, as ye see all its multitudinous proofs of the wisdom of God, that there you have the wisdom of Christ; for he was the creator of it" (*NPSP* 3:202, italics in the original).

11. Hebrews 2:10, "For it became him, for whom are all things, and by whom are all things, in bringing many sons unto glory, to make the captain of their salvation perfect through sufferings."

1. For a rationale explaining the numbering of this sermon, see the previous sermon, "Christ the Power and Wisdom of God."

2. On May 17, 1857, Charles preached an additional sermon on 1 Cor 1:24 entitled "Christ—the Power and Wisdom of God" (*NPSP* 3, Sermon 132). As in the previous sermon, there is enough overlapping content and structural similarity to suggest Charles's 1857 sermon was an expansion of the sermons in this notebook.

3. Isaiah 9:6, "For unto us a child is born, unto us a son is given: and the government shall be upon his shoulder: and his name shall be called Wonderful, Counsellor, The mighty God, The everlasting Father, The Prince of Peace."

4. The lack of margin space suggests the number 1 was an afterthought. Charles likely added it after writing the sentence "He is the power of God since by him the worlds were made."

5. Charles inserted an apostrophe between the letters "d" and "s" in the word "world's." The apostrophe has been deleted to reflect the plural, not possessive, rendering of the word. An alternative reading of this line is "He is the power of God since by him the world [was] made."

6. "The pillars of the earth were placed in their everlasting sockets by the omnipotent right hand of Christ" (*NPSP* 3:201).

7. Colossians 1:16, "For by him were all things created, that are in heaven, and that are in earth, visible and invisible, whether they be thrones, or dominions, or principalities, or powers: all things were created by him, and for him."

8. Charles likely had in mind John 1:3, "All things were made by him; and without him was not any thing made that was made."

9. Hebrews 1:3, "Who being the brightness of his glory, and the express image of his person, and upholding all things by the word of his power, when he had by himself purged our sins, sat down on the right hand of the Majesty on high."

10. "When the voice of Jesus startled the shades of Hades, and rent the bonds of death, with 'Lazarus come forth!' and when the carcass rotten in the tomb was woke up to life, there was proof of his divine power and godhead" (*NPSP* 3:202). Cf. John 11.

11. "The winds hushed by his finger uplifted, the waves calmed by his voice, so that they became solid as marble beneath his tread" (*NPSP* 3:202). Cf. Matt 8:23–27; Mark 4:34–41.

12. Cf. Matt 14:22–33; Mark 6:45–56; John 6:16–24.

13. Cf. Matt 14:13–21; Mark 6:30–44; Luke 9:10–17; John 6.

14. "At last he yielded up his life, and was buried in the tomb. Not long, however, did he sleep; for he gave another proof of his divine power and godhead, when starting from his slumber, he affrighted the guards with the majesty of his grandeur, not being holden by the bonds of death, they being like green withes before our conquering Samson, who had meanwhile pulled up the gates of hell, and carried them on his shoulders far away" (*NPSP* 3:202). Cf. Luke 24; 1 Corinthians 15.

15. Charles reversed the letters "r" and "u" in the word "cursed" (see also his treatment of the word "vice-gerent" in his sermon "The Unclean Spirit Returning" [Sermon 168]).

16. The question mark after the word "God" was smeared toward the lower right side of the page.

17. An illegible letter was written beneath the "R" in the word "Romish." If this letter is a lowercase "r," Charles likely failed to capitalize the word originally.

18. Charles was likely referring to the religious persecutions of the English Puritans and others, including his great-grandfather's grandfather Job Spurgeon, a Quaker from Dedham who was imprisoned for almost four months for not paying a fine for attending a Nonconformist meeting (*Autobiography* 1:8). "The good bark of the Church has had to plough her way through seas of blood, and those who have manned her have been bespattered with the bloody spray; yea, they have had to man her and keep her in motion, by laying down their lives unto the death. Mark the bitter persecution of the Church of Christ, from the time of Nero to the days of Mary, and further on, through the days of Charles the Second, and of those kings of unhappy memory, who had not as yet learned how to spell 'toleration.' From the dragoons of Claverhouse, right straight away to the gladiatorial shows of Rome, what a long series of persecutions has the gospel had?" (*NPSP* 3:203).

19. See "Oh That Men Would Praise the Lord" (Notebook 2, Sermon 105).

20. An illegible letter was written inside the bowl of the letter "o."

21. "Unbelief towards the Gospel of Christ is the most unreasonable thing in all the world, because the reason which the unbeliever gives for his unbelief is fairly met by the character and constitution of the Gospel of Christ. . . . While the gospel can be understood by the poorest and the most illiterate, while there are shallows in it where a lamb may wade, there are depths where leviathan may swim" (*NPSP* 3:201, 205). "I remember saying once, and as I cannot say it better I will repeat it, that before I knew the Gospel I gathered up a heterogeneous mass of all kinds of knowledge from here, there, and everywhere; a bit of chemistry, a bit of botany, and a bit of astronomy, and a bit of this, that, and the other. I put them altogether, in one great confused chaos. When I learned the Gospel, I got a shelf in my head to put everything away upon just where it should be. It seemed to me as if, when I had discovered Christ and him crucified, I had got the centre of the system, so that I could see every other science revolving round in order. . . . Begin with any other science you like, and truth will seem to be awry. Begin with the science of Christ crucified, and you will begin with the sun, you will see every other science moving round it in complete harmony. The greatest mind in the world will be evolved by beginning at the right end" (*NPSP* 3:207).

22. "If you want not this power of Christ, and this wisdom of Christ now, you will want them in a few short moments, when God shall come to judge the quick and the dead, when you shall stand before his bar, and when all the deeds that you have done shall be read before an assembled world. You will want religion then. Oh that you had grace to tremble now" (*NPSP* 3:208).

23. Charles unusually inserted the period before the number 256. He also wrote an ampersand between the two numbers. For a second instance in which he displays this tendency in this notebook, see his sermon "The Church of Antioch" (Sermon 172).

1. On the very last page of this notebook Charles recorded, "The 4 texts given me by an aged Sister are: John XX. 16. No. 175. Zech XIV. 6.7. No. 176. John XIII. 23. No. 183. Isa. XLI. 10. The 14th is similar. No. 170." In other words, the four texts given by the "aged Sister" to Charles to preach are (in numerical order): "Fear Not, Thou Worm Jacob" (Sermon 170); "Mary with Jesus in the Garden" (Sermon 175); "Light at Eventide" (Sermon 176); and "Leaning on Jesus['s] Bosom" (Sermon 183). Charles preached from all these texts at her request with the exception of this sermon. Instead of preaching on verse 10 as she requested, Charles preached on Isa 41:14, which he deemed was "similar." Who was the "aged Sister"? Unfortunately, there is no record of her in Charles's autobiography, his letters to his family members during this season of his ministry, or in his biographies. Nor is there recorded in this notebook the reason she requested these four texts to be preached by Charles.

2. Charles preached two additional sermons on Isa 41:14. On Sunday morning, October 4, 1857, he preached a sermon entitled "Fear Not" (*NPSP* 3, Sermon 156). That evening, he preached a sermon on Isa 41:14b entitled "Thy Redeemer" (*NPSP* 3, Sermon 157). There is enough overlapping content in Charles's morning sermon to suggest he expanded on the sermon in this notebook. The evening sermon shares little overlapping content, as Charles focused the majority of his attention on the second portion of the passage.

3. Charles may have attempted to pluralize the word "husband" before striking through the beginnings of the letter "s."

4. Charles did not include an apostrophe between the letters "y" and "s" in the word "days." An apostrophe has been added to show possession.

5. The letter "o" in the word "foresaw" is bolded and smeared toward the bottom of the page.

6. Cf. 2 Kgs 24:15; Esth 2:6; Jer 22:25. See "Little Children Keep Yourselves from Idols" (Sermon 153).

7. Charles wrote the word "enemies." However, the word has been changed to "enemy's" to show possession.

8. A dark stain appears above the second "l" in the word "intellect." It is likely the result of the aging of the notebook.

9. As in his previous sermon, "Christ the Power of God" (Sermon 169b), the lack of margin space suggests the number 1 was an afterthought. Charles likely decided to begin his list after writing the words "In Earthliness."

10. "Your emptiness is but the preparation of your being filled, and your casting down is but the making ready for your lifting up" (*NPSP* 3:391).

11. The bolded "s" differs in pressure from the handwriting surrounding it and was either added afterward or was the result of Charles dipping his stylus into the ink.

12. "I am so little, that I shrink into nothingness when I behold the Almightiness of Jehovah" (*NPSP* 3:391).

13. An alternative reading of this line is "Our own consequence appears great when we are in sin. Little, indeed, [when we are] under conviction, less when we believe, and smaller as we grow in grace."

14. Charles wrote the word "hopping," but it has been changed to "hoping" to reflect his intention. If "hopping" is retained, the sentence could read "There is the devil, hopping [around] to pick us up." Cf. 1 Pet 5:8.

15. "Periodic tornadoes and hurricanes will sweep o'er the Christian; he will be subjected to as many trials in his spirit as trials in his flesh. This much I know, if it be not so with all of you it is so with me. I have to speak to-day to myself; and whilst I shall be endeavouring to encourage those who are distressed and down-hearted, I shall be preaching, I trust, to myself, for I need something which shall cheer my heart—why I cannot tell, wherefore I do not know, but I have a thorn in the flesh, a messenger of Satan to buffet me; my soul is cast down within me, I feel as if I had rather die than live; all that God hath done by me seems to be forgotten, and my spirit flags and my courage breaks down with the thought of that which is to come. I need your prayers; I need God's Holy Spirit; and I felt that I could not preach to-day, unless I should preach in such a way as to encourage you and to encourage myself in the good work and labour of the Lord Jesus Christ" (*NPSP* 3:390).

16. Two illegible letters were written beneath the letters "f" and "e" in the word "defenceless." (Charles originally spelled the word "defenceless.") Additional

markings, likely caused by accidental smearing, can be seen also in this line. There are no imprint marks on the opposite page to suggest Charles closed the notebook before the ink could dry.

17. Multiple smudges appear throughout the final two lines on the page. In the absence of their imprint on the opposing page, the cause of these smudges is unknown.

18. Charles first spelled this word "strenghh." He corrected the misspelling by adding the letters "t" and "h" to construct the word "strength."

19. A dark stain, likely the result of the aging process of the manuscript, appears beneath the letters "t" and "h" in the word "thee." Additionally, although Charles did not include closing quotation marks around the phrase "I will help thee," they have been added for consistency.

20. "What miserable wretches the most faithful Christians are when they once begin doubting and fearing! It is a trade I never like to meddle with, because it never pays the expenses, and never brings in any profit" (*NPSP* 3:396).

21. "Doubt the Eternal, distrust the Omnipotent? Oh, traitorous fear! thinkest thou that the arm which piled the heavens, and sustains the pillars of the earth shall ever be palsied? Shall the brow which eternal ages have rolled over without scathing it, at last be furrowed by old age? What! shall the Eternal fail thee? Shall the faithful Promiser break his oath?" (*NPSP* 3:396).

22. See the previous two sermons, "Christ the Power and Wisdom of God" (Sermon 169a) and "Christ the Power of God" (Sermon 169b).

23. "O poor puny Christian that is overcome by every straw, that stumbles at every stone! Then, Christian men, behave like men! It is childish to doubt; it is manhood's glory to trust. Plant your foot upon the immoveable Rock of Ages; lift your eye to heaven; scorn the world; never play craven; bend your fist in the world's face, and bid defiance to it and hell, and you are a man, and noble" (*NPSP* 3:396–97).

24. Charles was referencing Shadrach, Meshach, and Abed-nego in Dan 3:30.

25. Charles wrote the word "least." However, the immediate context and also the use of the word on the following page suggests Charles intended to write the word

"lest." For additional examples of this tendency, see "The Watchman, His Work, Warning, and Promise" (Notebook 2, Sermon 120); "Christ's Sheep" (Notebook 2, Sermon 132); and "By Faith Jericho Fell" (Notebook 2, Sermon 133).

26. "Ah, I have often cried to God and desired that I might feel happy before I began to preach—that I might feel I could preach to the people. I could never get it at all. And yet sometimes God hath been pleased to cheer me as I have gone along, and given me strength that has been equal to my day. So it must be with you. God will come in when you want him—not one minute before, nor yet one minute later" (*NPSP* 3:395).

27. The word "of" is written in superscript above the line and between the words "because" and "our." Charles indicated its location with a caret.

28. "How easy it is, my brethren, for you and I to fly up! How hard to keep down! That demon of pride was born with us, and it will not die one hour before us. It is so woven into the very warp and woof of our nature, that till we are wrapped in our winding-sheets we shall never hear the last of it" (*NPSP* 3:393).

1.   This is the only time Charles preached a sermon on Isa 64:1–2.

2.   Cf. Isa 5:13.

3.   This word is also spelled "diverse."

4.   Cf. Acts 1:11; 3:19–21; 1 Cor 4:5; Phil 1:10; Col 3:4; 1 Thess 1:9–10; 1 Tim 6:13–16; Heb 9:28; Jas 5:7–9; 1 Pet 2:12; 1 John 2:28; Rev 3:11; 16:15; 22:20–21.

5.   A likely accidental vertical stroke appears above the letter "n" in the word "manner."

6.   Cf. Rev 8:8.   7.   Cf. Rev 8:12.

8.   Cf. Joel 2:31; Acts 2:20; Rev 6:12.

9.   Cf. Rev 16:3.   10.   Cf. Isa 34:4; 2 Pet 3:10–12; Rev 6:14.

11.   Cf. Rev 20:11.   12.   Cf. Rev 1:7; 18:19.

13.   Cf. Rev 6:10; 14:10; 16.   14.   Cf. Revelation 6.

15.   The word "burthen" is the archaic form of "burden." In his personal library Charles owned John Gill's collection of Tobias Crisp's sermons in which the word "burthen" is found: "There may be a heavy burthen laid upon the back of a child, and yet it may with ease go under it; because there is a greater strength that bears it up, it doth not lie upon the child. So long as Christ bears up your weight, it shall be easy to you" (John Gill, *Christ Alone Exalted, in the Perfection and Encouragement of the Saints, Notwithstanding Sins and Trials; Being the Complete Works of Tobias Crisp, D.D. Sometime Minister of the Gospel, at Brinkworth, in Wiltshire; Containing Fifty-Two Sermons, on Several Select Texts of Scripture. To Which Are Added Notes Explanatory of Several Passages in Them, with Memoirs of the Doctor's Life, &c. A New Edition, Being the Seventh. Vol. I* [London: printed for John Bennett, 1832, The Spurgeon Library], 136).

16.   Contraction, "overrun."

17.   The letter "c" appears beneath the "h" in the word "horrid." Charles may have prematurely begun writing the word "crime."

18.   Charles wrote the word "ours," though he likely intended to write "our." If he did intend to write "ours," the phrase could read "Ours [is] ingratitude."

19. Cf. Rev 3:15–17.

20. Before Charles struck through the letter "s" at the end of the word "relations," he may have intended to write "relationship."

21. The context suggests Charles did not intend to use the word "want" here to mean "lack," as he does elsewhere, but instead "desire." See also "Zeal in Religion Commended" (Sermon 154).

22. A vertical smear descends three lines beneath the base of the letter "p" in the word "professors."

23. Cf. Ezek 36:26.

24. An alternative reading of this line is "He melts and makes [the] stony heart flow down."

25. Charles may have been referencing Benjamin Franklin's famous Philadelphia kite experiment in 1752. Michael Schiffer explains, "For the electrical experiment Franklin made his own kite, using wooden arms of cedar covered by a large silk handkerchief. . . . To collect charge, he affixed a pointed wire, more than a foot long, to the kite's tip. The celebrated key was tied to the twine string with a silk ribbon. . . . After rain moistened the string, it conducted enough charge to be easily detected when Franklin's knuckle approached the key. From the key he then charged a Leyden jar, which enabled him to reproduce common electrical effects" (Michael Brian Schiffer, *Draw the Lightning Down: Benjamin Franklin and Electrical Technology in the Age of Enlightenment* [Berkeley: University of California Press, 2003], 168). Charles later referenced Franklin's experiment: "To use a very simple figure, you remember how Franklin, when he knew there was an electric fluid in the cloud, sped his kite and brought down the lightning. Well now, there is the everlasting power of God up yonder, and I must learn to let my faith get up into the clouds to bring down the divine power to me" (*MTP* 24:647). A less likely interpretation is that Charles was referring to telegraph wires, which had been invented in his parents' generation and perfected when he was child.

26. For additional statements about mountains and molehills in Charles's later sermons, see *MTP* 14:711; *MTP* 30:476; and *MTP* 31:466.

27. Cf. Rev 22:20.

1.   This is the only time Charles preached a sermon on Acts 11:26.

2.   "To be accustomed; to use; to be used" (Johnson's *Dictionary*, s.v. "wont").

3.   To make the subject and verb agree, an alternative reading of this line is "But though these have interest, what [are they] compared with. . . ."

4.   An alternative reading of this line is "What is it compared with the interest [that is attached] to this book of Acts?"

5.   Given the capitalization of the word "History," Charles may have been referring to a publication he owned in his personal library: John Lingard, *The History of England, from the First Invasion by the Romans to the Accession of William and Mary in 1688, The Fifth Edition. Revised and Considerably Enlarged, in Ten Volumes* (London: Charles Dolman, 1849, The Spurgeon Library).

6.   Charles likely had the following publication in mind: John Foxe, *An Universal History of Christian Martyrdom, Being a Complete and Authentic Account of the Lives, Sufferings, and Triumphant Deaths of the Primitive as Well as Protestant Martyrs, in All Parts of the World, from the Birth of the Blessed Saviour to the Latest Periods of Pagan and Catholic Persecution: Together with a Summary of the Doctrines, Prejudices, Blasphemies, and Superstitions of the Modern Church of Rome. With Notes, Commentaries, and Illustrations by the Rev. J. Milner, M. A. Assisted by the Communications of Several Learned and Eminent Ministers of the Gospel, Which Have Never Before Been Published. A New Edition Greatly Improved and Corrected* (London: George Routledge, 1845, The Spurgeon Library).

7.   Charles was likely referencing Acts 7:54–60.

8.   Charles owned numerous publications in his personal library on the subjects of voyages, traveling, and adventures: Daniel Defoe, *The Life and Adventures of Robinson Crusoe, of York, Mariner. With an Account of His Travels Round Three Parts of the Globe. With Twelve Illustrations by Thomas Stothard, R. A. and a Portrait of Daniel Defoe* (London: John Hogg, 1883, The Spurgeon Library); William H. Edwards, *A Voyage Up the River Amazon, Including a Residence at Pará* (London: John Murray, 1847, The Spurgeon Library); Francis B. Head, *Rough Notes Taken During Some Rapid Journeys Across the Pampas and Among the Andes* (4th ed.; London: John Murray, 1846, The Spurgeon Library); John Todd, *California and Its Wonders. New Edition, Carefully Revised and Brought Down to the Present Time. With 17 Illustrations* (London;

Edinburgh; and New York: T. Nelson and Sons, 1880, The Spurgeon Library); Henry William Haygarth, *Recollections of Bush Life in Australia, During a Residence of Eight Years in the Interior* (London: John Murray, 1848, The Spurgeon Library); Percy B. St. John, *The North Pole, and What Has Been Done to Reach It: A Narrative of the Various Arctic Explorations Undertaken by All Nations, from the Earliest Period to the Present Time; and the Expedition Preparing to Be Sent Out in the "Discovery" and "Alert," Under the Command of Captain Narnes, R.N. with a Map of the Polar Seas* (London: C. H. Clarke, 1875, The Spurgeon Library); William Shrubsole, *Christian Memoirs; in the Form of a New Pilgrimage to the Heavenly Jerusalem: Containing, by way of Allegorical Dialogues on the Most Interesting Subjects, and Adventures of Eminently Religious Persons. The Third Edition: Corrected. With the Life of the Author* (London: printed for W. Baynes by William Nicholson, 1807, The Spurgeon Library); and Thomas Davis, *Hymns, Old and New. For Church and Home, and for Travel by Land or Sea: Consisting of 223 Selected, and 260 Original Hymns. Second Edition* (London: printed by Woodfall and Kinder: Longman and Green, 1864, The Spurgeon Library).

9. For an example of this publication around the time Charles preached the sermon above, see *The Christian Times* (London), July 23, 1852.

10. Charles may have been thinking of a quotation by George Whitefield that he cited on numerous occasions throughout his ministry: "I am not particularly anxious about my own name, whether that shall endure for ever or not, provided it is recorded in my Master's book. George Whitefield, when asked whether he would found a denomination, said, 'No; brother John Wesley may do as he pleases, but let my name perish; let Christ's name last for ever.' Amen to that! Let my name perish; but let Christ's name last for ever. I shall be quite contented for you to go away and forget me" (Charles H. Spurgeon, *Exeter Hall Sermons: Sermons Delivered in Exeter Hall, Strand; During the Enlargement of New Park Street Chapel, Southwark* [London: Alabaster & Passmore and James Paul, 1855], 212; also printed in *NPSP* 1, Sermon 27). See also "Spurgeonism Again" (*ST* June 1866:281–84); "Spurgeonism," *The Nation* (June 13, 1857); "Spurgeonism," Dundee, Perth, and Cupar *Advertiser* (April 2, 1861); and *MTP* 60:300. Not long before his death in southern France, Charles gave instructions on how he wanted to be buried. He whispered to his secretary, Joseph W. Harrald, "Remember, a plain slab, with C. H. S. on it; nothing more" (*Autobiography* 4:377). Charles's marble tomb is one of the largest in West Norwood Cemetery in London.

11. Cf. Acts 11:22.   12. Cf. Acts 11:25.

13. Charles was referencing Barnabas, Simeon (called Niger), Lucius of Cyrene, Manaen, and Paul (cf. Acts 13:1).

14. The two missionaries were Paul and Barnabas (cf. Acts 13:2).

15. Charles originally wrote the word "tas." It is likely he intended to write "'twas," but afterward inserted the letter "w" to form the word "was."

16. Charles may have had in mind Waterbeach Chapel.

17. The phrase "and a congregation" was likely added afterward.

18. An alternative reading of this line is "He had a fullness [of] faith and [of] the Holy Ghost."

19. It is unclear which verse Charles was quoting with the words "all prayer." Cf. Acts 1:14; 6:4.

20. Charles originally spelled this word "stiled." However, the letter "i" was converted into a "y" in pencil, likely by Charles when he was redacting these sermon notebooks for publication in 1857.

21. An alternative reading of this line is "[It will be a] blessed time when this shall return and we shall be gathered in one." For an additional reference to Christian unity, see "Can Two Walk Together Unless They Are Agreed?" (Notebook 1, Sermon 76).

22. In a letter to his sister Caroline Louisa approximately two years before this sermon was preached, Charles wrote, "If anyone is called by the name of Christian, that is better than all these great words: it is the best name in the world, except the name of our Lord Jesus Christ" (*Autobiography* 1:194).

23. Cf. Acts 13:1.

24. Charles originally wrote the word "owe" before changing the letter "e" to an "n" to construct the word "owns."

25. This is the second time in this notebook that Charles inserted an ampersand between the numbers at the conclusion of his sermons (see also "Fear Not Thou Worm, Jacob" [Sermon 170]).

1.   On May 27, 1855, Charles preached an additional sermon on 2 Cor 2:15–16 entitled "The Two Effects of the Gospel" (*NPSP* 1, Sermon 26). There is enough overlapping content to suggest Charles had in mind the outline above when writing his later sermon.

2.   "Ah! with this thought a minister may lay his head upon his pillow: 'God makes manifest the savour of his knowledge in every place.' With this he may shut his eyes when his career is over, and with this he may open them in heaven" (*NPSP* 1:197).

3.   Charles was referring to the apostle Paul. Cf. Acts 13:50.

4.   "Picture Paul, the aged, the man who had been beaten five times with 'forty stripes save one,' who had been dragged forth for dead, the man of great sufferings, who had passed through whole seas of persecution—only think of him saying, at the close of his ministerial career, 'Now thanks be unto God, which always causeth us to triumph in Christ!' to triumph when shiprecked, to triumph when scourged, to triumph in the stocks, to triumph under the stones, to triumph amidst the hiss of the world, to triumph when he was driven from the city and shook off the dust from his feet, to triumph at all times in Christ Jesus!" (*NPSP* 1:197).

5.   "The minister is not responsible for his success. He *is* responsible for what he preaches; he is accountable for his life and actions; but he is not responsible for other people. If I do but preach God's word, if there never were a soul saved, the King would say, 'Well done, good and faithful servant!' If I do but tell my message, if none should listen to it, he would say, 'Thou hast fought the good fight: receive thy crown'" (*NPSP* 1:202, italics in the original).

6.   Charles originally wrote the word "the" before adding the letters "s" and "e" to construct the word "these." A less likely interpretation of this redaction is that Charles intended to change the word "the" into the word "those."

7.   "Now a fisherman is not responsible for the quantity of fish he catches, but for the way he fishes. That is a mercy for some ministers, I am sure, for they have neither caught fish, nor even attracted any round their nets. They have been spending all their life fishing with most elegant silk lines, and gold and silver hooks; they always use nicely polished phrases; but the fish will not bite for all

that, whereas we of a rougher order have put the hook into the jaws of hundreds. However, if we cast the gospel net in the right place, even if we catch none, the Master will find no fault with us. He will say, 'Fisherman! didst thou labour? Didst thou throw the net into the sea in the time of storms?' 'Yes, my Lord, I did.' 'What hast thou caught?' 'Only one or two.' 'Well, I could have sent thee a shoal, if it so pleased me; it is not thy fault; I will give in my sovereignty where I please; or withhold when I choose; but as for thee, thou has well laboured, therefore there is thy reward.' . . . If we mean right, and if with all our heart we strive to do the right thing as minister if we never see any effect, still shall we receive the crown" (*NPSP* 1:202).

8.   Stippling, likely accidental, appears at the base of the descender of the letter "f" in the word "fill."

9.   A smudge surrounds the word "to." The source of the ink may be the stippling around the base of the letter "f" in the word "fill" in the line above.

10. In his previous sermon Charles similarly compared Christians to angels: "And surely, 'tis a title which an angel might be envious of" ("The Church of Antioch" [Sermon 172]).

11. Charles contrasted the office of the priest in the Jewish tradition with the office of the preacher/pastor in his day. A completion of his thought in this sentence may be, "It was glorious to be a priest, a minister of the Mosaic ritual. But to preach the gospel of light and life [is better]."

12. "Man-made ministers are of no use in this world, and the sooner we get rid of them the better. Their way is this: they prepare their manuscripts very carefully, then read it on the Sunday most sweetly in *sotto voce*, and so the people go away pleased. But that is not God's way of preaching. . . . A man ought to feel first that he has a solemn call to it; next, he ought to know that he really possesses the Spirit of God, and that when he speaks there is an influence upon him that enables him to speak as God would have him, otherwise out of the pulpit he should go directly" (*NPSP* 1:203, italics in the original).

13. "Usefulness to all in causing the well being of the world in preserving the earth from destruction" ("The Path of the Just" [Notebook 1, Sermon 35]).

14. With regard to the danger of ministerial popularity, Charles later said, "There is a minister; when he first began his ministry he could say, 'God is my witness I have but one object, that I may free my skirts from the blood of every one of my hearers, that I may preach the gospel faithfully and honour my Master.' In a little time, tempted by Satan, he changes his tone and talks like this, 'I must keep my congregation up. If I preach such hard doctrine, they won't come. Did not one of the newspapers criticise me, and did not some of my people go away from me because of it? I must mind what I am at. I must keep this thing going. I must look out a little sharper, and prune my speech down. I must adopt a little gentler style, or preach a new-fashioned doctrine; for I must keep my popularity up. What is to become of me if I go down? People will say, "Up like a rocket, down like the stick," and then shall all my enemies laugh.' Ah, when once a man begins to care so much as a snap of the finger about the world, it is all over with him" (*NPSP* 4:478).

15. After moving to London, Charles was accused of being "a nine days' wonder—a comet that has suddenly shot across the religious atmosphere. He has gone up like a rocket and ere long will come down like a stick" (*The Sheffield and Rotherham Independent*, April 28, 1855). Twenty-four years later, on May 20, 1879, Charles referenced this comment, saying, "I well recollect when we were called 'a nine days' wonder,' and our critics prophesied that our work would speedily collapse. . . . The nine days have lasted considerably long;—may nine such days follow them in God's infinite mercy" (*MTP* 25:281–82).

16. Cf. Matt 18:15; 2 Cor 2:7; Gal 6:1.

17. During his first year in London, approximately two years after Charles preached the above sermon, a cholera outbreak killed 10,000 people. He recounted, "All day, and sometimes all night long, I went about from house to house, and saw men and women dying, and, oh, how glad they were to see my face. When many were afraid to enter their houses lest they should catch the deadly disease, we who had no fear about such things found ourselves most gladly listened to when we spoke of Christ and of things Divine" (*Autobiography* 1:371).

18. "To lose my Prayer-book, as I have often told you, is the worst thing that can happen to me. To have no one to pray for me would place me in a dreadful condition. . . . All our perils are nothing, so long as we have prayer. But increase my congregation; give me the polite and the noble,—give me influence and

understanding,—and I should fail to do anything without a praying church. My people! shall I ever lose your prayers?" (*NPSP* 1:204). Charles also said, "What shall I do if you cease to pray for me? Let me know the day when you give up praying for me, for then I must give up preaching, and I must cry, 'O my God, take me home, for my work is done!'" (*Autobiography* 2:335). The following quotations range from the middle to late seasons of Charles's ministry and give further meaning to his belief in the necessity of prayer: "Prayer has become as essential to me as the heaving of my lungs, and the beating of my pulse" (*MTP* 49:476); "God keeps a file for our prayers—they are not blown away by the wind, they are treasured in the King's archives" (*Morning and Evening*, March 29, PM); "We must get rid of the icicles that hang about our lips. We must ask the Lord to thaw the ice-caves of our soul and to make our hearts like a furnace of fire heated seven times hotter" (*MTP* 13:79); "We cannot commune with God, who is a consuming fire, if there is no fire in our prayers" (*MTP* 28:547); "You are no Christian if you do not pray. A prayerless soul is a Christless soul" (*MTP* 48:483); and "Prayer does move the arm that moves the world" (*MTP* 41:524).

Rom. VIII. 1. — No Condemnation to Christians. 174

There are two sorts of Christians now-a-days — One sort love ever to hear exhortations to duty, & the other continually cry out "comfort". Now these are like two farmers — one always at work, never thanks God for the crop, & often grumbles — the other is always looking at the wheatstack & the mow, goes on in a poor way for work, yet rests quite easy in what he has got already — Now in this sermon let us put the two together and both look at what we have & what we must do.

I. Here is a glorious declaration. "There is therefore now no condemnation."

1. Here is freedom from condemnation — joyful news to those who sit in prison & tremble, least they should hear the sentence of condemnation.

It does not say there is no "accusation" against us.

It does not say there is no "corruption" or "nothing worthy of condemnation", nothing wrong."

Nor does it say they shall have no affliction, trouble or fear of condemnation — but no condemnation.

2. Here moreover is perfect freedom from it, for there is no condemnation, "not one" says the original There are many illegal ones but not one just one.

Why neither Father, nor Son, nor Spirit, can do it for they are all engaged to save. Love will not condemn, and justice cannot — for it has nothing

174

NO CONDEMNATION
to CHRISTIANS
Romans 8:1[1]

"There is therefore now no condemnation to them which are in Christ Jesus, who walk not after the flesh, but after the Spirit."

There are two sorts of Christians now-a-days. One sort love ever to hear exhortations to duty and the other continually cry out, "[C]omfort." Now, these are like two farmers. One, always at work, never thanks God for the crop and often grumbles. The other is always looking at the wheat-stack and the mow,[2] goes on in a poor way for work yet rests quite easy in what he has got already.

Now in this sermon, let us put the two together and both look at what we have and what we must do.

I.   HERE IS A GLORIOUS DECLARATION. *"There is therefore now no condemnation."*

1.   Here is freedom from condemnation, joyful news to those who sit in prison and tremble, lest[3] they should hear the sentence of condemnation. It does not say there[4] is no "accusation" against us.[5] It does not say there is no "corruption" or "nothing worthy of condemnation," ["]nothing wrong." Nor does it say they shall have no affliction, trouble,[6] or fear of condemnation. But "no condemnation."

2.   Here, moreover, is perfect freedom from it, for there is no condemnation. "Not one," says the original. There are many illegal ones, but not one just one. Why, neither Father, nor Son, nor Spirit can do it, for they are all engaged to save. Love will not condemn, and justice cannot, for it has nothing

to condemn us for — The surety has borne the curse,
has given perfect obedience — & now the law is
satisfied for Christ has fulfilled the law.
3. Here also you have present justification.
Not there shall not be — but there is not — now.
Since Jesus has died, has risen, has lived a
perfect life & finished all his engagements.
There once was, but there is not now, & never shall
be one single Condemnation. —

II The secret name of the inheritors of this mercy
"to them that are in Christ Jesus"
Not those in him by profession who may be lost.
This blessing like every other comes through Christ.
We are in him.
By Election — chosen, enrolled, given, beloved.
In him — when he hung on the cross, when he
was buried & rose again, to ascend on high.
In him — as the Refuge of their souls.
In him — by faith — by simple trust — by love
by consecration — by sweet communion.

III. The open character of the "uncondemnable"
"who walk not after the flesh, but after the Spirit
1 What is meant by after the flesh?
The flesh means — the common course of the world

to condemn us for. The surety has borne the curse, has given perfect obedience. And now the lion is satisfied, for Christ has fulfilled the law.[7]

3. Here also you have present justification. Not, there shall not be. But there is not now[8] since Jesus has died, has risen, has lived a perfect life, and finished all his engagements. There once was, but there is not now and never shall be one, single condemnation.

II. THE SECRET NAME OF THE INHERITORS OF THIS MERCY, *"to them that are in Christ Jesus."*

Not those in him by profession who may be lost. This[9] blessing like every other comes through Christ. We are in him:

By Election,[10] chosen, enrolled, given, beloved.

In him when he hung on the cross, when he was buried, and rose again to ascend on high.[11]

In him as the Refuge of their souls.[12]

In him by faith, by simple trust, by love, by consecration, by sweet communion.[13]

III. THE OPEN CHARACTER OF THE *"uncondemnable," "who walk not after the flesh, but after the Spirit.["]*

1.[14] What is meant by after the flesh?

The flesh means the common course of the world,

which like dead flesh - corrupts, putrifies & is abominable
it means - the native desires of our mind — men
who never deny themselves walk after the flesh.
2 What is meant by after the Spirit?
after the new & divine nature given or after the prompt-
-ings of the Holy Spirit.

Fleshy		Spirit
proudly	————	humbly
self-confidently	————	believingly
wickedly	————	righteously.
carelessly		carefully.

3 To walk - means our general tenour, the
whole lump of life — many steps in all are
amiss — but the main drift decides it.
Here is not the season of our justification, but
the character we must strive to bear.

1 Do we answer this description? then rejoice all —
2. Do you not? then you are condemned already.
Strive oh Christian to walk better!
for you are more favoured, then love more.
Holy Spirit, blow through me!

270

which like dead flesh corrupts, putrifies,[15] and is abominable. It means the native desires of our mind. Men who never deny themselves walk after the flesh.[16]

2. What is meant by after the Spirit?[17]

After the new and divine nature given. Or, after the promptings of the Holy Spirit.[18]

Fleshy:	Spirit:
proudly	humbly
self-confidently	believingly
wickedly	righteously
carelessly	carefully

3. To walk means our general tenour, the whole lump of life. Many steps in all are amiss, but the main drift decides it.

Here is not the reason of our justification but the character we must strive to bear.[19]

1. Do we answer this description? Then rejoice, all.[20]

2. Do you not? Then you are condemned already.[21]

Strive, oh Christian, to walk better!

For you are more favoured. Then, love more.

270 <u>Holy Spirit, blow through me!</u>

1. Charles preached two additional sermons on Rom 8:1. In Notebook 9, Charles preached a sermon entitled "No Condemnation" (Notebook 9, Sermon 399) and on July 31, 1884, he preached a sermon entitled "In Christ No Condemnation" (*MTP* 32, Sermon 1917). The sermon in Notebook 9 shares little overlapping structure and content with the sermon above. However, Charles's 1884 sermon contains enough overlapping content (particularly *MTP* 32:473–80) to suggest Charles had in mind his early outline when writing his later sermon.

2. "A loft or chamber where hay or corn is laid up: hay in *mow*, is hay laid up in a house; hay in *rick*, is hay heaped together in a field" (Johnson's *Dictionary*, s.v. "mow," italics in the original).

3. Charles originally wrote the word "least"; however, the context suggests he intended to write the word "lest."

4. Charles originally wrote the word "their" before adding the letters "r" and "e" to construct the word "there."

5. "The devil says there is condemnation, and therefore he accuses us day and night" (*MTP* 32:478).

6. Cf. John 16:33.

7. "Paul is always a reasoned and a great logician. Here he seems to declare his certainty. 'What I say I can prove. There is no condemnation to them that are in Christ Jesus, and I can prove it to a demonstration.' Brethren, the demonstrations of mathematics are not more clear and certain than the inference that if we are in Christ, and Christ died in our stead, there can be no condemnation for us. Cool calculation may be used here. This is no raving fanaticism, but the unquestionable deduction of fair argument:—if Jesus was condemned in my stead, there can be no condemnation for me" (*MTP* 32:478).

8. An alternative reading of this line is "Not, there *shall* not be. But there *is* not now" (emphasis added).

9. Charles originally wrote the word "the" before converting the letter "e" into the "i" to construct the word "This."

10. See "Election" (Notebook 1, Sermon 10).

11. "I am not going into any deep theological disquisitions; I speak very simply and with a view to practical results. He that believes in the Lord Jesus Christ is in Christ. *By an act of simple dependence* upon Jesus he realizes his position as being in Christ. By nature I am in myself, and in sin, and I am, therefore, condemned; but when the grace of God awakens me up to know my ruined state, then I fly to Christ. I trust alone in his blood and righteousness, and he becomes to me the cleft of the rock, wherein I hide myself from the storm of vengeance justly due to me for my many offences" (*MTP* 32:473, italics in the original).

12. "The Lord Jesus is typified by the city of refuge. You and I are like the manslayer who was pursued by the avenger; and we are never safe till we pass the gate of the city of refuge—I mean, till we are completely enclosed by the Lord Jesus. Inside the walls of the city the manslayer was secure, and within our Saviour's wounds we are safe" (*MTP* 32:473). Cf. "Religion, the Foundation of Confidence" (Notebook 2, Sermon 106); Pss 46:1–3; 91:2; Jer 16:19.

13. "We are actually one with Christ by living experience. Beloved, if it be so, that we died in Christ, then we shall not be put to death again for the sin for which we have already died in him. . . . This union with Christ is often mentioned in Scripture under the form of a marriage, but it is also described under other symbols: we are one with Christ as a branch is one with the vine, as a stone is one with the foundation, and especially as a member of the body is one with the head. Now it is not possible if I am a member of Christ that I should be under condemnation until he is condemned. Is my head acquitted? Then my hand is acquitted. So long as a man's head is above water you cannot drown his feet; and as long as Christ, the Head of the mystical body, rises about the torrent of condemnation, there is no condemning even the least and feeblest member of his body" (*MTP* 32:474, 475).

14. Given the lack of margin space, the number 1 on this page and the numbers 2 and 3 on the following page were likely added afterward.

15. An alternative spelling of this word is "putrefies."

16. Cf. Rom 8:5.

17. "Observe carefully that the flesh is there: he does not walk after it, but it is there. It is there, striving and warring, vexing and grieving, and it will be there till he is taken up into heaven. It is there as an alien and detested force, and not there so as to have dominion over him. He does not walk after it, nor practically obey it. He does not accept it as his guide, nor allow it to drive him into rebellion" (*MTP* 32:477).

18. "What a wonderful power is that which dwells in every believer, checking him when he would do wrong, encouraging him to do right, leading him in the paths of righteousness for Christ's name's sake! Happy men to have such a Conductor!" (*MTP* 32:477).

19. "But go and proclaim the dying love of Jesus; tell them that free grace reigns, and that undeserved mercy saves the sinner through faith in Christ, and that the moment he believes in Jesus there is no condemnation to him, and you shall see miracles accomplished" (*MTP* 32:480).

20. Charles intended to write either "Then [all] rejoice" or "Then, rejoice [with] all." The former interpretation of this line is more likely.

21. "The breasts of wicked men are steeled rather than softened by a sense of condemnation; but once let the Holy Spirit remove the burden of their guilt, and they will be dissolved by love" (*MTP* 32:480).

175.   John XX.16.   Mary with Jesus in the garden.
This text is one of 4 — which were solemnly com-
-mitted to me on Wednesday. Oct 13- 1852 by an old
sister in the faith then lying on her bed, which
I believe to be the bed of death. — May the
God who put them into her mind, also hear her
prayer and mine that they may become the seed
of many souls — Hear our prayers. Oh God.

Let us come and behold the sight.
'Ere the first ray of the morning sun had given
light to the earth — the much-forgiven & much-loving
Mary goes alone to the sepulchre of her Lord.
She seeth the stone rolled away & runs to Peter
& John with the news — they come at her call —
— they see and depart, but the first there stays
last — as much as to say I will not go till I
find him. She weeps as doubtless she had
done ever since his death, but now afresh
because she knew not to what insult they might
expose the body — dead yet dear to her. She had
hoped to have at least the melancholy consolation
of embalming the body, & her companions are behind
bearing the spices &c but ah it is gone. — She
can scarce believe Peter & John, nor ēen her own
eyes, therefore she stoops down & looks into

374

175

MARY *with* JESUS *in the* GARDEN
John 20:16[1]

"Jesus saith unto her, Mary. She turned herself, and saith unto him, Rabboni, which is to say, Master."

This text is one of four[2] which were solemnly committed to[3] me on Wednesday, Oct. 13, 1852,[4] by an old sister in the faith then lying on her bed, which I believe to be the bed of death. May the God who put them into her mind also hear her prayer and mine, that they may become the seed of many souls. Hear our prayers, Oh God.[5]

Let us come and behold the sight.

'Ere the first ray of the morning sun had given light to the earth, the much-forgiven[6] and much-loving Mary goes alone to the sepulchre of her Lord.[7] She seeth the stone rolled away and runs to Peter and John with the news.

They come at her call.[8] They see and[9] depart.[10] But the first there stays last, as much as to say, I will not go till I find him.[11] She weeps as doubtless she had done ever since his death,[12] but now afresh because she knew not to what insult they might expose the body dead, yet dear to her.[13]

She had hoped to have at least the melancholy consolation of embalming the body and her companions are behind, bearing the spices, etc.[14] But ah, it is gone. She can scarce believe Peter and John, nor e'en[15] her own eyes. Therefore, she stoops[16] down and looks into that dreary sepulchre. She sees two angels – but what are they – The sight might dazzle and amaze were it not that she has ~~other~~ griefs more weighty than such a sight could remove. The angels who sat at the head & foot were such as we want in that very position – to guard our head & foot from sin. They say to her "Woman, why weepest thou? Perhaps from surprise to see her weep at that which gives the firmest ground for rejoicing, even his resurrection – as also from sympathy – this is a grace that becomes even angels & is the orna- -ment of good men. — "Alas" says she "they have taken my Lord I know not whither". To take him away was grievous, but not to know where his body was, to what insult exposed, was grievous indeed She turns away to weep – and there stands the living person of that Lord whose corpse she wept – her prayer is more than answered – seeking she has found more than she sought. but she sees not. her tearful eyes, & rending heart, obscure her vision & ~~his~~ unheeded. He speaks & says the very words of the angels with a more piteous accent. But she recognizes not the voice, the heart is almost bursting, & but one object has engrossed her. She hardly thinks – but concludes it is the gardener. She sobs out "Sir, if thou hast borne him hence! – <u>him</u> the name she needs not mention, so it <u>seems</u> to her, <u>him</u> there was but one to her that dreary sepulchre. She sees two angels,[17] but what are they? The sight might dazzle and amaze were it not that she has griefs more[18] weighty than such a sight could remove.

The angels who sat at the head and foot were such as we want in that very position to guard our head and foot from sin. They say to her, "Woman, why weepest thou?["][19] perhaps from surprise to see her weep at that which gives the firmest ground for rejoicing, even his resurrection, as also from sympathy.[20] This is a grace that becomes even angels[21] and is the ornament of good men.

"Alas," says she,[22] "they have taken my Lord I know not whither."[23]

To take him away was grievous but not to know where his body was, to what insult exposed,[24] was grievous indeed.

She turns away to weep and there stands[25] the living person of that Lord whose corpse she wept.[26] Her prayer is more than answered, seeking she has found more than she sought.[27] But she sees not. Her tearful eyes and rending heart obscure her vision, and he's[28] unheeded.

He speaks and says the very words of the angels, with a more piteous accent. But she recognizes not the voice. The heart is almost bursting and but one object has engrossed her. She hardly thinks but concludes it is the gardener.[29]

She sobs out, "Sir, if thou hast borne <u>him</u>, hence!"[30]

<u>Him</u>. The name she needs not mention, so it seems to her. <u>Him</u>. There was but one to her,

Her all in all & she supposes that he was so to all.
Tell me.' I will take him away – Surely she cannot
lift the weight, but love seems omnipotent. She
can do anything for him who cured one so dreadfully possessed. What strength of love! what want
of faith! ——— She knew not the voice when
it spake to her as a woman even though there
were 7 words – But when but one personal
word came to her she knows – "Mary" said
Jesus. Ah what a world flashed by in one
moment. Rabboni.!' she cries in extacy – yet
Rabboni? is it thou? the little faith broke in.
But it is he & lo she would embrace him
but at his request she goes to his disciples.
Now Oh. Lord. help me to address.
I. The fors-aken Christian – whose Lord
seems to be gone & doubt comes in.
Is your Lord away? Then do you sit at home.
No if you be a true disciple, you will be up
before the dawn, to seek him where he
may be found, even at the sepulchre.
Shouldest thou not find him, if thou art
a forgiven one thou wilt say, I will tarry
here & weeping thou wilt stay beside the
sepulchre, hoping that in the way thou wilt

Her all in all, and she supposes that he was so to all.

"Tell me! I will take him away."[31] Surely, she cannot lift the weight,[32] but love seems omnipotent. She can do anything for him who cured one so dreadfully possessed.[33] What strength of love! What want of faith!

She knew[34] not the voice when it spake to her as a woman, even though there were 7 words.[35] But when but one personal word came to her, she knows.

"Mary,"[36] said Jesus.[37] Ah, what a world flashed by in one moment.

"Rabboni!!" she cries in extacy.[38] Yet Rabboni? is it thou?[39] The little faith broke in.[40]

But it is he, and lo, she would embrace him. But at his request, she goes to his disciples.[41]

Now, oh Lord, help me to address:

I. THE FORSAKEN CHRISTIAN WHOSE LORD SEEMS TO BE GONE AND DOUBT COMES IN.

Is your Lord away? Then do you sit at home? No, if you be a true disciple, you will be up before the dawn to seek him where he may be found, even at the sepulchre. Shouldest thou not find him? If thou art a forgiven one, thou wilt say, I will tarry here. And weeping, thou wilt stay beside the sepulchre, hoping that in the way thou wilt see thine absent one. Ah! how thou wilt weep & stoop & stoop & weep again. Thy one question of men or angels will be "Saw ye him whom my soul loveth?" Oh that I knew where I might find him. We wonder why thou mournest when Jesus is so near, but then thy poor eye is so weak. Wipe thine eye one moment & behold! Jesus is near thee, he has not cast thee off, see! there he stands! But still thou seest not & the voice of promise is all in vain, though it is as sweet as the droppings of the honey-comb. Let Jesus now speak one word and call thee by name. "Mary" & thy sleep would break, Thy sorrows melt & thou shouldest claim him as indeed "Rabboni" Thy Master, Thy Lord. —

II. God of Gods — Aid me in speaking to the penitent. Thou hast a lump of sin on thy back which is indeed intolerable & thou seekest deliverance. Well thou knowest who can cure, even Jesus. Go then to his sepulchre by prayer — go rather to his cross, his throne. Seek him early, with streaming eyes, & longing soul. Thou sayest "So I do" but yet you find him not, go again then even seven times. Thy one stiff neck, now stoops & in the dust thou seekest mercy, but it is in vain. The world laughs at thy griefs & says "Why weepest thou?" The saints, the ministers who guard the doctrine & the precept of Jesus, say to thee "Why weepest thou see thine absent one. Ah! how thou will weep and stoop and stoop and weep again. Thy one question of men or angels will be, "Saw ye him whom my soul loveth?"[42] Oh, that I knew where I might find him. We wonder why thou mournest when Jesus is so near. But then, thy poor eye is so weak.

Wipe thine eye one moment! and behold! Jesus is near thee. He has not cast thee off.[43] See! there he stands! But still thou seest not and the voice of promise is all in vain, though it is as sweet as the droppings of the honey-comb.[44]

Let Jesus now speak one word and call thee by name, "Mary," and thy sleep would break, thy sorrows melt, and thou shouldest claim him as ~~in~~ indeed,[45] "Rabboni," thy Master, thy Lord.

II. GOD OF GODS, AID ME IN SPEAKING TO THE PENITENT.

Thou hast a lump of sin on thy back, which is indeed intolerable and thou seekest deliverance. Well, thou knowest who can cure, even Jesus. Go then to his sepulchre by prayer. Go rather to his cross, his throne.

Seek him early with streaming eyes and longing soul. Thou sayest, "So I do," but yet, you find him not. Go again then, even seven times.[46] Thy one stiff ~~necks~~[47] now stoops and in the dust thou seekest mercy. But it is in vain.

The world laughs at thy griefs and says, "Why weepest thou?" The saints, the ministers who guard the doctrine, and the precept of Jesus,[48] say to thee, "Why weepest thou?"

And to all, there is one reply "Oh that I knew where I
might find him!" Thou weepest, thou longest,
thy spirit fainteth, thy heart & thy flesh crieth out.
& poor soul thou dost not yet discern that
Jesus the sinner's friend is at thy elbow.
He speaks in the gospel to all sinners with the
sweetest utterance, but thou dost not discern
a present Saviour. But open thy eyes &
look, hear the word to thee "Mary!". —
Ah if thou can't thou art blessed & thy
soul wilt rejoice & answering "Rabboni".
the covenant mercies are thine.

"'tis done, the great transaction's done"
Blessed be he who thus to sinful man displays
abounding grace. Sweet hour in which
he first spoke my name in melting tones.
Sure rocks would flow at such a word.
And the whole earth ~~earth~~ embrace its Lord.
Lions would cease the lambs to tear
And vultures peaceful plumage wear.
Lord speak by me to some – to many
Through Jesus who died –
amen

271 . 273 . 276.

And to all, there is one reply, "Oh, that I knew where I might find him!"

Thou weepest, thou longest, thy spirit fainteth, thy heart and thy flesh crieth out. And poor soul, thou dost not yet discern that Jesus, the sinner's friend,[49] is at thy elbow. He speaks in the gospel to all sinners with the sweetest utterance. But thou dost not discern a present Saviour. But open thy eyes and look. Hear the word to thee, "Mary!" Ah, if thou can'st,[50] thou art blessed and thy soul will rejoice and, answering "Rabboni," the covenant mercies are thine.

"[]Tis done, the great[51] transaction's done."[52]

Blessed be he who thus to sinful man displays abounding grace. Sweet hour in which he first spoke my name in melting tones.[53]

Sure[ly], rocks would flow at such a word
And the whole earth ~~earth~~[54] embrace its Lord.
Lions would cease the lambs to tear.
And vultures peaceful plumage wear.[55]

Lord, speak by me to some, to many.

Through Jesus who died.

Amen

271. 273. 276.

1. Charles preached on John 20:16 and its surrounding verses five additional times throughout his ministry. On December 31, 1882, he preached the sermon "Supposing Him to Be the Gardener" (*MTP* 29, Sermon 1699); on October 24, 1889, he preached the sermon "Magdalene at the Sepulchre: An Instructive Scene" (*MTP* 35, Sermon 2119); on February 4, 1888, he preached the sermon "Noli Me Tangere" (*MTP* 44, Sermon 2561); in 1859, he preached the sermon "Christ's Manifestation to Mary Magdalene" (*MTP* 47, Sermon 2733); and on June 13, 1875, he preached the sermon "A Handkerchief" (*MTP* 51, Sermon 2956). There is enough overlapping content and structural similarity in Charles's 1889 sermon to suggest he had in mind his early outline when writing this later sermon. Of the five later sermons, only "Magdalene at the Sepulchre: An Instructive Scene" contains enough overlapping content to suggest Charles had this early sermon in mind during its composition.

2. On the last page of this notebook, Charles recorded, "The 4 texts given me by an aged Sister are: John XX. 16. No. 175. Zech XIV. 6.7. No. 176. John XIII. 23. No. 183. Isa. XLI. 10. The 14th is similar. No. 170." In other words, the four texts given by the "aged Sister" to Charles to preach are (in numerical order): "Fear Not, Thou Worm Jacob" (Sermon 170); "Mary with Jesus in the Garden" (Sermon 175); "Light at Eventide" (Sermon 176); and "Leaning on Jesus['s] Bosom" (Sermon 183). Charles preached from all these texts at her request with the exception of Sermon 170. Instead of preaching on verse 10 as she requested, Charles preached on Isa 41:14, which he deemed was "similar." Who was the "aged Sister?" Unfortunately, there is no record of her in Charles's autobiography, his letters to his family members during this season of his ministry, or in his biographies. Nor is there recorded in this notebook the reason she requested these four texts to be preached by Charles.

3. Charles originally wrote the word "by" before he struck through the descender and tail of the letter "y" to construct the word "to."

4. The date "1852" was written above the word "by."

5. These six sets of dashes signal the conclusion of Charles's personal remarks and are the second instance in this notebook of this type of division (see also "Boast Not Thyself of To-morrow" [Sermon 150]).

6.   Cf. Luke 8:1–3.   7.   Cf. John 20:1.

8.   Cf. John 20:3.

9.   The letters "n" and "d" in the word "and" are faded. Charles replenished the ink on the tip of his writing instrument and reinforced the letter "d."

10. "In thinking over this subject, I have come to the conclusion that Mary Magdalene was selected to see Christ first because she loved him most. John loved Jesus much, but Mary loved him more. John looked into the empty sepulchre, and then went away home; but Mary stood there, and wept, until her risen Lord appeared to her" (*MTP* 47:302). Cf. John 20:10.

11. "There she stands, to weep if she cannot find her Lord, for she feels that nothing else will content her; she must wait at the sepulchre until she finds him. And, my dear friends, if there is anyone here who *will* find Christ, it is the one who *must* find him" (*MTP* 44:134, italics in the original). "John was able to go home, because he had seen and believed. Peter went home all the more readily because a cloud darkened the sky. Mary was of another order from either of these: she loved, and longed to see him whom she loved. Whether he be dead or alive, she would find him. When you are seeking the Lord, it brings out your individuality. Every truly anxious soul must seek the Lord in his own way. There are not two Mary Magdalenes; and Mary differs from John and Peter" (*MTP* 35:674).

12. Cf. Matt 27:56; Mark 15:40; John 19:25.

13. An alternative reading of this line is "She weeps, as doubtless she had done ever since his death, but now afresh because she knew not to what insult they might expose the [dead, yet dear] body to her."

14. Cf. John 19:40.   15.   Contraction, "even."

16. "Mary did something more, which was according to her own mode of action—'*she stooped down, and looked into the sepulchre.*' They that would find Christ must stoop to look for him. They must not merely wait for him, but look for him on their knees" (*MTP* 35:674–75, italics in the original).

17. Cf. John 20:12.

18. An illegible letter is written beneath the letter "m" in the word "more." If this letter was the stem of a "t," Charles may have intended to write the word "too." Thus, the sentence would read "[S]he has ~~other~~ griefs too weighty."

19. John 20:15a, "Jesus saith unto her, Woman, why weepest thou? whom seekest thou?"

20. "Those shining ones do not appear to have comforted her at all. She went on weeping. She told them why she wept, but she did not, therefore, cease her tears. And, believe me, if the angels of heaven cannot content a heart which is seeking after Jesus, you may depend upon it that the angels of the churches cannot do so. We may preach as best we can, but the words of man will never satisfy the cravings of the heart. The seeker needs Jesus: Jesus only, but Jesus certainly" (*MTP* 35:676).

21. For previous examples in which Charles compared angels to humans, see "The Church of Antioch" (Sermon 172) and "Who Is Sufficient for These Things?" (Sermon 173).

22. Charles struck through an illegible mark above and between the words "says" and "she." He possibly closed his quotation marks prematurely before striking through them and extending them before the word "they."

23. "When she spoke to Peter and John, in the second verse, she said, 'They have taken away *the* Lord out of the sepulchre'; but when she addressed the angels, she said, 'They have taken away *my* Lord, and I know not where they have laid him.' It might not be necessary to say, '*my* Lord' to the two apostles, who knew exactly what she was; but she had not seen those angels before, and she would not let them go without their knowing that Jesus was her Lord, her very own" (*MTP* 35:677, italics in the original). John 20:13, "And they say unto her, Woman, why weepest thou? She saith unto them, Because they have taken away my Lord, and I know not where they have laid him."

24. An alternative reading of this phrase is "to what insult [it was] exposed."

25. "If she had seen him lying down, with the image of death upon his face, she would have known him; but to see Jesus *standing*, was far more than she could have hoped for. She had seen his lifeless body taken down by Joseph and Nicodemus, and she had helped to wrap him in spices and fine linen; but to see him standing,

alive, was more than she could have dreamed of. The rapture was too great for her to expect or believe; and we marvel not that it is written 'she knew not that it was Jesus'" (*MTP* 35:679, italics in the original).

26. An alternative reading of this sentence is "She turns away to weep, and there stands the living person of that Lord [for] whose corpse she wept."

27. Cf. Matt 7:7; Luke 9:11.

28. Charles likely wrote the word "his" before he inserted the letter "e" over the "i" and converted the tittle into an apostrophe to construct the contraction "he's."

29. "Go back to Eden for a minute. When Adam was the gardener, what happened? The Lord God walked in the garden in the cool of the day. But 'supposing HIM to be the gardener,' then we shall have the Lord God dwelling among us, and revealing himself in all the glory of his power, and the plenitude of his Father's heart; making us to know him, that we may be filled with all the fulness of God. What joy is this! One other thought. 'Supposing him to be the gardener,' and God to come and walk among the trees of the garden, then I expect he will remove the whole of the garden upward with himself to fairer skies; for he rose, and his people must rise with him. I expect a blessed transplantation of all these flowers below to a clearer atmosphere above, away from all this smoke and fog and damp, up where the sun is never clouded, where flowers never wither, where fruits never decay" (*MTP* 29:24 , capitalization in the original).

30. John 20:15b, "She, supposing him to be the gardener, saith unto him, Sir, if thou have borne him hence, tell me where thou hast laid him."

31. John 20:15c, "[T]ell me where thou hast laid him, and I will take him away."

32. "Why, Mary, you could not bear away so great a load! You would fall beneath the weight of a man's corpse! You are not strong enough for the sad task! Ah! but she thought that she could bear the blessed burden, and she meant to try! . . . A heart that is burning with love has about it a seven-fold energy, whose capacity it would be hard to calculate. It would seem a grim and terrible task for a woman, at early morning, to be carrying from its grave the corpse of one who had been hanged upon a tree; but she offers herself for the deed, and is even eager for it. To a soul that would fain find Christ, nothing is too hot or

too heavy, nothing is too cold or too sickening. We would do anything, refuse nothing, and suffer everything, if we might but clasp him in our arms, our Jesus and our all" (*MTP* 35:681).

33. According to Luke 8:2, Jesus expelled seven demons from Mary Magdalene. Three lines beneath, Charles may have had this number in mind when noting that Jesus spoke seven words to her.

34. Charles originally wrote the word "know" before adding the bowl of the letter "e" to construct the word "knew." To confirm this redaction, see Charles's use of the present tense three lines below.

35. The seven words in John 20:15b were "Woman, why weepest thou? whom seekest thou?"

36. "When a soul knows that Jesus knows its name, it soon begins to know Jesus for itself. . . . One glance of his eye darted the light of God into her spirit. 'Mary!' was the Open Sesame of her heart and mind" (*MTP* 35:683).

37. John 20:16a, "Jesus saith unto her, Mary." "Only one word! Jesus can preach a perfect sermon in one word. O dear friends, when you cannot say much to an anxious enquirer, say a single word. Who knows what that one word may do?" (*MTP* 35:682).

38. John 20:16b, "She turned herself, and saith unto him, Rabboni; which is to say, Master."

39. The phrase "Yet Rabboni? is it thou?" does not appear in the passage. For other instances in which Charles paraphrases or imagines the dialogue of his characters, see "The Physician and His Patients" (Notebook 1, Sermon 74); "Present Your Bodies, Etc." (Notebook 2, Sermon 93); "The Minister's Commission" (Notebook 2, Sermon 110); and *MTP* 22:591; 35:187; and 46:401. Charles may have learned this rhetorical device by reading the sermons of Anglican preacher John Stephenson, whom Charles cited in his sermon "The Church and Its Boast" (Notebook 1, Sermon 75). Cf. John Stevenson, *Christ on the Cross: An Exposition of the Twenty-Second Psalm* (2nd ed.; London: Tyler & Reed, originally published 1842, 1844), 126–27.

40. An alternative reading of this line, with added punctuation, is "'Rabboni!!' she cries in extacy. 'Yet Rabboni? Is it thou?' The little faith broke in."

41. John 20:17–18, "Jesus saith unto her, Touch me not; for I am not yet ascended to my Father: but go to my brethren, and say unto them, I ascend unto my Father, and your Father; and to my God, and your God. Mary Magdalene came and told the disciples that she had seen the Lord, and that he had spoken these things unto her." "We may blunder, again, when we are very near to Christ, by seeking after that which we really do not need. Was it wrong for Mary to try to touch the Lord? Certainly not, for he permitted Thomas to put his finger into the print of the nails, and to thrust his hand into his side. He also said to all the disciples, 'Handle me, and see; for a spirit hath not flesh and bones as ye see me have.' It would have been wrong if Thomas and the other apostles had not touched the Master, yet the Lord refused that touch to Mary. She did not need it; she knew that he was the Christ, and that he was risen from the dead; Thomas doubted it, and the other disciples had some lingering questions, hence they were allowed to have certain signs which Mary did not need, and which the Saviour did not let her have" (*MTP* 44:135).

42. A modernized reading is "Have you seen him whom my soul loves?"

43. Cf. John 15:6.   44. Cf. Ps 19:10.

45. Charles originally wrote the word "imdeed." To correct this misspelling, he struck through the first stem of the letter "m" to construct the letter "n" and to construct the word "indeed."

46. Charles wrote "seven," likely signifying the seven demons Jesus expelled from Mary Magdalene and also because of the seven words Jesus said to her in John 20:15b: "Woman, why weepest thou? whom seekest thou?"

47. Charles likely struck through the letter "s" in the word "necks" to make his subject and verb agree.

48. Depending on the insertion of the second comma, an alternative reading of this line is "The saints, the ministers who guard the doctrine and the precept of Jesus, say to thee, 'Why weepest thou?'"

49. Cf. Matt 9:10–11; Mark 2:16; John 15:15.

50. The word "can'st" is the archaic form of the second-person singular present tense of the word "can." For additional instances in which Charles uses this word in Notebook 3, see "The Golden Crown of Holiness" (Sermon 149) and "Boast Not Thyself of To-morrow" (Sermon 150).

51. Charles originally did not construct the bowl of the "e" in the word "great." This literary tendency also appears in the word "realities" in his sermon "The Certain Judgment" (Sermon 136); in the word "widely" in his sermon "God's Dealings with the Antediluvians (Sermon 138); in the word "prudence" in his sermon "The Harvest and the Vintage" (Sermon 144); in the word "perceived" in his sermon "The Washing of the Disciples' Feet by Jesus" (Sermon 156); and in the abbreviation "Jer" in his sermon "Absolute Sovereignty" (Sermon 177).

52. This sentence is taken from the third stanza of the hymn "O Happy Day That Fixed My Choice" by English Nonconformist preacher Philip Doddridge (1702–1751). The full stanza is "'Tis done! the great transaction's done: / I am the Lord's, and He is mine; / He drew me, and I followed on, / Charmed to confess the voice divine" (*A Collection of Hymns for the Use of the People Called Bible Christians* [London: Bible Christian Book-Room, 1889, The Spurgeon Library], 767). From an early age Charles had familiarized himself with the works of Doddridge, particularly his *Rise and Progress of Religion* and *The Family Expositor.* On August 22, 1850, approximately two years before preaching the sermon above, Charles wrote the following words in a letter to his father: "I am studying through Romans in the Greek, with Barnes, Doddridge and Chalmers, for my commentaries" (Angus Library and Archive, Regent's Park College, Oxford University, D/SPU 1, Letter 6). See also "Salvation" (Notebook 1, Sermon 11), in which Charles used Doddridge's exposition of Heb 7:25.

53. Charles is likely referencing his conversion experience in the Primitive Methodist Chapel in Colchester, which he later allocated an entire chapter in his autobiography to recount (*Autobiography* 1:97–115). He wrote, "He has done that for me which none but a God could do. He has subdued my stubborn will, melted a heart of adamant, broken a chain of steel, opened the gates of brass, and snapped the bars of iron" (*Autobiography* 1:113). With regard to the phrase "melting tones," Charles later said, "There is no sinner's heart so stout and stubborn

but that, if God shall thrust at him, he shall soon find his heart melt like wax in the midst of his bowels. The eternal God never yet came into contact with men, either in the way of grace or vengeance, but he made them feel that he was not a man like themselves, with whom they could wrestle and contend, but that he was infinitely greater than the very strongest of them" (*MTP* 42:92). See also *NPSP* 1:41 and *NPSP* 5:472.

54. Charles struck through the repetitive word "earth." For additional instances of dittography, see "The Affliction of Ahaz" (Notebook 1, Sermon 57); "The Dog and Swine" (Notebook 2, Sermon 85); "Prove Me Now Herewith" (Notebook 2, Sermon 109); "The Downfall of Dagon" (Notebook 2, Sermon 124); "The Joy of Heaven" (Sermon 147); and "Complaint, Prayer, and Answer" (Sermon 155).

55. This poem was likely original to Charles. For an additional example of his poetry in the early notebooks, see the final page of Notebook 6.

Zech. XIV. 6.7.   Light at eventide.   176

This is another of the 4 texts committed to me.
Oh that may God may be pleased to help me.

There are many things in this chapter which are
now obscure but the day shall reveal it.
I shall apply this passage

I. As a promise to the Church.

That after the death of Jesus, & the proclamation
of the gospel, her sun shall commence rising
first with feeble rays, then more brightly, until there
shall be universal twilight. when though
much darkness remain there shall also be
much light contending with it. At last in
the latter day there shall be a positive actual
light — then sun being then near rising in
the second coming of Jesus.

II. In relation to God's providential dealings
          with his people. —

There is much in our outward circumstances
that is dark & painful, but never positive
night.   For faith makes a moon to reflect
the rays of God. & true love to God gives light
in the greatest darkness.   We often fear that
these things are against us but we ought not
to distrust, nor even to fear, but ever to remember that though dark to us they are not so really

176

LIGHT *at* EVENTIDE
Zechariah 14:6–7[1]

"And it shall come to pass in that day, that the light shall not be clear, nor dark: but it shall be one day which shall be known to the Lord, not day or night: but it shall come to pass, that at evening time it shall be light."

This is another of the 4 texts[2] ~~o~~committed[3] to me. Oh, that my[4] God may[5] be pleased to help me.

There are many things[6] in this chapter which are now obscure, but the day shall reveal it.

I shall apply this passage:

I.   AS A PROMISE TO THE CHURCH.

That after the death of Jesus and the proclamation of the gospel, her sun shall commence rising, first with feeble rays, then more brightly[7] until there shall be universal twilight. When, though much darkness remain, there shall also be much light contending[8] with it. At last, in the latter day there shall be a positive actual light, then sun, being then near rising in the second coming of Jesus.[9]

II. IN RELATION TO GOD'S PROVIDENTIAL DEALINGS[10] WITH HIS PEOPLE.

There is much in our outward circumstances that is dark and painful, but never positive night. For faith makes a moon to reflect the[11] rays of God and true love to God gives light in the greatest darkness.

We often fear that these things are against us. But we ought not to distrust nor even to fear, but ever to remember that though dark to us, they are not so really.[12]

X   + Consider.

1. That these varied scenes to us all chaos are to
God – one day, without any confusion & that all
these work one great design, our lasting benefit

2. That these light afflictions are but for a time
but for one short day, but for a moment.

3. That these are known to the Lord, who
will therefore succour or deliver, for if he knows
the trouble, he knows the way out of it –
        In all our temporal trials we may
confidently expect deliverance, it shall
come when the thick shades are gathering.
When night's black wings appear to spread
o'er the sky, & gloomy darkness gathers then
contrary to expectation the sun shall rise
        (Deliverance comes at eventide.

III. In relation to the inward experience
        of the saints. – . – . –––– . ––––
Once in the sinner's heart nought but Egyptian
darkness was to be found. In God's time the
burning mountain of Sinai threw a horrid glare
athwart the gloom & made the blackness
more terrific. Soon a stray ray from the sun
of righteousness lit up the scene a moment –
then another, but then all was black again
save the flames & lightening of Sinai. Once
more a faint light appeared, but died

And[13] consider:

1.[14] That these varied scenes to us all chaos, are to God one day without any confusion.[15] And that all these work one great design, our lasting[16] benefit.

2. That these light afflictions are but for a time,[17] but for one short day, ~~aye~~[18] but for a moment.

3. That these are known to the Lord who will, therefore, succour or deliver. For if he knows the trouble, he knows the way out of it.

In all our temporal trials we may confidently expect deliverance. It shall come when the thick shades are gathering, when night's black wings appear to spread o'er[19] the sky and gloomy darkness gathers. Then, contrary to expectation, the sun shall rise.[20]

Deliverance comes at eventide.

III. IN RELATION TO THE INWARD EXPERIENCE OF THE SAINTS.

Once, in the sinner's heart, nought[21] but Egyptian darkness was to be found.[22] In God's time, the burning mountain of Sinai threw a horrid glare athwart~~h~~ the gloom[23] and made the blackness more terrific. Soon, a stray ray from the sun of righteousness lit up the scene [for] a moment, then another. But then, all was black again, save the flames and lightenings[24] of Sinai. Once more a faint light appeared but died away as if unable to penetrate the shades. The poor soul all trembling at the gloom, kindles a fire & for a moment smiles amid the sparks, but a swift whirlwind swept it all away, clouds & darkness thicken, the earthquake shakes the mountains & there remains only a fearful looking for of judgment — — just then the sun arises & the beams of grace dispel our black despair.

Our constant every day feeling is like this — there is light & darkness too, it is both, & yet neither. Sometimes sin prevails, the clouds obscure the sky — tenfold night is near — but yet even then light shineth — (Doubt, Distrust, all rise & threaten destruction but they shall not. The path of the just shines more & more. There is design in these shadings, they are short & known to God & we hope to be able in days to come to see more light as evening gathers.

IV. Let us inspect the precious promise.
   "At evening time, it shall be light".
1. In man's extremity is felt God's power.
2. As we grow old, God's grace sustaineth.
3. In the hour of death — our sun rises, & in heaven the full morning bursteth on our ravished eyes.

277

away as if unable to penetrate the shades. The poor soul, all trembling at the gloom, kindles a fire and for a moment smiles amid the sparks. But a swift whirlwind swept it all away. Clouds and darkness thicken, the earthquake shakes the mountains, and there remains only a fearful looking for of judgment. Just then, the sun arises and the beams of grace dispel our black despair.

Our constant every day feeling is like this. There is light and darkness too. It is both, and yet neither. Sometimes sin prevails. The clouds obscure the sky, tenfold night is near. But yet, even then light shineth.

Doubt, Distrust, all rise and threaten destruction, but they shall not. The path of the just shines more and more. There is design in these shadings. They are short and known to God, and we hope to be able in days to come to see more light as evening gathers.

IV. LET US INSPECT THE PRECIOUS PROMISE, *"At evening time, it shall be light."*

1. In man's extremity is felt God's power.

2. As we grow old, God's grace sustaineth.[25]

3. In the hour of death, our sun rises.[26] And in heaven, the full morning bursteth on our ravished eyes.

277

1. Charles preached two additional sermons on Zech 14:6–7. On October 25, 1857, Charles preached a sermon entitled "Light at Evening Time" (*NPSP* 3, Sermon 160) and on April 20, 1917, his sermon "Light at Evening Time" (*MTP* 62, Sermon 3508) was posthumously published. There is not enough overlapping content or structural similarity to suggest Charles had in mind his early sermon when writing his later two sermons.

2. On the last page of this notebook, Charles recorded: "The 4 texts given me by an aged Sister are: John XX. 16. No. 175. Zech XIV. 6.7. No. 176. John XIII. 23. No. 183. Isa. XLI. 10. The 14th is similar. No. 170." In other words, the four texts given by the "aged Sister" to Charles to preach are (in numerical order): "Fear Not, Thou Worm Jacob" (Sermon 170), "Mary with Jesus in the Garden" (Sermon 175), "Light at Eventide" (Sermon 176), and "Leaning on Jesus['s] Bosom" (Sermon 183). Charles preached from all these texts at her request with the exception of Sermon 170. Instead of preaching on verse 10 as she requested, Charles preached on Isa 41:14, which he deemed was "similar." Who was the "aged Sister?" Unfortunately, there is no record of her in Charles's autobiography, his letters to his family members during this season of his ministry, or in his biographies. Nor is there recorded in this notebook the reason she requested these four texts to be preached by Charles.

3. Charles struck through the letter "o" at the beginning of the word "committed." He may have originally intended to write the word "offered."

4. Charles bolded the word "my," likely because either he misspelled it or he prematurely wrote the word "God." Before his redaction, Charles may have intended the sentence to read "Oh, that God may be pleased to help me."

5. An illegible letter appears beneath the letter "m" in the word "may."

6. Charles wrote the stem of the letter "l" or "k" before the "g" in the word "things." He may have accidently written the word "think" before correcting the misspelling.

7. Charles wrote the word "brightly" in superscript above and between the words "more" and "until." He indicated the location of this word with a caret below the line.

8. Charles originally wrote the stem of the letter "t" in the word "contending" before changing it to the letter "d."

9. Cf. Acts 1:11; Rev 1:7–8.

10. The letters "ings" in the word "dealings" are smudged.

11. Charles reinforced the bowl of the letter "e" to construct the word "the."

12. Cf. Ps 139:12.

13. Charles wrote and struck through the letter "f" in the margin before the ampersand. He may have begun to write the word "for."

14. Charles likely began writing Roman numeral I before writing the number 1.

15. An alternative reading of this line is "That these varied scenes to us [are] all chaos, [but] to God [are] one day without any confusion."

16. A smudge appears above the word "lasting."

17. "No child of God can be very long without trouble of some kind or other, for sure it is that the road to heaven will always be rough. . . . There is a pilgrimage, and a weary pilgrimage too, which must be taken before you can obtain entrance into those gates. Still, in all their trials, God's people always find it true that at evening time it shall be light. Are you suffering from temporal troubles? You cannot expect to be without these. They are hard to bear. This, however, should cheer you, that God is as much engaged to succour and support you in your temporal, as he is in your spiritual interests. Beloved, the very hairs of your head are all numbered. Not a sparrow falls on the ground without your Father knowing it" (*MTP* 62:185).

18. The word "aye" is the archaic word for "yes." If Charles had retained the word "aye" instead of striking through it, a modernized reading of this phrase may be "but for one short day, [yes], but for a moment."

19. Contraction, "over."

20. Cf. Ps 30:5.

21. A modernized translation of the word "nought" is "nothing."

22. A modernized reading of this sentence is "In the sinner's heart, once nothing was to be found but Egyptian darkness." Cf. Exod 10:21–23.

23. Cf. Exod 19:18.

24. An alternative spelling of the word "lightenings" is "lightnings." A series of horizontal dots appear above the word "lightenings."

25. Cf. Isa 46:4.

26. "Never fear dying, beloved. Dying is the last, but the least, matter that a Christian has to be anxious about. Fear living—that is a hard battle to fight; a stern discipline to endure; a rough voyage to undergo. You may well invoke God's omnipotence to your aid. But to die, that is to end the strife, to finish your course, to enter the calm heaven. Your Captain, your Leader, your Pilot is with you. One moment, and it is over: 'A gentle wafting to immortal life.' It is the lingering pulse of life that makes the pains and groans. Death ends them all" (*MTP* 62:188–89).

177. Jer XVIII . 6 – 10 .   Absolute sovereignty .

This is a high & hazardous subject, but seeing it
is a Scriptural one , I venture . Here I need more
than at other times the inspiration of the Holy One
I find I cannot touch some men unless I enter
into the den in which they lurk , — moreover
the doctrine has been the means of the salvation
of many as Jonathan Edwards testifies — Yet I
go cautiously, & prayerfully, trusting on the great
right-guiding Spirit, even the Holy Ghost.

Jeremiah is directed to go to the potter's house for
a sermon , with the clay before him he would
have truth more vividly impressed on his own
mind & could bring it out more clearly to others.

He saw the potter put the clay on the wheel &
since it was marred by some hard stone or grit
he changed his model at will, & formed a vessel
for dishonour instead of a vessel for honour.

Here are clearly shewn.

I . God's right to save or to destroy .

God has other rights, indeed he has a right to do
what he will with his own . since he is Creator
But as this seems to be the most eminent
prerogative & the one mentioned in the next
4 verses. I shall confine myself to that.

1 God has a right to destroy, punish & damn
man — — & that because man is a sinner
As Creator God had a right to demand

177

ABSOLUTE SOVEREIGNTY
Jeremiah[1] *18:6—10*[2]

"O house of Israel, cannot I do with you as this potter? saith the Lord. *Behold, as the clay is in the potter's hand, so are ye in mine hand, O house of Israel. At what instant I shall speak concerning a nation, and concerning a kingdom, to pluck up, and to pull down, and to destroy it; if that nation, against whom I have pronounced, turn from their evil, I will repent of the evil that I thought to do unto them. And at what instant shall I speak concerning a nation, and concerning a kingdom, to build and to plant it; if it do evil in my sight, that it obey not my voice, then I will repent of the good wherewith I said I would benefit them."*

This is a high and hazardous subject. But seeing it is a Scriptural one, I venture. Here I need more than at other times the inspiration of the Holy One. I find I cannot touch some men unless I enter into the den in which they lurk. Moreover, the doctrine has been the means of the salvation of many,[3] as Jonathan Edwards testifies.[4] Yet, I go cautiously and prayerfully, trusting on the great, right-guiding Spirit,[5] even the Holy Ghost.

Jeremiah is directed to go to the potter's house for a sermon. With the clay before him, he would have truth more vividly impressed on his own mind and could bring it out more clearly to others.

He saw the potter put the clay on the wheel and since it was marred by some hard stone or grit; he changed his model at will and formed a vessel for dishonour instead of a vessel for honour.

Here are clearly shown:

I. GOD'S RIGHT TO SAVE OR DESTROY.

God has other rights. Indeed he has a right to do[6] what he will with his own since he is Creator. But as this seems to be the most eminent prerogative and the one mentioned in the next 4 verses, I shall confine myself to that.

1.[7] God has a right to destroy, punish, and damn man. And that because man is a sinner. As Creator, God[8] had a right to demand

obedience of us & to fix a penalty to disobedience.
Now since we have broken that law we are now
in his hands to do as he will with us.
If you consider against what a law we have sinned
& how often, & with what aggravations of light
& knowledge — you must own he has a right to damn you

2. God has a right to forgive, save, & glorify man
This right he derives not alone from his own
nature for on that footing he never exercises
it — but from the satisfaction he has made to
law & justice. His right to save is as large
as his right to destroy. It may be exercised
on none, on all, on some, just as he wills.
If we consider that he promotes morality, holiness,
man's happiness, & the interest of the universe
when he saves a sinner we may cheerfully
admit that he has a right to save.
II. God's power to save or to destroy.
The cavillers at his rights, cannot abridge his
powers with all their arguments.
1. He has power to destroy. does he but stay
our breath we die & who can deliver. not the
multitudes of the wicked, nor the hosts of
hell, nor art, nor power can save if he destroy
2. He has power to save & he only. The power
is all centred in him. The most stubborn soul
he can subdue. The law he can silence. Satan
he can baffle. & death & hell o'ercome. He is
able to save to the uttermost.

obedience[9] of us and to fix a penalty for disobedience. Now since we have broken that law, we are now in his hands to do as he will with us.[10] If you consider against what a law we have sinned, and how often and with what aggravations of light and knowledge, you must own he has a right to damn you.

2. God has a right to forgive, save, and glorify man. This right he derives, not alone from his own nature, for on that footing he never exercises it, but from the satisfaction he has made to law and justice. His right to save is as large as his right to destroy. It may be exercised on none, on all, on some, just as he wills.

If we consider that he promotes morality, holiness, man's happiness, and the sinterest[11] of the universe when he saves a sinner, we may cheerfully admit that he has a right to save.

II. GOD'S POWER TO SAVE OR TO DESTROY.

The cavillers[12] at his rights cannot abridge his powers with all their arguments.

1. He has power to destroy. Does he but stay our breath, we die. And who can deliver? Not the multitudes of the wicked, nor the hosts of hell, nor art, nor power can save if he destroy.

2. He has power to save, and he only. The power is all centred in him. The most stubborn soul he can subdue, the law he can silence, Satan he can baffle, and death and hell o'ercome.[13] He is able to save to the uttermost.[14]

Thus far God's rights & God's powers — the two alike infinite so that he cannot overstep the one, nor can anything withstand the other. let us now notice two of the actual decrees he has made.

Penitent sinners shall find mercy.
This is founded on sovereignty, he might have said I will not have mercy. or he might have said industrious sinners, or little sinners, or those who perform ceremonies but it is not so.
Notice the decree is large, reaching to monster sinners, yea those on whom the sentence is all but passed — It is a just decree, for how could he have mercy on men going on in sin — would not this increase sin exceedingly.

Imperitent sinners shall be damned.
This again is sovereignty — but yet infinite justice Not all the promises, the blood of Christ, nor outward duties can save one, impenitent man Is not this a just decree for what else can be done with obstinate & hardened rebels. Shall God take them to heaven unholy, or make a purgatory for them. No. They shall be damned so runs the absolute decree. They shall perish who repent not.
Great God — save since thou can'st —
For Jesus' sake, Amen.

278.

Thus far, God's rights and God's powers.[15] The two [are] alike infinite so that he cannot overstep the one, nor can anything withstand the other.[16]

Let us now notice two of the actual decrees he has made:

Penitent sinners shall find mercy.

This is founded on sovereignty. He might have said, I will not have mercy. Or he might have said, Industrious sinners, or little sinners, or those who perform ceremonies. But it is not so.

Notice the decree is large, reaching to monster sinners, yea, those on whom the sentence is all but passed.[17] It is just a decree. For how could he have mercy on men going on in sin? Would not this increase[18] sin exceedingly?

Impenitent sinners shall be damned.

This again is sovereignty. But yet [also] infinite justice. Not all the promises, the blood of Christ, nor outward duties can save one, impenitent man. Is not this a just decree? For what else can be done with obstinate and hardened rebels?

Shall God take them to heaven unholy or make a purgatory[19] for them? No. They shall be damned, so runs the absolute decree. They shall perish who repent not.[20]

Great God, save since thou can'st.[21]

For Jesus'[s] sake.   Amen

278.

1. Charles did not construct the bowl of the letter "e" in the abbreviation "Jer." He corrected this mistake by reinforcing the letters "e" and "r."

2. This is the only time Charles preached a sermon on Jer 18:6–10. For additional sermons and books on the sovereignty of God in Charles's ministry, see "God's Sovereignty" (Notebook 1, Sermon 18); "Absolute Sovereignty" (Sermon 177); "Divine Sovereignty" (*NPSP* 2, Sermon 77); "Testimony to Free and Sovereign Grace" (*MTP* 33, Sermon 1953); "The Sequel to Divine Sovereignty" (*MTP* 58, Sermon 3284); and "A Defence of Calvinism" (*Autobiography* 1:167–78). In 1866 Charles said, "No doctrine in the whole word of God has more excited the hatred of mankind than the truth of the absolute sovereignty of God" (*MTP* 58:13). A definition of God's sovereignty may be borrowed from James Smith of Cheltenham who gave an address at the Metropolitan Tabernacle on April 11, 1861. Charles published Smith's address, which was entitled "Effectual Calling," in *The Metropolitan Tabernacle Pulpit*: "The way we put it is—God is the Creator, he has a right to do as he wills; he is Sovereign, there is no law above him, he has a right to make and to unmake, and when man hath sinned, he has a right to save or to destroy. If he can save, and yet not impair his justice, heaven shall ring with songs; if he destroy, and yet his goodness be not marred, then hell itself with its deep bass of misery, shall swell the mighty rollings of his glorious praise" (*MTP* 7:322). The doctrine of God's sovereignty played a significant role in Charles's theology, so much so that he reprinted Elisha Cole's *A Practical Discourse of God's Sovereignty* and recommended it "to the attention of our friends" (*MTP* 13:vii).

3. "One week-night, when I was sitting in the house of God, I was not thinking much about the preacher's sermon, for I did not believe it. The thought struck me, '*How did you come to be a Christian?*' I sought the Lord. '*But how did you come to seek the Lord?*' The truth flashed across my mind in a moment,—I should not have sought Him unless there had been some previous influence in my mind to *make me* seek Him. I prayed, thought I; but then I asked myself, *How came I to pray?* I was induced to pray by reading the Scriptures. *How came I to read the Scriptures?* I did read them; but what led me to do so? Then, in a moment, I saw that God was at the bottom of it all, and that He was the Author of my faith; and so the whole doctrine of grace opened up to me, and from that doctrine I have not departed to this day, and I desire to make this my constant confession, 'I ascribe my change wholly to God'" (*Autobiography* 1:168–69, italics in the original).

4. "[God] not only is sovereign, and has a sovereign right to dispose and order in that affair; and he not only might proceed in a sovereign way, if he would, and nobody could charge him with exceeding his right; but he actually does so; he exercises the right which he has. . . . God can either bestow salvation on any of the children of men, or refuse it, without any prejudice to the glory of any of his attributes, except where he has been pleased to declare, that he will or will not bestow it" (Jonathan Edwards, Henry Rogers, and Sereno E. Dwight, *The Works of Jonathan Edwards with an Essay on His Genius and Writings by Henry Rogers: and a Memoir by Sereno E. Dwight* [rev. ed.; ed. Edward Hickman; 2 vols.; London: Ball, Arnold, and Co., 1840, The Spurgeon Library], 2:850). Edwards added, "Let us with the greatest humility adore the awful and absolute sovereignty of God. As we have just shown, it is an eminent attribute of the Divine Being, that he is sovereign over such excellent beings in that of their eternal salvation. The infinite greatness of God, and his exaltation above us, appears in nothing more, than in his sovereignty" (2:853).

5. Cf. John 16:13.

6. Depending on the placement of the comma, the line may also read "God has other rights indeed. He has a right to do. . . ."

7. The lack of margin space suggests Charles likely wrote the number 1 afterward.

8. A smudge appears before the letter "G" in the word "God." The ink of this smudge may have originated from the letter "h" in the word "had." This smudge can also be seen before the word "to" in the same line.

9. Charles exaggerated the bowl of the letter "e" in the word "obedience."

10. In his sermon "Sinners in the Hands of an Angry God," Jonathan Edwards said, "Your wickedness makes you as it were heavy as lead, and to tend downwards with great weight and pressure towards hell; and if God should let you go, you would immediately sink and swiftly descend and plunge into the bottomless gulf; and your healthy constitution, and your own care and prudence, and best contrivance, and all your righteousness, would have no more influence to uphold you and keep you out of hell, than a spider's web would have to stop a falling rock" (*The Works of Jonathan Edwards*, 2:9).

11. Charles struck through the letter "s" at the beginning of the word "interest." He possibly intended to write either the word "sin" or "sinner" as he did in the line following.

12. "A man fond of making objections; an unfair adversary; a captious disputant" (Johnson's *Dictionary*, s.v. "caviller").

13. Contraction, "overcome."

14. Hebrews 7:25, "Wherefore he is able also to save them to the uttermost that come unto God by him, seeing he ever liveth to make intercession for them."

15. The context suggests the alternative reading of this sentence could be "Thus far, [we have seen] God's rights and God's powers," or "Thus far, [I have addressed] God's rights and God's powers."

16. An alternative reading of these sentences is "Thus far, God's rights and God's powers—the two alike infinite—[are such] that he cannot overstep the one, nor can anything withstand the other."

17. As in the abbreviation "Jer" at the beginning of this sermon, Charles reinforced the bowl of the letter "e" in the word "passed."

18. Charles originally wrote the letter "e" instead of the "i" at the beginning of the word "increase." For the other instance in this notebook in which Charles misspelled this word, see "I Glory in Infirmities" (Sermon 165).

19. See "Justification by Imputed Righteousness" (Notebook 2, Sermon 117).

20. Luke 13:3, "I tell you, Nay: but, except ye repent, ye shall all likewise perish."

21. The word "can'st" is the archaic form of the word "can." For an additional use of this word in this notebook, see "Mary with Jesus in the Garden" (Sermon 175). Cf. Zeph 3:17.

1. Kings . X . 6. 7. 8 .   The Queen of Sheba .   178.

I. I will draw a parallel between Solomon & Jesus.
   1. He was a king over all Israel.
   2. He was celebrated for his wisdom.
   3. He had immense riches.
   4. He made all around him rich.
   5. He built the temple — so Jesus Heaven &c.
II. I will commend the queen of Sheba's conduct.
   She heard but was not content with hearing.
   She had great riches but she loved wisdom more.
   The way was toilsome but she ventured.
   She was willing to give much for wisdom.
   She went into Solomon's presence & saw.
It was knowledge of God she wanted. She
noted all particulars considering that all was
worthy of it. She went to duty much the better.
III. I will assure you of her success.
   In every-thing else report says too much.
   Of Jesus himself. His love, his wisdom.
   Of the enjoyments of believers the bible.
   Of the security & safety of God's people.
   Of the joys & glories of heaven.
   Try him sinners ! Try him !!
283

178

THE QUEEN *of* SHEBA
1 Kings 10:6–8[1]

"And she said to the king, It was a true report that I heard in mine own land of thy acts and of thy wisdom. Howbeit, I believed not the words, until I came, and mine eyes had seen it: and, behold, the half was not told me: thy wisdom and prosperity exceedeth the fame which I heard. Happy are thy men, happy are these thy servants, which stand continually before thee, and that hear thy wisdom."

I. I WILL DRAW A PARALLEL BETWEEN SOLOMON AND JESUS.[2]

    1. He was a king over all Israel.[3]

    2. He was celebrated for his wisdom.[4]

    3. He had immense riches.[5]

    4. He made all around him rich.[6]

    5. He built the temple.[7] So Jesus, Heaven,[8] etc.[9]

II. I WILL COMMEND THE QUEEN OF SHEBA'S CONDUCT.

She heard, but was not content with hearing.[10]

She had great riches,[11] but she loved wisdom more.

The way was toilsome, but she ventured.[12]

She was willing to give much for wisdom.[13]

She went into Solomon's presence and saw.

It was knowledge of God she wanted. She noted all particulars,[14] considering that all was worthy of it. She went to duty much the better.

III. I WILL ASSURE YOU OF HER SUCCESS.

In everything[15] else [the] report says, too, much

    Of Jesus himself. His love, his wisdom.

    Of the enjoyments of believers, the[16] Bible.

    Of the security and safety of God's people.

    Of the joys and glories of heaven.[17]

        Try him, sinners! Try him!![18]

283

1. This is the only time Charles preached a sermon on 1 Kgs 10:6–8. For additional sermons on the Queen of Sheba from Charles's later ministry, see also "The Queen of the South, or the Earnest Enquirer" (*MTP* 9, Sermon 533); "The Queen of Sheba, a Sign" (*MTP* 48, Sermon 2777); and "The Queen of Sheba" (*MTP* 59, Sermon 3351). There is enough overlapping content with his 1881 sermon "Greater Than Solomon" (*MTP* 27, Sermon 1600) to suggest Charles may have had this early sermon in mind when writing his later sermon. See also "A Greater Than Solomon" (*MTP* 55, Sermon 3166). A dark ink spot, likely caused by a malfunction of the writing instrument, appears over the letter "s" in the word "Kings."

2. "When the Saviour himself gives us a comparison it is a clear proof that a likeness was originally intended by the Holy Spirit, and therefore we may say without hesitation that Solomon was meant to be a type of Christ" (*MTP* 27:295).

3. Cf. 1 Kgs 4:1.

4. "*He intermeddled with all knowledge*, and was a master in all sciences. . . . Yes; but our Saviour knows infinitely more than Solomon. I want you to-night to come to him just as the Queen of Sheba came to Solomon, only for weightier reasons. . . . Solomon might *have* wisdom, but he could not *be* wisdom to others; Christ Jesus is that to the full" (*MTP* 27:296–97, italics in the original). Cf. 1 Kgs 4:31.

5. "But, oh, when you consider all the wealth of Solomon, what poor stuff it is compared with the riches that are treasured up in Christ Jesus. . . . All the wealth of eternity and infinity is his; how can you say that you are poor while all that he has is yours?" (*MTP* 27:298–99). Cf. 1 Kgs 9:26–28; 10:7, 25.

6. "Beloved, he who died upon the cross, and was indebted to a friend for a grave; he who was stripped even to the last rag ere he died; he who possessed no wealth but that of sorrow and sympathy, yet had about him the power to make many rich, and he has made multitudes rich—rich to all the intents of everlasting bliss; and therefore he must be rich himself. Is he not rich who enriches millions?" (*MTP* 27:298).

7. "Solomon built the temple, which was one of the seven wonders of the world in its time. A very marvellous building it must have been, but I will not stay to describe it, for time fails us. In addition to this he erected for himself palaces, constructed fortifications, and made aqueducts and great pools to bring streams from the mountains to the various towns. . . . He was a marvellous man. Earth

has not seen his like. And yet a greater [man] than Solomon is here, for Christ has brought the living water from the throne of God right down to thirsty men, being himself the eternal aqueduct through which the heavenly current streams. Christ has built fortresses and munitions of defence, behind which his children stand secure against the wrath of hell; and he has founded and is daily finishing a wondrous temple, his church, of which his people are the living stones, fashioned, polished, rendered beautiful—a temple which God himself shall inhabit" (*MTP* 27:299–300). Cf. 1 Kings 6; 2 Chronicles 3.

8. "In the blackest midnight, when the ebon darkness stands thick and hard as granite before you, believe that, at the mystic touch of Christ, the whole of it shall pass away, and at the brightness of his rising the eternal light shall dawn, never to be quenched" (*MTP* 27:301).

9. Cf. John 2:21; 1 Cor 3:16; 6:9, 16.

10. *"Her interest in Solomon was readily awakened.* She heard different reports concerning him, and she took an interest in them. She heard that he was the wisest of kings. Then she thought within herself, 'I would like to know wherein he is wise, and be a partaker of his wisdom'" (*MTP* 55:494, italics in the original).

11. Cf. 2 Chr 9:1.

12. "She did not send an ambassador to see if it was true. That might have helped her, but it would not have satisfied her. Neither did she wait to pick up further evidence from others. But, long as the distance was, she set off to see for herself" (*MTP* 55:498).

13. "He gave her abundance in return. In the exchange I do not suppose she was a loser; but still her heart was so full of thankfulness for what she had learnt that she could not but make an offering unto the king who had been her instructor. I wish all Christians would imitate her in this. If we have salvation from Christ let us never count the giving of our substance to him to be any hardship. Let us not need to be pressed to give, or begged to give, or incited to give by the example of other people; but let us do it conscientiously, out of love to him, doing it as unto him" (*MTP* 55:502).

14. Cf. 1 Kgs 10:1.

15. Charles hyphenated the word "everything."

16. The period before the word "the" is smeared to the right, likely by accident.

17. "Oh, dear brethren, I invite you all—and I ask that I may be able myself—to give the Lord, who is greater than Solomon, our whole being, every power of thought and expression—every faculty of affection or of judgment—all that we are and all that we have; for if we gave Christ our gold and nothing more he could not accept it. He want ourselves,—to live from morning's light to evening's shade for him, to eat and drink and sleep to his glory, to do all to his honour. This is the obligation of the Christian, and this his truest privilege. May the Spirit of God help us up to this" (*MTP* 55:503).

18. "I wish you would even come and try Christ with your hard questions, as this queen of Sheba did Solomon. *Come and see whether he can forgive great sins. Come and see whether he can help you in great trials. Come and bring to him your great doubts and your grievous distresses. Come and tell to him your despair and your horrible thoughts, and the blasphemous suggestions that creep through your mind. Come and see whether he is a Saviour able to save you.* It will be a new thing if he shall have to say, 'Thou art beyond my power. Thou hast sinned beyond the reach of my love.' Come and try him, I say, with your hardest question and most difficult case, and you shall only prove the truth of this word, 'Him that cometh to me I will in no wise cast out'" (*MTP* 55:498, italics in the original). "Oh, that all loved him! Alas that so many do not! What strange monsters! Why, if you do not love Christ, what are you at? You hearts of stone, will you not break? If his dying love do not break them, what will? If you cannot see the beauties of Jesus, what can you see? You blind bats! O you that know not the music of his name, you are deaf. O you that do not rejoice in him, you are dead. What are you at, that you are spared through the pleadings of his love, and yet do not love him? God have mercy upon you, and bring you to delight yourselves in Christ, and trust him!" (*MTP* 27:304).

179.　　　Numbers XII . 3.　　The meekness of Moses.

It has been objected that Moses could hardly be modest if the author of this verse, & that to assume so great a virtue is at once to declare our pride. But Ezra or some inspired scribe may have added it or since Moses was but the instrument of God, he may have been impelled to put into words not only his own faults but this virtue also . . . .

I.　　Wherein consists the virtue of meekness.

It is a compound virtue who ingredients are Humility & gentleness.

1. Humility, a low opinion of one's self, will ever be united with gentleness in some degree. But a man may be humble & not meek. as Luther. This will not alone produce such meekness as that of Moses.

2. Gentleness, must accompany humility But even this alone is not meekness. since gentleness may arise from fear, or hypocrity but Humility combined with gentleness constitute the Christian virtue of meekness.

II. In what great instance Moses displayed his meekness . . –

1 In his dealings with Pharoah who was tried by such a multitude of plagues & yet was hard. He lied many times & yet Moses did not

179

THE MEEKNESS *of* MOSES
Numbers 12:3[1]

"(Now the man Moses was very meek, above all the men which were upon the face of the earth.)"

It has been objected that Moses could hardly be modest if [he is] the author of this verse.[2] And that to assume so great a virtue is at once to declare our pride.

But Ezra or some inspired scribe may have added it, or since Moses was but the instrument of God, he may have been impelled to put into words not only his own faults but this virtue also.[3]

I. WHEREIN CONSISTS THE VIRTUE OF MEEKNESS.

It is a compound virtue who[se] ingredients are Humility and gentleness.

1. Humility,[4] a low opinion of one's self, will ever be united with gentleness in some degree. But a man may be humble and not meek. As Luther.[5] This will not alone produce such meekness as that of Moses.

2. Gentleness[6] must accompany humility. But even this alone is not meekness since gentleness may arise from fear or hypocrisy. But Humility combined with gentleness constitute[s] the Christian virtue of meekness.

II. IN WHAT GREAT INSTANCE MOSES DISPLAYED HIS MEEKNESS.

1. In his dealings with Pharoah[7] who was tried by such a multitude of plagues and yet was hard. He[8] lied many times and yet Moses did not

give forth one wrathful word. but even prayed for him

2. At the Red Sea. when the people complained so unbelievingly of God & so unjustly of him, yet he did not give them scarce a reproof, but pityingly comforted.

3. When they murmured for bread. Exod. XVI. he merely took it to God & answered his words.
When they complained for water. Ex. XVII. He answered in a few mild gentle words.

4 When Eldad & Medad prophesied how humble & meek was Moses' reply to Joshua. Numb. XI. 29.

5. When Miriam & Aaron spoke against Moses' wife, this was a touch in a tender place. Num. XII. Coming too from his own kindred it was severe. Moreover they questioned his mission but there is no word of reproach, simply an earnest prayer

6. When the people seemed to be near the land & just arrived at the goal of his hopes, he was disappointed by the false report of the spies. Num. XIII. He only fell on his face in prayer.

III. What rendered Moses so meek.
I think that though his disposition was not passionate, yet it was not so gentle as to be the cause of all this meekness. Besides his natural temper was not so very gentle.
He slew the Egyptian & hid him.
He broke the tables of stone
He smote the rock twice now though perhaps the two first were not wrong yet they show some warmth of temper & spirit.

420

give forth one wrathful word, but even prayed for him.

2. At the Red Sea when the people complained so unbelievingly of God and so unjustly of him, yet he did not give them scarce a reproof, but pityingly comforted.[9]

3. When they murmured for bread. Exod. XVI.[10] He merely took it to God and answered his words. When they complained for water. Ex. XVII.[11] He answered in a few mild gentle words.

4. When Eldad and Medad prophesied. How humble and meek was Moses'[s] reply to Joshua. Numb. XI. 29.[12]

5. When Miriam and Aaron spoke against Moses['s] wife. This was a touch in a tender place. Num. XII.[13] Coming too from his own kindred, it was severe. Moreover, they questioned his mission. But there is no word of reproach, simply an earnest prayer.[14]

6. When the people seemed to be near the land and just arrived at the goal of his hopes, he was disappointed by the false report of the spies. Num. XIII.[15] He only fell on his face in prayer.[16]

III. WHAT RENDERED MOSES SO MEEK?

I think that though his disposition was not passionate, yet it was not so gentle as to be the cause of all this meekness. Besides, his natural temper was not so very gentle.

He slew the Egyptian and hid him.[17]

He broke the tables[18] of stone.[19]

He smote the rock twice.[20]

Now, though perhaps the two first were not wrong, yet they show some warmth of temper and spirit.[21]

Moreover Moses was a Man subject to the same passions as we, he was angry & sinned not Wroth with ~~sabbath~~ breakers. Ex. XVI. 20. Those who kept the manna wroth with Dathan & Abiram. Num. XVI. 15.

He was very angry with the calf-worshippers. Ex. XXXII.
But in these he sinned not, we should be angry when God is disobeyed. Moses was not one who was gentle out of carelessness. But the secret of his meekness. Say.

1. In an intimate acquaintance with the law by this he was made to feel his own undeservingness. The mercy of God was magnified in his forgiveness. He felt that he could not deal harshly with others. Did we study the law of God more we too should grow in meekness. Moses knew it well, he transcribed it.

2. In the eye which he ever had to the recompence of the reward — for this he left Egypt & doubtless for this he could well bear the little inconveniences of this present world. If we thought more of this, we should be more meek.

3. In his eminent prayerfulness. He took all his burdens to his God & thus gained more profit by words of prayer than by words of anger.

When at his first appearance they complained. Ex. V. 22. He went to God.
At the Red Sea his prayer went up. Ex XIV. 15.
For water, he cried to God. Ex. XVII. 4
The fire was quenched at Taberah Num. XI. 2
When the spies lied he fell on his face. Num. XIV. 5
When Korah rebelled he fell on his face. Num XVI. 4

His falling on the face is a sovereign remedy for hasty spirits, stay a moment to pray & then proceed. This would be a good rule for all of us.

Moreover, Moses was a Man subject to the same passions as we. He was angry and sinned not.

> Wroth[22] with ~~Sabbath breakers~~.[23] Ex. XVI. 20.[24] Those who kept the manna.[25]

> Wroth with Dathan and Abiram. Num. XVI. 15.[26]

> He was very angry with the calf worshippers. Ex. XXXII.[27]

But in these he sinned not. We should be angry when God is disobeyed. Moses was not one who was gentle out of carelessness. But the secret of his meekness [was], Say:

1. In an intimate acquaintance with the law. By this he was made to feel his own undeservingness.[28] The mercy of God was magnified in his forgiveness. He felt that he could not deal harshly with others.[29] Did we study the law of God more, we too should grow in meekness.[30] Moses knew it well. He transcribed it.

2.[31] In the eye which he ever had to the recompence[32] of the reward.[33] For this he left Egypt and doubtless for this he could well bear the little inconveniences of this present world. If we thought more of this, we should be more meek.

3. In his eminent prayerfulness. He took all his burdens to his God and thus gained more profit by words of prayer than by words of anger.

> | When at his first appearance they complained. | Ex. V. 22.[34] |
> | He went to God.[35] | |
> | At the Red Sea, his prayer went up. | Ex. XIV. 15.[36] |
> | For water he cried to God. | Ex. XVII. 4[37] |
> | The fire was quenched at Taberah. | Num. XI. 2[38] |
> | When the spies lied, he fell on his face. | Num. XIV. 5[39] |
> | When Korah rebelled, he fell on his face. | Num. XVI. 4[40] |

This falling on the face is a sovereign remedy for hasty spirits. Stay a moment to pray and then proceed. This would be a good rule for all of us.

4. In his communion with God — on the mount in the tabernacle — the desert — &c &c. He felt a divine influence all day long from these visits. The man who communes much with God will be meek.

IV. What advantages are gained by meekness.

In Moses' case much benefit followed.

1. He was thus fitted to rule so turbulent & ignorant a people — none but a meek man could.

2. He was well fitted to be the dispenser of the law which is in itself most terrific, & so God acted kindly, in committing it to the meekest of men. He was spared many troubles by it — —

In relation to ourselves we may remark.

1. That the contrary is highly unbecoming in a forgiven sinner, a follower of Jesus, an heir of heaven & that this grace is the distinguishing ornament of a Christian.

2. That the want of this gives much pain to us, brings dis-grace on the cause & displeases God.

3. That there is no man who will not find it very serviceable whether, as master, servant, parent, child, man of business, friend &c —

4. That by the diligent perseverance in the road which Moses took we shall arrive at the same end. by divine grace.

285

Lord, revive my stupid soul.

4.[41] In his communion with God on the mount,[42] in the tabernacle,[43] the desert,[44] etc. etc. He felt a divine influence all day long from these visits. The man who communes much with God will be meek.

IV. WHAT ADVANTAGES ARE GAINED BY MEEKNESS?

In Moses'[s] case, much benefit followed.

1. He was thus fitted to rule so turbulent and ignorant a people. None but a meek man could.

2. He was well fitted to be the dispenser of the law, which is in itself most terrific. And so God acted kindly in committing it to the meekest of men. He was spared many troubles by it.

In relation to ourselves we may remark:

1. That the contrary is highly unbecoming in a forgiven sinner, a follower of Jesus, an heir of heaven. And that this grace is the distinguishing ornament of[45] a Christian.

2. That the want of this gives much pain to us, brings disgrace on the cause, and displeases God.

3. That there is no man who will not find it very serviceable whether as master, servant, parent, child, man of business, friend, etc.

4. That by the diligent perseverance in the road which Moses took we shall arrive at the same end by divine grace.

<u>Lord, revive my stupid soul.</u>

285

1. This is the only time Charles preached a sermon on Num 12:3. For additional sermons on Moses from Charles's later ministry, see "Moses' Decision" (*MTP* 18, Sermon 1063); "The Hiding of Moses by Faith" (*MTP* 24, Sermon 1421); "The Prophet like unto Moses" (*MTP* 25, Sermon 1487); "The Death of Moses" (*MTP* 33, Sermon 1966); "Moses: His Faith and Decision" (*MTP* 34, Sermon 2030); "The Shining of the Face of Moses" (*MTP* 36, Sermon 2143); "Moses' Dying Charge to Israel" (*MTP* 40, Sermon 2345); and "The Mediation of Moses" (*MTP* 41, Sermon 2398).

2. John Gill noted, "[T]his is to be considered, not as a self-commendation of *Moses*, but as testimony of his character by God himself" (Gill, *An Exposition of the Old Testament*, 1:705, italics in the original). Ninety years later Matthew Pool wrote, "The holy penmen of Scripture are not to be measured or censured by other pro-fane writers, because they are guided by special instinct in every thing they write; and as they ofttimes publish their own and their near relations' greatest faults, where it may be useful to the honour of God, and the edification of the church in after-ages; so it is not strange if for the same reasons sometimes they commend themselves, especially when they are forced to it by the insolence and contempt of their adversaries, which was Moses'[s] case here" (Matthew Pool, *Annotations upon the Holy Bible; Wherein the Sacred Text Is Inserted, and Various Readings Annexed, Together with the Parallel Scriptures; The More Difficult Terms in Each Verse Are Explained, Seeming Contradictions Reconciled, Questions and Doubts Resolved, and the Whole Text Opened. In Three Volumes. Vol. I.* [London: James Nisbet and Co., 1853, The Spurgeon Library], 286). Gill and Pool both mention the possibility of Ezra's involvement (see Gill, *An Exposition of the Old Testament* 1:705 and Pool, *Annotations upon the Holy Bible* 1:286).

3. A line of stippling appears after the word "also." Charles likely expounded upon this introduction before beginning his first Roman numeral.

4. "I believe every Christian man has a choice between being humble and being humbled" (*MTP* 30:533).

5. Charles later lauded Martin Luther, whose "brave spirit overturned the tyranny of error which had so long held the nations in bondage" (*MTP* 29:613). Charles added, "He was not the man to conceal truth because it was dangerous to avow it" (*MTP* 29:633). He also noted Luther's gentleness, humility, and dependence on God. During an acute season of suffering, Charles preached, "I have found it a blessed thing, in my own experience, to plead before God that I am His

child. When, some months ago, I was racked with pain to an extreme degree, so that I could no longer bear it without crying out, I asked all to go from the room, and leave me alone; and then . . . I talked to the Lord as Luther would have done, and pleaded His Fatherhood in real earnest" (*Autobiography* 3:247). In 1855, Charles confessed, "I have often admired Martin Luther, and wondered at his composure. When all men spoke so ill of him, what did he say? Turn to that Psalm —'God is our refuge and strength, a very present help in time of trouble; therefore we will not fear. Though the earth be removed, and though the mountains be carried into the midst of the sea.' In a far inferior manner, I have been called to stand up in the position of Martin Luther, and have been made the butt of slander, a mark for laughter and scorn" (*NPSP* 1:90).

6. "If you can only keep as firm as Isaac did, never losing your temper, but always being gentle, and meek, and kind, you will conquer; and you who are to-day despised, will yet come to be honoured" (*MTP* 38:18).

7. Charles misspelled this word. It should read "Pharaoh."

8. The letter "e" in the word "He" was smeared to the bottom left of the page, likely by accident.

9. Exodus 14:13–14, "And Moses said unto the people, Fear ye not, stand still, and see the salvation of the LORD, which he will shew to you to day: for the Egyptians whom ye have seen to day, ye shall see them again no more for ever. The LORD shall fight for you, and ye shall hold your peace."

10. Exodus 16:2–3, "And the whole congregation of the children of Israel murmured against Moses and Aaron in the wilderness: and the children of Israel said unto them, Would to God we had died by the hand of the LORD in the land of Egypt, when we sat by the flesh pots, and when we did eat bread to the full; for ye have brought us forth into this wilderness, to kill this whole assembly with hunger."

11. Exodus 17:2–3, "Wherefore the people did chide with Moses, and said, Give us water that we may drink. And Moses said unto them, Why chide ye with me? wherefore do ye tempt the LORD? And the people thirsted there for water; and the people murmured against Moses, and said, Wherefore is this that thou hast brought us up out of Egypt, to kill us and our children and our cattle with thirst?"

12. Numbers 11:29, "And Moses said unto him, Enviest thou for my sake? would

God that all the Lord's people were prophets, and that the Lord would put his spirit upon them!"

13. Numbers 12:1–2, "And Miriam and Aaron spake against Moses because of the Ethiopian woman whom he had married: for he had married an Ethiopian woman. And they said, Hath the Lord indeed spoken only by Moses? hath he not spoken also by us? And the Lord heard it."

14. Num 12:13.   15. Num 13:25–33.

16. Num 14:5.   17. Exod 2:11–15.

18. Charles may have intended to write the word "tablets" instead of "tables."

19. Exod 32:19.   20. Num 20:11.

21. When Charles noted "perhaps the first two were not wrong," he was possibly referring to Exod 17:6 and the first strike upon the rock in Num 20:11.

22. "Angry; out of use" (Johnson's *Dictionary*, s.v. "wroth").

23. Cf. Num 15:32–36.

24. Exodus 16:20, "Notwithstanding they hearkened not unto Moses; but some of them left of it until the morning, and it bred worms, and stank: and Moses was wroth with them."

25. The phrase "Those who kept the manna" differs in size and characteristic from the preceding line and was likely added afterward.

26. Numbers 16:15, "And Moses was very wroth, and said unto the Lord, Respect not thou their offering: I have not taken one ass from them, neither have I hurt one of them."

27. Exodus 32:19–20, "And it came to pass, as soon as he came nigh unto the camp, that he saw the calf, and the dancing: and Moses' anger waxed hot, and he cast the tables out of his hands, and brake them beneath the mount. And he took the calf which they had made, and burnt it in the fire, and ground it to powder, and strawed it upon the water, and made the children of Israel drink of it."

28. Charles prematurely wrote the long "s" before smudging through it to add the letter "e."

29. John Gill wrote, Moses was "seldom angry, and when he was, it was generally, if not always, when the honour of God was concerned, and not on account of his own person and character; though it must not be said of him, that he was perfect in this respect, or free from passion, or from blame at any time on account of it, but when compared with others, he was the meekest man that ever lived" (Gill, *An Exposition of the Old Testament* 1:705).

30. A modernized reading of this line is "If we studied the law of God more, we too should grow in meekness."

31. The number 2 was smudged, likely by accident.

32. This word may also be spelled "recompense."

33. Cf. Heb 11:24–26.

34. Exodus 5:22, "And Moses returned unto the Lord, and said, Lord, wherefore hast thou so evil entreated this people? why is it that thou hast sent me?"

35. The phrase "He went to God" differs in size from the preceding line and was likely added afterward.

36. Exodus 14:15, "And the Lord said unto Moses, Wherefore criest thou unto me? speak unto the children of Israel, that they go forward."

37. Exodus 17:4, "And Moses cried unto the Lord, saying, What shall I do unto this people? they be almost ready to stone me."

38. Numbers 11:2, "And the people cried unto Moses; and when Moses prayed unto the Lord, the fire was quenched."

39. Numbers 14:5, "Then Moses and Aaron fell on their faces before all the assembly of the congregation of the children of Israel."

40. Numbers 16:4, "And when Moses heard it, he fell upon his face."

41. Charles originally wrote the number 3 before changing it to 4.

42. Cf. Exodus 19; 24:12–31:18.

43. Cf. Exod 33:7–11.   44. Cf. Numbers 14.

45. The letter "f" in the word "of" was smudged to the right side of the page, likely by accident.

180. <u>II Kings II</u>. 16. More for us than against us.

The servant had sense enough to see his danger but faith he wanted & therefore could not see his safety. What shall <u>we</u> do? Should have said. What shall <u>God</u> do? We do nothing, Elijah might say. We leave that to God our work is to trust.   This sentence may cheer

1. In regard to the justification of a convinced sinner, much is against the hope of pardon, but the blood of Jesus overcomes all.

2. In regard to temporal troubles.

3. In regard to our sanctification; our own heart, Satan, the world, our friends are against us but. the Spirit, the word, the Father the angels, the saints, the promises are for us.

4. In prospect of death we shall find even there that if dangers double, grace shall quadruple & help us quite through.

5. The Church universal may lay this up as a precious word, when infidels, Catholics Puseyites, heathens, Arians &c are at her, a mightier is on our side. Then fear not but onward, onward, right on

<u>Help. Great & Mighty one</u>

279. 280. 384.

180

MORE *for* US THAN AGAINST US
2 Kings 6:16[1]

"And he answered, Fear not: for they that be with us are more than they that be with them."

The servant had sense enough to see his danger, but faith he wanted[2] and therefore could not see his safety.[3] What shall we do?[4] Should have said, What shall God do?[5] We do nothing. Elijah[6] might say we leave that to God. Our work is to trust.[7]

This sentence may cheer:

1. In regard to the justification of a convinced sinner.[8] Much is against the hope of pardon, but the blood of Jesus overcomes all.[9]

2. In regard to temporal troubles.[10]

3. In regard to our sanctification, our own heart, Satan, the world. Our friends are against us but the Spirit,[11] the Word,[12] the Father, the angels, the saints, the promises, are for us.

4. In prospect of death we shall find even there that if dangers double, grace shall quadruple and help us quite through.[13]

5. The Church universal[14] may lay this up as a precious word when infidels, Catholics, Puseyites,[15] heathens, Arian[16] etc. are at her.

A mightier is on our side.[17] Then fear not, but onward, onward, right on.[18]

Help. Great and Mighty One

279. 280. 384.

1. Charles did not completely construct the upward stroke of Roman numeral VI, and it takes the appearance of II. However, the correct Scripture reference for this sermon is 2 Kgs 6:16, one Charles never preached a sermon from again. He did preach two later sermons on 2 Kgs 6:17: "Young Man! A Prayer for You" (*MTP* 37, Sermon 2215) and "Eyes Opened" (*MTP* 54, Sermon 3117).

2. An alternative reading of this phrase is "but faith he lacked." Johnson defined the word "want" in this sense: "to be without something fit or necessary"; "to be defective in something"; "to fall short of; not to contain"; "to be without; not to have"; "to need; to have need of; to lack"; "to fail; to be deficient"; and "to be missed; to be not had" (Johnson's *Dictionary*).

3. "The young man was at that time in the peculiar condition of seeing, and yet not seeing. He saw the enemy surrounding the city, but not the greater host of the Lord's angels who protected the man of God. . . . He could see the danger, but he could not see the deliverance" (*MTP* 37:397).

4. "Perhaps I am addressing some, at this time, who are very friendly to the cause of God, and are even connected with it by relationship or occupation; they cheerfully lend a hand at any time in holy service so far as they can, and they wish prosperity to the cause of true religion. Yet their eyes have not been opened to see spiritual things; or, at least, not sufficiently opened to see the gracious and divine side of them. They see enough to perceive that they are in danger from a great enemy. They perceive that it is no easy thing to fight the battle of life: in the prospect of it they cry, 'How shall we do?' They perceive that it is a difficult thing for a man to stand up for holiness, for truth, for integrity, for purity, and to maintain a gracious character throughout the whole of life. They seem to themselves to be environed with opposing forces in their business, in their temperament, in their companionships, and perhaps in their families. As for the cause of godliness, it seems hemmed in by adversaries; and they ask—What is to be done? Is not the matter desperate? Might it not be as well to surrender at once? For any such timid one I would present to God the prayer of Elisha: 'Oh, that the prayer might be answered at this hour!'" (*MTP* 27:397–98).

5. "Do not try to hold up your tallow candles to reveal the chariots of fire, nor parade your vain philosophy, as if that could clear away the darkness of the soul. Leave room for God to work; and, in a moment, at the touch of his finger, in

response to the prayers of his people, the wondrous work shall be accomplished" (*MTP* 37:402–3).

6. Charles was mistaken in writing the name Elijah. The main subject of his text was instead Elisha.

7. "If we could see what Elisha saw, we should be quiet and serene as Elisha was. But most men have not this calmness of mind because they have not the spiritual eyesight which would bring it to them" (*MTP* 54:530). Charles may have intended the stippled smudge after the word "trust" to indicate a break in the introduction.

8. "Oh my hearers, as yet strangers to the things of God; if the Lord would open your eyes at once, you would be astonished indeed; for as yet you have no idea, you cannot have any idea, what the spiritual life is, nor what spiritual realities must be: neither can you have any true idea of them till you are quickened of the Lord. You may talk about spiritual subjects, and discuss them, and think yourselves theologians; but you resemble deaf persons criticizing music, and blind men describing pictures. You are not qualified even to express an opinion upon the matter till you are created anew in Christ Jesus, and brought within range of the spiritual and the heavenly" (*MTP* 37:401).

9. "We need to pray—Lord, open their eyes, that they may see; for seeing, they do not see; and hearing, they do not perceive! Blessed be the Lord, how sweetly they do see it the moment their eyes are opened by his own omnipotent touch! Then they wonder that they did not see it before, and call themselves ten thousand fools for not perceiving what is so plain. . . . I hope, beloved fellow-Christians, that you are praying while I am speaking; praying, I mean, for those around you, and for all the blind souls that wander among the graves of earth: 'Lord, open their eyes, that they may see!' He that made the eye can open it. Sin cannot so darken the mind but that God can pour light into it. If we cannot make men see, we can at least lead them to the Master Oculist, who can rectify their sight" (*MTP* 37:400). Cf. Rom 3:25; 5:9; Eph 1:7; Heb 9:14; 10:19, 22; 13:12; 1 John 1:17; Rev 1:5.

10. Cf. Matt 6:25–34; Rom 8:28.

11. A faint fingerprint, likely belonging to Charles, appears on the word "Spirit."

12. Charles did not capitalize the word "word." However, for consistency the word has been capitalized.

13. "The young may die: but the old must" (*MTP* 41:477). "It is a very natural thing that man should fear to die, for man was not originally created to die" (*MTP* 55:1). "When Baxter lay a dying, and his friends came to see him, almost the last word he said was in answer to the question, 'Dear Mr. Baxter, how are you?' 'Almost well,' said he, and so it is. Death cures; it is the best medicine, for they who die are not only almost well, but healed for ever" (*MTP* 18:101). Charles died at the age of fifty-seven in Menton, France, on January 31, 1892, after falling into a coma at the Hotel Beau-Rivage.

14. The Universal church, in Charles's view, was "Any company of Christian men, gathered together in holy bonds of communion for the purpose of receiving God's ordinances, and preaching what they regard to be God's truths," and it contains "all them that love the Lord Jesus Christ in sincerity and in truth" (*NPSP* 4:210). Just before his death in 1892, Charles reflected, "I had no idea that Christian people, of every church, would spontaneously and importunately plead for the prolonging of my life. I feel myself a debtor to all God's people on this earth. Each section of the church seemed to vie with all the rest in sending words of comfort to my wife, and in presenting intercession to God on my behalf. If anyone had prophesied, twenty years ago, that a dissenting minister, and a very outspoken one, too, would be prayed for in many parish churches, and in Westminster Abbey and St. Paul's Cathedral, it would not have been believed; but it was so. There is more love in the hearts of Christian people than they know themselves. We mistake our divergences of judgment for differences of heart; but they are far from being the same thing. In these days of infidel criticism, believers of all sorts will be driven into sincere unity. For my part, I believe that all spiritual persons are already one. When our Lord prayed that his church might be one, his prayer was answered, and his true people are even now, in spirit and in truth, one in him" (*ST* February 1892:52).

15. Edward Bouverie Pusey (1800–1882) was a prominent Anglican who gave leadership to the Oxford Movement, which was a resurgence of conservative Anglicanism at Oxford University sparked by John Keble's 1833 sermon "National Apostasy" (see R. W. Church, *The Oxford Movement: Twelve Years 1833–1845*, vol. 6 [London: MacMillan, 1897]). Pusey championed the doctrine of baptismal regeneration, as seen in his *Tract for the Times by Members of the University of Oxford*, no. 67: Scriptural Views of Holy Baptism, part I ([2nd ed.; London: J. G. F. & J. Rivington; Oxford: J. H. Parker, 1840], 4). For a recent work on

Pusey, see Rowan Strong and Carol Engelhardt Herringer, eds., *Edward Bouverie Pusey and the Oxford Movement*, Anthem Nineteenth-Century Series (London: Anthem Press, 2012). On one occasion Charles remembered hearing a "Mr. Jay, of Bath" preach sermons against Puseyism, saying, "You do need a Mediator between yourselves and God, but you do not need a Mediator between yourselves and Christ" (*Autobiography* 1:208). Mr. Jay also said, "Puseyism is a lie" (*MTP* 26:386–87). For additional references to Puseyism, see "Salvation in God Only" (Notebook 1, Sermon 24); "The Fight and the Weapons" (Notebook 1, Sermon 37a); "Justification by Imputed Righteousness" (Notebook 2, Sermon 117); and "Come Ye Out from Among Them" (Notebook 2, Sermon 119).

16. Arius (AD 250–336) was a heretic in the early church who believed Jesus Christ was the first creation of God and therefore less than equally God (see Harry R. Boer, *A Short History of the Early Church* [Grand Rapids, MI: Eerdmans, 1976], 167). Charles summarized Arius's Christology in the following words: "There was Arius; he would receive Christ as a good man, but not as God" (*MTP* 41:161). He also said Arius "sought to rob Christ of his true glory, and reduce him to the level of mere man" (*MTP* 46:159). See also Lewis Ayres, *Nicaea and Its Legacy: An Approach to Fourth-Century Trinitarian Theology* (Oxford: Oxford University Press, 2004). Charles likely read about Arius in his personal copy of Henry B. Smith and Philip Schaff, eds., *Theological and Philosophical Library: A Series of Text-Books, Original and Translated for Colleges and Universities: The Creeds of the Greek and Latin Churches* (London: Hodder and Stoughton, 1878, The Spurgeon Library). For additional references to Arius, see "What Think Ye of Christ" (Notebook 1, Sermon 70); *NPSP* 4:358; *ST* March 1887:123, and *ST* April 1887:166.

17. An alternative reading of this line is "A Mightier [One] is on our side" or "A Mightier [God] is on our side."

18. "Perhaps, within a month, some of you, to whom I now speak, may be in so severe a fight that you will be almost driven to throw down your weapons in utter despair, saying, 'How can I stand against so many?—I that am so feeble?' I beseech you, remember this warning. Have not I told you of it? I would plead with you to play the man. Gird up the loins of your mind; be sober, and hope to the end; for if the Lord has opened your eyes, you will perceive that you are on the winning side" (*MTP* 37:407).

Matt III. 11.   The Baptism of the Spirit.   181.

This text is what some may call a Baptistical one.
I am not one who often brings this prominent.
All know that I endeavour to preach unity:
but my warrant for taking this text is the fact
that it is the word of God. Let us regard it as
such & if by the help of the Holy Spirit I may
be able to speak only what is in the text, I
trust my hearers will agree to take the same.
Here are two Baptisms spoken of.

I. Water-baptism — what does this text say of it.
1. This verse declares that baptism with water
is not a saving ordinance, for when administered
even by John, it was only baptism with water,
and was of no use whatever without the other
baptism.   The Fire-Baptism.
2. This verse declares that repentance is
necessary to the right administration of the
water-baptism here spoken of & therefore it
must be the baptism of adults since only they
can repent. Indeed the Church of England
admits that repentance & faith are necessary.
3. This verse teaches that the right adminis-
-tration of the ordinance does not depend on
the character or intention of the administrator.
He gives no efficacy to it. Why did not Jesus
do it if this were true? We can go no further
than the sign. We baptize with water.

181

THE BAPTISM *of the* SPIRIT
Matthew 3:11[1]

"I indeed baptize you with water unto repentance; but he that cometh after me is mightier than I, whose shoes I am not worthy to bear: he shall baptize you with the Holy Ghost, and with fire:"

This text is what some may call a Baptistical one. I am not one who often brings this prominent.[2] All know that I endeavor to preach[3] unity:[4] but my warrant for taking this text is the fact that it is the Word[5] of God. Let us regard it as such, and if by the help of the Holy Spirit I may be able to speak only what is in the text, I trust my hearers will agree to take the same.

Here are two Baptisms spoken of:

I. WATER-BAPTISM. WHAT DOES THIS TEXT SAY OF IT?

    1.   This verse declares that baptism with water is not a saving ordinance,[6] for when administered even by John it was only baptism with water and was of no use whatever without the other baptism, The Fire-Baptism.

    2.   This verse declares that repentance is necessary to the right administration of the water-baptism[7] here spoken of, and therefore it must be the baptism of adults since only they can repent.[8] Indeed, the Church of England admits that repentance[9] and faith are necessary.[10]

    3.   This verse teaches that the right administration[11] of the ordinance does not depend on the character or intention of the administrator.[12] He gives no efficacy to it. Why did not Jesus do it if this were true? We can go no further than the sign. We baptize with water.

4. There seems to be some evidence here of the truth of the doctrine that baptism is by immersion — for can we imagine that we are to be sprinkled with the Holy Ghost, surely we need & must have an entire burial & immersion in its fiery operations. So must it be with water. Much water — much spirit. If it means little water, then a little Holy Spirit.

Now let us leave the water, the naval combat, & go to where we are agreed.

II. Fire — Baptism, what does the text say of that.

1. It declares that it is the more important of the two, for the servant could baptize with water but the mighty Master has to take the other in hand & he only can do it,

2. It declares that the Holy Ghost is necessary in this baptism as well as Jesus Christ. If Jesus be the Baptizer. the Holy Spirit is that in which the soul is baptized.

3. It declares in what manner the Holy Spirit acts in the conversion of men, when Jesus plunges them into its influence.

1 The first effect is a sense of acute pain, the soul suffers often such agonies as are well expressed by the sharp pains of burning.

2. Next comes more enlighten-ment caused by the flame burning around. — the soul is

4. There seems to be some evidence[13] here of the truth of the doctrine that baptism is by immersion. For can we imagine that we are to be sprinkled with the Holy Ghost? Surely we need and must have an entire burial and immersion in its fiery operations. So must it be with water. Much water, much Spirit.[14] If it means little water, then a little Holy Spirit.

Now, let us leave the water, the naval combat, and go to where we are agreed.

II. FIRE-BAPTISM. WHAT DOES THE TEXT SAY OF THAT?

1. It declares that it is the more important of the two, for the servant could baptize with water but the mighty Master has to take the other in hand, and he only can do it.

2. It declares that the Holy Ghost is necessary in this baptism, as well as Jesus Christ. If Jesus be the Baptizer, the Holy Spirit is that in which the soul is baptized.

3. It declares in what manner the Holy Spirit acts in the conversion of men when Jesus plunges them into its influence.[15]

    1.[16] The first effect is a sense of acute pain the soul suffers often.[17] Such agonies as are well expressed by the sharp pains of burning.

    2. Next comes more enlightenment[18] caused by the flame burning around. The soul is

put into a glare of light where its blackness is revealed by the same light the refuges of lies are discovered to be nothing more than vanities — & by & by the glorious salvation of Jesus is dis-cerned & understood.

3. Then comes its quick, lively, energetic force, not lieing idle but spreading, having life in itself & giving life to the whole man in regeneration. —

4. Soon comes comfort & warmth, but it is the same Spirit — who worketh variously.

give me not a little of this.

5. Yet ever there must remain the fire giving life, zeal, might — — As well as consuming the dross which remaineth in the regenerate Burning the dry parts, spreading as fire doth from little to great & greater still. :

now all this is the Holy Ghost's doing. This greatest, Fire Baptism is of him alone.

1. You who are not baptized be so.

2. Baptized persons, seek to know that you have the Fire-Baptism — be holy, zealous, let your hearts ascend as the flames toward heaven

3. All men — be Fire-Baptists even if you will not be Water-Baptists.

Oh God! may I feel this for
<u>Jesus' blood sake</u>

284

put into a glare[19] of light where its blackness is revealed by the same light. The refuges of lies are discovered to be nothing more than vanities, and by and by the glorious salvation of Jesus is discerned[20] and understood.

3. Then comes its quick, lively, energetic force. Not lieing idle, but spreading, having life in itself and giving life to the whole man in regeneration.

4. Soon comes comfort and warmth, but it is the same Spirit who worketh variously. Give me not a little of this.[21]

5. Yet ever there must remain the fire giving life, zeal,[22] might. As well as consuming the dross which remaineth in the regenerate. Burning the dry parts, spreading as fire doth from little to great and greater still.

Now all this is the Holy Ghost's doing. This greatest **Fire-Baptism** is of him alone.

1. You who are not baptized, be so.

2. Baptized persons, seek to know that you have the Fire-Baptism. Be holy, zealous. Let your hearts ascend as the flames toward heaven.

3. All men, be Fire-Baptists even if you will not be Water-Baptists.

Oh God! may I feel this, for

Jesus' blood sake.

284

1. This is the only time Charles preached a sermon on Matt 3:11.

2. Why did Charles qualify his stance on believer's baptism to his Baptist congregation at Waterbeach Baptist Chapel? One reason could be that his ever-expanding number of visitors came from Anglican or Methodist congregations. Whatever the case, Charles was aware of "the naval combat" of this issue and felt pressure in his introduction to this sermon to justify his stance on immersive baptism and at the conclusion said, "All men, be Fire-Baptists even if you will not be Water-Baptists."

3. A pencil mark appears below the word "preach" and also above the word "this" in the line above. These strokes, likely in the hand of Charles, may be evidence that he edited this manuscript for publication in 1857.

4. For additional references to church unity, see "Pleasure in the Stones of Zion" (Notebook 1, Sermon 53); "Can Two Walk Together Unless They Are Agreed?" (Notebook 1, Sermon 76); "David in the Cave of Adullam" (Notebook 2, Sermon 116); *NPSP* 3:213; *NPSP* 4:166; *MTP* 27:198, *MTP* 28:628; *MTP* 58:150; and *Autobiography* 4:168. Cf. John 17:21; 1 Cor 12:13.

5. As in the previous sermon, "More for Us Than Against Us" (Sermon 180), the word "Word" in references to the Bible has been capitalized for consistency.

6. Fourteen-year-old Charles likely had been exposed to the doctrine of baptismal regeneration as a student at St. Augustine College, an Anglican school in Maidstone where he was educated from 1848 to 1849. Charles's opposition to this doctrine resulted in his highly controversial sermon in 1864, "Baptismal Regeneration" (*MTP* 10, Sermon 573), which became one of his most popular sermons in his lifetime. By 1899, 230,000 copies of this sermon had been sold (*Autobiography* 3:82). In this sermon Charles said, "[I]f I should provoke some hostility—if I through speaking what I believe to be the truth lose the friendship of some and stir up the enmity of more, I cannot help it. The burden of the Lord is upon me, and I must deliver my soul" (*MTP* 10:314). He also said, "We hold that persons are not saved by baptism, for we think, first of all, that *it seems out of character with the spiritual religion which Christ came to teach*, that he should make salvation depend upon mere ceremony" (*MTP* 10:317, italics in original) and "I do beseech you to remember that you must have a new heart and a right

spirit, and baptism cannot give you these. You must turn from your sins and follow after Christ; you must have such a faith as shall make your life holy and your speech devout, or else you have not the faith of God's elect, and into God's kingdom you shall never come (*MTP* 10:323). With regard to this point, John Gill, in his treatise *Infant-Baptism a Part and Pillar of Popery*, wrote, "This old leaven yet remains in some Protestant churches, who have retained it from *Rome*; hence a child when baptized is declared to be regenerate, and thanks are returned to God that it is regenerate; and it is taught, when capable of being catechized, to say, that in its baptism it was 'made a child of God, a member of Christ, and an inheritor of the kingdom of heaven;' which has a tendency to take off all concern in persons when grown up, about an inward work of grace, in regeneration and sanctification, as a meetness for heaven, and to encourage a presumption in them, notwithstanding their apparent want of grace, that they are members of Christ, and shall never perish; are children and heirs of God, and shall certainly inherit eternal life" (John Gill, *A Collection of Sermons and Tracts: In Two Volumes. Containing, Vol. I. I. Annual Sermons. II. Occasional Sermons. III. Funeral Sermons. Vol. II. I. Ordination Sermons. II. Polemical Tracts. III. Dissertations. Several of Which Were Never Before Printed. To Which Are Prefixed, Memoirs of the Life, Writings, and Character of the Author. Vol. II* [London: printed for George Keith in Gracechurch-Street, 1773], 521, italics in the original). For two academic treatments of the Baptismal Regeneration Controversy, see Tom Nettles, *Living by Revealed Truth: The Life and Pastoral Theology of Charles Haddon Spurgeon* (Ross-shire, Scotland: Christian Focus Publications, 2013), 513–17; and Larry Michael, "The Effects of Controversy on the Evangelistic Ministry of C. H. Spurgeon" (PhD diss., The Southern Baptist Theological Seminary, 1988), 148–86.

7.   In Charles's diary entry for April 6, 1850, he recorded, "Had some serious thoughts about baptism" (*Autobiography* 1:129). He was baptized less than one month later. On May 3, 1850, fifteen-year-old Charles woke early in Newmarket before departing at 11:00 AM for the village of Isleham some eight miles away. "What a walk it was!" Charles reflected. "What thoughts and prayers thronged my soul during that morning's journey!" (1:151). At 1:00 PM, he arrived at the River Lark. The site had been used first for baptism in 1798. In Charles's day five churches in the area used the location for baptisms. Charles described the River Lark as "a beautiful stream, dividing Cambridgeshire from Suffolk, and is dear to local anglers" (ibid.). He claimed to have forgotten the content of the

service because "my thoughts were in the water, sometimes with my Lord in joy, and sometimes with myself in trembling awe at making so public a confession" (1:152). After he escorted two women into the water, he himself was baptized by a Mr. Cantlow. Charles reflected, "It was a new experience to me, never having seen a baptism before, and I was afraid of making some mistake. The wind blew down the river with a cutting blast, as my turn came to wade into the flood; but after I had walked a few steps, and noted the people on the ferry-boat, and in boats, and on either shore, I felt as if Heaven, and earth, and hell, might all gaze upon me; for I was not ashamed, there and then, to own myself a follower of the Lamb. My timidity was washed away; it floated down the river into the sea, and must have been devoured by the fishes, for I have never felt anything of the kind since. Baptism also loosed my tongue, and from that day it has never been quiet. I lost a thousand fears in that River Lark" (ibid.). That same day Charles recorded the following words in his diary: "Blest pool! Sweet emblem of my death to all the world! May I, henceforward, live alone for Jesus! Accept my body and soul as a poor sacrifice, tie me unto Thee; in Thy strength I now devote myself to Thy service for ever; never may I shrink from owning Thy name!" (1:135). On July 9, 1882, Charles reflected on his baptism: "Well do I remember that May morning when I walked into the river at Isleham Ferry, and thus declared publically that I belonged to the Lord Jesus Christ. By that act of immersion, I felt that I had crossed the Rubicon, and there was no possibility of ever going back. I had burned the boats behind me, so that I could not retreat, nor have I ever wanted to do so. It did not matter to me how many spectators looked on me that day, nor whether they were angels, men, or devils. I wanted them all to witness that, henceforth, I was Christ's servant,—that I bore in my body the marks of the Lord Jesus, the water-mark which could never be taken out" (*MTP* 45:546). For additional sermons on baptism, see "Faith Before Baptism" (Notebook 9, Sermon 396); "Baptism—a Burial" (*MTP* 27, Sermon 1627); and "Baptism Essential to Obedience" (*MTP* 39, Sermon 2339). See also "An Exhortation to Bravery" (Notebook 1, Sermon 72); *NPSP* 4:170; and *MTP* 17:156.

8. Numerous books in Spurgeon's personal library address the New Testament practice of baptism by immersion, including Philip Schaff's *The Teaching of the Twelve Apostles* in which Schaff wrote, "Nothing is said of Infant Baptism. The reference to instruction and the direction of fasting show that the writer has in view only the Baptism of catechumens, or Adult believers. Christianity always begins by

preaching the gospel to such as can hear, understand and believe. Baptism follows as a solemn act of introduction into fellowship with Christ and the privileges and duties of church-membership. In Baptism has no sense and would be worse than useless where there is no Christian family or Christian congregation to fulfil the conditions of Baptism and to guarantee a Christian nurture. Hence in the Apostolic and the whole ante-Nicene age to the time of Constantine, Baptism of believing converts was the rule, and is to this day on every missionary field. Hence in the New Testament the baptized are addressed as people who have died and risen with Christ, and who have put on Christ" (Philip Schaff, *The Oldest Church Manual Called the Teaching of the Twelve Apostles. ΔΙΔΑΧΗ ΤΩΝ ΔΩΔΕΚΑ ΑΠΟΣΤΟΛΩΝ. The Didache and Kindred Documents in the Original. With Translations and Discussions of Post-Apostolic Teaching, Baptism, Worship and Discipline, and with Illustrations and Fac-similes of the Jerusalem Manuscript* [New York: Funk & Wagnalls, 1885, The Spurgeon Library], 31, capitalization in the original).

9. Charles did not originally construct the entirety of the letter "e" at the end of the word "repentance." He reinforced the letter by increasing the size of its bowl.

10. In his *Exposition of the Thirty-Nine Articles*, Thomas Rogers noted the necessity of faith in baptism in Article XI, Proposition II, saying, "*Only by faith are we accounted righteous before God*" (Thomas Rogers, *The Catholic Doctrine of the Church of England, an Exposition of the Thirty-Nine Articles. Edited for the Parker Society, by the Rev. J. J. S. Perowne, M. A., Fellow of Corpus Christi College, Cambridge* [Cambridge: printed at The University Press, 1854, The Spurgeon Library], 111, italics in the original). In the chapter entitled "The Ministration of Baptism to Such as Are of Riper Years, and Able to Answer for Themselves," Charles's 1832 edition of *The Book of Common Prayer* reads, "Doubt ye not therefore, but earnestly believe, that [God] will favourably receive *these* present *persons*, truly repenting, and coming unto him by faith; that he will grant *them* remission of *their* sins, and bestow upon *them* the holy Ghost; that he will give *them* the blessing of eternal life, and make *them* partakers of his everlasting kingdom" (*The Book of Common Prayer, and Administration of the Sacraments, and Other Rites and Ceremonies of the Church, According to the Use of the United Church of England and Ireland: Together with the Psalter or Psalms of David, Pointed as They Are to Be Sung or Said in Churches* [Cambridge: printed by John Smith, Printer to the University, 1832, The Spurgeon Library], n.p., italics in the original). Moreover, a prayer from the chapter entitled "The Ministration of Publick

Baptism of Infants, to Be Used in the Church," reads, "Almighty and immortal God, the aid of all that need, the helper of all that flee to thee for succour, the life of them that believe, and the resurrection of the dead; We call upon thee for *this Infant*, that *he*, coming to thy holy Baptism, may receive remission of *his* sins by spiritual regeneration. Receive *him*, O Lord, as thou hast promised by thy well-behaved Son, saying, Ask, and ye shall have; seek, and ye shall find; knock, and it shall be opened unto you: So give now unto us that ask; let us that seek find; open the gate unto us that knock; that *this Infant* may enjoy the everlasting benediction of thy heavenly washing, and may come to the eternal kingdom which thou hast promised by Christ our Lord. *Amen*" (*The Book of Common Prayer*, "The Ministration of Publick Baptism of Infants," italics in the original).

11. Charles hyphenated the word "administration" and rolled the remainder of the word onto the next line.

12. "The sacraments—in this case baptism—are effective by the simple fact that they are administered. This means that their validity is not dependent on the minister who performs the ceremony" (Gregg Allison, *Historical Theology: An Introduction to Christian Doctrine* [Grand Rapids, MI: Zondervan, 2011], 620–21). Thomas Rogers also noted the sacramental function of "*ex opera operato*" in Article XXVI of *The Thirty-Nine Articles* (Thomas Rogers, *Exposition of the Thirty-Nine Articles*, 269, italics in the original).

13. A dark smudge, likely accidental, appears over the word "evidence." The source of the ink for the smudge was likely the tittle of the letter "i." The additional discoloration was likely due to the aging process of the manuscript.

14. Since Charles was referring to the Holy Spirit, the word "Spirit" has been capitalized here and also on the following page for consistency.

15. "The Holy Dove has often been greatly grieved, but he has never spread his wings to depart. This is still the dispensation of the Spirit. You hardly need to pray to have the Spirit poured out; for that has been done. What you need is, a baptism of the Holy Spirit; namely, to go down personally into that glorious flood which has been poured forth. Oh, to be immersed into the Holy Ghost, and into fire: covered with his holy influence, 'plunged in the Godhead's deepest sea, and lost in his immensity!'" (*MTP* 36:251).

16. The left-leaning tilt of the number 1 is unusual. Charles may have not originally intended this stroke to be a number at all. However, when comparing this stroke to the number 4 on the following page, it is more likely that Charles originally intended this number to be 4.

17. "A spiritual experience which is thoroughly flavoured with a deep and bitter sense of sin is of great value to him that hath had it" (*Autobiography* 1:76).

18. Charles hyphenated the word "enlighten-ment." However, the word has been conjoined for consistency.

19. A smudge appears above the word "glare." The source of the ink is from the opposite page above the word "evidence" and was likely caused by the tittle of the letter "i."

20. Charles originally hyphenated the word "dis-cerned."

21. Charles may not have said the words "Give me not a little of this" in his sermon but instead intended this line to be a prayer between himself and God, as was likely the case for his concluding prayer below.

22. The capital letter "G" appears beneath the letter "z" in the word "zeal." Charles likely had the word "God" or "Godliness" in mind.

182.   Heb XII. 15,16,17. Profane Esau.

In all times there have been immense temptations to apostacy.   In Paul's days fiery troubles, later the splendours of Rome, again the persecutions of men, & now the pleasures, sins, & jeers of the world. That any persevere is owing wholly to the almighty power of divine grace & that not one true believer has ever apostatized, is an amazing proof of God's fidelity & omnipotence.

We have need of every promise, threat, or caution so that we may be prevented from going back.

This text may be styled. Paul's three warnings. Three danger signals. —

I. "Looking diligently, lest any man fail of the grace of God." —   This is a warning more especially, against secret apostacy. —

' To fail of the grace of God. means.

1. To be found at last unconverted, not to have the root of the matter, not to gain saving grace.   To miss of grace & so of glory.

2. Having professed to have grace, they were not to belie their profession by openly going back when tried. This many mere professors did & in so doing may be said to fail of grace.

3. But the words may mean "fall from the grace of God" — & as such must be addressed to real Christians, warning them not to

182

PROFANE ESAU
Hebrews 12:15–17[1]

"Looking diligently lest any man fail of the grace of God; lest any root of bitterness springing up trouble you, and thereby many be defiled; lest there be any fornicator, or profane person, as Esau, who for one morsel of meat sold his birthright. For ye know how that afterward, when he would have inherited the blessing, he was rejected; for he found no place of repentance, though he sought it carefully with tears."

In all times, there have been immense temptations to apostacy. In Paul's days, fiery troubles.[2] Later the splendours of Rome.[3] Again the persecution of the men. And now, the pleasures, sins, and jeers of the world.[4]

That any persevere is owing wholly to the almighty power of divine grace; and that not one true believer has ever apostatized[5] is an amazing proof of God's fidelity and omnipotence.

We have need of every promise, threat, or caution so that we may be prevented from going back.[6]

This text may be styled Paul's three warnings. Three danger signals.

I. "LOOKING DILIGENTLY LEST ANY MAN FAIL OF THE GRACE OF GOD."

This is a warning more especially against secret apostacy.[7]

To fail of the grace of God means:

1. To be found at the last unconverted. Not to have the root of the matter.[8] Not to gain saving grace. To miss of grace, and so, of glory.

2. Having professed to have grace, they were not to belie their profession by openly going back when tried. This many mere professors did and, in so doing, may be said to fail of grace.[9]

3. But the words[10] may mean "fall from the grace of God,"[11] and as such must be addressed to real Christians, warning them not to

turn back. Not that he imagined that true ones would, but even they must be warned against it. We tell Christians not to apostatize in order that our caution may be the means of fulfilling the promise that they shall not. We should walk even more circumspectly than if we could fall finally — How useful this warning was may be gathered from the deaths of the many martyrs who overcame the most dreadful trials.

— We must "look" if we would not apostatize — & not be asleep, the watchful sentinel is safe.

— We must "look diligently" not a wink of the eye or a random glance, but a diligent watch

— All must watch; "lest any man", says Paul for all are in danger & only looking saves.

True Christians shall not fail in grace for this bankruptcy is either the effect—

Of a small stock in trade a bad beginning	But true Christians begin aright, with faith, repentance & regeneration.
Or unforseen disaster not to be avoided	This never happens to a Xn for all things work together for his good.
Or want of skill & wisdom	Now God giveth us this & manages for us.
Or extravagant waste. Sin or dishonesty	Now some do this, but not the heirs of heaven, for they are kept by the power of God through faith unto salvation

turn back. Not that he imagined that true ones would, but even they must be warned against it. We tell Christians not to apostatize in order that our caution may be the means of fulfilling the promise that they shall not.[12] We should walk even more circumspectly[13] than if we could fall finally.

How useful this warning was may be gathered from the deaths of the many martyrs who overcame the most dreadful trials.

— We must "<u>look</u>" if we would not apostatize and not be asleep.[14] The watchful sentinel is safe.

— We must "<u>look diligently.</u>" Not a wink of the eye or a random glance, but a diligent watch.

— All must watch; "<u>lest any man</u>," says Paul. For all are in danger and only looking[15] saves.

True Christians shall not fail in grace, for this bankruptcy is either the effect:

Of a small stock in trade a bad beginning	But true Christians begin aright, with faith, repentance, and regeneration.
Or unforeseen disaster not to be avoided	This never happens to a Xn,[16] for all things work together for his good.[17]
Or want of skills and wisdom	Now God giveth us this and manages for us.
Or extravagant waste, sin, or dishonesty	Now some do this, but not the heirs of heaven, for they are kept by the power

of God through faith unto salvation.

II. The second signal which in these times of fog we need — is —

"Lest any root of bitterness springing up trouble you, & thereby many be defiled"

This caution relates more to apostacy in the Church, from love, Sins against the Church. Secret apostacy grows to this, nor tarries here but often becomes open & awful crime.

There are roots of bitterness in all our hearts & in every Church, & if we cannot eradicate them yet we must nip their tops & cut off their shoots. What roots of bitterness do we know of.

1. Our evil tempers & passions are.
2. Our differences of opinion sometimes are.
3. All hypocrites, formalists, & backsliders.
4. Evil doctrines & practises — allowance in any known error. ——— ———

These roots of bitterness have 2 bad effects.

1. They are a great trouble to the Church.
2. They are a defilement — to our religion
                              to the brethren —
                              to inquirers & hearers.

we are to look diligently after these roots of bitterness. Let us give them to the devil's swine but let us have nothing to do with them. You must look closely for mischief has small roots, though large shoots.

II. THE SECOND SIGNAL, WHICH IN THESE TIMES OF FOG WE NEED,[18] IS *"Lest any root of bitterness springing up trouble you, and thereby many be defiled."*

This caution relates more to apostacy in the Church from love, Sins against the Church. Secret apostacy grows to this, nor tarries here, but often becomes open and awful crime.

There are roots of bitterness in all our hearts and in every Church. And if we cannot eradicate them, yet we must nip their tops and cut off their shoots.[19]

What roots of bitterness do we know of:

1. Our evil tempers and passions are.
2. Our differences of opinion sometimes are.
3. All hypocrites, formalist, and backsliders[20] are.
4. Evil doctrines and practises, allowance in any known error.

These roots of bitterness have 2 bad effects:

1. They are a great trouble to the Church.
2. They are a defilement: to our religion
                            to the brethren
                            to inquirers and hearers

We are to look diligently after these roots of bitterness. Let us give them to the devil's swine, but let us have nothing to do with them. You must look closely, for mischief has small roots, though large shoots.

III. Signal the third – the loudest report of all
2. Charges of powder. The danger is immense.

This last has more reference to open apostacy,
into gross sin with the vile ones of the world.

Let professors take heed of two dangers.

1. Fornication – love of women, lasciviousness, an
evil to which alas we are prone, & by which many
of the mighty have fallen. To those of us who
are young it is as the Siren's rock. the abhorred
of the Lord shall be dashed thereon. but may
God save me & you from its horrors.

2. Worldliness – here called profanity – the
despising of religion – giving up the joys of
God's children & eternal inheritances for a few
hours of sin, a bauble, a mess of pottage, a
mere nothing. Alas how many who appeared
true have turned aside for drunkenness,
dishonesty, business, wealth. – these are profane.

Esau is here introduced as a solemn
warning – he believed not in the value of the
birthright, he sneered at the covenant blessings,
he sold it for one meal. God sealed the
bargain & when in after ages he sought of
his father the blessing, he could not obtain it
for he sold it – & tears could not blot out the
bargain made with his brother Jacob.

His case is similar to those who like him
enjoy the ordinances, have some chance of heaven,

III. SIGNAL THE THIRD, THE LOUDEST REPORT[21] OF ALL. 2 CHARGES OF POWDER. THE DANGER IS IMMENSE.

This[22] last has more reference to open apostacy into gross sin with the vile ones of the world.

Let professors take heed of[23] two dangers:

1. Fornication, love of women, lasciviousness, an evil to which alas we are prone and by which many of the mighty have fallen.[24] To those of us who are young, it is as the Siren's rock,[25] the abhorred of the Lord shall be dashed thereon. But may God save me and you from its horrors.

2. Worldliness, here called profanity, the despising of religion, giving up the joys of God's children and eternal inheritances for a few hours of sin, a bauble, a mess of pottage,[26] a mere nothing. Alas, how many who appeared true have turned aside for drunkenness, dishonesty, business, wealth. These are profane.

Esau is here introduced as a solemn warning. He believed not in the value of the birthright. He sneered at the covenant blessings. He sold it for one meal.[27]

God sealed the bargain, and when in after ages[28] he sought of his father the blessing, he could not obtain it for he sold it. And tears could not blot out the bargain made with his brother, Jacob.[29]

His case is similar to those who, like him, enjoy the ordinances, have some chance of heaven,

seem to come near its gates, yet after a time
prefer the sins & pleasures of the world & turn back.
these will one day desire the now-despised
grace but if their day of probation be past
there remains no place of repentance.
Not tears, nor groans, can win the lost
inheritance —   Yet, oh poor saint, or
poor sinner say not this is thy case..for
1. Every penitent has room for repentance
in the promise. now Esau had none.
2. He wanted his father to repent, but
God is moved on earth, more easily than man.
3. You never had a birthright to sell
& if Satan bought it the bargain is not
legal, if thou believest, for then thou
wilt die & be a new man.—
    Yet oh backslider, yea oh thou my soul
beware lest holding the world thou
shouldest lost Christ & thy hour of grace
pass away unimproved.
        Great God, for Jesus sake, keep me
            & all thy saints in thy hand.
291.

seem to come near its gates, yet after a time prefer[30] the sins and pleasures of the world and turn back. These will one day desire the now-despised grace. But if their[31] day of probation[32] be past, there remains no place of repentance. Not tears, nor groans, can win the lost inheritance.

Yet, Oh poor saint, or poor sinner, say not this is thy case, for:

1. Every penitent has room for repentance in the promise. Now Esau had none.

2. He wanted his father to repent, but God is moved on earth more easily than man.

3. You never had a birthright to sell. And if Satan bought it, the bargain is not legal. If thou believest, for then thou[33] wilt die and be a new man.

Yet, Oh backslider,[34] yea, oh thou my soul beware, lest holding the world thou shouldest lose Christ and thy hour of grace pass away unimproved.

Great God, for Jesus['s] sake, keep me

and all thy saints in thy hand.[35]

291.

1. On June 10, 1870, Charles preached an additional sermon on Heb 12:14–15 entitled "The Winnowing Fan" (*MTP* 16, Sermon 940). There is enough overlapping content and structural similarity to suggest Charles had his early sermon in mind when writing his later one.

2. Charles likely had in mind the persecution that occurred under Emperor Nero. Charles's copy of John Foxe's *Book of Martyrs* reads, "This monarch reigned for the space of five years with tolerable credit to himself; but then gave way to the greatest extravagance of temper, and to the most atrocious barbarities. Among other diabolical outrages, he ordered that the city of Rome should be set on fire, which was done by his officers, guards, and servants. While the city was in flames, he went up to the tower of Maecenas, played upon his harp, sung the song of the burning of Troy, and declared, 'That he wished the ruin of all things before his death.' . . . Nero, finding that his conduct was greatly blamed, and a severe odium cast upon him, determined to charge the whole upon the Christians, at once to excuse himself, and have an opportunity of fresh persecutions. The barbarities inflicted upon the Christians, during the first persecution, were such as excited the sympathy of even the Romans themselves. Nero nicely refined upon cruelty, and contrived all manner of punishments for his victims. He had some sewed up in the skins of wild beasts, and then worried by dogs till they expired; and others dressed in shirts made stiff with wax, fixed to axletrees, and set on fire in his garden" (John Foxe, *An Universal History of Christian Martyrdom, Being a Complete and Authentic Account of the Lives, Sufferings, and Triumphant Deaths of the Primitive as Well as Protestant Martyrs, in All Parts of the World, from the Birth of the Blessed Saviour to the Latest Periods of Pagan and Catholic Persecution: Together with a Summary of the Doctrines, Prejudices, Blasphemies, and Superstitions of the Modern Church of Rome. Originally Composed by John Fox, M.A. With Notes, Commentaries, and Illustrations by the Rev. J. Milner, M.A. Assisted by the Communications of Several Learned and Eminent Ministers of the Gospel, Which Have Never Before Been Published. A New Edition Greatly Improved and Corrected* [London: George Routledge, 1845, The Spurgeon Library], 25–26). Cf. 1 Pet 4:12.

3. "Further down in history there came the time of the Church's most awful dearth. She had sinned. Led by the princely hand of Constantine to the altar of infamous adultery, she prostituted herself to a connexion with the State, and committed fornication with the kings of the earth. From that day forth the Spirit of God forsook her, and in the brightness of his splendour he shone not upon her. Her

vigour died when the imperial hand was laid upon her. Whatever a royal hand may do to diseased men, it always brings the king's evil upon the Church. No ills of poverty or persecution can equal the injurious effects of State alliance upon the Church of God. Her freedom is evaporated, her discipline becomes a pretence, her faults cannot be remedied, her progress in reformation is prohibited, her glory is departed. The Christian Church, when linked with the Roman power, soon declined, till the truth became dim and holiness was stained" (*MTP* 7:612).

4. See "The Little Fire and Great Combustion" (Notebook 1, Sermon 54).

5. Cf. 1 John 2:19.

6. "Well did the apostle declare that the righteous scarcely are saved. It is no child's-play to be a Christian. The Christian life is beyond the poet's meaning, real and earnest. The hills of difficulty which lie before us are no molehills, and the giants and dragons with which we must contend are no phantoms of a disordered brain. When we reach heaven, what monuments of grace we shall be, and how shall we throughout eternity emulate one another's praises, each one feeling himself to be the deepest debtor to sovereign grace!" (*MTP* 16:385).

7. "Perhaps a more dangerous way of failing of the grace of God may be this. Some have maintained an admirable character to all appearance all their lives, and yet have failed of the grace of God because of some secret sin. They persuaded even themselves that they were believers, and yet they were not truly so; they had no inward holiness, they allowed one sin to get the mastery, they indulged in an unsanctified passion, and so though they were laid in the grave like sheep, they died with a false hope, and missed eternal life. This is a most dreadful state to be in, and perhaps some of us are in it" (*MTP* 16:393).

8. Cf. Matt 13:1–23; Mark 4:1–20; Luke 8:1–15.

9. Cf. 2 Tim 4:9–10.

10. The word "words" was smeared before the ink could dry.

11. Charles's reference to the phrase "fall from the grace of God" may have been inspired by the marginalia of Heb 12:15 in his Bible (see *The Holy Bible, According to the Authorized Version; with Notes, Explanatory and Practical; Taken Principally from the*

Most Eminent Writers of the United Church of England and Ireland: Together with Appropriate Introductions, Tables, Indexes, Maps, and Plans: Prepared and Arranged by the Rev. George D'Oyly, B.D. and the Rev. Richard Mant, D.D. Domestick Chaplains to His Grace the Lord Archbishop of Canterbury. Under the Direction of the Society for Promoting Christian Knowledge. For the Use of Families. Vol. II [Oxford: printed for the Society at the Clarendon Press by Bensley, Cooke, and Collingwood, Printers to the University, sold by F. C. and J. Rivington, Booksellers to the Society, 1817, The Spurgeon Library], Heb 12:15). He may have also seen this phrasing of Heb 12:15 in Charles John Ellicott, ed., *A Biblical Commentary for English Readers, by Various Writers. Vol. VIII. Ephesians to Revelation* (London, Paris, New York, and Melbourne: Cassell and Company, n.d.), 340, which reads, "*[W]hether any one by falling back from the grace of God*" (italics in the original).

12. "Those who reject the doctrine frequently tell us that there are many cautions in the word of God against apostatizing, and that those cautions can have no meaning if it be true that the righteous shall hold on his way. But what if those cautions are the means in the hand of God of keeping his people from wandering? What if they are used to excite a holy fear in the minds of his children, and so become the means of preventing the evil which they denounce[?] I would also remind you that in the Epistle to the Hebrews, which contains the most solemn warnings against apostasy, the apostle always takes care to add words which show that he did not believe that those whom he warned would actually apostatize" (*MTP* 23:363).

13. "Nobody ever grew holy without consenting, desiring, and agonising to be holy. Sin will grow without sowing, but holiness needs cultivation" (*MTP* 16:390).

14. Cf. Matt 25:1–13.

15. Charles may have had his own conversion experience in mind in the Primitive Methodist Chapel on Artillery Street in Colchester when a layman preached a sermon on Isa 45:22, "Look unto me, and be ye saved, all the ends of the earth: for I am God, and there is none else." Charles reflected, "Then he looked at me under the gallery, and I daresay, with so few present, he knew me to be a stranger. Just fixing his eyes on me, as if he knew all my heart, he said, 'Young man, you look very miserable . . . and you always will be miserable—miserable in life, and miserable in death,— if you don't obey my text; but if you obey now, this

moment, you will be saved. . . . Young man, look to Jesus Christ. Look! Look! Look! You have nothin' to do but to look and live" (*Autobiography* 1:106). Charles said, "I had been waiting to do fifty things, but when I heard that word, 'Look!' what a charming word it seemed to me! Oh! I looked until I could almost have looked my eyes away" (ibid.).

16. Abbr., "Christian."   17.   Cf. Rom 8:28–29.

18. Charles inserted a colon after the word "need." Afterward, he included the verb "is" with two dashes.

19. Cf. Song 2:15.

20. "If laziness is detestable to good men, much more must it be to God" (*MTP* 16:391).

21. "Sound; loud noise; repercussion" (Johnson's *Dictionary*, s.v. "report").

22. Charles originally wrote the word "These" before striking through the final "e" and changing the letter "e" in the middle of the word to "i."

23. A pencil mark was written above the word "of" and also above the word "dangers" in the line below. These marks likely evidence Charles's attempt to edit the manuscript for publication in 1857.

24. Cf. 2 Samuel 11.

25. The Sirens refer to those in book 12 of Homer's *Odyssey*, a work Charles personally owned. The *Odyssey* reads, "O friends, oh ever partners of my woes, / Attend while I what Heaven foredooms disclose. / Hear all! Fate hangs o'er all; on you it lies / To live or perish! to be safe, be wise! / In flowery meads the sportive Sirens play, / Touch the soft lyre, and tune the vocal lay; / Me, me alone, with fetters firmly bound, / The gods allow to hear the dangerous sound. / Hear and obey; if freedom I demand, / Be every fetter strain'd, be added band to band. / While yet I speak the winged galley flies, / And lo! the Siren shores like mists arise. / Sunk were at once the winds; the air above, / And waves below, at once forgot to move: / Some demon calm'd the air and smooth'd the deep, / Hush'd the loud winds, and charm'd the waves to sleep. / Now every sail we furl, each oar we ply: / Lash'd by

the stroke, the frothy waters fly. / The ductile wax with busy hands I mould, / And cleft in fragments, and the fragments roll'd: / The aëriel region now grew warm with day, / The wax dissolved beneath the burning ray; / Then every ear I barr'd against the strain, / And from access of frenzy lock'd the brain, / Now round the masts my mates the fetters roll'd, / And bound me limb by limb with fold on fold. / Then bending to the stroke, the active train / Plunge all at once their oars, and cleave the main, / While to the shore the rapid vessel flies, / Our swift approach the Siren choir decries; / Celestial music warbles from their tongue, / And thus the sweet deluders tune the song. . . . Thus the sweet charmers warbled o'er the main; / My soul takes wing to meet the heavenly strain; / I give the sign, and struggle to be free: / Swift row my mates, and shoot along the sea; / New chains they add, and rapid urge the way, / Till, dying off, the distant sounds decay: / Then scudding swiftly from the dangerous ground, / The deafen'd ear unlock'd, the chains unbound" (Alexander Pope, trans., *The Odyssey of Homer. With Notes by the Rev. Theodore Alois Buckley, M.A., F.S.A. and Flaxman's Designs* in the Chandos Classics [London: Frederick Warne and Co., n.d., The Spurgeon Library], 170–72). Around the time he preached this sermon, Charles also owned a copy of *The Iliad of Homer* and inscribed on the inside front cover, "Charles Spurgeon. July. 1852" (Alexander Pope, trans., *The Iliad of Homer* [Edinburgh: printed by and for James Hunter, 1796, The Spurgeon Library]).

26. "Any thing boiled or decocted for food" (Johnson's *Dictionary*, s.v. "pottage").

27. Cf. Gen 25:29–34.

28. A smear, likely accidental, covers the letter "s" in the word "ages."

29. Cf. Heb 12:17.

30. Charles originally wrote the word "the" before changing it to the word "prefer."

31. An illegible letter appears beneath the letter "t" in the word "their."

32. By writing "But if their day of probation be past," Charles was referring to the earthly life of the ungodly prior to the Day of Judgment. On March 4, 1855, he wrote, "There be many who are sleeping the sluggard's sleep, who are resting upon the bed of sloth; but an awful waking shall it be to them, when they shall find that the time of their probation has been wasted; that the golden sands of their life

have dropped unheeded from the hour-glass; and that they have come into that world where there are no acts of pardon passed, no hope, no refuge, no salvation" (*NPSP* 1:86). The word "probation" was similarly used by Charles's contemporary Elisha Bates (1781–1861), who wrote, "On the manner in which we pass the time of our probation here, our final happiness or misery depends" (Elisha Bates, *The Doctrines of Friends; or, the Principles of the Christian Religion, as Held by the Society of Friends* [orig. published: Mount Pleasant, OH; reprinted Leeds, 1829], 32).

33. Charles struck through the final arm of the letter "w" in the word "thow" to form the letter "u," thereby constructing the correct spelling of the word "thou."

34. "If there be in this house to-day any who have backslidden, I beg them to mourn indeed, and put their trust in Jesus, and begin" (*MTP* 16:396).

35. See "Final Perseverance Certain" (Notebook 2, Sermon 82).

John. XIII. 23. Leaning on Jesus bosom. 183.

This text is another of the 4 given by the aged sister mentioned before. she declared that this was the position she ever occupied & that Jesus was her pillow. I will by the Holy Spirit's aid make some remarks.

I. On Jesus special love to John.

II. On the position John occupied.

III. I would endeavour to apply the subject

I. Jesus special love to John. "That disciple whom Jesus loved" this was John, too modest to put his name. see John C. 21. V 20.24. Jesus loved all the disciples but John more especially.

Some men deny that God has any favourites or loves one part of mankind better than another they speak of Universal benevolence, which is right enough, but beyond this there is special love, displaying itself in the Election, redemption, calling, sanctification, & salvation of a chosen race.

Among these Chosen, elect ones there is yet still a diversity of degrees of love. Elect out of the elect stand the twelve apostles to whom especial commissions, authority, grace & blessings were given. Out of these twelve there was a chosen trio. Peter, James & John who enjoyed especial favours. These saw the damsel raised Mark. V. 37. These witnessed the transfiguration. Mark. IX. 2. These went to Gethsemane & saw his agony, bloody sweat, & intercession. Mark. XIV. 33.

183

LEANING *on* JESUS['S] BOSOM

John 13:23[1]

"Now there was leaning on Jesus' bosom one of his disciples, whom Jesus loved."

This text is another of the 4 given by the aged sister mentioned before.[2] She declared that this was the position she ever occupied and that Jesus was her pillow. I will, by the Holy Spirit's aid, make some remarks:

I. ON JESUS['S] SPECIAL LOVE TO JOHN.

II. ON THE POSITION JOHN OCCUPIED.

III. I WOULD ENDEAVOUR TO APPLY THE SUBJECT.

I. JESUS['S] SPECIAL LOVE TO JOHN. *"That disciple whom Jesus loved."*

This was John, too modest to put his name.[3] See John 21.V[4] 20.24.[5] Jesus loved all the disciples, but John more especially.

Some men deny that God has any favourites or loves one part of mankind better than another. They speak of Universal benevolence,[6] which is right enough. But beyond this, there is special love, displaying itself in the Election, redemption, calling, sanctification, and salvation of a chosen race.

Among these Chosen, elect ones there is yet still a diversity of degrees of love. Elect out of the elect[7] stand the twelve apostles to whom especial commissions, authority, grace, and blessings were given.

Out of these twelve there was a chosen trio, Peter, James, and John, who enjoyed especial favours.

These saw the damsel raised.	Mark. V. 37.[8]
These witnessed the transfiguration.	Mark. IX. 2.[9]
These went to Gethsemane and saw his agony, bloody sweat, and intercession.	Mark. XIV. 33.[10]

Probably Jesus had no more to witness these since he was not anxious for great publicity; & this number 3 that from their testimony the facts might be well established. These three were the three first mighties of the Son of David. Doubtless they were all eminent as preachers. Peter for boldness & zeal & the other two were named sons of thunder. Perhaps too, our Lord gave Peter these special favours, not only because he loved his honest though hasty zeal, but also because he foresaw the fall he would have & the need then of much comfort & help.

James, was the first among the apostles who gained the martyr's fiery crown, dieing by Herod's sword. Perhaps his noble preaching marked him as the first victim. Our Lord gave him much, because a trial unto death was at hand.

But John was "that disciple whom Jesus loved", he, the man best beloved, the chief among the three mighties. He is stiled so many times in this book. He alone leaned on Jesus bosom, he ~~entered~~ stood & the foot of the cross, he entertained Mary, the mother of Jesus. Saw the blood & water flow from the side. He alone according to history, out of the twelve, died a natural death. He lived to be 100 years old. He had the visions of the apocalypse made to him in Patmos. & was a man greatly beloved.

Probably Jesus had no more to witness these since he was not anxious for great publicity. And this number 3, that from their testimony, the facts might be well established.[11]

These three were the three first mighties of the Son of David.[12] Doubtless, they were all eminent as preachers. Peter for boldness and zeal, and the other two were named sons of thunder.

Perhaps too, our Lord gave Peter these special favours, not only because he loved his honest-though-hasty[13] zeal, but also because he foresaw the fall he would have and the need then of much comfort and help.

James was the first among the apostles who gained the martyr's fiery crown, dieing by Herod's sword.[14] Perhaps his noble preaching marked him as the first victim. Our Lord gave him much because a trial unto death was at hand.

But John was "that[15] disciple whom Jesus loved."[16] He, the man best beloved, the chief among the three mighties.[17] He is stiled[18] so many times in this book. He alone leaned on Jesus['s] bosom.[19] He ~~entered~~[20] stood a[t][21] the foot of the cross. He entertained Mary,[22] the mother of Jesus. Saw the blood and water flow from the side.[23] He alone, according to history, out of the twelve, died a natural death. He lived to be 100 years[24] old. He had the visions of the apocalypse made to him in Patmos[25] and was a man greatly beloved.[26]

Now why did Jesus single out John to be the one he favoured most & loved best.

1. Perhaps there was not one other person who could have born it. Peter would have been haughty perhaps. but his loving temper made him behave so that none could wish to dislodge him.

2. Perhaps our Lord foreseeing that the Catholics would make Peter their head — made John even greater than he, to shut up their foolish mouth.

3. John was young & Jesus carries such in his bosom, young persons if converted often have a greater portion of grace than those saved at later periods of life. Christ hereby defeats the notion that age of body is age of soul and shews that striplings can outstrip the Fathers.

4. But, above all, John had a meek, loving gentle nature, akin to that of his Master. Kindred souls soon join in union. Jesus could not hold such communion with bold Peter, or unbelieving Thomas, as he could with John. In proportion as we are like-minded we shall receive like love. Jesus first gives us graces & then rewards us for them.

II. Let us notice John's position.

"Leaning on Jesus bosom."

He sat next his Lord, spoke to him, & leaned on him, John was the bosom friend of Jesus. John wished to catch every word his Master dropped

Now, why did Jesus single out John to be the one he favoured most and loved best?

1. Perhaps there was not one other person who could have born it. Peter would have been haughty perhaps, but his loving temper made[27] him behave so that none could wish to dislodge him.[28]

2. Perhaps our Lord, foreseeing that the Catholics would make Peter their head, made John even greater than he to shut up their foolish mouth.[29]

3. John was young, and Jesus carries such in his bosom. Young persons, if converted, often have a greater portion of grace than those saved at later[30] periods of life.[31] Christ hereby defeats the notion that age of body is age of soul and shews that striplings[32] can outstrip[33] the Fathers.

4. But above all, John had a meek, loving, gentle nature akin to that of his Master. Kindred souls soon join in union. Jesus could not hold such communion with bold Peter or unbelieving Thomas as he could with John. In proportion as we are like-minded, we shall receive like love.[34] Jesus first gives us graces and then rewards us for them.

II. LET US NOTICE JOHN'S POSITION. *"Leaning on Jesus['s] bosom."*

He sat next [to] his Lord, spoke[35] to him, and leaned on him. John was the bosom friend of Jesus.[36] John wished to catch every word his Master dropped.

What an honour? The greatest surely of all.
  But such an honour as all, who are true
disciples, in some measure enjoy. ——
  To lean on Jesus bosom implies
1. That we are at peace, are friends, are brethren
2. That there is much mutual love.
3. That we rely implicitly on him, & trust all in
   his hands with cheerful confidence.
4. That our cares are all dismissed,
5. That we enjoy communion with him.
  Sweet to lean here in trial, in death
in all times & every varied season. ✤
  III. Now. Oh. My Father Apply it –
To 1. In whose bosom do you lean in trouble.
Sinners 2. Do you rest content without Jesus love?
  3. On whom will you lean at last.

To 1. Cultivate a loving spirit.
Saints 2. Cultivate a leaning spirit.
  3. Eat the Lord's supper with your head
   where John's was, at least your heart
   there.
    Great God. I entreat thee bless – for the sake
        of him on whom we lean

292.296.

What an honour? The greatest surely of all.

But such an honour as all who are true disciples in some measure enjoy.

To lean on Jesus['s] bosom implies:

1. That we are at peace, are friends, are brethren.

2. That there is much mutual love.

3. That we rely implicitly on him and trust all in his hands with cheerful confidence.[37]

4. That our cares are all dismissed.

5. That we enjoy communion with him.

Sweet to lean here in trial, in death, in all times and every varied season.[38]

III. NOW. OH MY FATHER, APPLY IT.

To Sinners

1. In whose bosom do you lean in trouble?

2. Do you rest content without Jesus'[s] love?

3. On whom will you lean at last?

To Saints

1. Cultivate a loving spirit.

2. Cultivate a leaning spirit.

3. Eat the Lord's Supper with your head where John's was, at least your heart there.

> Great God, I entreat thee bless. For the sake
>
> of him on whom we lean.

292. 296.

1. In 1888 Charles preached an additional sermon on John 13:23–26 entitled "On His Breast" (*MTP* 34, Sermon 2052). There is enough overlapping content and structural similarity to suggest Charles had in mind his early sermon when writing his 1888 sermon.

2. On the last page of this notebook, Charles recorded, "The 4 texts given me by an aged Sister are: John XX. 16. No. 175. Zech XIV. 6.7. No. 176. John XIII. 23. No. 183. Isa. XLI. 10. The 14th is similar. No. 170." In other words, the four texts given by the "aged Sister" to Charles to preach are (in numerical order): "Fear Not, Thou Worm Jacob" (Sermon 170), "Mary with Jesus in the Garden" (Sermon 175), "Light at Eventide" (Sermon 176), and "Leaning on Jesus['s] Bosom" (Sermon 183). Charles preached from all these texts at her request with the exception of Sermon 170. Instead of preaching on verse 10 as she requested, Charles preached on Isa 41:14, which he deemed was "similar." Who was the "aged Sister?" Unfortunately, there is no record of her in Charles's autobiography, his letters to his family members during this season of his ministry, or in his biographies. Nor is there recorded in this notebook the reason she requested these four texts to be preached by Charles other than what is found in this sermon, that "Jesus was her pillow."

3. "So John drops his own birth-given name, as it were, and takes this title instead of it—'that disciple whom Jesus loves.' He wears it as a Knight of the Garter, or of the Golden Fleece, wears the mark of his sovereign's esteem. He took it for his honour; and yet, beloved, there was not a grain of boasting in it, nor even an approach to glorifying in the flesh. A sense of love makes us happy, but not haughty. . . . So precious has its nearness to Jesus made it, that perhaps next to the name of Jesus no name is sweeter than that of John. As Ivan, or Evan, it has a most evangelical, gospel sound. It is common in many forms throughout Christendom, and many of the noblest disciples have worn it, from John Chrysostom to John Calvin, and from John Bunyan to John Welsey, and John Newton. In any case the honour of being loved by Jesus is greater than the name John; and happy are they who can claim it!" (*MTP* 34:617, 618).

4. It is unclear why Charles wrote Roman numeral V between the numbers 21 and 20.

5. John 21:20–24, "Then Peter, turning about, seeth the disciple whom Jesus loved following; which also leaned on his breast at supper, and said, Lord, which

is he that betrayeth thee? Peter seeing him saith to Jesus, Lord, and what shall this man do? Jesus saith unto him, If I will that he tarry till I come, what is that to thee? follow thou me. Then went this saying abroad among the brethren, that that disciple should not die: yet Jesus said not unto him, He shall not die; but, If I will that he tarry till I come, what is that to thee? This is the disciple which testifieth of these things, and wrote these things: and we know that his testimony is true." Before the number 21, Charles inserted what appears to be the capital letter "C." More likely, he intended this stroke to be an open parenthesis, which he did not close after the number 24.

6. "Never let us doubt the universal benevolence of God. Let us hold it as a fundamental doctrine that 'the Lord is good to all; and his tender mercies are over all his works;' and let us firmly believe that, if any man shall be consigned to eternal misery, it will be because it is just that he should so suffer, and he has brought his terrible doom upon his own head; for as the apostle Peter tells us, God is 'not willing that any should perish, but that all should come to repentance.' Yet we must never forget that, inside this universal love, there is a private, secret, distinguishing, discriminating love, which is set upon those whom God chose, before the foundation of the world, to be his own peculiar people" (*MTP* 52:530).

7. "We believe in the doctrine of election, but the principle of election goes to be carried farther than some suppose. There is an election in the midst of the election, and another within that. The wider circle contains the inner, and a still more select circlet forms the innermost ring of all. The Lord had a people around him who were his disciples. Within them he had the twelve. Within the twelve he had three. Within the three he had one disciple whom he loved" (*MTP* 34:614).

8. Mark 5:37, "And he suffered no man to follow him, save Peter, and James, and John the brother of James."

9. Mark 9:2, "And after six days Jesus taketh with him Peter, and James, and John, and leadeth them up into an high mountain apart by themselves: and he was transfigured before them."

10. Mark 14:33, "And he taketh with him Peter and James and John, and began to be sore amazed, and to be very heavy."

11.   Cf. Deut 17:6; 19:15; Matt 18:16; 2 Cor 13:1; 1 John 5:7.

12.   Cf. 2 Sam 23:8–12.

13.   For clarity, hyphens have been added to the adjectival phrase "honest-though-hasty."

14.   Acts 12:2, "And he killed James the brother of John with the sword."

15.   Charles originally wrote the word "the" before converting it to the word "that."

16.   "Why did our blessed Lord love John better than others? I can only reply that he exercises a sovereignty of choice, and it is not for us to ask the why and wherefore of the movements of the sacred heart. Surely, nothing should be left so free as the love of the Son of God. Let him love whom he wills; he has an unquestionable right to do so" (*MTP* 34:616).

17.   "Jesus still has his Johns, whom he peculiarly loves. He loves Peter and Nicodemus, and Nathanael, and all of them; but still there are some who know his love more than others, live in it more than others, drink into it more than others, reflect it more than others, and become more conformed to it, and saturated with it, and perfumed with it, than others are. There are first as well as last" (*MTP* 34:615).

18.   The word "stiled" is the antiquated form of the word "styled," which Samuel Johnson defined as "manner of writing with regard to language" and "manner of speaking appropriate to particular characters" (Johnson's *Dictionary*, s.v. "style").

19.   "If you are living far away in the cold regions of broken fellowship, then I am sure you have but very little conscious enjoyment of the love of Jesus Christ your Lord. The dearest must be the nearest" (*MTP* 34:619).

20.   Before striking through the word "entered," Charles may have had in mind John's visit to the empty tomb in John 20:8: "Then went in also that other disciple, which came first to the sepulchre, and he saw and believed."

21.   Charles originally wrote an ampersand. However, the context suggests he intended to write the word "at."

22. John 19:25–27, "Now there stood by the cross of Jesus his mother, and his mother's sister, Mary the wife of Cleophas, and Mary Magdalene. When Jesus therefore saw his mother, and the disciple standing by, whom he loved, he saith unto his mother, Woman, behold thy son! Then saith he to the disciple, Behold thy mother! And from that hour that disciple took her unto his own home."

23. John 19:34, "But one of the soldiers with a spear pierced his side, and forthwith came there out blood and water." See also "Jesus'[s] Dead Body Whilst on the Cross" (Notebook 2, Sermon 107).

24. Charles may have gleaned this information from John Foxe, who wrote that John "was the only apostle who escaped a violent death, and lived the longest of any, he being nearly 100 years of age at the time of his death" (John Foxe, *An Universal History of Christian Martyrdom*, 25). The letter "y" in the word "years" was smudged, likely by accident.

25. Revelation 1:9, "I John, who also am your brother, and companion in tribulation, and in the kingdom and patience of Jesus Christ, was in the isle that is called Patmos, for the word of God, and for the testimony of Jesus Christ."

26. "Our blessed Lord did not love John because of any excess of talent; for albeit that John's Apocalypse and his Gospel are, in some respects, the highest parts of revealed Scripture, being both the simplest and the most mysterious portions of Holy Writ; yet we should not say that John betrayed evidence of so great a mind in itself, naturally, or by education, as Paul had. He had as much talent as his Lord gave him, but there was nothing about him so special that he should for that cause have been loved; and to dismiss the thought with a word, Jesus never loves men on account of talent, and we should be unwise if we ourselves did so" (*MTP* 34:615).

27. Pencil marks appear above the words "made" and "been" in the line above. These lines may be evidence that Charles edited these sermons for publication in 1857.

28. "John, like his Lord, had much love. He may have lacked some qualities in which Peter, and James, and others excelled, but he towered above them all in love. He was full of tenderness, and therefore his Master at once selected him to be his choicest companion and his dearest friend" (*MTP* 34:616).

29. See "Salvation in God Only" (Notebook 1, Sermon 24).

30. Charles originally constructed the bowl of the letter "o" beneath the letter "l" in the word "later." He may have intended to write the word "older."

31. "I am afraid our sermons often go over the heads of the younger folk, who, nevertheless, may be as true Christians as the older ones. Blessed is he that can so speak as to be understood of a child! Blessed is that godly woman who in her class so adapts herself to girlish modes of thought that the truth from her heart streams into the children's hearts without let or hindrance. We ought especially to feed the young because this work is so profitable. Do what we may with persons converted late in life, we can never make much of them. We are very glad of them for their own sakes; but at seventy what remains even if they live another ten years? Train up a child, and he may have fifty years of holy service before him. We are glad to welcome those who come into the vineyard at the eleventh hour, but they have hardly taken their pruning-hook and their spade before the sun goes down, and their short day's work is ended. The time spent in training the late convert is greater than the space reserved for his actual service: but you take a child-convert and teach him well, and as early piety often becomes eminent piety, and that eminent piety may have a stretch of years before it in which God may be glorified and others may be blessed, such work is profitable in a high degree. It is also most beneficial work to ourselves. It exercises our humility and helps to keep us lowly and meek. It also trains our patience; let those who doubt this try it; for even young Christians exercise the patience of those who believe in them and are therefore anxious that they should justify their confidence. If you want big-souled, large-hearted men or women, look for them among those who are much engaged among the young, bearing with their follies, and sympathizing with their weaknesses for Jesus' sake" (*MTP* 28:569–70).

32. "A youth; one in the state of adolescence" (Johnson's *Dictionary*, s.v. "stripling").

33. "To outgo; to leave behind in a race" (Johnson's *Dictionary*, s.v. "outstrip").

34. "You know the way, then, to the heart of Christ. Let your own heart be full of love, and you will know his love. He loves you, you know, altogether apart from anything that is in you, of his own rich and sovereign grace; but for the special

manifestation of that love, for your personal enjoyment of it, to fit you for such enjoyment, you must have much love to him. You greatly need, not a great head, but a great heart. You must have, not more knowledge, but more affection; not a higher rank in society, but a higher rank in the power to love Jesus and to love your fellow-men. Less of self, and more of Jesus, and then you shall enjoy more of his love" (*MTP* 34:616).

35. The words "spoke" and "him" in the line below were smeared toward the left side of the page, likely from the same sweeping motion.

36. Cf. John 13:23.

37. "It was a bold thing, surely, for John to lean his head on Christ's bosom. Our Lord did not say, 'Nay, John; nay. I am thy Master, and thy Lord. Dost thou do this to me as if I were thine equal?' No. The meaning of that blessed text, 'Him that cometh to me I will in no wise cast out,' runs in other directions beside that which we generally think of. If you come to Jesus in the most intense manner, he will not repulse you. If your head shall come into his bosom, he will not cast your head out. If you can get your very heart into his heart and come closer to him than even John dared to do—if you carry that coming beyond all previous comings, yet Jesus neither will nor can resent the nearest approaches of any one of his believing people. We lose a great deal of Christ's loving fellowship because we are so formal and distant towards him. We seem to think that he came among men to show them their distance from God, and not to be as a brother to them, to reveal God to them. Jesus seeks to reach our hearts, he stoops to our littleness; let us pluck up courage to draw near to him. . . . Lean on him. Lean on the bosom of the Christ of God, who loveth us, and hath given himself for us. Make a confidant as well as a confidence of your Lord" (*MTP* 34:620).

38. Charles's illustration to the right of the word "season" may be an eagle or fleur-de-lis. This is the first symbol of its kind Charles has recorded thus far in the notebooks.

Isa LIII. 5. By his stripes we are healed. 184

This chapter contains so clear a revelation of the suffering of our Lord, that we seem while reading it, as if we were reading an account of it when past, rather than a prophecy of the future.

I. The disease implied.

1. Brought on by the slow poison of sin.
2. Tainting all our blood & all our members.
3. Descending from Father to Son.
4. Universal among all men.
5. Incurable by nature's arts

II. The Physician.

1. Wise & skilful.
2. Impartial in his visits.
3. Always at home & ready.
4. Gratis — Gratis.

III. The Medicine.

Stripes on his own back. gall for his own lips. We are cured. The Redeemed on high exclaim. As to justification so are all believers. But in sanctification the medecine to counteract the slow poison, is also gradual in it's operation. Nevertheless it is sure & we shall be healed

289. 303.

BY HIS STRIPES WE ARE HEALED

Isaiah 53:5[1]

"But he was wounded for our transgressions, he was bruised for our iniquities: the chastisement of our peace was upon him; and with his stripes we are healed."

This chapter contains so clear[2] a revelation[3] of the sufferings[4] of our Lord[5] that we seem while reading it as if we were reading an account[6] of it when past rather than a prophecy of the future.

I. THE DISEASE IMPLIED.

    1. Brought on by the slow poison of sin.[7]

    2. Tainting all our blood and all our members.[8]

    3. Descending from[9] Father to Son.[10]

    4. Universal among all men.[11]

    5. Incurable by nature's arts.

II. THE PHYSICIAN.

    1. Wise and skilful.[12]

    2. Impartial in his visits.[13]

    3. Always at home and ready.[14]

    4. Gratis. Gratis.[15]

III. THE MEDICINE.

Stripes on his own back.[16] Gall for his own lips.[17] We are cured, the Redeemed on high exclaim.[18] As to justification, so are all believers.

But in sanctification, the medicine to counteract the slow poison is also gradual in its operation.[19]

Nevertheless, it is sure and we shall be healed.[20]

289. 303.

1. Charles preached five additional sermons on Isa 53:5. On October 4, 1868, he preached a sermon entitled "The Universal Remedy" (*MTP* 14, Sermon 834); on September 1, 1872, he preached a sermon entitled "A Simple Remedy" (*MTP* 18, Sermon 1068); on May 28, 1876, he preached a sermon entitled "A Dire Disease Strangely Cured" (*MTP* 50, Sermon 2887); on April 20, 1885, he preached a sermon entitled "Christopathy" (*MTP* 43, Sermon 2499); and on January 1, 1888, he preached a sermon entitled "Number Two-Thousand; or, Healing by the Stripes of Jesus" (*MTP* 33, Sermon 2000). Each of these sermons contains enough overlapping content and structural similarity to suggest Charles had in mind his early sermon when writing these later sermons.

2. Charles bolded the word "clear," likely because he intended to reinforce its spelling. He reinforced the bowl of the letter "e" and also the letters "a" and "r."

3. The letter "a" has been replaced in pencil with the letter "e," just above it, likely by Charles. This may be evidence he edited this sermon in hopes of publishing it in 1857.

4. "Brethren, whenever we come to talk about the passion of our Lord,—and that subject is clearly brought before us here by the two words, 'his stripes,'—our feelings should be deeply solemn, and our attention intensely earnest. Put off thy shoes from thy feet when thou drawest near to this burning bush, for God is in it. . . . You smote him, dear friend, and you wounded him; therefore, do not rest until you can say, 'with his stripes I am healed'" (*MTP* 43:13).

5. "Satan, too, struck at him. I think I see the Arch-fiend ascend from the pit with haste, and, lifting himself upon his dragon wings, come forward to strike the Saviour, daring to inflict upon his soul the accursed temptations of hell. He smote him in the desert, and in the garden, till beneath that smiting great drops of blood crimsoned his face. But this was nothing, compared with the fact that he was smitten of God. Oh, what a word is that! If God were to lay his finger on anyone of us this morning, only his finger, we should be struck with sickness, paralysis, aye, and death. Then think of God smiting! God must smite sin wherever he sees it; it is just that he should do so; it is as much an essential part of God's nature that he should crush sin, as that he should love, for, indeed, it is only love in another form that makes him hate that which is evil. So when he saw our sin laid upon his Son, he smote him with the blows of a cruel One,

till beneath that smiting his Son cried out, 'My God, my God, why hast thou forsaken me'? He was bearing in that moment all the crushing blows of that great sword of vengeance" (*MTP* 18:487).

6. Pencil markings, likely in the hand of Charles, appear at the end of the word "account" and above the word "while" in the line above. These markings suggest Charles likely edited his sermon in preparation for publication.

7. "If we could see sin as it appears to the all-discerning eye of the Eternal, we should be more shocked at the sight of sin than by a vision of hell; for there is in hell something which purity approves, it is the vindication of righteousness, it is justice triumphant; but in sin itself there is abomination, and only abomination; it is something out of joint with the whole system of the universe; it is a miasma dangerous to all spiritual life; a plague, a pest full of dangers to everything that breathes. Sin is a monster, a hideous thing, a thing which God will not look upon, and which pure eyes cannot behold but with the utmost detestation. A flood of tears is the proper medium through which a Christian should look at sin" (*MTP* 14:556).

8. "Sin is abnormal; a sort of cancerous growth, which ought not to be within the soul. Sin is disturbing to manhood: sin unmans a man. Sin is sadly destructive to man; it takes the crown from his head, the light from his mind, and the joy from his heart. We may name many grievous diseases which are the destroyers of our race, but the greatest of these is sin: sin, indeed, is the fatal egg from which all other sicknesses have been hatched" (*MTP* 33:710).

9. The tail of the letter "f" in the word "from" was smeared toward the upper left of the page, likely by accident.

10. The capitalization of the words "Father" and "Son" seem to imply God the Father and Christ the Son. However, the context makes clear Charles did not intend the Trinitarian relationship (see *NPSP* 6:191; *MTP* 16:637; *MTP* 32:541; and *MTP* 54:557) but instead, the transmission of original sin from fathers to sons (see *NPSP* 1:96; *MTP* 14:296; *MTP* 22:545; and *MTP* 38:327). "We are all sinful, sinful through and through, corrupt with evil passions and depraved desires. Our fathers were fallen men, and so are we, and so will our children be" (*MTP* 18:483). Cf. Rom 5:12–14.

11.	"Sin is a contagious disease, which passes from one to another. It is hereditary; it is universal; it is incurable; it is a mortal malady; it is a disease which no human physician can heal. Death, which ends all bodily pain, cannot cure this disease; it displays its utmost power in eternity" (*MTP* 43:18).

12.	"Surgeons usually give us pain while trying to cure us, but here is a Physician who bears the pain himself, and thereby heals us" (*MTP* 43:18).

13.	"Everywhere, at this present hour, we meet with some form or other of sickness; no place, however healthful, is free from cases of disease. As for moral disease, it is all around us, and we are thankful to add that the remedy is everywhere within reach. The Beloved Physician has prepared a healing medicine which can be reached by all classes, which is available in every climate, at every hour, under every circumstance, and effectual in every case wherever it is received" (*MTP* 18:481).

14.	"I do not believe there is anything that can so effectually make the ice within us melt, and so speedily thaw the great glaciers of our inner nature, as the love of Jesus Christ" (*MTP* 14:558).

15.	"For nothing; without a recompence" (Johnson's *Dictionary*, s.v. "gratis"). "My sins, they ceased to be, centuries ago; my debts, my Saviour paid them before I was born, and nailed up the receipted bill to his Cross, and I can see it there. The handwriting of ordinances that was contrary to us, he took it away and nailed it to his Cross. I can see it, and while I read the long list of my sin—oh, how long, what a roll it wanted to contain them,—yet I see at the bottom, 'The blood of Jesus Christ his Son cleanseth us from all sin.' It matters not how long that roll was; the debt is all discharged" (*MTP* 18:488).

16.	"I take the term 'stripes' to comprehend all the physical and spiritual sufferings of our Lord, with especial reference to those chastisements of our peace which preceded rather than actually caused his sin-atoning death: it is by these that our souls are healed" (*MTP* 14:554). Cf. Ps 129:3; Isa 53:5; Matt 27:26; John 19:1.

17.	Cf. Ps 69:21; Matt 27:34.

18.	An alternative reading of these two sentences is "We are cured. The Redeemed on high exclaim."

19. "I dare not limit my Master's power as to how far he may subdue sin even in this life in the believer, but I expect never to be perfect till I shuffle off this mortal coil" (*MTP* 14:561).

20. "'With his stripes we are healed.' These six words contain the marrow of the gospel, and yet scarcely one of them contains a second syllable. They are words for plain people, and in them there is no affectation of mystery or straining after the profound. . . . Sicknesses are not healed by eloquence" (*MTP* 18:481–82). "Beloved, if you know that Jesus has healed you, serve him, by telling others about the healing medicine. Whisper it in the ear of one; tell it in your houses to the twos; preach it, if you can, to the hundreds of thousands; print it in the papers; write it with your pen; spread it through every nook and corner of the land. Tell it to your children; tell it to your servants; have none around you ignorant of it. Hang it up everywhere in letters of boldest type. 'With his stripes we are healed.' Oh, sound it! sound it! sound it loud as the trump of doom! and make men's ears to hear it, whether they will or no!" (*MTP* 18:492).

185.   1 Cor XV. 42.43.44.   The resurrection body.

No rational person can deny the existence of a soul in man.   And this being discovered, nature gives a gleam of light sufficient to teach the immortality of the soul. Reason & Revelation alike declare that the soul dies not : but the resurrection of the body is an idea that nature never knew, a novelty to reason an absurdity. Yet faith accepts it as a certain fact, a glorious promise.

The body shall be raised. ~~Enoch~~, Elias & Jesus. are the forerunners.   The transfiguration & resurrection of Jesus were pledges & preludes.

How are they raised? cries out the sneering infidel —   Faith answers, By that same power that raises the buried grain, & in a manner as mysterious as the corn rises from its tomb.   In what body do they come? The unbeliever questions.   And Paul replies That bodies are not necessarily all of one nature

He declares the nature of the new body & teaches that its fashion shall be the same as that of our ascended Lord.   We strip off the rags of this body, to put on the robes of Heaven

I. The present body is corruptible : but the one to come is incorruptible.

Sin infects us from our cradle to the tomb. but there our body shall be untainted with sin. Here we are liable to accident, loss of reason, disease & death but there — corruption is not known.

185

THE RESURRECTION BODY
1 Corinthians 15:42–44[1]

"So also is the resurrection of the dead. It is sown in corruption, it is raised in incorruption: it is sown in dishonour, it is raised in glory; it is sown in weakness; it is raised in power; it is sown a natural body, it is raised a spiritual body. There is a natural body, and there is a spiritual body."

No rational person can deny the existence of a soul in man. And this being discovered, nature gives a gleam of light sufficient to teach the immortality of the soul. Reason and Revelation alike declare tha[t][2] the soul dies not. But the resurrection of the body is an idea that nature never knew, a novelty, to reason an absurdity.[3] Yet faith accepts it as a certain fact, a glorious promise.

The body shall be raised. ~~Enoch~~,[4] Elias[5] and Jesus are the forerunners. The transfiguration[6] and resurrection[7] of Jesus were pledges and preludes.

How are they raised?[8] cries out the sneering infidel. Faith answers, By that same power that raises the buried grain and in a manner as mysterious as the corn rises from its tomb.

In what body do they come? the unbeliever questions. And Paul replies that bodies[9] are not necessarily all of one nature. He declares the nature of the new body and teaches that its fashion shall be the same as that of our ascended Lord.[10] We strip off the rags of this body to put on the robes of Heaven.

I. THE PRESENT BODY IS CORRUPTIBLE, BUT THE ONE TO COME IS INCORRUPTIBLE.[11]

Sin infects us from our cradle to the tomb. But there, our body shall be untainted with sin. Here, we are liable to accident, loss of reason, disease and death. But there, corruption is not known.

This body becomes the worms carousel, it moulders & decays, but that will know no worm or decay.

II. This body is dishonourable; that glorious —

Our birth, our helpless ignorance, our youthful folly, our animal alliance — all are dishonouring.

But there no childhood, no helplessness, no ignorance alliance with angels not with animals.

The funeral however well conducted or respectfully attended, or solemnized with regal pomp is still the evidence that the body is dishonourable, loathesome, bearing sin's brand of death. But there it shall be raised not in honor alone but glory. God's people in persecution, died amid contumely & were buried, if buried at all, in an ignominious way, but when they rise how great the change. Glory shall be theirs.

III. This body is weak. but that has power.

The spirit in another world shall be gigantic compared with what we are now. So also the body.

How subject to fatigue, how soon sick even in life's prime. In old age how tottering & feeble. At the hour of death unable to lift perhaps even the hand, entirely helpless, a mass of feebleness.

When dead, no strength remaineth, all is fled the eye is glazed; the head bowed down, the ear hears not, nor can it lift even one finger.

But there strength shall come into the frame. the infant shall be strong, the faint revive, the eyes young, the sick, hale & mighty, the dead shall burst the bands of the grave & stand mighty through their God, able to run without weariness & fly forever on his errands without ceasing.

This body becomes the worm's carousel, it moulders and decays, but that [body] will know no worm or decay.

II. THIS BODY IS DISHONOURABLE; THAT [BODY] GLORIOUS.

Our birth, our helpless ignorance, our youthful folly, our animal alliance, all are dishonouring. But there, no childhood, no helplessness, no ignorance. Alliance with angels, not with animals.

The funeral, however well conducted or respectfully attended or solemnized with regal pomp, is still the evidence that the body is dishonourable, loathesome, bearing sin's brand of death. But there, it shall be raised not in honor alone but glory. God's people in persecution died amid contumely[12] and were buried, if buried at all in an ignominious way. But when they rise, how great the change. Glory shall be theirs.

III. THIS BODY IS WEAK. BUT THAT [BODY] HAS POWER.[13]

The spirit in another world shall be gigantic compared with what we are now. So also the body. How subject to fatigue. How soon sick, even in life's prime. In old age, how tottering and feeble. At the hour of death, unable to lift perhaps even the hand. Entirely helpless, a mass of feebleness.

When dead, no strength[14] remaineth. All is fled, the eye is glazed, the head bowed down, the ear hears not, nor can it lift even one finger.

But there, strength shall come into the frame. The infant shall be strong, the faint revive, the aged young, the sick hale[15] and mighty. The dead shall burst the bands of the grave and stand mighty through their God, able to run without weariness[16] and fly forever on his errands without ceasings.

IV. It is here a natural body - but there spiritual
not pure spirit, but ethereal refined matter.
Incapable of pain, exhaustion, or decay. Fitted to
render us congeners of seraphim & cherubim. —
We know how much spiritual pleasures excel
natural — just by so much — will our bodies be
exceeded by their after existences. This chrysalis
shall cease to lie motionless & shall be a winged
glorious, creature ——— The body here pulls
down our soul & becomes its clog, there it shall
be a swift chariot, with glowing wheels assisting
the spirit's flight. — how meats & drinks afford
a nourishment not found within — but then our
bodies shall have their strength within themselves.
We shall feast on the ambrosia & nectar of immortal love.
live on the honey dews & sunbeams of eternal delight.

1. Christian why fear to die? — to be immortal
2. Friend — why weep the friend rendered for ever rich
3. Christian - why ever be downcast? Since Heaven is your home

Sinner — this is not thine - not one word of
it — thy body too shall rise. body & soul in hell
shall be tortured. Both enlarged, expanded to
a vast degree — thou shalt feel pains thou
knowest nothing whatever of —— Repent.
God help me. Amen

294.

IV. IT IS HERE A NATURAL BODY, BUT THERE, SPIRITUAL.

Not pure spirit, but ethereal refined matter.[17] Incapable of pain, exhaustion, or decay. Fitted to render us congeners[18] of seraphim and cherubim. We know how much spiritual pleasures excel natural. Just by so much will our bodies be exceeded by their after existences. This chrysalis[19] shall cease to lie motionless and shall be a winged glorious creature.

The body here pulls down our soul and becomes its clog. There, it shall be a swift chariot with glowing wheels assisting the spirit's flight. Now, meats[20] and drinks afford a nourishment not found within. But then, our bodies shall have their strength within themselves. We shall feast on the[21] ambrosia[22] and nectar of immortal love, live on the honey dews and sunbeams of eternal delight.

1. Christian, why fear to die, to be immortal?

2. Friend, why weep? The friend rendered for ever rich.

3. Christian, why ever be downcast? Since Heaven is your home.

Sinner, this is not thine, not one word of it. Thy body too shall rise. Body and soul in hell shall be tortured.[23] Both enlarged, expanded to a vast degree. Thou shalt feel pains thou knowest nothing whatever of. Repent.

God help me. Amen

294.

1. This is the only time Charles preached a sermon on 1 Cor 15:42–44.

2. Due to a lack of space in the margin, Charles did not fully construct the final letter "t" in the word "that."

3. Depending on the placement of punctuation, an alternative reading of this line is "But the resurrection of the body is an idea that nature never knew, a novelty to reason, an absurdity."

4. Charles may have struck through the name "Enoch" because, according to Heb 11:5, "By faith Enoch was translated that he should not see death; and was not found, because God had translated him." Cf. Gen 5:24.

5. In Hebrew, the name אֵלִיָּהוּ (Elijah) was transliterated into Greek as Ἠλιας (cf. Luke 5:26) and into English as "Elias" (see Edward Robinson, trans., *A Hebrew and English Lexicon of the Old Testament, Including the Biblical Chaldee. Translated from the Latin of William Gesenius* [Boston: Crocker and Brewster; New York: Leavitt, Lord & Co.; Andover: printed by Gould and Newman, 1836, The Spurgeon Library], 62; and S. T. Bloomfield, *The Greek New Testament. With English Notes, Critical, Philological, and Exegetical, Especially Adapted to the Use of Theological Students, and Ministers. In Two Volumes. Vol. I* [9th ed.; London: Longman, Brown, Green, and Longmans, 1855, The Spurgeon Library], 391). Cf. 2 Kgs 2:11.

6. Cf. Matt 17:1–9; Mark 9:2; Luke 9:28–36.

7. Cf. Matt 28:1–8; Mark 16:1–8; Luke 24:1–13; John 20:1–9.

8. Cf. 1 Cor 15:35.

9. By prematurely writing the letter "e" immediately after the "d" in the word "bodies," it seems Charles's mind jumped ahead of his pen. See also "God's Binding the Floods" (Sermon 186).

10. Cf. 1 Cor 15:42–49.   11. Cf. 1 Cor 15:53–54.

12. "Rudeness; contemptuousness; bitterness of language; reproach" (Johnson's *Dictionary*, s.v. "contumely").

13. Cf. 1 Cor 15:43.

14. The letter "t" in the word "strength" is smeared, likely by accident or due to a malfunction of Charles's writing instrument.

15. "Healthy; sound; hearty; well complexioned" (Johnson's *Dictionary*, s.v. "hale").

16. Charles used the long "s" in the word "weariness." For an additional example of this tendency, see "Inventory and Title of Our Treasures" (Notebook 2, Sermon 92).

17. Charles was likely quoting Matthew Henry who, in his commentary on 1 Cor 15:35–50, wrote, "Ours is at present a vile body, Phil. iii. 21. Nothing is more loathsome than a dead body; it is thrown into the grave as a despised and broken vessel, in which there is no pleasure. But at the resurrection a glory will be put into it; it will be made like the glorious body of our Saviour; it will be purged from all the dregs of earth, and refined into an ethereal substance" (Matthew Henry, *An Exposition of the New Testament: Wherein Each Chapter Is Summed Up in Its Contents: The Sacred Text Inserted at Large in Distinct Paragraphs: Each Paragraph Reduced to Its Proper Heads: The Sense Given, and Largely Illustrated: With Practical Remarks and Observations. With Preface by the Rev. C. H. Spurgeon. Vol. VIII. I. Corinthians—Philippians* [London: Thomas C. Jack; Edinburgh: Grange Publishing Works, n.d., The Spurgeon Library], 145).

18. "Of the same kind or nature" (Johnson's *Dictionary*, s.v. "congener"). Cf. Matt 22:30; Mark 12:25.

19. "A term used by some naturalists for aurelia, or the first apparent change of the maggot of any species of insects" (Johnson's *Dictionary*, s.v. "chrysalis").

20. Stippling appears above and below the word "meats." The reason for Charles's stippling is unknown.

21. Charles inserted the word "the" between the words "on" and "ambrosia" and indicated its location by a caret beneath the line.

22. "The imaginary food of the gods, from which every thing eminently pleasing to the smell or taste is called *ambrosia*" (Johnson's *Dictionary*, s.v. "ambrosia," italics in the original).

23. An alternative reading of this line is "[Your] body and soul in hell shall be tortured."

Job. XXVIII 11.   God's binding the floods.   186

Though this verse originally refers to the miners' staying the floods from bursting into the mine, it may with truthfulness be applied to God — who holds the waters in the hollow of his hand. Let us consider the subject both naturally & spiritually & may we be instructed by the Holy Spirit, the best teacher.

I. In Nature.
How true this sentence is, <u>"He bindeth the floods from overflowing"</u>
Some men imagine that God created a world & thrust it into space, & left it to be governed as they say by laws. They do not remember that his constant power is necessary to render the laws of any service — but deny a constant providence

But here it is asserted plainly that he does this & consequently all natural operations

We cannot better grasp the text than by thinking on (1) The Tides of the Sea. You behold the armies of waves, in ranks, marching to attack the shore. One by one they die, but another fills up the unbroken line. On, On they come & inexperience might tremble lest they should devastate the lands. Over rocks & upon cliffs they dash & what mortal can resist. They stay their headlong career. They hesitate, expecting the commands of the King on high. The word is spoken & they retreat, with unaverted front like fierce warriors, retreating leisurely ---

492

GOD'S BINDING *the* FLOODS

Job 28:11[1]

"He bindeth the floods from overflowing; and the thing that is hid bringeth he forth to light."

Though this verse originally refers to the miners' staying the floods from bursting into the mine,[2] it may with truthfulness be applied to God who holds the waters in the hollow of his hand.[3]

Let us consider the subject both naturally and spiritually, and may we be instructed by the Holy Spirit, the best teacher.

I.   IN NATURE, HOW TRUE THIS SENTENCE IS, ~~HE~~ *"He bindeth the floods from overflowing."*

Some men imagine that God created a world and thrust it into space and left it to be governed, as they say, by laws.[4] They do not remember that his constant power is necessary to render the laws of any service, but deny a constant providence.[5]

But here, it is asserted plainly that he does this and consequently all natural operations. We cannot better grasp the text than by thinking on:

(1) The Tides of the Sea.

> You behold the armies of waves in ranks marching to attack the shore. One by one they die, but another fills up the unbroken line. On, On they come, and inexperience might tremble lest they should devastate the lands.

> Over rocks and upon cliffs they dash. And what mortal can resist? They stay their headlong career. They hesitate, expecting the commands of the king on high. The word[6] is spoken and they retreat with unaverted front like fierce warriors retreating leisurely.

2. Launch on the sea & witness a Storm.
The harsh winds sound the blast of the onset,
the giant multitudes of waves, leap even to
heaven in their fury; the horrid clouds
are gathering on the brow of tempest, who
with one hand hides the sun, & with the
other hurls lightning & bolts of thunder.
The timid moon, with her train of stars
fly from the scene. & leave the trembling
mariner, alone, in darkness. reeling as a
drunken man. The spray Ocean grasps
the little bark & the rough hand drips
spray & waterfloods upon it. The mouth
of the deep yawns & sucks in the ship,
other jaws of mighty width are closing on
it but it escapes as by a miracle.
The Miracle repeated oft saves the poor vessel
till the storm subsides & the desired
haven comes in view.
3. Go to those countries which lying lower than
the sea are protected by the mounds which
with much labour man has made, or walk
by the side of our rivers whose channels are
above the surrounding country. Imagine
the desolation should the sea burst its prison
walls & avenge our encroachment on its territory
by a devastating invasion of ours.

2. Launch on the sea and witness a **Storm**.

> The harsh winds sound the blast of the onset. The giant multitudes of waves leap even to heaven in their fury. ~~the~~ Horrid clouds ~~are~~[7] ~~gathering~~ on the brow of tempest, who with one hand hides the sun and with the other hurls lightning and bolts of thunder.

> The timid moon with her train of stars fly from the scene and leave the trembling mariner alone in darkness, reeling as a drunken man.[8] ~~The spray~~ Ocean grasps the little bark and ~~this~~[9] rough hand drips spray~~s~~ and waterfloods upon it. The mouth of the deep yawns and sucks in the ship. ~~t~~Her[10] jaws of mighty width are closing on it, but it escapes as by a miracle.

> The miracle repeated oft saves the poor vessel[11] till the storm subsides and the desired haven comes in view.

3. Go to those countries which, lying lower than the sea, are protected by the mounds which with much labour man has made. Or walk by the side of our rivers whose channels are above the surrounding country. Imagine the desolation should the sea burst its prison walls and avenge our encroachment on its territories by a devastating invasion of ours.

Though our industry is the means, yet to him be the praise for every hours salvation from the water floods.

4. Consider the Caverns beneath our feet, filled with water; the Fountains whence come our springs & wells, — Should the Almighty liberate these, joyful would they ascend to these regions, & instead of blessing, curse our earth. He seals these, though if unloosed they would soon sweep away rebellious man. He binds & ever will —

5. Look to the Clouds, whence Rain comes down, we have seen the torrents fall. The Clouds were not emptied by their long outpouring but recommenced pouring down their showers. While heaven wept, the earth was swollen with the moisture. God could cause unceasing descents of rain, but the bow forbids the fear we else might well entertain — the cisterns are restrained, the sun appears.

"He bindeth the floods from overflowing"

1. This subject should show us how entirely we are in the hands of God. Where can we go to escape, the rain, the bursting river, the ocean should it o'erstep the present decree we are entirely in the power of God.

2. It should teach us to admire the faithful- -ness of God. who could. but will not because of his promise. Easily, in many ways he could overflood us, but he rather binds the water floods.

Though our industry is the means, yet to him be the praise for every hour[']s salvation from the water floods.

4. Consider the Caverns beneath our feet filled with water, the Fountains whence come our springs and wells. Should the Almighty liberate these, joyful[12] would they ascend to these regions,[13] and instead of blessing, curse our earth.[14] He seals these, though if unloosed, they would soon sweep away rebellious man. He binds and ever will.

5. Look at the Clouds whence Rain comes down. We have seen the torrents fall. The clouds were not emptied by their long outpouring, but recommenced, pouring down their showers. While heaven wept, the earth was swollen with the moisture. God could cause unceasing descents of rain, but the bow forbids the fear we else might well entertain.[15] The cisterns are restrained. The sun appears.

"He bindeth the floods from overflowing."

1. This subject should show us how entirely we are in the hands of God. Where can we go to escape the rain, the bursting river, the[16] ocean should it o'erstep[17] the present decree? We are entirely in the power of God.

2. It should teach us to admire the faithfulness of God, who could, but will not, because of his promise. Easily in many ways, he could overflood us, but he rather binds the waterfloods.

3. Moreover, the promise though it forbids our destruction as a whole, does not forbid partial deluges, or floods that may damage but not ruin. Should he sink England still the promises would not be broken, or should a flood over the earth destroy much property & life & yet spare many — the promise would be still unviolated. The earth however will never wholly perish by a watery deluge. But let us bless God that we are not the victims of such a flood as the promise allows & that still "He bindeth the floods from overflowing"

II. Spiritually. this verse has much meaning whilst we like not the torturing scheme which finds a spiritual meaning every-where; we would not cramp a sentence into barely literal meaning when a natural figure appears in it.

1. Think of the fiery deluge of God's wrath. which long suffering mercy binds up so long. What if he had let things follow their courses where should we be, where our race, where the ungodly, the profane. truly, he bindeth up the floods.

3. Moreover, the promise, though it forbids our destruction as a whole,[18] does not forbid partial[19] deluges or floods that may damage but not ruin. Should he sink England, still the promises would not be broken. Or should a flood over the earth destroy much property and life and yet spare many, the promise would be still unviolated.

    The earth, however, will never wholly perish by a watery deluge.[20] But let us bless God that we are not the victims of such a flood as the promise allows and that still "He bindeth the floods from overflowing."

II. SPIRITUALLY, THIS VERSE HAS MUCH MEANING.

Whilst we like not the torturing scheme, which finds a spiritual meaning every-where, we would not cramp a sentence into barely literal meaning when a natural figure appears in it.[21]

1. Think of the fiery deluge of God's wrath, which longsuffering mercy binds up so long.[22] What if he had let things follow their courses? Where should we be? Where our race? Where the ungodly, the profane? Truly, he bindeth up the floods.

2. Behold the streams of iniquity which with muddy current ~~stream~~ bear contagion & death to souls. See! they run along our streets, even by the door. They rage, they rave, of old they played furiously but persecution now is hushed, in some sort.

Why are not men worse? why are not all devils? why even so much morality? why do not error & superstition more abound? why any of the true religion? — verily because

He bindeth up the floods from overflowing

3. Look within our own hearts, even we who are regenerate, behold the caverns of evil, the floods of sin. of evil affections, desires, imaginations. See our own weakness, proneness to evil, aversion to good, our lust, pride, self love How is it we have held on till now? Why have we not fearfully fallen? How hope for final perseverance? Truly. He bindeth up the floods from overflowing

4. Declare ye pilgrims who have been in the deep rivers, in the struggling billows Your troubles have not drowned you, they were not greater than you could bear No trouble has been so great as your fears imagined. For good all has tended. Remember in future days to comfort yourselves with the sure word of testimony

He bindeth up the floods from overflowing

2. Behold the streams of iniquity, which with muddy current ~~stream~~,[23] bear contagion and death to souls. See! They run along our streets,[24] even by the door. They rage, they rave. Of old they played furiously, but persecution now is hushed in some sort.

   Why are not men worse? Why are not all devils? Why even so much morality?[25] Why do not error and superstition more abound? Why any of the true religion?[26] Verily, because <u>He bindeth up the floods from overflowing</u>.

3. Look within our own hearts, even we who are regenerate. Behold the caverns of evil, the floods of sin, of evil affections, desires, imaginations. See our own weakness, proneness to evil, aversion to good, our lust, pride, self love.

   How is it we have held on till now? Why have we not fearfully fallen? How hope for final perseverance?[27] Truly, <u>He bindeth up the floods from overflowing</u>.

4. Declare, ye pilgrims who have been in the deep rivers, in the struggling billows. Your troubles have not drowned you. They were not greater than you could bear. No trouble has been so great as your fears imagined. For good all has tended.

   Remember in future days to comfort yourselves with the sure word of testimony.

<u>He bindeth up the floods from overflowing</u>.

5. Visit the saint's deathbed, how is he so calm, so placid! Are the rivers dried! Is there no pain, no pang, no death! Yes there are all these but they overflow not. They are not gone, they are to be passed by all. But "they shall not overflow thee" runs the promise, & whether we cross dry-shod or wade deeper in the black stream. Still, "He bindeth up the floods from overflowing"

1. Christian rejoice! know thy perfect safety. Rejoice! in this rainbow promise, for to thee the flood cannot come with power to destroy. Doubt not but trust.

2. Sinner be grateful that the flood has not burst on thy deserving soul, but tremble lest soon it should. Say who can bind thy floods but the one whom thou refusest. Be at one with him who "bindeth up the floods from overflowing"

298. 301. 302.

May He unloose my tongue.
But bind my wandering heart.
Through the Ascended Jesus.

5. Visit the saint's deathbed. How is he so calm, so placid? Are the rivers dried? Is there no pain, no pang, no death?

Yes, there are all these, but they overflow not. They are not gone. They are to be passed by all. But "they shall not overflow thee" runs the promise. And whether we cross dry-shod[28] or wade deeper in the black stream, still, "He bindeth up the floods from overflowing."

1. Christian, rejoice! Know thy perfect safety! Rejoice! in this rainbow promise, for to thee the flood cannot come with power to destroy.[29] Doubt not, but trust.

2. Sinner, be grateful that the flood has not burst on thy deserving soul, but tremble, lest soon it should. Say, who can bind thy floods but the one whom thou refusest? Be at one with him who "bindeth up the floods from overflowing

May He unloose my tongue.

But bind my wandering heart.[30]

Through the Ascended Jesus.

298. 301. 302.

1. This is the only time Charles preached a sermon on Job 28:11.

2. Charles may have consulted John Gill who, in his commentary on Job 28:11, wrote, "As the miner finds ways and means of cutting through rocks, and draining and carrying off the waters in his mine; so he makes use of other methods of restraining and keeping back the waters from coming into and overflowing his works" (Gill, *An Exposition of the Old Testament*, 3:389).

3. Cf. Isa 40:12.

4. Charles often preached against deistic claims that God is Creator only and not Sustainer. "A religion that has not God in it is irreligion. Atheism cannot bring you to heaven, nor can any form of deism, even though it be baptized into the name of Christianity. If God be not Chief, Head, King, Lord, Sovereign, you are not in the right road" (*MTP* 36:368). For the remainder of his ministry, Charles never wavered from his belief in theodicy. On August 25, 1861, he said, "To gather up all in one, the calamities of earthquake, the devastations of storm, the extirpations of war, and all the terrible catastrophes of plague, have only been co-workers with God—slaves compelled to tug the galley of divine purpose across the sea of time. From every evil good has come, and the more the evil has accumulated the more hath God glorified himself in bringing out at last his grand, his everlasting design" (*MTP* 7:467). For additional references to deism in his early sermon notebooks, see "Ignorance, Its Evils" (Notebook 1, Sermon 31); "The Little Fire and Great Combustion" (Notebook 1, Sermon 54); "What Think Ye of Christ?" (Notebook 1, Sermon 71); and "The Day of God" (Notebook 2, Sermon 115).

5. Cf. Col 1:17; Heb 1:3.

6. An ink blot appears above the word "word," likely caused by accident.

7. Charles originally wrote, "The Horrid clouds are gathering on the brow of ~~the~~ tempest." With his strike-throughs, the sentence reads "Horrid clouds gather on the brow of [the] tempest."

8. Cf. Ps 107:27.

9. Charles originally wrote the word "these" before striking through the letter "t" and converting the letter "e" into an "i" to construct the word "his."

10. Charles originally wrote an ampersand before striking through it to construct the word "her."

11. Due to lack of space in the margin, Charles did not fully construct the final letters of the word "vessel."

12. It is not clear why Charles inserted a tittle above the letter "o" in the word "joyful."

13. An alternative reading of this phrase is "Should the Almighty liberate these, joyful[ly] would they ascend to these regions."

14. Cf. Gen 7:11.   15.   Cf. Gen 9:8–17.

16. Charles did not originally fully construct the letter "e" in the word "the." He reinforced the spelling of the word by enlarging the bowl of the letter.

17. Contraction, "overstep."

18. Cf. Gen 9:11.

19. Due to lack of space in the margin, Charles did not fully construct the final letters in the word "partial."

20. Cf. Gen 9:11.

21. In his lecture "On Spiritualizing," Charles warned his students about the dangers of overspiritualizing the text. He said, "I counsel you to employ spiritualizing within certain limits and boundaries, but I pray you do not, under cover of this advice, rush headlong into incessant and injudicious 'imaginings' as George Fox would call them. Do not drown yourselves because you are recommended to bathe, or hang yourselves on an oak because *tannin* is described as a valuable astringent. An allowable thing carried to excess is a vice, even as a fire is a good servant in the grate, but a bad master when raging in a burning house. Too much even of a good thing surfeits and disgusts, and in no case is this fact more sure than in the one before us" (*Lectures* 1:103, italics in the original). Charles offered his students the following five principles when spiritualizing Scripture: "*Do not violently strain a text by illegitimate spiritualizing*" (ibid., italics in the original).

"*Never spiritualize upon indelicate subjects*" (ibid., 106, italics in the original). "*Never spiritualize for the sake of showing what an uncommonly clever fellow you are*" (ibid., 107, italics in the original). "*In no case allow your audience to forget that the narratives which you spiritualize are facts*" (ibid., 108, italics in the original). And, "The faculty which turns to spiritualizing will be well employed *in generalizing the great universal principles evolved by minute and separate facts*" (ibid., 110, italics in the original). On April 19, 1873, Charles offered additional insight into his cautious use of allegory: "As for the *allegories*. What a world of nonsense have people talked about the allegories of Scripture, trying to make things run on all fours that were meant to walk erect. Alas, for those silly expounders who without the genius of old Origen, imitated his worst faults. What can I say that would be censure severe enough upon Origen himself, who never could read a chapter but he must needs twist it from its plain sense to make a mystery of it. We have all heard, I dare say, of the divine who was foolish enough to take the three baskets full of sweet meats that were upon the head of Pharaoh's baker, and to say that they represented the Trinity. . . . Was God's Book ever meant to be a toy for the amusement of childish imagination[?] Surely, no. The strong meat of allegory must be for half-inspired saints like John Bunyan, and those masters in Israel who are not to be carried away upon the back of every figure, but who can ride their figures like good horsemen, with a bit in the mouth of the allegory, and make it keep in a straight road and bear them safely on to their destination" (*MTP* 9:233, italics in the original).

22. Cf. 2 Pet 3:10–13.

23. Charles likely struck through the word "streams" because he had already used the word streams in the line above.

24. Charles prematurely wrote the stem of the letter "t" before the "e" in the word "streets." For an additional instance in this notebook of Charles's mind jumping ahead of his pen, see his previous sermon, "The Resurrection Body" (Sermon 185).

25. An alternative reading of this line is "Why even [is there] so much morality?"

26. An alternative reading of this line is "Why [does] any of the true religion [exist at all]?"

27. Due to lack of space in the margin, Charles wrote the final letters "rance" in the word "perseverance" beneath the line.

28. Cf. Exod 14:22; Josh 3:14–17.

29. Cf. Gen 9:8–17.

30. Charles was quoting from the third stanza of the famous hymn "Come, Thou Fount of Every Blessing" by Robert Robinson: "1. Come, Thou fount of every blessing, / Tune my heart to sing Thy grace, / Steams of mercy, never ceasing, / Call for songs of loudest praise. / Teach me some melodious sonnet, / Sung by flaming tongues above: / Praise the Mount—oh fix me on it, / Mount of God's unchanging love. / 2. Here I raise my Ebenezer; / Hither by Thine help I'm come; / And I hope, by Thy good pleasure, / Safely to arrive at home. / Jesus sought me when a stranger, / Wandering from the fold of God; / He, to rescue me from danger, / Interposed his precious blood. / 3. Oh to grace how great a debtor / Daily I'm constrain'd to be! / Let that grace, now, like a fetter, / Bind my wandering heart to Thee. / Prone to wander, Lord, I feel it; / Prone to leave the God I love— / Here's my heart, oh take and seal it, / Seal it for Thy courts above" (C. H. Spurgeon, comp., *Our Own Hymn-Book. A Collection of Psalms and Hymns for Public, Social, and Private Worship* [London: Passmore & Alabaster, 1885, The Spurgeon Library], Hymn 1035). At the conclusion of this hymn, Charles did not cite Robinson but instead he wrote "Selina, Countess of Huntingdon, 1760." The authorship of this hymn was widely debated in the nineteenth century (see John Julian, *A Dictionary of Hymnology. Setting Forth the Origin and History of Christian Hymns of All Ages and Nations. With Special Reference to Those Contained in the Hymn Books of English-Speaking Countries, and Now in Common Use. Together with Biographical and Critical Notices of their Authors and Translators and Historical Articles on National and Denominational Hymnody, Breviaries, Missals, Primers, Psalters, Sequences, &c., &c., &c.* [New York: Charles Scribner's Sons, 1892], 252). Julian traced the history of both versions of the hymn and noted, "These facts conclusively show that the author was Robert Robinson, and *not* Selina, Countess of Huntingdon" (252, italics in the original). Charles's predecessor at New Park Street Chapel, John Rippon, also believed Robinson was the author of this hymn (see John Rippon, *A Selection of Hymns from the Best Authors, Including a Great Number of Originals; Intended as an Appendix to Dr. Watts's Psalms and Hymns. With a Number of Additional Hymns, and Suitable Tune[s] Adapted to the Whole from "The Psalmist"* [new ed.; London: Arthur

Hall, Virtue, & Co.; Simpkin, Marshall, & Co.; Whittaker & Co.; Hamilton & Co.; Houlston & Wright, Paternoster Row, 1858, The Spurgeon Library], Hymn 509). For additional references to the phrase "bind my wandering heart," see *MTP* 17:363; *MTP* 31:269; *MTP* 38:185; and *Autobiography* 1:138.

Matt. X. 38. Following Jesus with a Cross on our back.

Some understand Justification by faith, as if it gave us a release from duties but Scripture affirms that the conversion of a man makes him even more a debtor. & brings peculiar duties upon him.

Doctrine — We must follow Christ & that bearing a cross.

I. Following Christ ——. as our Master, Teacher, Guide, Captain & Exemplar. — trace him — from youth to manhood, follow him in all points from the cradle to the grave.

II. Why is the Cross necessary?
1. All enterprises have difficulties.
2. Even the most quiet life has its storms.
3. From bad to good is ever a rough journey.
4. Our aim is so great — we so slow — enemies so great
5. Moreover these troubles act as cures of sin.

III. What cross must we bear?
1. Justification by faith is a sad cross to flesh & blood.
2. Mortification of sin is cutting work.
3. Patience under affliction, endurance of persecution.
4. Perseverance or holding on & out.
5. Self Denial in many matters.

IV. Let me urge you to shoulder the cross.
1. For Jesus sake & example.
2. For fear of the loss of heaven.
3. By the horrible dread of hell.

Young, old — the Lord awaken ye —

Amen

357

187

FOLLOWING JESUS *with* *a* CROSS *on* OUR BACK
Matthew 10:38[1]

"And he that taketh not his cross, and followeth after me, is not worthy of me."

Some understand justification by faith as if it gave us a release from duties,[2] but Scripture affirms that the conversion of a man makes him even more a debtor and brings peculiar duties upon him.

Doctrine. We must follow Christ, and that, bearing a cross.

I. FOLLOWING CHRIST AS OUR MASTER,[3] TEACHER,[4] GUIDE, CAPTAIN, AND EXEMPLAR.[5]

Trace him from youth to manhood. Follow him in all points from the cradle to the grave.

II. WHY IS THE CROSS NECESSARY?
1. All enterprises have difficulties.
2. Even the most quiet life has its storms.
3. From bad to good is ever a rough journey.
4. Our aim is so great. We, so slow.[6] Enemies so great.
5. Moreover, these troubles act as cures of sin.

III. WHAT CROSS MUST WE BEAR?
1. Justification by faith is a sad cross to flesh and blood.
2. Mortification of sin is cutting work.[7]
3. Patience under affliction, endurance of persecution.
4. Perseverance,[8] or holding on and out.
5. Self Denial in many matters.

IV. LET ME URGE YOU TO SHOULDER THE CROSS.
1. For Jesus['s] sake and example.
2. For fear of the loss of heaven.
3. By the horrible dread of hell.

Young, old, the Lord awaken ye.

Amen

357

1. This is the only time Charles preached a sermon on Matt 10:38.

2. Charles often referenced the dangers of Antinomianism, which leads to lasciviousness. In his 1866 sermon "Temptations on the Pinnacle" (*MTP* 12, Sermon 689), he said, "And so, dear friends, let us, when Satan tells us a Christian is all right and always safe, go where he may; let us respond to that, that it is true the Christian is safe in the way of duty, and will be kept in the path of God's commands, but he that presumptuously runneth in the teeth of God's will, and disobeyeth the Most High, must look to it lest a lion tear him to pieces. Brethren, it is a precious doctrine that they are safe, but it is a damnable inference from it, that therefore they may live as they list. It is a glorious truth that God will keep his people, but it is an abominable falsehood that sin will do them no harm. Remember that God gives us liberty, not license, and while he gives us protection he will not allow us presumption" (*MTP* 12:259). Ten years later he said, "If the judge of all the earth could possibly forgive sin while men continue to indulge in it, I do not see how the world could be inhabited; it would become a den of beasts, wild and without restraint, raging against all goodness and even against themselves. The very pillars of society would be moved if sin could be at the same time indulged by the sinner and pardoned by the Lord" (*MTP* 22:88). For additional references to Antinomianism in Charles's early sermon notebooks, see "Pleasure in the Stone of Zion" (Notebook 1, Sermon 53) and "Making Shipwreck of Faith" (Notebook 1, Sermon 161).

3. Cf. John 20:28; 1 Cor 8:6; 2 Cor 4:5; Phil 2:9–11; Col 3:17; Rev 17:14.

4. Cf. Matt 4:23; 5:2; 7:29; Mark 6:34; Luke 4:15; 5:3; John 3:2; 7:14; 8:2; 13:13.

5. Cf. John 13:13–16; 1 Cor 11:1; Eph 5:1–2; Phil 2:1–8; 1 Pet 2:20–22; 1 John 2:6.

6. An alternative reading of this line is "Our aim is so great [and] we [are] so slow."

7. Cf. Rom 8:13; Gal 5:25; Eph 4:20–24; Col 3:5.

8. See "Final Perseverance" (Notebook 1, Sermon 8) and "Final Perseverance Certain" (Notebook 2, Sermon 82).

[blank][1]

The 4 texts given me by an aged Sister, are.
John. XX. 16   No. 175 .   Zech XIV. 6. 7.   No. 176.
John XIII. 23. No. 183 .   Isa XLI. 10.
                               The 14th is similar,   No. 170

Praise, Praise, unto him who causeth
the river to run on still. though as
some say unfed by natural streams.
God doeth good & all the good herein is
every atom his. Bear witness oh paper! of
my thanks for these instances of grace

The 4 texts given me by an aged Sister[2] are:

John. XX. 16[3]	No. 175.[4]	Zech XIV. 6.7.[5] No. 176.[6]
John XIII. 23.[7]	No. 183.[8]	Isa XLI. 10.[9]
		The 14th is similar. No. 170[10]

Praise. Praise unto him who causeth
the river to run on still, though as
some say, unfed by natural streams.
God doeth good and all the good herein is
every atom his. Bear witness, oh paper! of
my thanks for these instances of grace.[11]

1. The darkened corners on this page are imprints of the tape applied to the corners of the opposite page, likely applied by Spurgeon's College in order to attach the back cover of the notebook. The aging process of the manuscript caused the dark spot on the left.

2. Charles preached from all these texts at her request with the exception of Sermon 170. Who was the "aged Sister?" Unfortunately, there is no record of her in Charles's autobiography, his letters to his family members during this season of his ministry, or in his biographies. Nor is there recorded in this notebook the reason she requested these four texts to be preached by Charles. She was likely a member of Waterbeach Chapel.

3. John 20:6, "Then cometh Simon Peter following him, and went into the sepulchre, and seeth the linen clothes lie."

4. "Mary with Jesus in the Garden" (Sermon 175).

5. Zechariah 14:6–7, "And it shall come to pass in that day, that the light shall not be clear, nor dark: but it shall be one day which shall be known to the LORD, not day, nor night: but it shall come to pass, that at evening time it shall be light."

6. "Light at Eventide" (Sermon 176).

7. John 13:23, "Now there was leaning on Jesus' bosom one of his disciples, whom Jesus loved."

8. "Leaning on Jesus['s] Bosom" (Sermon 183).

9. Isaiah 41:10, "Fear thou not; for I am with thee: be not dismayed; for I am thy God: I will strengthen thee; yea, I will help thee; yea, I will uphold thee with the right hand of my righteousness." Charles did not preach from Isa 41:10, as the "aged sister" requested. Instead, he preached from Isa 41:14, which he deemed was "similar."

10. "Fear Not, Thou Worm Jacob" (Sermon 170).

11. Charles included this paragraph in volume 1 of his *Autobiography* with the updated punctuation and capitalization: "Praise, praise, unto Him who causeth the river

to run on still,—though, as some say, unfed by natural streams. God doeth good, and all the good herein is every atom His. Bear witness, oh, paper, of my thanks for these instances of grace!" (*Autobiography* 1:225).

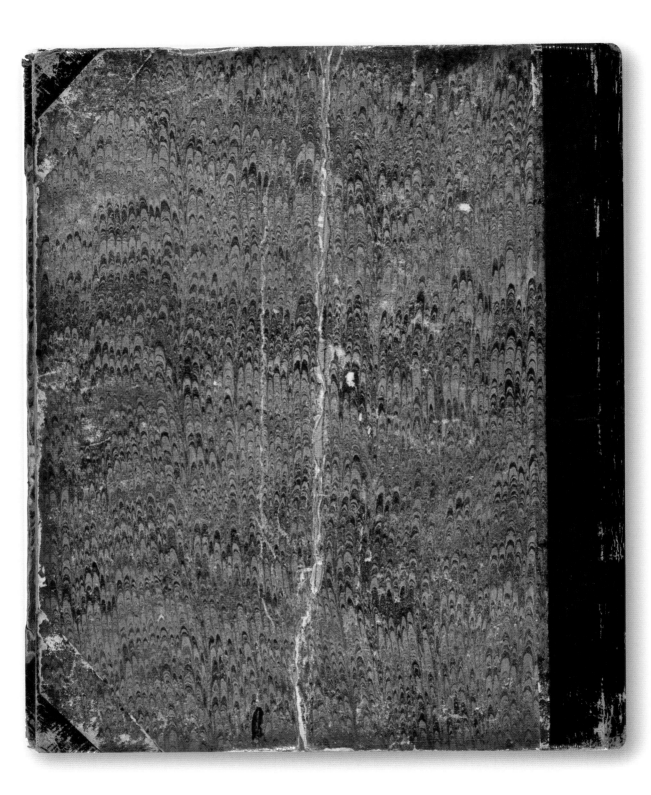

ABOUT THE EDITOR

CHRISTIAN T. GEORGE

(PhD, University of St. Andrews, Scotland) serves as curator of The Spurgeon Library and associate professor of historical theology at Midwestern Baptist Theological Seminary in Kansas City, Missouri. For more information, visit www.spurgeon.org.

SCRIPTURE INDEX

PSALMS

PROVERBS

ECCLESIASTES

SONG OF SOLOMON

ISAIAH

ACTS

SUBJECT INDEX